William McDougall:

Explorer of the Mind

Studies in Psychical Research

Compiled and Edited by
Raymond Van Over and Laura Oteri
in Collaboration with
Professor Angus McDougall

with a Biographical Introduction
by J. Wainwright Evans
and Foreword by Eileen J. Garrett

Helix Press

Garrett Publications

29 West 57th Street

New York, N. Y. 10019

Acknowledgments

The Editors would like to note with deep appreciation the valuable editorial assistance of J. Fraser Nicol, T. W. Coward, Virginia Camp, C. C. Chambers, Virginia Blount, and W. R. A. Akins.

Contents

PART III

PART IV

Editorial Note

In order to present the author's writings as originally published, no attempt has been made to alter English spellings, capitalization of certain nouns, varied footnote and reference styling and the like in order to be consistent with current American usage. The obvious typographical errors and omissions have, of course, been corrected.

Foreword

by Eileen J. Garrett

Professor William McDougall, who died November 28, 1938, was the head of the Psychology Department at Duke University where he established the Parapsychology Laboratory and sustained the work of its co-founder, Dr. J. B. Rhine, during the laboratory's primary phase. This important contribution became the link between psychical research and the quantitative (statistically based) study of ESP. Ironically, few of the students of recent years remember Prof. McDougall as the originator of quantitative research with the Zener cards that came into national prominence during Dr. Rhine's years as head of the Parapsychology Laboratory.

A pioneer in physiology and social psychology, Prof. McDougall was attracted to psychical research by William James's work in mediumship with Mrs. Piper.

During the early days of my own work in psychical research under the guidance of Mr. Hewat McKenzie at the College of Psychic Science, London, I met Prof. McDougall, who frequently dropped in to quietly pursue his own continuing interest in survival of mind after bodily death. He was also interested in hypnotism and knew that I had spent a year undergoing hypnosis in order to insure my complete separation from the "control" personalities developed under stringent discipline by Mr. McKenzie.

My respect and admiration for Prof. McDougall has grown with the years. Long after his death, and the death of Mr. McKenzie, I continued to keep in touch with their wives, who shared their husbands' deep and continuing concern for the future of psychical research. They were the links with these two men widely apart in character though not in aims: McKenzie, who, finding himself at odds with his church, gave up his theological studies to follow a career in engineering, and McDougall, who so often found himself at odds with the orthodox scientific establishment.

1

Introduction

William McDougall: Explorer of the Mind

by J. Wainwright Evans

Back around the turn of the century, a brilliant, immensely learned, but prickly and unorthodox young British biologist named William McDougall launched a lively attack on the sacrosanct dogmas of associational psychology, a strictly mechanistic way of thought that was then sweeping the scientific world. He considered such materialism intellectually disreputable, and he said so.

Contemporary orthodox scientists saw McDougall as an arrogant, cocky, and rather impudent youngster butting his head against the stone wall of what they were sure was Established Truth. The mechanistic thinkers paid little attention to this upstart, though they found him annoying, like a buzzing fly—a fly, as it turned out, with a sting.

McDougall's thought was not new; he simply became an especially articulate leader among a group of like-minded thinkers and investigators. Furthermore, as Sir Cyril Burt [1] has pointed out in his introduction to McDougall's *Psychology: The Study of Behavior*, McDougall "found British psychology still a branch of general philosophy; he left it a firmly established member of the biological sciences." This in itself was an enormous feat, but what marked him off from most of his fellow dissenters was his capacity for generating lively controversy.

For the most part, McDougall's opponents were older men, strongly entrenched behind great reputations and speaking with authority. They had made materialism fashionable. Science, according to them, had arrived to answer all the age-old questions about man and his destiny and to deal solely with tangible facts in place of idealistic and fuzzy metaphysical pipe dreams. What were they to think of this young biologist who, asserting himself as a serious scientist, did not shrink from the notion that man might have a soul, who experimented with a questionable brand of quackery called hypnosis, who showed an interest in the horrifying superstitions of psychical research, and who even went so far as to opine that consciousness was not just an epiphenomenal mist hanging like a cloud over a concatenation of atoms bumping each other in the brain centers?

It was especially disconcerting that this bright youngster obviously had as much respect for physical facts as the toughest materialist, but he refused to make gods of them.

In later years, when McDougall had traveled along his chosen road far enough to line up his conclusions,[2] he put it this way: "I had come to see more and more clearly that the main defect of the psychologies with which I had struggled in the opening years of the century was their acceptance, or their compromise with, the mechanistic biology, and their consequent neglect of the purposive or teleological aspect of all mental life. I seemed to see clearly that, whatever theory of the relation of mind to matter (of the psychophysical relation) one might hold, any psychology that ignored, or failed to bring out clearly, the fundamentally purposive nature of mental activity, was doomed to sterility. . . . The most essential character of life-processes seemed to be their goal-seeking nature."

It was fortunate for McDougall that he loved a good fight, since this kind of thinking so shocked the orthodox. By instinct and temperament he was a rebel. As he noted[2] quite unrepentantly in 1930, looking back over his career: "Whenever I have found a theory widely accepted in the scientific world, especially when it has acquired something of the nature of a popular dogma among scientists, I have found myself repelled into skepticism."

The crude materialism of the early 20th century was just such a dogma, and to McDougall it seemed to erase all meaning and purpose from life. It had been dominant both in science and philosophy ever since the findings of men like Darwin and Huxley had burst upon the scientific and religious world like an atomic bomb—one whose fallout promised to be permanent.

Here was Darwin with the facts of natural selection all neatly ticketed and verified. Here was the brilliant Huxley, with surely one of the keenest minds on record, to support him. And massed solidly behind these two were other influential thinkers for whom the definiteness of mechanistic concepts had a strong appeal.

As they saw it, the picture was devastatingly simple. Man was a machine— a strictly mechanical, cause-and-effect machine; his brain and nervous system were a glorified computer, a wonder in cybernetics (although the word was yet to be invented). Man was merely a wonderfully complex automaton, a robot incapable of acting with any genuinely intelligent purpose.

True, all this could produce a tantalizingly reasonable facsimile of goal-seeking intelligence but not the real thing. Why? Because purposiveness implied something lying outside the orbit of mechanical processes and was therefore impossible. So-called "consciousness" was just a mechanical effect *pretending* to be conscious. It might be described as a kind of impersonal cerebral weather; just as one says "It rains," so one might say "It thinks"— nothing *personal* about it, nothing at all! Man came out of nowhere and was bound there. He was something less than nothing—a cipher, so to speak, from which in due time death would knock off even the rim. How ridiculous, then, for this doll-like puppet of fate called man to delude himself with the notion that "I think" is a more believable concept than "It thinks"!

McDougall, for all his unswerving respect for physical facts, was unable to share the satisfaction of the mechanists in their philosophy of absolute zero. He saw such thinking as a gigantic negativism. In his view, the old religious orthodoxies (with which, incidentally, McDougall himself was not in accord) had gone gray and anemic in the withering breath of such concepts, which had themselves become unbending dogmas. And nothing constructive was being offered to take the place of religious beliefs that had at least fed men's souls.

The hopelessness of it all was well summed up with poignant and disturbing beauty in Fitzgerald's translation of Omar Khayyám:

> "A Moment's Halt—a momentary taste
> Of BEING from the Well amid the Waste—
> And Lo! the phantom caravan has reach'd
> The NOTHING it set out from—Oh, make haste!"

To young William McDougall, that conception was a poison that robbed life of purpose, meaning, incentives and goals. As he saw it, the materialists were crude reasoners talking nonsense. When he set out to pay them his disrespects, he usually managed to be polite about it but not always; and he laid on with especial relish in his not-too-polite comments on Dr. John Watson and his "crude behaviorism" when behaviorism became fashionable as a vociferous super-materialism.

What gave all this special value for parapsychology as we know it today was that McDougall's way of thought made him hospitable to psychical research, even leading him to reflect in his later years that, if he had been financially able to do it, he might have chosen to give all his time and energy to work in that field.

Both as a psychologist and as a parapsychologist, McDougall was driven by his growing realization that materialistic thought was bringing despair to thousands simply because it seemed to shut off all possibility of survival after death. He thought it possible that prolonged scientific investigation might eventually produce conclusive proof of such survival—indeed, he believed that psychical research had already achieved something very close to this proof.

Undoubtedly it was this attitude of mind that caused him, after nearly thirty years of active interest in psychical research, to sponsor energetically the work of Dr. J. B. Rhine in that field at Duke University. As head of the University's Department of Psychology in 1927, McDougall brought Rhine to Duke and there helped him establish the first parapsychology laboratory in the world. Thus parapsychology owes McDougall a debt which it would be hard to overestimate.

In 1926, in his great paper, *Psychical Research as a University Study*,[3] McDougall said: "If Mind in any manner and degree transcends the physical world and its laws, surely it may somehow and somewhere be possible to obtain direct evidence of the fact by the methods of science, by observation of phenomena and by reasoning from them! . . . Psychical Research proposes, then, to go out and seek such phenomena, namely, phenomena pointing directly to the transcendence of Mind, and, if possible, to provoke them experimentally. . . . To believe in the transcendence of Mind is a moral need of mankind in general. . . . The great public . . . are much concerned to know what kind and degree of influence Mind can exert upon bodily processes, what truth there is in the claims of many sects and schools of mental healers. They do keenly desire to know whether there is a kernel of truth in the widely accepted claims of communication with departed friends; whether each of us, as science tells us, is forever shut off from all his fellows by the distorting and inadequate means of communication provided by the sense-organs and muscular system; whether there is not some common stock of memory and experience upon which men may draw in ways not recognized by Science; whether at death each of us is wholly exterminated; whether ghost stories are founded only on illusion and other forms of error. . . .

"Unfortunately there is a multitude of persons who for the sake of filthy lucre take advantage of these eager desires, these strong emotional needs, and of the prevailing lack of sure knowledge, to falsify, obscure and fabricate the evidence. . . .

"The whole civilized world increasingly becomes the scene of a confused welter of amateur investigation . . . and of woeful blindness or wilful deception. . . ."

Then he illustrated his point by reference to telepathy as crucial to psychical research. "Does telepathy occur? That is to say—Do we, do minds, communicate with one another in any manner and degree otherwise than through the sense-organs and through the bodily organs of expression and the physical media which science recognizes?"

Belief in telepathy, he observed, "is held by all intelligent Christians; for it is implied in the practice of prayer and communion. . . .

"I am . . . a person of the kind that deals in probabilities and degrees of probability. . . . In my view the evidence for telepathy is very strong; and I foretell that it will become stronger and stronger. . . . In my opinion there has been gathered a very weighty mass of evidence indicating that human personality does not always at death wholly cease to be a source of influence upon the living. I am inclined to regard as part of this evidence the occurrence of ghostly apparitions. . . . I hold that a case has been made out for clairvoyance of such strength that further investigation is imperatively needed; and I would say the same of many of the alleged supernormal phenomena of mediumship. . . . I feel very strongly that the evidence for [such phenomena] is such that the scientific world is not justified in merely pooh-poohing it, but rather is called upon to seek out and investigate alleged cases with the utmost care and impartiality."

Thus did McDougall urge psychical research as a university study at a Clark University symposium on the question. What he did later to establish parapsychological research at Duke University stemmed directly from that statement, one of the most important in his career.

William McDougall was born in 1871 in Chadderton, England, a small town in Lancashire not far south of the Scottish border. He died in 1938 in Durham, North Carolina, at the age of sixty-seven; he was then head of the psychology department at Duke.

He relates tersely[2] that his paternal great-grandfather "began life, I am told, as a cobbler in his native wilds. He seems to have been a man of some spirit and originality, for he eloped across the border with an heiress and settled down in the north of England." The family from his great-grandfather down was as Scotch as oatmeal.

One of the old man's sons, William's grandfather, began an impressive display of the McDougall potentialities. With no inherited background of intellectuality, he became owner and headmaster of an old-fashioned boarding school for boys. His keen, self-generated interest in science made him a pupil of John Dalton, author of the atomic theory in chemistry; of Angus Smith, also famous in chemistry; and of Sir James Simpson, Edinburgh physician who first used chloroform as an anesthetic. This McDougall built up a chemical factory that became the foundation of the family fortunes; to that he added an iron foundry and a paper-pulp factory. In short, there was money in the McDougall family—important because it eventually gave William the means and independence to consider and pursue unorthodox ideas with complete indifference to what anyone thought.

Of his mother, "a pure Saxon type," McDougall remarks that she "lacked the touch of erratic originality so strong in her husband," and he says "I thus represent that blend of the Mediterranean and Nordic races which has produced the English people."

To this blending and to what he considered the predominance of the Mediterranean strain in himself, McDougall attributed the fact "that I have never felt myself to be altogether and typically English." He added, "I have never fitted neatly into any social group . . . have always stood outside, critical and ill-content. I have participated in the life of many groups, scientific, medical, academic, and social, but have belonged to none. Consequently, the list of my acquaintances on both sides of the Atlantic is immense; but I have very few intimates, and have always stood alone in my intellectual interests. This isolation has been an involuntary outcome of my nature, which I have learned to accept as inevitable." In short, McDougall recognized himself as a lone wolf— or perhaps a bit like Kipling's "Cat who walked by himself."

He was from the start something of a prodigy. In a private boys' school where he was sent at five years of age, he ranked for some years as the youngest pupil. He excelled in Euclid; he took on Latin and French when he was six and found them easy. By the time he left this school at fourteen he was an omnivorous, eager and nonstoppable reader of the better English novelists and of scientific classics. He was fascinated by Thomas Huxley's book on physiography. He read Hume and Gibbon, both of them "bugbears to the prevailing nonconformist conscience." His parents encouraged him in all this, and the house was kept well supplied with current magazines and books.

At about this time, the family moved to Manchester for the sake of better schools. The family income was about £2,000 a year—a lot of money in those days—and the ménage included four or more servants. Fortunately for himself then and for the scientific world later, the boy grew up in a home where ample income encouraged achievement; and he was of a disposition to take full advantage of the opportunities thus given him.

At fourteen, he went with his older brother to the German university at Weimar, where he learned German and attended theater and opera but didn't do too well in his studies—by reason of the language difficulty and differences in methods of instruction. At fifteen, in 1886, he returned to England and entered the recently founded University of Manchester.

He took languages, history, mathematics and, above all, biology, which was to be his continuing passion. Before his graduation in general science at 17, he had applied his spongelike memory to Spencer, Darwin and Huxley, to Lyell's *Principles of Geology*, and to other standard works of science.

And now he began to do some independent thinking about religion—not a small venture in a day when a wrong guess was popularly believed to place the guesser's immortal soul in peril.

His father saw to it that the boy attended church regularly, but very soon, while William did not reject religion, his tough-mindedness brought him to conclude that Christian theology was a "monstrous system of delusions." The controversy between the evolutionary theory and religion was at its height. He eagerly read Huxley's memorable attacks on Gladstone's religious orthodoxy and sided with Huxley.

Yet he never felt himself to be an atheist. Agnosticism (the word had been invented by Huxley) struck him as about right. His father, presumably a bit shocked by these developments, nevertheless wisely refrained from trying to influence him. "My indulgent, erratic, rather brilliant father had never ruled me," he said. "I had no resentment against the Church, and no father-complex to prompt me to rebellion."[2] Thus the relationship was one of mutual tolerance.

The results of that tolerance for his later thinking were important. For instance, he never accepted Freud's structure of the father-complex, which he regarded as mythological and unreal, as a universal factor in human life. Later he found in Freud's conceptions of the Unconscious much that he could agree with and use. But his approval of Freud remained markedly limited.

"My agnosticism was not militant, aggressively negative, or hostile to religion," he noted in his autobiography. "I said *ignoramus*, but I could not follow Dubois Reymond in adding *ignorabimus*. It seemed to me that most of the men who took life seriously and worked for the improvement of the life of mankind were in one sense or another Christians. And so, though the moral and historical bases of Christianity seemed to me incapable of resisting any serious examination, I did not feel that the intellectual was either justified in attacking religion or required to make a public display of his own skepticism. I saw that, though it was impossible to prove the truth of any of the propositions thought or implied by the churches, it was equally impossible to prove that there was no truth in them."[2]

His scholarship and thought were greatly enriched by his ardent study of geology in his fourth year at Manchester, and he saw in paleontology one of the great approaches to the study of evolution. Though he worked prodigiously at his studies, he found time to excel in athletics. He was outstanding in Rugby football, on the track and as a rower. "In the vacations," he reported, "I rode, swam, played tennis and climbed mountains."

Along with all this, he developed aesthetic sensibilities of a sort rare in persons immersed in predominantly scientific work. Perhaps as a reaction against the smoky ugliness of heavily industrialized Manchester, he became a passionate rather than a casual lover of natural beauty. He spent many holidays with his family in the Western Highlands, in the Lake Country, in the Welsh mountains and in the Alps. "I became a disciple of Wordsworth," he said, "before I had read his poetry."

From Manchester, which now seemed to him provincial as well as ugly, he set his sights on the two most important of England's seats of learning, Oxford and Cambridge—both good, both ancient, both steeped in tradition. In addition, their academic and social prestige would be useful to his career, and both were turning to the study of science.

He chose Cambridge because it seemed to him, even more than Oxford, the home of first-rate minds: Chaucer, Milton, Cromwell, Pitt, Newton, Gray, Wordsworth, Tennyson, Darwin. Clearly this was the place for a young man who had set his sights on the best. Moreover, Cambridge appealed to the aesthetic side of his nature. He thrilled to its lovely courts and buildings and to the rural simplicity of the little town which now he was going to share with the great men whose memories lingered there.

When he arrived at Cambridge in December, 1889, he was a freshman of nineteen years. His fellow freshmen were relatively immature boys, fresh from school, whereas he had already graduated from a provincial university with first-class honors and was in many ways extraordinarily mature. All of this, plus his natural brilliance and his enormous capacity for work, enabled him with far less effort than most of his fellow students to meet the high academic standards. As a result, he led what he called a double life; he "joined clubs, rowed in the college boat, wined, sang, and played cards"— remarkably combining work with play, although he regarded the play as somewhat childish.

"The dons," he commented, "seeing my participation in the social and athletic life of the college, wrote me down as a lost soul," but they soon discovered their mistake. This half-frivolous young man with energy to burn casually jumped into the first class in both Latin and Greek at the end of the first term, although he had studied no Greek before coming to Cambridge.

As a result of such scholarly achievements, he built up close and sympathetic companionships with some of the faculty. "During this freshman year," wrote McDougall a little dryly, "in my desire to be and do as other freshmen, I even accepted compulsory attendance at the college chapel."

And then at the end of that year he suffered a tragic loss which lastingly embittered him, freezing his dissent from religious orthodoxy into permanent form for the rest of his life. His adored mother died, painfully, of cancer.

His attitude was one of angry resentment. "This incident," he wrote, "completed the destruction of any remaining orthodox belief in a beneficent Providence. That a gentle woman whose whole life had been the blameless and faithful discharge of her natural duties, involving constant self-sacrifice, patient self-control, and active effort on behalf of others, that such a woman should die such a death was an unforgivable outrage—if there were any personal and all-powerful Director of our destinies. The moral of it for me was that mankind must rely on their own efforts to ameliorate their lot; prayer as a petition for help or protection from evil was a childish substitute for personal effort. Only scientific research could mitigate such horrors in the future. I was sobered and turned back from my boyish activities to more serious effort. I ceased to attend college chapel. When the Dean demanded an explanation, I told him my conscience would no longer allow me to participate; and he wisely let me go."[2]

It was then that McDougall decided to work for a medical degree and to specialize in psychology. He had two reasons: first, he wanted knowledge of medicine; second, although he did not intend to go into medical practice, he knew he might have to turn to it to make a living. He could not count for financial independence on his father's resources, which now were dwindling.

At this point the record shows a part of McDougall's true nature quite as revealing as his achievements in the field of science. In his mind, it becomes clear, the aesthetic and the purely intellectual met, merged and mingled in a way far from common among men of his type. Charmed with the rural beauty of the country around Cambridge, he wrote, "I caught in those fields and marshes some of 'the vision splendid' which now for me has faded 'into the light of common day.' Not the least of the pleasures of . . . a walk was the return to the beautiful old college where Wordsworth had dwelt and where I was often conscious that just beyond the college wall was the statue of Newton, 'with his prism and silent face, marble index of a mind forever voyaging through strange seas of thought, alone.' "[2]

It is worth noting that McDougall apparently takes it for granted that the reader's own knowledge of his chief idol among the poets makes it unnecessary to pinpoint the line as coming from "The Prelude."

That in turn suggests an interesting question: Why was McDougall so passionately devoted to Wordsworth? Particularly, why his apparently special interest in "The Prelude"? The answer may be that Wordsworth, in that autobiographical poem, put into magnificent poetic form the introspective psychology of which McDougall was a master in prose.

Consider, for example, what F. W. H. Myers has to say at the end of his chapter on "Genius," in his great classic, *Human Personality and Its Survival of Bodily Death:*

"I believe . . . that true, though vague, impressions of a world beyond the range of sense are actually received . . . by men of genius of certain types. . . . Chiefly, perhaps, of the philosopher and the poet must we need feel that if any genius reaches out into an interpenetrating spiritual world, *theirs* must do so; that *they* ought to have some message corroborating, even though but in vague general fashion, the results to which sensitives have been led by a plainer if narrower way.

"For our present purposes, however, one single poet—almost one single poem—will practically suffice. In whatever rank Wordsworth may be placed as an artist in language, there can be no doubt as to his conscientious veracity as an introspective psychologist. 'The Prelude, or Growth of a Poet's Mind' is . . . unique . . . a deliberate, persistent attempt to tell the truth, the whole truth, and nothing but the truth, about exactly those emotions and intuitions which differentiate the poet from common men."

McDougall, then, communed with Wordsworth as one psychologist to another—each of them reaching out for whatever it is that lies beyond the ranges that limit our ordinary human vision. Here, perhaps, is one of the roots of McDougall's interest in psychical research. Wordsworth spoke to that interest.

Unlike many whose absorption in physical science causes them to lose interest in great imaginative literature, McDougall's devotion to great poetry was an outstanding factor in his life. He fed on it, and he chose to feed chiefly on a poet ranked by critics with Shakespeare and Milton. His devotion to great poetry grew rather than diminished with his immersion in science.

Precisely the opposite had happened to one of McDougall's scientific idols, Darwin. Darwin, after starting life with a cultured man's normal interest in literature, later became so immersed in gathering and classifying scientific facts that, as he himself wrote, "Now for many years I cannot endure to read a line of poetry; I have tried lately to read Shakespeare, and found it so intolerably dull that it nauseated me." In contrast, McDougall went in the opposite direction; he came aesthetically more and more alive. That fact may help to account for his energetic rejection of the materialism that apparently satisfied Darwin.

In the introduction that McDougall wrote for the first issue of the *Journal of Parapsychology*,[4] dated March, 1937, he said, with a grim hint of his own readiness for combat with the mechanists, "Such research demands from its devotees . . . a disinterested pursuit of truth, and readiness in such pursuit to face incredulity rooted in massive traditional prejudices, scorn, ridicule, jeers, and loss of reputation; it involves facing the most subtle problems of logic and scientific method, and grave risks of self-deception in spite of the best intentions." And once again he called upon a poet to make his meaning clear. "It requires, in short, such severe discipline as may lift the devoted worker almost to the level of Robert Browning's grammarian." His creed as a scientist and a scholar comes to the surface like a cork in that reference to Browning's poem, "A Grammarian's Funeral," about a medieval scholar who worked himself to death in his pursuit of the truth:

"Left play for work, and grappled with the world,
    Bent on escaping:
'What's in the scroll,' quoth he, 'thou keepest furled?
    Show me their shaping. . . .' "

Such was his own passionate ideal when, as head of the Department of Psychology at Duke University, he sponsored the great research in parapsychology that began in 1927 and continued there until recently under the leadership of Dr. J. B. Rhine.

Summing up McDougall's achievements, all in the tradition of Browning's Grammarian, Charles Spearman of the University of London says in a biographical sketch:[5] "All his native ability was utilized to the utmost. By the time he had finished all his education, he must have been as nearly as possible omniscient. His university subjects included languages, history, mathematics, biology, geology, poetry, metaphysics and ethics, followed up in London by a study for the medical degree which included not only all the regular courses but also all the special courses available."

McDougall, with his usual blunt directness, said much the same thing with no false modesty: "There is perhaps no man living who has had a more intensive and varied training in the natural sciences; and what intellectual faults and virtues I possess must be largely due to this long process of education through study of natural sciences. I suspect that to it I owe something uncompromising in my pursuit of truth, an incapacity to be content with one kind of truth in science, another in philosophy or religion."

All his life, as if possessed by some daemon whose business it was to spur him on, McDougall carried a load of work under which anyone of lesser capacity would have foundered, but he managed it easily. Intellectually, he was ambidextrous; physically he was as tough as they come. Tides of energy and ambition raced through him that gave him more funneled and concentrated power than he knew what to do with.

As evidence of the surge of sheer spiritual and physical energy that drove him, he mentions offhand how "on one wild morning I jumped out of bed at four o'clock and caught the newspaper-train [from London] to Cornwall in order to see the storm break on the cliffs."[2] Imagine that, in contrast to the slugabed extra forty winks the average healthy young man would choose!

Again, "During those years in London I was still a practicing disciple of Wordsworth. I had rooms looking onto the grounds of Westminster Abbey. The Thames embankment was my favorite walk; and often in summertime I saw the dawn break over the City from Waterloo Bridge and could say, 'Earth has not anything to show more fair.' Often, after a day in the laboratory, I would take the train into the heart of Surrey and walk over the downs, sometimes returning only at breakfast time."

A former student of psychology at Duke tells a story he heard from Dr. Rhine about a walk Rhine took with McDougall in the beautiful North Carolina forest surrounding the Duke campus. They were following a path that had been cleared along an underground pipeline right-of-way. At one point, the ground sloped steeply downward toward a stream just ahead and rose again to the same level on the other side. The pipe, however, emerged from the ground and bridged the stream for a distance of about three hundred yards, its midway point about thirty feet above the stream. Without changing his measured pace, McDougall calmly walked across this hazardous foot-bridge—a smooth metal pathway from which even youngsters turned back. He did it apparently as a matter of course and without deeming the feat even worthy of comment.

The incident is characteristic. McDougall, with unlimited energy, was ready for any challenge that might come along. He took such situations literally in his stride.

This relish for meeting challenges, big or little, showed up on many occasions. McDougall had a biting tongue and at one time reflected that, if he should go into the practice of law as for a time he thought of doing, the gift might enable him to make a lot of money.

It is interesting to speculate on what a swath he would have cut in legal practice—with the resources of his phenomenally broad learning in science and philosophy, a mind like a razor and a plentiful supply of the "youthful arrogance" which he often mentioned, with wry humor, as one of his liabilities. It was really a combination of self-confidence and determination; his former associates agree that "arrogant" is not at all the appropriate word for his powerful and impressive personality.

Whatever the quality, however, it often was a liability just as McDougall said. It frequently enraged his adversaries, and, when he made some well-acidulated attack on their "crude" or "bizarre" or "intellectually disreputable" way of mechanistic thinking, they would even the score by conspiring to politely ignore his books or to jeer at them.

In debate, he himself was never impolite—well, hardly ever, but he could not conceal his contempt for the Watson behaviorists, who were in the saddle in the United States when he came to Harvard in 1920 to take the chair once filled by the matchless William James.

The behaviorists, on their part, subjected him to criticism and sarcastic ridicule, and many an unpleasant incident resulted, especially in those early years at Harvard. One point of attack, naturally, was his known interest in psychical research. When his antagonists struck, he replied promptly. His stock in trade was cold logic combined with a passionate but restrained emotional intensity that turned the cold logic into something like hot ice, blistering his jeering opponents. They did not love him for that.

Long before he reached Harvard, however, McDougall tangled at Oxford with people who should have approved of him. His concept of consciousness as "purposive" and "goal-seeking" once again led to the controversy, but, paradoxically, it was his attempts to prove the concept by using experimental methods to investigate the human soul that outraged some self-styled idealists at Oxford, who thereupon joined the mechanists in sniping at him. The incident occurred when McDougall held the Wilde Readership in Mental Philosophy at Oxford, a position he had requested and had been granted.

"The post had its drawbacks," McDougall says dryly in his account of the matter.[2] "It was, I think, T. H. Huxley who said that, if he had to devise a punishment for a very wicked scientist, he would condemn him to be a professor of science at Oxford."

McDougall's classes were small at first, but the attendance rose quickly to two hundred when he began to lecture on the experimental uses of hypnotism and used actual platform demonstrations. It was sensational and dramatic, partly because reputable scientists of that day (around 1904) rated hypnotism as little short of a Black Art—at best a mess of superstition and quackery.

Dr. Henry Wilde, the aged manufacturer of electromagnetic devices, who had founded the readership, was outraged by the very idea that mental life might be experimentally studied; the hypnotism demonstrations were the last straw. He promptly went after McDougall's scalp. The only thing, so the story goes, that saved McDougall from being summarily fired was the intervention of Sir William Osler, Regius Professor of Medicine.

The result of all this pulling and hauling, however, was that McDougall became one of the leaders of a small but influential group of British psychologists who had more or less thrown off the yoke of the orthodox mechanistic psychology. Long before his death in 1938, McDougall had the satisfaction of seeing the old associational psychology far less dominant than it had been—in no small degree because of his attacks on it. Today extreme behaviorism, which went furthest in upholding mechanistic concepts, seems to be singing small and losing ground.

The discoveries of modern physics, curiously, have contributed heavily to this state of affairs. Modern electronic developments have transformed the supposedly indivisible, non-splittable atom of Newtonian physics into the neutrons, protons, and the like that combine to form what may be called the modern atom. Matter thus becomes an aggregate of such electronic forces.

Even the old principle of physical determinism has been modified by the discovery of the "uncertainty principle," which finds that the movements of electrons are literally unpredictable, both in mathematical theory and in fact. It may not be putting it too strongly to say that modern physics has turned on its own mechanistic offspring to rend them. The old notion of a strictly mechanical universe, moving along with no goals in sight and no intelligent purpose, would seem incompatible with modern physics.

But these developments were far in the future when McDougall was fighting

his lonely battle for "purposiveness." Purposiveness? Goal seeking?—
Orthodox scientists were shocked. What did this brash youngster mean—
a-talking one day like a fact-respecting, materialistic biologist, and then revers-
ing himself and making noises like an animist or some other pipe-dreaming
crank? Clearly he had a foot in both camps. It just wasn't regular! And
then, further enraging the orthodox, he began turning his attention hopefully
to psychical research, which rated as next to Black Art in the materialistic
lexicon.

Looking back in 1930, he wrote: "I have served on the council of the
English Society [Society for Physical Research, London] for many years.
I have presided over it and over the American Society, and have taken an
active part in founding the new Boston Society. And, though my contacts
with the field in America have brought many disagreeable incidents, I do not
repent. I have given the minimum of support which, as a psychologist occupying a position of some slight influence, I could give without reproaching
myself with cowardice. If I had not found it necessary to earn some income,
I should perhaps have chosen to give all my time and energy to work in this
field."[2]

As McDougall admits in his remarkable book *Body and Mind, A History
and a Defense of Animism,*[6] he had to watch his step for fear his enthusiasm
and his hopes for psychical research would sweep him off his feet and into
premature and unscientific commitments. Characteristically, in those days he
was careful to refer not to "supernormal phenomena," but to "alleged supernormal phenomena." Yet he made it plain that he considered it highly probable that the "alleged" phenomena were valid.

"At the present day," he wrote in *Body and Mind,* "no one undertaking to
review the psycho-physical problem can ignore the results of these investigations without laying himself open to the charge of culpable ignorance or unscientific prejudice."[6] He continued: "The principle aim of the Society for
Psychical Research has been to obtain, if possible, empirical evidence that
human personality may and does survive in some sense and degree the death
of the body. A considerable mass of evidence pointing in this direction has
been accumulated. Its nature is such that many of those who have devoted
attention to the work and have had a full and firsthand acquaintance with the
investigations and their results, have become convinced that survival is a
fact. And among these persons so convinced are several who, in respect to
their competence to form a sane and critical judgment on this difficult question, cannot be rated inferior to any other persons."

It was characteristic of his scientific tough-mindedness that he went on to
say, cautiously, "Nevertheless, in my judgment, the evidence is not of such a
nature that it can be stated in a form which should produce conviction in

the mind of any impartial inquirer. Again and again the evidential character of the observations has fallen just short of perfection; the objections that stand between us and the acceptance of the conclusion seem to tremble and sway; but still they are not cast down, the critical blow has not been struck; and, perhaps, they will remain erect in spite of all efforts."

Later [6] he pointed out, "If Animism is the only solution of the psycho-physical problem compatible with a belief in any continuance of the personality after death, the empirical proof [through psychical research] of such continuance would be the verification of Animism; it would be proof that the differences between the living human organism and the corpse are due to the presence or operation within the former of some factor or principle which is different from the body and capable of existing independently of it.

"But though, in my judgment, this verification of Animism has not been furnished by 'psychical research,' a very important positive result has been achieved by it, namely, it has established the occurrence of phenomena that are incompatible with the mechanistic assumption. I refer especially to the phenomena of telepathy."

For McDougall, telepathy seemed the least debatable of psychic phenomena. It was the keystone of the arch, so to speak, and acceptance of telepathy seemed a possible justification for qualified acceptance of other phenomena less clearly established.

In other words, if the validity of a thing so incompatible with mechanistic concepts as telepathy could be regarded as established, then other phenomena less clearly established might be accepted as so highly probable as to satisfy the demands of common sense—though still short of being fully proved.

Since 1911, when McDougall wrote *Body and Mind*, the researches of Dr. Rhine and scores of others have tended to put psychical research, or parapsychology, on an increasingly firm foundation. Further evidence has been presented not only on behalf of telepathy but also of clairvoyance and, if perhaps to a lesser degree, of precognition and psychokinesis.

As late as 1930, after thirty years of psychical research, McDougall remained skeptical of the so-called physical phenomena but kept an open mind on the subject. His acceptance of telepathy and "also of some of the other 'mental phenomena' " grew stronger.[2]

One point he made is the difference between the evidential value of telepathy between persons at no great distance from each other and those cases where it occurs under experimental conditions at great distances. He said "The explanation of telepathy at close quarters by the hypothesis of 'brain-waves' transmitted through the ether cannot be absolutely rejected. But to my mind the difficulties are so great that the hypothesis is incredible. It is usual to support this hypothesis by pointing to the facts of wireless telegraphy."

And then he went on to mention the famous "cross-correspondences" reported in the *Proceedings of the S.P.R.*, from 1907 onward. The explanation for these extensively documented phenomena seems to lie either in communication from surviving personalities of the dead, or in the assumption that there has been telepathic communication of complex and subtle thoughts between living persons "separated by hundreds and even thousands of miles, thoughts of which neither is conscious or has been conscious at any time, so far as can be ascertained." This presented the skeptics with a dilemma—a choice between survival after death, in which they do not believe, and telepathy, in which they also do not believe. Either choice "is fatal to the mechanistic scheme of things." Physical "brain waves" *at such distances* in the expression of one's thought become "wholly incredible," and fraud as an explanation becomes likewise incredible in view of the character of the persons involved. Thus McDougall faced down the critics, whether coming or going.[6]

As another evidence against mechanistic concepts, McDougall cited the known fact that "the mind may exert an influence over the organic processes of the body far greater than any that had been generally recognized by physiologists. Especially noteworthy are the production of blisters, erythemata, and ecchymoses, of the skin (the so-called stigmata) in positions and of definite shapes determined by verbal suggestions [especially in hypnosis] and the rapid healing of wounds or burns with almost complete suppression of inflammation; and with these may be put the complete suppression or prevention of pain, even pain of such severity as normally accompanies a major surgical operation."[6]

Since McDougall wrote those words, the use of hypnotism in surgery, childbirth and the like, including even heart surgery, has become a commonplace.

McDougall concluded that this evidence of the mind's power to influence the body goes far "to justify the belief that the normal processes of growth and repair are in some sense controlled by mind, or by a teleological principle of which our conscious intelligence is but one mode of manifestation among others."

In the same book, *Body and Mind*, McDougall came out flatly for the old-fashioned notion that man has a soul, a concept more or less summed up in the phrase "unity of consciousness." This concept seemed to him unintelligible "unless we postulate . . . *some ground other than bodily organization.*" [Italics mine.]

Of the genesis of *Body and Mind*, McDougall said in his Autobiography:[2] "I had become more and more convinced that . . . in all living things there is some factor which does not work in accordance with mechanistic principles and which has its own peculiar nature and organization. . . . Souls were out of fashion, as James has said. But I had a predilection for unfashionable doctrines. And, seeing that so many scientists seem to find satisfaction in shocking the bourgeois, I would shock [the scientists] by putting up a defense of an exploded superstition. In this spirit of defiance I wrote my *Body and Mind* and gave it, defiantly, the subtitle *A History and Defense of Animism.*"

McDougall's was a concept of consciousness as *personal* and individual. "Consciousness as we know it runs always and only in personal streams," he said. As a corollary, he rejected the notion of the world "as consisting of conscious processes forming one vast system of consciousness, every part of which is in functional relationship to every other. . . ." The contrary conception of consciousness as personal and consequently individual is, perhaps, a natural consequence of McDougall's own intensely individualistic and personal stance in the matter of living.[6]

Apparently he looked on consciousness as unique in the sense that it obviously can't be defined in terms of anything else.

Lack of space forbids any attempt here to describe more fully McDougall's brand of animism. Only his books—in particular *Body and Mind* and *Social Psychology*—can do justice to his purposive (hormic) psychology, but it *is* appropriate here to raise a question. Why are McDougall's books so little known to the general public, to the thousands who might be expected to welcome his special brand of "positive thinking"? Why do readers who are familiar with William James pass McDougall by, thereby overlooking a mind similarly devoted to the affirmation of man's purposes? That question has puzzled many of McDougall's admirers, and it puzzled him.

Despite McDougall's own disappointment at his lack of wide popularity, however, he can hardly be said to have been ignored. His *Social Psychology* (1908)[7] sold more than 100,000 copies in the first twenty years after publication and achieved twenty-four editions by the time of McDougall's death in 1938. Of it, Gardner Murphy said "This book marked the beginning of a new social psychology; it swept everything before it." Today it is available in University Paperbacks. An astonishingly versatile, nimble-witted, wide-ranging book, it contains, in the chapter entitled "Hormic Psychology" an account of McDougall's concept of the purposive nature of consciousness that is not only notable for clarity, cogency and force, but is shot through with an emotional power that makes it very moving. His writing style here is, as always, restrained, precise and given to understatement, but the restraint merely adds to the impression of a tremendous head of steam behind the carefully chosen words. The book explores all sorts of bypaths, including, for instance, a highly original speculation on the biological and psychological reasons for human laughter and its function in life.

Another of his books that achieved a circulation of 100,000 is the condensed

Psychology: The Study of Behavior (Home University Library, Oxford), with an introduction by Sir Cyril Burt, one of his Oxford colleagues.[1]

Yet to McDougall his recognition seemed cruelly limited. He attributed public neglect in the case of *Body and Mind* to that same "spirit of defiance" which drove him to write it and of which he said a little ruefully in his *Autobiography*,[2] "This, perhaps, is the most accentuated illustration of that uncompromising arrogance which I have already mentioned. The publication of this book, like that of my *Social Psychology*, was like dropping a stone into some bottomless pit. I waited to catch some reverberation; but in vain. Each book received, I think, one favorable mention in the press; and that was all. I never could discover that anyone in Oxford had read either of them. And my colleagues, with one or two exceptions, seemed to be shaking their heads very gravely.

"About this time I began to find it difficult to believe in the value of my work, a difficulty that has grown steadily greater. I was much tempted to turn to medical practice before it should be too late."

Just when he most needed a boost for his spirits, however, it came. In 1912 he was elected a Fellow of the Royal Society, and he straightway renewed his resolve to continue his work in the paths of pure science, however small his success might be.

He could not help contrasting his unpopularity, as he saw it, with what happened to "my model," William James. He wrote:[2] "It is on record that, within a few weeks after the publication of one of his less popular books, he received letters about it from some five hundred persons. Whereas, if I receive from those to whom I have sent copies of a newly published book three or four postal cards and a couple of letters, I feel that I have done pretty well. The more I write, the more antagonism I seem to provoke. . . . I have not been able to acquire James' magic touch, which made all his readers his friends. I suppose it is that my uncompromising arrogance shows through, in spite of the taming it has undergone."

McDougall was, of course, being less than just to himself. He was not "arrogant," but his stiffly uncompromising streak contrasted with the easy charm and geniality of James, the "magic touch that made all his readers his friends." McDougall himself felt that magic, even at the times when he did not agree with James.

Consider, for example, McDougall's blunt rejection of prayer after his mother's death and his unqualified opinion of it "as a childish substitute for personal effort." Along with that went his forthright rejection of "religious belief" in the sense of "some theocratic governance of the world."

"I do not doubt," he said, "that if we could see good grounds for accepting such theocratic belief as William James inclined to, such belief would be of moral value. The mystical experience of the few who attain to it seems to suffice for their conviction. But . . . I see . . . no sufficient ground for such belief, though in a vague way I share the desire. The desire of belief in theocracy . . . if it proceeds from lack of courage to stand alone in the world . . . seems to me of no great merit. . . . If it leads us to distort the evidence, to blind ourselves to any part of it, to weigh it with less than the strictest honesty, such desire and such belief are morally stultified."

This rigorous point of view may or may not be the right one, but, right or wrong, it conveys little comfort to people longing at heart for some crumb of hope that prayer, for example, may reasonably be regarded as a channel through which, as James put it, "higher energies filter in."

James said in "Conclusions," the final chapter of *The Varieties of Religious Experience:* "What the more characteristically divine facts are, *apart from the actual inflow of energy in the faith-state and the prayer-state* [my italics], I know not. But the over-belief on which I am ready to make my personal venture is that they exist. . . . The practical needs and experiences of religion seem to me sufficiently met by the belief that beyond each man and in a fashion continuous with him there exists a higher power which is friendly to him and to his ideals."

In other words, James found a justification in his thinking for *faith,* as is well illustrated in his famous essay, *The Will to Believe.* The temperament of the two men was different in this. McDougall's loss of his mother, moreover, would seem to have cut him off from ability, in religion at least, to accept faith as valid, compatible with intellectual honesty. Yet in this he seems not to have been wholly consistent.

In his paper, "Psychical Research as a University Study," for example, he says, "I am not the sort of person who holds a great number of clear-cut positive and negative beliefs. I am rather a person of the kind that deals in probabilities and degrees of probability." So was James. The difference seems to be that McDougall, rather arbitrarily as it seems to some, drew the line at "theocratic belief." For him that was no longer a "probability," but he did admit that acceptance of a "probability" was, in a degree, an act of faith.

Perhaps, then, McDougall's unbending sternness and his refusal to play along with an attitude of mind that, for deep-rooted emotional reasons, he considered intellectually dishonest may account in part for the fact that his public often found him cold and stern when personally he was quite otherwise. His own deep affection for William James is reflected in his mention of a visit from James in 1908 as "one of the greatest pleasures of my life." Previously they had met in Rome in 1906. McDougall said:[2] "I felt that his visit was both a great compliment to me and a new evidence of the man's profound kindliness. . . . In 1910 I tried to express my appreciation of James in a short memoir contributed to the *Proceedings of the Society of Psychical Research*. James and [G. P.] Stout are the only two men of whom I have felt myself to be in some degree the disciple and humble pupil."

Unlike James, McDougall somehow erected a wall between himself and those who did not know him well. And, by his own account, those who knew him well were few indeed. Nobody called him Bill. Perhaps the mere fact that he was so intent on his purposes and ideas made him seem formidable to those meeting him casually or for the first time.

As part of his rather overwhelming personality, McDougall had a resonant bass voice, and he could be awesome on the lecture platform. Dr. R. C. Oldfield, of the Institute for Experimental Research at Oxford, has reported with some humor on McDougall as a reader at Oxford:[8]

"McDougall's presence and delivery were impressive. Indeed, it has been suggested by at least one of his regular hearers that, for the female moiety of his audience, the interest of the subject matter was notably reinforced by the view afforded of his fine head and countenance. The end of the lecture was a moment when he could be approached personally, and one student who thus presented himself and his psychological interest [Jack Flugel, later to become a psychology professor] received an invitation to visit the laboratory then and there. Walking up the High with McDougall, he inquired with respectful curiosity what he might expect to see there. 'You may expect something in the nature of research,' was the stony reply. Perhaps this was not so crushing in intention as it must have seemed in fact, but the would-be disciple hurriedly reminded himself of another appointment. Happily, Professor Flugel's interest in psychology was already established on a sturdy basis and survived this mortifying episode."

Sir Cyril Burt, who was closely associated with McDougall and his work, has kindly amplified on McDougall's Oxford days in a letter to me. His account based on jottings in his diaries, gives such a vivid picture of McDougall both as a lecture-room personality and as a researcher that with Sir Cyril's permission I quote him in full. Under the title "Reminiscences of William McDougall," Sir Cyril says:

"I first met McDougall in 1903, when as an undergraduate, I decided to take Psychology as a "Special Subject" for the second part of my degree examination. At that time he held a post in Sully's new laboratory at University College, London, and merely came up to Oxford twice a week to deliver lectures. The first course was advertised as dealing with 'Moral Psychology,' and the second with 'Body and Mind.' They consisted in fact of the preliminary drafts of his books—*Social Psychology* and *Body and Mind*.

"For the first of the series the lecture hall was reasonably full; for the second it was crowded. In those days women students who attended university lectures were chaperoned by their college tutors and required to sit apart from the men. Hence I was embarrassed to observe that, with the exception of a youth near the door, I was the only male. McDougall, who (as I subsequently discovered) had no notion of time, kept his audience waiting for nearly twenty minutes. When at last he mounted the platform in gown and mortarboard and then removed the cap from his head, an audible gasp floated up from the feminine section. One young lady murmured quite breathlessly: 'Oh, but that head should be modelled in marble!' McDougall in those days wore his ginger hair almost as long as the contemporary Beatle; his muscular torso was an impressive contrast to the stooping and bespectacled figure cut by the average lecturer; and his glance, as it swept the audience hall, was positively imperial. The ladies immediately opened their notebooks, not to make notes on the lecture, but to sketch those handsome features.

"At the end of the lecture my mind was made up, and I boldly asked him there and then if I could 'read with him' for my special subject. He agreed, and explained that his system would 'combine the Oxford and the German.' I was to read William James's *Principles*—one chapter per week—and discuss it with him at a 'tutorial' on Monday afternoons; but on Wednesdays I should be set to learn experimental techniques, like a student in a German laboratory, by embarking on a research of my own; while on Fridays I should act as subject for other research workers. At first the only other research worker was McDougall himself, who was then carrying out experiments on color visions and on apperception. Presently, however, the other male listener in the lecture hall, Jack Flugel, turned up; and together we undertook an elaborate research, standardizing intelligence tests for Galton's projected school surveys.

"The following year McDougall built a home on Boar's Hill, a couple of miles outside Oxford; and we began to see much more of him. For somewhat different reasons we were all three interested in psychical research, and attempted—with varying results—a number of experiments in telepathy. Dr. F. C. S. Schiller, another admirer of William James, occasionally joined us, and suggested using the statistical methods of comparison and analysis proposed by Oliver Lodge—who at that time was President of the British Psychical Research Society, an office subsequently held by both Schiller and McDougall.

"Of the various topics which the founders of the Society had put forward as calling urgently for research, the one which McDougall believed was most amenable to scientific study was that of hypnosis. By its means, he thought, it might be possible to train 'mediums,' to induce telepathic states, and possibly even communicate with the dead. In those days few people—whether psychologists, physicians, scientists, or philosophers—thought that hypnotism was anything more than a music-hall stunt. McDougall accordingly decided to give a series of public lectures on 'Hypnotism and Suggestion.' He had little difficulty in hypnotizing almost anyone who did not know him too intimately. Indeed, with that commanding presence and imperial glance it seemed natural, even to skeptics, that he should bring it off. And his demonstrations were decidedly impressive—sometimes almost hair-raising. The medical members of the university considered such exhibitions 'unprofessional,' and clerical members ascribed them to the Devil. McDougall accordingly had to abandon public performances; but we continued our sessions in private.

"His most remarkable 'subject' was a brilliant student of philosophy who was completely blind. One evening, under hypnosis, and speaking with an unfamiliar voice, he announced that he was the Egyptian carpenter who carved certain tablets 'in the hollow tomb of the King in his Den . . . an eagle and a hand and a zigzag . . . and the God on the steps with the bright white crown . . . King of the upper and the lower world.' His vivid description of the interior of the tomb was quite awe-inspiring, but seemed to savor somewhat of the imaginative fiction of those days. We were astonished, some eight or nine months later, to read a very similar account first in the newspapers and then in the publications of the Egyptian Exploration Society. At about the time of the séance, it appeared, Sir Flinders Petrie had been excavating the cenotaph of a king of the First Dynasty called Semti (*c.* 3200 B.C.), whose 'Horus name' was Den. (A hand is the hieroglyphic for D and a horizontal zigzag the hieroglyphic for N, as carved in his cartouche. The 'eagle' or rather hawk over the cartouche is the symbol of Horus, the sky-god, from whom the kings were descended. Den Semti, a great fighter and a patron of the arts, was the first to assume the title of 'King of Upper and Lower Egypt.') In the tomb was a tablet representing the king dancing before Osiris (the father of Horus)—who was often entitled 'the God on the steps,' and was so represented, wearing his emblematic white crown. There is in the British Museum a small but very lifelike ivory figure, representing the First Dynasty king wearing a white crown, which may quite possibly date from Semti's reign.

"The student himself claimed to know nothing of ancient Egypt beyond what was in the Bible; and, owing to his blindness, his reading was extremely restricted. I remember heated arguments in favor of five possible hypotheses: (i) an actual communication from the surviving mind or spirit of the Egyptian of the period, or possibly a reincarnation; (ii) a set of coincidences, with details probably drawn by hearsay from current fiction or the newspapers;

(iii) fraud, based on the same sources; (iv) clairvoyance or precognition; and (v) telepathy.

"Sir Flinders Petrie, the archaeologist, wholly rejected the notion that *he* might have communicated the information by telepathy to an unknown recipient in Oxford, and apparently favored (ii) or (iii). McDougall, with his usual caution, was noncommittal. In those days he was particularly eager to emphasize the unrecognized importance of unconscious mental processes; without any intention to deceive, he argued, the student might be unconsciously reconstructing data from forgotten memories of what he had heard about Egyptian explorations; and he recalled that he himself had frequently been present in the Common Room at University College when Petrie had been discussing his plans or his finds, and so might (a) have unconsciously overheard what was going on at Abydos, and (b) have unconsciously transmitted it telepathically to the student. The more we studied the available data, however, the more we were struck with the numerous discrepancies; and it became clear that occasional incidents of this type could claim no evidential value.

"In the hope of gaining more light on the hypnotic state McDougall suggested that I should allow myself to be hypnotized, and subsequently report my introspections. We spent almost all the afternoons of a whole month in these attempts. I was very amenable to suggestion: I never lost consciousness, but I often lost my self-control. I remember roaring with laughter at this dignified don waving his fingertips before my sleepy eyes, like Svengali on the stage; however, my 'symptoms' were rather coolly received. What was worse, I completely lost my sense of time. During the last week of our experiments I was performing every evening with an amateur dramatic society at an Oxford theater. McDougall promised to release me a couple of hours before the curtain was due to rise. But, as I have said, he had no notion of time, and even declared (on the basis of a Dunne-like theory) that he 'didn't believe in it.' As a result, I had to race down Boar's Hill at breakneck speed on my bicycle, and sometimes had to go on for the very first scene with practically no make-up.

"McDougall, however, with his keen interest in applied psychology, devoted far more time to experiments on the results of suggestion under normal conditions. He believed that many of the effects attributed to alcohol and other drugs were largely due to unconscious suggestion, and was constantly preaching the need to use controls. He showed uncanny skill in concocting drinks with cayenne, apple juice, chemical essences and soda water, such as the inexperienced youngsters who were his 'patients' would accept as a draught of champagne or a cocktail. (In the days of Prohibition he might easily have made a fortune.) I have seen the only female student he ever accepted—

a friend of his wife and a prim and proper lecturer at a women's college—laughing, shouting and lurching about like an intoxicated undergraduate—all as a result of a few harmless glasses poured from a labeled bottle which had originally contained Scotch whisky.

"McDougall, Flugel, and I travelled together to attend the International Congress of Psychology at Geneva in 1912. All the famous psychologists from every part of the world seemed to be present. As a final treat the Swiss organizers put us on board their newest steamboat to be taken the whole length of that beautiful lake and back. At the Isle of Clarens a wind got up; and McDougall dryly inquired, 'What future would there be for the young science of psychology if, thanks to the prayers of the Oxford clergy, the boat went down with all hands on board?' I remember how Flugel joined a small crowd on the deck to listen to Ernest Jones expounding the novel doctrines of Freud, while McDougall (who later declared he had thought of most of them himself long ago and rejected half) stood in the prow and related Flournoy's account of his experiments with his latest medium, Hélène Smith, who during a recent trance had given a firsthand description of life on the planet Mars. I have always kept in mind McDougall's own comments—virtually a lecture on how *not* to carry out a research in paranormal psychology.

"His personal losses during the first World War and the American attacks on his views which he had to face at Harvard deeply distressed him; and on his return he seemed quite a different man. He cheered up a little after he went to Duke; and used to come over once a year to England, staying at his son's charming cottage on the slopes of the Chilterns. He showed me over it with pride; and at first was full of the doings of Rhine and others, and his own experiments on the Lamarckian hypotheses. But, owing perhaps to his increasing deafness, he gradually became more reticent than ever. He gloomily anticipated a second world war, but hoped, so he said, he would not survive to witness it. Nor did he.

"To McDougall both British psychologists and British psychology owe a vast debt which has never been fully recognized. I could relate innumerable stories about many acts of kindness to his students, of which they never learned until much later and then only by accident. But his services to psychology were still more far-reaching. In other countries, when psychology changed from a branch of philosophy to an experimental science, it adopted the general materialistic basis that had become so popular among scientists toward the close of the nineteenth century. The fact that this did not happen in Britain is due primarily to McDougall. He was the first experimental psychologist which this country produced. Yet, unlike many who followed him, he never became *purely* an experimentalist. Indeed, he was forever emphasizing the limitations of the mechanistic approach. The reaction (which set in only after he died) against the more materialistic type of behaviorism is gradually justifying his criticisms, and is following, almost unawares, the paths which he originally mapped out. How often, when we hear of some recent discovery or interpretation which the present generation hails as new, do those of us who remember McDougall's teaching exclaim: 'But McDougall told us that over sixty years ago!' "

Such incidental sidelights on McDougall make clear that all his life he had to put up with his own deceivingly crusty exterior. But the sweetness of character that lay behind that crust nevertheless constantly comes to view when one examines his life and career.

At the beginning of the first World War, he unhesitatingly dropped his work and enlisted as a private in the French Army.[2] "I found myself," he says, "driving an ambulance and dodging German shells on the western front." Later, because of his training in psychology, he was made a major in the Royal Army Medical Corps and put in charge of shell-shock patients in need of skilled mental treatment. He called his patients "a most strange, wonderful, and pitiful collection of nervously disordered soldiers, mostly purely functional. . . . One thing was clear—successful treatment required the exploration and fullest possible laying bare of the causes of the trouble. . . . Sympathetic rapport with the patient was the main thing, not the mysterious 'transference' of a mythical 'father fixation' of the 'libido'; but, under the circumstances, a very natural and simple human relation. It is true that I felt like the father of a multitude of helpless children, hopelessly stumbling on the brink of hell; and that they for the most part were very docile and dependent and grateful. It was a wonderful experience for a psychologist. . . . I was giving my whole time and energy to work that was indisputably worthwhile."

In short, McDougall threw Freudian jargon and concepts to the wind, substituting instead the marked common sense, tenderness and compassion that were part of his nature. The same note is apparent in his account of his reactions when he was part of the Cambridge Anthropological Expedition to the Torres Straits off the coast of New Guinea in 1899.[2] The purpose was to make a complete survey of the sensory endowments of the Negroid inhabitants of the islands; among the important results of the study was a theory proposed by McDougall "of the common origin and diffusion from a common center (in Asia north of the Himalaya) of the religion of the Kayans (a dominant tribe in the heart of Borneo) and of the religion of ancient Rome."

"I found it easy to make sympathetic contact with such people," he said, adding, "Looking back, I cannot now understand why I rejected this alluring prospect [the temptation to make field anthropology his life work]. I remember that my conscious ground of rejection was characteristically arrogant. I said to myself, 'That field is too easy for me'; and turned back to my original scheme of direct attack on the secrets of human nature."

There once again is the curious ambivalence that made him "arrogant," crusty and formidable at one time and capable of warm fellowship with some of the most primitive people on earth at another time.

His account of his marriage is another example. James Ward, to whose lectures he had listened at Oxford, advised him to attend the lectures of G. E. Müller at Göttingen—"one of the very few instances," said McDougall, "in which I have accepted advice."[2]

"My choice," he continued, "was determined by what might seem an ir-relevant consideration. I had, against my principles, fallen suddenly in love and become engaged to marry, and Göttingen promised to be a better scene for a year's honeymoon than Paris, Vienna or any other large city. We spent a delightful year in quaint, quiet Göttingen. My marriage at the compara-tively early age of twenty-nine was against my considered principles . . . but I have never regretted the step. It might be thought that for a charming girl to marry an intellectual monstrosity like myself would be like making a bed-fellow of a hedgehog. But my wife has proved equal to the task she under-took. In intellect and temperament we were as unlike as possible, pure com-plementaries: I introverted, reserved, outwardly cold and arrogant, severely disciplined, absorbed in abstruse intellectualities; she extroverted, all warmth and sympathy and charm and intuitive understanding. To do one's duty by a wife and five children does require the expenditure of considerable time and energy that might *possibly* be given to purely intellectual tasks. But I have always found delight and recreation in my home; I have never ceased to grow more grateful to my wife for her influence upon me and her perfect exercise of the privileges of her position; and I realize that she has saved me from entanglements which, if I had followed my principle, might well have wrecked me. Then, too, I have learned more psychology from her intuitive under-standing of persons than from any, perhaps all, of the great authors. I ven-ture to think that the success of our marriage has been partly due to my recognition that the intellectual is apt to ruin his domestic relations by per-mitting himself to regard them as of less importance than his work. At a very early stage I resolved to avoid that error."[2]

After World War I, McDougall continued his medical work with shell-shock cases until 1919. He then returned to Oxford where he resumed teaching and took up practice in the out-patient department of the Oxford City Hospital.

He had long since rejected the ideas of Freud, though he agreed with some of Freud's doctrine. He put Jung in a somewhat different category; after the war, he was psychoanalyzed by Jung in Zurich—"so far," he said, "as that process is possible for so hopelessly normal a personality as mine. I made an effort to be as open-minded as possible; and came away enlightened but not convinced."[2]

Jung was much interested in psychical research; and, since McDougall had been a member of the British Society for Psychical Research since 1901, and was elected president of the Society at about that time (1920), it may be presumed that he and Jung had some illuminating discussions of the subject. But McDougall says nothing about that.

At about this time, with some thirty-five notebooks crammed with observations, he felt they must be put into a book. He turned to the writing of *Group Mind,* for which he considered his *Social Psychology* an introduction.[2] The general idea was that any group—such as a nation—possesses an organization, mainly mental, which resides not in any one individual, but is rather an organized system of interacting energies, a sort of super-personality.

Partly, McDougall thought, because of its title, and partly because of his "arrogance," the book was unfavorably received, so that his notion of a magnum opus went aglimmering. He found it increasingly hard to believe in the value of his work. Then his spirits were lifted by an invitation to occupy James's old chair in the Department of Philosophy and Psychology at Harvard. James had died in 1910. Hugo Münsterberg had followed him in the Harvard post but had died during the war. Now in 1921 it was McDougall's turn to occupy what he regarded as "the premier post in America."

There were other reasons for accepting the offer. McDougall was bitter against the English climate, blaming it for his total deafness in one ear and for the loss of one of his children from rheumatic fever. In his forty-ninth year, he came to the United States.[2]

He found the atmosphere at Harvard far less hospitable than he had expected. His *Group Mind* had drawn a hostile and stinging review there, and the behaviorists, firmly in the saddle, instantly opened attack. The situation was made worse by the fact that most of the Harvard graduate students had been trained in the prevailing mechanistic orthodoxies at other universities.

He increased his difficulties by allowing himself to be persuaded to give a lecture on national eugenics. Calling the lecture "Is America Safe for Democracy?" McDougall inevitably touched on racism and stirred up a hornet's nest. In his opinion, the lecture led to implacable hostility in the American press toward his later publications.

McDougall counterbalanced the ill will to some degree by making a few friends, and their encouragement made him feel once again that his work was useful. He began a laboratory investigation, using white rats, of the Lamarckian theory that environment causes changes in organisms according to need and that these characteristics are passed along to offspring—that acquired characteristics, in fact, may be inherited. "So, with a small group of graduate students," he reported rather ruefully, "I set out on this fool's experiment."[2] What drove him was the conviction that a positive result would be a heavy blow to the mechanistic biology. "It would," he felt, "place mind at the very heart of the evolutionary process, instead of leaving it as a by-product of that process, an unintelligible excrescence upon life."

Writing of the experiment nine years later, with the rats in their twenty-fourth generation, he felt that the work already gave promise of success. "If, in the next few years," he wrote, "this promise should be amply realized, the work will rank as by far my most important contribution to science; although the execution of it will have required little but great confidence in my own judgment and dogged persistence. This work has absorbed all the time and energy I have had for experimental research." [2]

The experiments were extended through forty-nine rat generations (lasting some sixteen years), and McDougall stated that the "later generations showed an increased facility, measured by a reduction in the amount of training required by nearly 90 per cent." He believed that this indication of "inheritance of an acquired characteristic" pointed to the conclusion that evolution is essentially purposive, not a mere mechanical process. He believed also that it "lent strong support to the idea of a non-material basis for racial as well as individual memory."

Commenting on this, Sir Cyril Burt says, "Few, I fancy, would nowadays consider this a conclusive or a permanent contribution. But the experiments certainly deserve to be repeated." [9]

It is not commonly realized that McDougall, through laboratory experimentation, arrived at conclusions which have played an important part in what is known today as "cybernetics."

"In his laboratory at Oxford," says Sir Cyril, [9] "he spent much of his time discussing, designing, and even constructing a variety of diagrammatic and working models, which might illustrate or reproduce typical activities of the human mind. In view of the renewed interest in such inventions, it will be of interest to note how far the theoretical principles on which he relied have since been adopted by contemporary mechanicians. . . .

"McDougall's earliest models, like those of Descartes, were conceived mainly in hydraulic terms: the essential work was done by 'currents' of nervous energy, flowing from a common 'reservoir,' and directed by variable sluice-gates situated at the cell-junctions or 'synapses.'" He maintained, says Burt, that "transmission across the synapses was . . . (as Fechner's experiments on discrimination suggested) a variable process which could only be expressed by probabilities."

"Here then," comments Burt, "was an inescapable element of indeterminacy . . ." demonstrating "that, at the very best, all that an external observer can ever do is to predict the *probable* performance of the reagent. . . . As [McDougall] remarked in discussing learning by trial and error, 'the earlier reactions of the higher cerebral levels have a random character, as though the choice was determined by blindly throwing dice: the problem therefore is—can consciousness increase efficiency by loading the dice?' All blueprints for an artificial brain should, he considered, be based in the future not on mechanistic but on 'probabilistic' principles. . . .

"The outcome of all these speculative efforts was that [McDougall] grew more and more firmly convinced that, as he had vaguely suspected from the outset, there would forever remain certain irreducible characteristics in human behavior which would defy all attempts at mechanistic explanation."

From his teaching days at Oxford until his death in Durham, while devoting himself to his work in psychology, McDougall ceaselessly supported psychical research. He contributed articles on the subject to the proceedings and journals of the British and American Societies and to other publications, and he urged the study of parapsychology as a university subject. When he decided that satisfactory standards were not being maintained by the American Society for Psychical Research, he joined Dr. Walter Franklin Prince, Dr. Elwood Worcester and others in founding the Boston Society for Psychic Research. He took part in the investigations of the controversial medium, "Margery." With the help, successively, of Dr. Gardner Murphy and Dr. G. H. Estabrooks, he introduced controlled experimentation in parapsychology at the Harvard Psychology Laboratory. Most important of all, he launched the work of Dr. J. B. Rhine at Duke.

In 1927 McDougall was asked by the late Dr. William Preston Few, then President of Duke University, to suggest a qualified person to head the psychology department there. McDougall made several suggestions, none of which were received favorably, and then proposed that he take the position himself, an offer that was immediately accepted.

McDougall was already well acquainted with Dr. J. B. Rhine and with his wife, Dr. Louisa E. Rhine, both of whom had taken doctorates in biology at the University of Chicago. They wanted to turn from biology to parapsychology and were interested in research that might lead to evidence of survival after death. In his foreword to Dr. Rhine's notable first book, *Extra-Sensory Perception* (1934),[10] McDougall tells of bringing the Rhines to Duke —thus initiating a research which has since become world famous and which at the same time made history in the field of parapsychology.

The experiments at Duke were made a matter of permanent record with the founding in 1937 of the *Journal of Parapsychology*, and the list of books that have evolved from the research is impressive. Besides *Extra-Sensory Perception*, they include J. B. Rhine's *New Frontiers of the Mind* (1937), *The Reach of the Mind* (1947), and *The New World of the Mind* (1953); Louisa E. Rhine's *Hidden Channels of the Mind* (1961), and *ESP in Life*

and Lab: Tracing Hidden Channels (1967) ; Parapsychology, Frontier Science
of the Mind (1957), by J. B. Rhine and J. Gaither Pratt; and J. G. Pratt's
own book, Parapsychology: An Insider's View of ESP (1964).

Only the first two of these books, Extra-Sensory Perception and New
Frontiers of the Mind, appeared in McDougall's lifetime, but, long before
the end of his life and despite what he considered the disappointing lack of
attention paid to his own writings, McDougall left a permanent mark on the
scientific and philosophic thought of his time.

For many years, he seemed to have a premonition that his physical inheritance from his mother presaged a relatively early death for him, and he hurried
himself into added effort and maximum production partly because he felt his
time was short. A fixed part of his routine, come what might, was a daily stint
of writing.

The disease that finally took him was indeed the same that had ended his
mother's life. He went with courage, but reluctantly. Shortly before he died,
he said protestingly to his friend and colleague, Dr. D. K. Adams, "Adams,
life is too damned short!"

In spite of that protest, he seems to have accepted his lot stoically. Like
Browning's Grammarian, he held his course unswervingly so long as life was
in him.

The last book he wrote, when he knew his time was short, was The Riddle
of Life; if he had added a subtitle, it might well have been The Riddle of
Death. He was consumingly curious about both.

For many days before the end, he asked constantly whether copies of the
new book, still on the press, had come from the publishers. At last the book
arrived, two days before he died. To his friend, the president of Duke University, he presented a copy inscribed "To William Preston Few from William
McDougall. Hail and Farewell."

REFERENCES

1. Burt, Sir Cyril: Introduction to McDougall's Psychology: The Study of Behavior. London: Williams and Norgate (Home University Library of Modern
   Knowledge), 1912, and London: Thornton Butterworth, 1937.
2. McDougall, William: Autobiographical sketch in A History of Psychology in
   Autobiography, edited by Carl Murchison. Worcester, Mass.: Clark University Press, 1930, and London: Oxford University Press, 1930.
3. ————: Psychical Research as a University Study, in The Case For and
   Against Psychical Research, edited by Carl Murchison. Worcester, Mass.:
   Clark University Press, 1927.
4. Journal of Parapsychology, Vol. 1, No. 1, March 1937. Editorial Introduction.
5. Spearman, Charles: The Life and Work of William McDougall. Character
   and Personality, Vol. 7, No. 3, 1939.

6. McDougall, William: *Body and Mind: A History and a Defense of Animism.* London: Methuen & Co., 1911; Sixth edition, 1923.
7. ———: *An Introduction to Social Psychology.* London: Methuen & Co., 1908, and in University Paperbacks, 1960, 1961, London: Methuen & Co. and New York: Barnes & Noble.
8. Oldfield, R. C.: Psychology in Oxford—1898-1949. *Bulletin of the British Psychological Society,* July and October 1950.
9. Burt, Sir Cyril: The Permanent Contributions of McDougall to Psychology. *British Journal of Educational Psychology,* Vol. XXV, Part I, February 1955.
10. Rhine, J. B.: *Extra-Sensory Perception.* Foreword by William McDougall. Boston: Boston Society for Psychic Research, 1934.

PART I

1.   A Plea For Psychical Research*

In all ages the mass of mankind has believed in the occurrence of certain phenomena which have excited wonder because they seem to show that a few persons possess supernormal capacities. As science has become more and more definitely mechanistic, it has become possible to define these alleged capacities negatively, to say that they include all those which seem to fall outside the limits of the possible as prescribed by a strictly mechanistic science. These alleged capacities fall into two distinct groups: (1) capacity for manifesting knowledge not obtained, directly or indirectly, through sense-perception; (2) the production of physical changes in ways that cannot be interpreted in terms of physical science as now understood and which seem to be irreconcilable with strictly mechanistic science.

We may speak of all alleged manifestations of these two classes as supernormal phenomena. If such phenomena, of either or both classes, really occur, they would seem to show that the categories of physical science are not adequate to the interpretation of life and mind. That is the essence of their claim upon the interest of men of science. For science does unmistakably claim, through the mouths of the great majority of its devotees, that its mechanistic categories are adequate to such interpretation; that the operations of mind do not transcend these categories, are not exceptions to its laws; that the world as described by mechanistic science is a closed system and that the phenomena of mind must be interpreted in a manner compatible with this mechanistic description of the world.

* Originally published in *The Forum*, Vol. 75 (1926), pp. 532-537.

The essential question raised by these alleged supernormal phenomena is this: Can we find in them empirical evidence that mind transcends the categories of mechanistic science?

Now I observe that the vast majority of civilized intelligent men always have accepted, and do still accept, the positive answer to this question. Indeed, their lives are controlled in some measure by this belief. For the vast majority still profess to accept religion of some kind, and to accept any religion is to accept this positive answer, to assert that mind is transcendent. It may be said that Pantheism is a religion which does not imply this belief. But it is clear that a mechanistic pantheism, such as that of Spinoza, can be called a religion only by exercising a degree of courtesy which amounts to an actual misuse of language.

I observe, also, that vast numbers of intelligent men, including all Christians, believe they have empirical evidence of this transcendence in the facts of prayer and worship and in what they regard as the historical bases of their religion. Furthermore, a smaller, but still a very large, number believe that they have empirical evidences of such transcendence of more striking and unmistakable kinds, and they base their religious beliefs largely upon such evidence.

Science on the other hand has asserted, more and more confidently throughout the modern period, that such evidences never have occurred and never can occur; that the alleged evidences always are and always will be illusory. It is not to be doubted, I think, that, if this verdict of science should become generally accepted, in the course of a few generations all religion will disappear from the civilized world, except as a subject for antiquarian and anthropological research.

This consideration is the ground of the importance claimed for psychical research. For psychical research is essentially the endeavor to answer this question: Can we find empirical evidence of the transcendence of mind?

If the answer should be clearly and finally positive, it will be a sure basis on which religions may continue to develop. If the answer should be finally negative, we must reconcile ourselves to the disappearance of all religion. Civilization must proceed to adjust itself on a new moral basis.

The determination of this issue lies with men of science. Here is a responsibility which they cannot repudiate without incurring grave reproach. Yet, with very few exceptions, they do repudiate it. They show a scornful hostility to psychical research, or, at the best, a strict neutrality which in practical effect is the reverse of benevolent.

There are those among the men of science who excuse this hostility by professing to know that the answer must be, in any event, in the negative, that alleged supernormal phenomena cannot occur because, by definition, they would be inconsistent with the strictly mechanistic scheme of the world, a scheme which is believed to be literally and finally true. This is to deduce the negative answer from a metaphysical dogma or prejudice.

Most of the men of science who maintain this dogmatic negative have been led to this position, I believe, not through any critical or philosophical reflection, but through the cumulative effect on them of the successive triumphs of mechanistic science. This is true more especially of the biologists. When they discover, to select one example, that the eggs of a sea-urchin can be induced to develop parthenogenetically by the addition of certain salts to the water in which they live, they are inspired with an unjustified confidence in the adequacy of physical and chemical principles to the explanation of all the phenomena of life and mind.

Another group of scientists who reject the possibility of any positive answer to our question consists of those who report that they approached it with an open mind. But they have found, they say, in every instance of alleged supernormal phenomena, that the supposed facts would not stand criticism but dissolved into error and fraud. They believe, therefore, that this will be true of every alleged instance if it be examined with sufficient care.

If every competent and scientifically trained investigator who has given serious attention to alleged supernormal phenomena, or even if a majority of such men, had reached this conclusion, the argument would be strong and would justify a fair degree of confidence in a negative answer to our great question. But what are the facts? They are exactly the opposite. During the last half century a number of men whose names stand high in the learned world have interested themselves in these alleged supernormal phenomena. Some of these are men of science of high standing—such men as Sir William Crookes, Lord Rayleigh, and Professor Charles Richet. Others are men of intellectual eminence who, although not technically men of science, are competent judges of the claims of science—men such as Henry Sidgwick, William James, Professor Bergson, Dr. F. C. S. Schiller, and Lord Balfour. Now the fact seems to be that no one such man has ever turned away from psychical research declaring himself satisfied of the truth of the negative answer. Instead, every one of them seems to have become more rather than less inclined to admit the positive answer. Some of them have been led, indeed, to assert the positive answer with the utmost confidence.

This state of affairs constitutes, I submit, strong ground for demanding systematic and sustained investigation, by the methods of science, into the alleged phenomena. And more, it constitutes strong ground for believing that eventually the positive answer will turn out to be the true one.

Consider the state of affairs throughout our western civilization. The world is divided into two acutely opposed parties. On the one hand, organized science, which formerly battled for the right to live, is now powerful and aggressive. It wields an immense authority and bears a correspondingly great responsibility. And it steadily maintains before the world the attitude that this question of the transcendence of mind is a closed one, that science has finally answered it in the negative and that no further investigation is needed.

On the other hand stands practically all the rest of mankind; nearly all that part of the learned world which is not directly concerned with natural science, all the representatives of religion, all the members of the various churches. This overwhelming majority continues to affirm its belief in the transcendence of mind, and, for the most part, attaches great practical importance to this belief.

Between these two parties, between the highly organized and efficient army of science which dogmatically denies and the vast public which confidently and somewhat uncritically affirms, we have a tiny group of men, a few score in number, who are trying to get at the truth, who are trying to gather and to evaluate all the empirical evidence that can be adduced.

This is not a satisfactory state of affairs. The social mind cannot be healthy while it is thus acutely divided on a matter which is rightly felt to be supremely important. Already there are signs that the tension between the two parties is becoming acute. The assembled bishops of the Episcopal Church of America have announced authoritatively the reality of spiritual healing. The English bishops have this aspect of the question under consideration and seem likely to agree with their American brothers. In certain States of this country we seem to be within sight of a time when State schools and universities will be forbidden to teach some, at least, of the conclusions and theories of science.

The representatives of science face this growing volume of discontent confidently and even scornfully. But is such confidence justified? Let us reflect that the position maintained by science is intrinsically weak, because it is not established by the principles of science, but rather, like the opposing creed, remains a matter of faith and of dogma rather than of demonstration. While this remains true, it is foolish for science to believe that its authority will suffice to dragoon the mass of mankind into acquiescence.

I would say to the army of science and especially to its leaders—Beware! Your position is not so strong as you seem to think it. There are within your ranks many who are not convinced of the justice of your attitude. There remains the possibility, even, of a crushing demonstration of the falsity of your position. The ruthless application of the methods of science may deal this blow at any moment. And if it falls, you will be made ridiculous before the world.

The time has come, I urge, when men of science should combine and, by a concentrated and sustained effort, settle this great question forever. It is not yet fifty years since a few pioneers began critically to examine the alleged evidences of the transcendence of mind. During these years a mere handful of competent persons have attempted to carry on the research, handicapped by the hostility of both the dogmatically opposed parties. If organized science would adopt, in this matter, the truly scientific attitude; if it would support psychical research freely and unreservedly, then every type of the alleged supernormal phenomena could be investigated adequately and evaluated critically. And if, after fifty years of psychical research thus supported and cultivated, no such evidence should be found to have withstood the application of scientific method, then, at last, science might be able to maintain, with justice, the attitude which at present it assumes dogmatically and uncritically.

If, on the other hand, the verdict after fifty years should be that some things do happen which cannot be reconciled with a strictly mechanistic science, that will not mean, as has sometimes been asserted, that science is thereby overthrown and destroyed. It may merely prove that mind is what all men, the few scientific extremists excepted, have always held it to be, namely a creative activity that cannot be brought within the bounds set by the mechanistic categories. And the recognition of this fact, if fact it be, may open a new door for the progress of science and may increase vastly its efficacy in the promotion of human welfare and in the harmonious development of our civilization.

2.   The Need for Psychical Research*

EDITORIAL NOTE.—In its original form this address was delivered in Boston, May 25, 1922, and was published in the Harvard Graduates' Magazine for September. Professor McDougall has slightly remodelled it at the request of the Journal, which desires to give it a wider circulation [*Journal A.S.P.R.*].

I have the honor to address you in the capacity of President of the American Society for Psychical Research. I propose simply to state the grounds on which, as it seems to me, the American Society for Psychical Research may fairly hope for and justly demand an increased measure of support from the educated people of this country.

I shall not delay to define what we mean by Psychical Research, nor to sketch the history of the profoundly interesting movement of thought which goes by that name. I will plunge at once into my topic, and will say briefly, first, why we should support Psychical Research in general, secondly, why this support should be given in particular to the work of the American Society for Psychical Research. There must be thousands of intelligent people, not now members of the Society, who agree with me in thinking that Psychical Research is in some manner and degree interesting. My aim is to stimulate that interest—to make clear the grounds which justify it— and to try to give the interest a more practical bent than perhaps it has had hitherto.

The extreme differences of opinion and attitude among us toward the phenomena with which Psychical Research is concerned make it necessary to emphasize differently the arguments directed to the holders of these di-

* Reprinted from *Jour. A.S.P.R.*, Vol. 17 (1923), pp. 4-14.

vergent views. We may divide intelligent persons into three main groups in this respect.

(1) There are those who refuse to support Psychical Research because they claim to know that there is "nothing in it," nothing to be discovered by it. Unfortunately, a considerable number of scientific men, among whom we might fairly expect to find at least the support of sympathy and approval, if not of cooperation, belong to this group. It might seem as though no argument in favor of Psychical Research could logically touch these persons unless their dogmatic negation can first be shaken. That, however, is not the case. This position of scientific indifference or hostility can be easily turned.

The function of the man of science is, not merely to discover truth for himself, but also to make truth prevail, to establish it in the body of traditional beliefs by which civilized society lives and by which alone it can hope to progress to a better state of things than it has yet attained. And Science cannot achieve this great purpose merely by adding one fact after another to the body of scientific truth. It must also examine critically any beliefs which are widely entertained by cultivated minds and by the popular mind and which are, or may seem to be, incompatible with scientific truth; and if on investigation these beliefs prove to be ill-founded, Science must give its authoritative verdict against them, and do what it can to overthrow them.

Any man of science who does not admit this to be a proper function and duty of organized science is not worthy of the name; he is merely a man who grubs in a laboratory for his own private and selfish reasons.

The men of science who are opposed to, or indifferent to, Psychical Research because they profess to know that there is "nothing in it" beyond illusion and delusion based on fraud, these men really stand upon their belief that the materialistic conception of the world is true. Only from belief in the literal truth of this view can their opinion of the futility of all Psychical Research be derived; only by that belief can their opinion be justified, in the present state of knowledge. Even then, if any man of science is convinced of the essential truth of Materialism, he is yet under obligation to approve and to give at least moral support to Psychical Research. For only by a well-organized and long-sustained course of scientific investigation into the phenomena of Psychical Research can it be proved that there is "nothing in them." That investigation is still only in an early stage; and, so far as it has gone, it certainly cannot be claimed to have yielded support to the materialistic philosophy.

If Materialism is true, let us ascertain the fact by all means; let the truth be told, though the heavens fall and all the gods also. And let us then hope that civilization may succeed in adjusting itself to this truth and by its aid may render human life better worth living. But at present it is clear that the civilized world is becoming more and more acutely divided on this question, the question of the truth of Materialism. This lack of sure knowledge, and the consequent wide and widening divergence of opinion is a scandal, a reproach to our boasted scientific culture, and an actual and increasing social danger. Here, then, is one good reason why the convinced scientific materialist should support Psychical Research.

But there is a second good reason. It is the investigation of the obscure and mysterious and unaccountable phenomena that leads on to great scientific discoveries. Psychical Research has already established phenomena which, if they are eventually to be brought within the boundaries of the materialistic scheme of things, will necessarily require and lead to great developments of that scheme, certainly in the biological, and almost as certainly in the physical, sciences. For this reason also, no matter how convinced he may be of the truth of Materialism, the man of science should support Psychical Research.

For these two good reasons, then, even the scientific materialists and those philosophers who camouflage their acceptance of the materialistic scheme by giving to things names other than those used by science—even they should give their approval and support to Psychical Research. And, if I were a convinced materialist, I should feel that there was no anomaly in my officiating as president of the American Society for Psychical Research and urging a more active support of its work. I should feel rather that I was merely undertaking an obligation that rests upon men of science.

(2) A second class of cultivated persons, and this is probably the largest class, professes to have no conviction as to the possible results of Psychical Research. Persons of this class are not prepared to swear that there is "nothing in it." Many of them are even inclined to believe that there is "something in it," and that Psychical Research may succeed in scientifically establishing the reality of certain forms of existence and happening which science at present officially ignores. But they remain indifferent, prepared to enjoy a good ghost story, or to listen with interest to what may seem *prima facie* a story of telepathic communication. Yet they refrain from supporting, or refuse to support, Psychical Research. Their attitude seems to be in the main—Why should I dabble in these things? I prefer to leave all such enquiry to those who have nothing better to do.

Now many persons of this class are not without interest in, or even zeal for, the moral welfare of mankind; and many of them are religiously minded, and perhaps professed Christians. How, then, do they justify their indifference when Psychical Research says, Here is the way, if there be any way, to establish the truth, or at least the possibility of the truth, of those beliefs in the reality of spirit and of moral purpose in the world order, on which our moral tradition and moral culture, in fact the whole of our civilization, are founded?

Such persons offer one of two answers. Some say—The reality of spirit, the truth that the world is in some sense a moral universe, and the guarantee of the conservation of moral values, these things have been supernaturally revealed once for all, and no further evidence is necessary.

To these our answer is that the evidence of revelation no longer suffices. It may suffice for you individually. But the world at large, especially our Western civilization, is unmistakably drifting away from these beliefs. More and more clearly and with increasing rapidity the purely materialistic view of the world is gaining acceptance, destroying the old beliefs. And Psychical Research, empirical enquiry into the contemporary evidences of modes of action and being that fall outside the materialistic scheme, such enquiry offers the only possible method of arresting this landslide, of establishing firmly once more in the hearts of men these essential beliefs, by which the development of our moral culture has been molded.

A different attitude is expressed by some of this open-minded but indifferent group. They admit that Materialism is spreading and that it is rapidly becoming the real working creed of the mass of civilized men. But—they say—What of it? Professor Kirsopp Lake gave eloquent expression to this attitude in his recent Ingersoll Lecture. And his expression is the more interesting in that he is a churchman and represents, I suppose, that advanced wing of religious heterodoxy which, as experience shows, becomes the orthodoxy of the quickly following generation. Professor Lake said—I look around and I see men who are essentially materialists leading good and wholesome lives, doing their part as good citizens. They have ceased to trouble about the salvation of their souls and are concerned merely to play the game, to live up to the moral standards they have been taught to accept. And, he added, perhaps they are all the better for this change of attitude. Coming from a leader of religious thought, this is interesting confirmation of what I said just now of the general spread of Materialism.

It was the more interesting because Professor Lake indicated that he himself shared to some degree in the general change of belief and attitude, especially as regards the belief in life after death. He indicated that in his view such life has become, in the light of modern knowledge, very improbable; though he added that, if Psychical Research can produce convincing evidence of its reality, his mind will be open to receive this truth, even though it might demand of him considerable intellectual readjustment. I agree entirely with Professor Lake in his diagnosis of the present tendency; but I am very skeptical in regard to his prognosis. For Professor Lake implied that, in his view, the decent standard of conduct maintained by so many of our fellow men, in spite of their materialistic outlook, affords ground for believing that civilization and morals may continue to thrive indefinitely on the basis of pure Materialism.

That seems to me a very questionable inference. Our civilization, our moral ideals and standards of conduct, have been built up on the basis and under the guidance of certain definite beliefs that are incompatible with Materialism, the belief that our lives have a significance and value that is greater than appears on the surface of things, the belief that we are members of an order of things that somehow is a moral order, and that the value of moral idealism and moral effort cannot be measured in terms of material comfort or the satisfactions of our animal nature. Our moral tradition is the product of such beliefs. There is no good reason to think that in the absence of such beliefs, any high moral tradition could have been evolved by any branch of the human race. Are we then justified in assuming that, if the foundations are sapped away, the superstructure of moral tradition will continue to stand unshaken and unimpaired, powerful to govern human conduct through the long ages to come?

I gravely doubt it. Any society which continued to prosper in that condition would be living on its capital, its capital of moral tradition. And it seems but too probable that that capital, unrenewed and unsustained by any beliefs other than those permitted by a strict Materialism, must undergo a gradual, or perhaps a rapid, attrition.

It is possible even now to point to one way in which the sapping of these beliefs has already seriously modified the moral tradition and influenced the conduct of men so as to constitute a very grave threat to the whole of our civilization. Professor Lake's cheerful, prosperous, decent-living materialists may well think it worth while to live up to the standards of honesty and helpfulness traditional in our society. Finding themselves in the world, through no choice of theirs, they wisely make the best of it; and they see that, in order to make the best of it, they must accept the moral obligations along with the material benefits conferred by civilization. But they are not sure whether in the long run the game is worth the candle, whether, if they had been given the choice, they would have chosen to take a hand in the game. Their attitude is apt to be something of the kind we may express in the words—Let me get through with my life honorably and decently—then after me the deluge. Perhaps few men or women formulate this attitude in words; but it is expressed unmistakably in one great outstanding fact of our civilization. Though each of us came into this life through no choice of his own, each of us can exert choice in the matter of perpetuating the life he bears. We can follow the course of nature and perpetuate our life in our children; or we can refuse to perpetuate it. We can refrain from exercising our privilege of creating new men and women. And the outstanding fact of the utmost significance and evil omen for our civilization is that thinking men and women are choosing more and more to refrain. This is the sign of the times which more than any other casts a dark shadow on the future. And can it be doubted that the decay of Religion, with the spread of Materialism, is at the root of this refusal to perpetuate the life we bear? Everywhere in History the two tendencies have appeared in close connection; and together they have destroyed the great civilizations in which they have grown strong.

The case may be simply stated in this way. If Materialism is true, human life, fundamentally and generally speaking, is not worth living; and men and women who believe Materialism to be true will not in the long run think themselves justified in creating, in calling to life, new individuals to meet the inevitable pains and sorrows and labors of life and the risks of many things far worse than death. Human life, as we know it, is a tragic and pathetic affair, which can only be redeemed by some belief, or at least some hope, in a larger significance than is compatible with the creed of Materialism, no matter in how nobly stoic a form it may be held. The fact cannot be gainsaid, and men and women acknowledge it by their actions.

This, I say, is the most ominous indication that a civilization which resigns itself wholly to Materialism lives upon and consumes its moral capital and is incapable of renewing it. Here perhaps I may venture on a word of personal explanation. I have two hobbies—Psychical Research and Eugenics. So far as I know, I am the only person alive today who takes an active interest in both of these movements. To most of you perhaps these two lines of scientific study have seemed entirely distinct and perhaps even opposed in spirit. I hope what I have said may serve to show you that, for my mind at least, these are the two main lines of approach to the most vital issue that confronts our civilization—two lines whose convergence may in the end prevent the utter collapse which now threatens.

The indifference to Psychical Research of this second group is, then, not justified. Unless Psychical Research—that is to say enquiry according to the strictest principles of empirical science—can discover facts incompatible with Materialism, Materialism will continue to spread. No other power can stop it; revealed religion and metaphysical philosophy are equally helpless before the advancing tide. And if that tide continues to rise and to advance as it is doing now, all the signs point to the view that it will be a destroying tide, that it will sweep away all the hard-won gains of humanity, all the moral traditions built up by the efforts of countless generations for the increase of truth, justice, and charity.

(3) The third group indifferent to the claims of Psychical Research is made up of persons who have become convinced, in one way or another, of the reality of the phenomena which Psychical Research investigates, especially those who believe they have sufficient evidence of the life after death and of communication between the living and the dead. They are the persons generally classed as "spiritualists." These fall into two classes; the first, those who are content merely to draw personal comfort and consolation from their belief. With such persons we are not much concerned. They may be classed with other persons who are concerned only with the salvation of their own souls.

But with the other subdivision of this group we are much concerned. Sir A. Conan Doyle may stand as the perfect type of this class. He is a public-minded man, earnestly concerned to gain general acceptance for what he holds to be the truths of Spiritualism. But, instead of supporting Psychical Research, he is indifferent to it; or rather, he is not merely indifferent, he is actually hostile to it. This is very unfortunate; for in this Sir A. Conan Doyle represents a large number of the very best of the spiritualists. This attitude of impatient hostility on the part of such persons is one of the greatest difficulties in the path of Psychical Research. For experience shows us that, of all those who enter upon the path of Psychical Research, a considerable proportion become lost to it, by passing over into this hostile camp. Having become personally convinced of the truth of the main tenets of Spiritualism, these persons cease to be interested in Research and devote themselves to propaganda. It is only too probable that many of those who listen to or will hereafter read this address are inclining to follow this course, that they are hesitating between Psychical Research and spiritualist propaganda. How are we to meet this very real difficulty? How may we hope to retain the support and cooperation of the already convinced? We cannot afford to lower our standards of evidence or relax the strictness of our rules of investigation, as these persons would have us do. We must continue to run the risk of estranging them by the rigidity of our scientific principles. We must continue to regard Research as of the first importance. Our only hope in respect of these persons is, I think, to convince them that, even from the point of view of their main purpose, namely, the spread of what they hold to be the truth, ours is the better plan. If what they would teach *are* truths, further research will establish them more firmly; if they cannot be verified by further research, they are not truths and ought not to be taught. And by mere propaganda, by popular lecturing and writing and discussion, they will never succeed in gaining general acceptance for their views. Sir A. Conan Doyle and those who share his attitude are attempting a perfectly impossible task. They will never convert the world to their view by the methods they are pursuing.

Organized Science has become tremendously powerful. Philosophy and Religion, which in former ages were the official dispensers of truth, have had to bow their proud heads before the triumphant march of the scientific method. We cannot hope to stem this conquering advance. We must be content to adopt and to apply the patient and slow but irresistible methods of Science. Science has seemed to many minds to lead more and more definitely to the strictly materialistic view of the world. But if that, as many of us believe, is a mistake, if Materialism is not the whole truth and the last word of Science, only the further progress of Science can make this clear to all. Only by the methods of Science can we hope to combat effectively the errors of Science.

Therefore we confidently say to those who are personally convinced of some or all of the tenets of Spiritualism—"Do not desert Psychical Research; stand by us, give us at least your moral support. Do not be impatient with our slow methods. Do not be offended by what seems to you our excess of caution, our obstinate skepticism. For our road is the only sure road." Fortunately we have a few striking examples in men who, although they themselves have attained to personal conviction, have continued unabated their active support of Psychical Research, such men as Richard Hodgson, Sir Oliver Lodge, Sir William Barrett. Theirs is the example we ask our spiritualist friends to follow.

Now a few words on the reasons why not only Psychical Research in general, but the American Society for Psychical Research in particular, should be supported. In this field of research, even more than in any other branch of science, organized cooperation is necessary. Psychical Research has to make head against the cold indifference and the open hostility of those who should be its friends, among the men of science on the one hand, and the spiritualists on the other. Therefore "psychic researchers" need to stand together for mutual moral support. But that is not the only or, perhaps, the chief reason for working together as an organized group. Two or three persons may get together for research, and by the strictest methods they may obtain the most convincing evidence of "psychic" happenings. Then they may publish a book or a magazine article reporting their observations. A few hundred persons will read it, mostly persons already convinced that such things do happen. And then the whole thing is quickly forgotten. The evidence is practically lost, so far as Science and public opinion are concerned.

It is only by bringing together all our evidence in one place, by submitting it to expert criticism, and by inviting the cooperation and corroboration of impartial experts, that any evidence, no matter how good its quality, can be given due weight and added to the growing mass of effective evidence. The American Society for Psychical Research exists to render possible, to facilitate in every way, such accumulation of evidence. And it is, though not perhaps the only society in this country having these aims, the chief of such societies. It offers the best guarantee of effective publication, effective criticism and cooperation. It has a small staff of able and zealous officers; and recently it has secured the cooperation and support, in an advisory capacity, of a Council which includes men of great eminence in science and letters. I feel sure that any support given to the Society, whether moral or material, will be in no danger of being wasted.

And there is yet another good reason why any one interested in Psychical Research should cooperate with the Society. It may properly be expected that I should say a few words about the dangers of Psychical Research. I will say only this. An active interest in Psychical Research is not without its dangers for those who make research in isolation or in isolated groups of two or three. There is danger under such circumstances of a warping of judgment, of loss of balance, a loss of due sense of proportion. I will venture to assert that the most effective defense against these dangers may be found in working cooperatively as members of the American Society for Psychical Research. In that way individual evidence may be brought into an atmosphere of mutual and helpful and cool criticism, which will be a sure safeguard against undue emotionalism and loss of critical balance. Here I may refer to the English Society for Psychical Research. During its existence of more than forty years, it has had the good fortune to have the active cooperation of a number of indefatigable workers. But there is no ground for thinking that any one of these has suffered in any degree any diminution of his intellectual integrity or emotional balance. These workers have been effectively protected against these dangers by the mutual criticism and friendly cooperation they have found within the Society. And the Society has not only protected them against these dangers that beset the isolated worker; but also it has protected them against a risk which all must run who take a hand in "Psychical Research," namely, the risk of imputation of loss of balance. The American Society is capable of doing the same for the "psychic researchers" of this country. I submit that it deserves most cordial support.

3. Presidential Address to the Society for Psychical Research*

I will not attempt to express my sense of the great honour you have done me in electing me to the presidency of this Society. That sense is much accentuated by the fact that my predecessor in this chair, whose loss we all deplore, was so great a man; a man of science so great that his name will remain among those few which the English people will ever cherish with pride and gratitude. Our Society was fortunate indeed in being able for many years to claim him as a member, and still more fortunate in that he consented to occupy this chair before he was called away.

In looking with mingled pride and humility at the list of former Presidents of the Society, I cannot avoid remarking that one only of them was primarily and professedly a psychologist. I mean of course William James, the man who more than all others has been for me the shining leader, the perfect exponent of scientific candour and courage.

I notice also that but few other names of professed psychologists appear on our roll of membership. I am moved by these facts to offer some slight apology and explanation on behalf of my professional colleagues; for surely they, beyond all other men of science, should have felt the call to support, if only by passive membership, the work and reputation of this Society. They, by special knowledge and training, are or should be better equipped than any others to evaluate the work of the Society, to criticise it, or, better still, actively to cooperate in it. The fact that the great majority of them stand aloof requires some consideration; for it is capable of being, and in some

* Delivered at a General Meeting of the Society on July 19, 1920. Published in *Proc. S.P.R.*, Vol. 31 (1921), pp. 105-123.

quarters has been, interpreted in a sense detrimental to our work. It may be said—here is a body of men on whose judgment the public may best rely in forming its opinion about Psychical Research, and that judgment seems to be adverse; for the bulk of them do not support the work, even to the small extent of joining the Society. This conclusion would, I think, be false. The explanation of the fact is in the main to be found in a different direction.

An open mind towards the phenomena which the Society investigates is far commoner, I am sure, among men of science, than appears to the general public. This opinion, which I venture to express in this highly responsible position, is founded not only upon my personal contacts with men of science, but also upon the fact that only one scientific creed logically permits the deduction that these alleged phenomena do not and *cannot* occur. That creed is dogmatic materialism: and although that creed can still claim a few confident exponents, it is distinctly out of fashion at the present time. However materialistic may be the dominant habit of thought among men of science, there are but few of them who will confess to a whole-hearted acceptance of materialism as a philosophic creed. The bulk of them are sufficiently well educated to know that as such it is untenable; and also to know that from it alone can they logically deduce the impossibility of the alleged phenomena. The grounds of the aloofness of so many men of science from the work of our Society, in spite of their minds being more or less open to conviction in its sphere, are many and complex. It would perhaps not be altogether unprofitable to attempt to describe and examine them. But for my present purpose I wish to point out one only of them, one by no means discreditable to those who are influenced by it. I mean a sense of responsibility towards the public. Men of science are afraid lest, if they give an inch in this matter, the public will take an ell and more. They are afraid that the least display of interest or acquiescence on their part may promote a great outburst of superstition on the part of the public, a relapse into belief in witchcraft, necromancy, and the black arts generally, with all the moral evils which must accompany the prevalence of such beliefs. For they know that it is only through the faithful work of men of science during very recent centuries that these debasing beliefs have been in large measure banished from a small part of the world; they know that, throughout the rest of the world, these superstitions continue to flourish, ready at any moment to invade and overwhelm those small areas of enlightenment. They know that such overwhelming of those areas must plunge their populations back among the grovelling fears and the cruel and hateful practices which have been the scourge and torment of mankind since that remote age when the race became endowed with the two-edged and dangerous weapon of imagination. Now the psychologists, just because they of all men must be regarded as best equipped to judge of these difficult matters, feel this responsibility more acutely than any other class of scientific men. Further—they feel a great responsibility for the reputation of their own science and are afraid of doing it an injury. Any physicist, like the great physicists who have adorned and strengthened this Society, may display an active interest in Psychical Research without the least risk of injury to the reputation of his science. Physical science stands firmly established in the esteem of all men; for it is clear to all that it has provided the material basis of our civilisation. Psychology stands in a very different position. It is only beginning to assert its position among the sciences; the general public and even some of our universities still regard its claim to be a science, and a science of high practical value, with doubt and suspicion. In face of this situation the academic psychologist is rightly cautious. His attitude may, I think, be succinctly and concretely expressed by saying that he is afraid of the left wing of our Society, and that, if the Society consisted only of its right wing, he would come in and co-operate cheerfully and profitably. But both wings are necessary to our Society; we cannot hope to fly to any good purpose on one alone. It has been the great virtue of our Society that, in spite of differences of opinion, sometimes acute, it has kept the allegiance of men and women of so widely different views in respect to its problems. My own conviction is that the risk I have indicated must be run. I myself belong very decidedly to the right wing; but I recognise the importance of the left; I recognise also the right of its members to their opinions, and I esteem the driving power and the freedom of speculation which come from the left as essential to the success of our work.

The importance of the work of our Society seems to me to justify the taking of some risk. But that work does not really add to the risk of relapse into barbaric superstition; rather it is our best defence against it. For Pandora's box has been opened, the lid has been slightly lifted, and we are bound to go on and to explore its remotest corner and cranny. It is not only or chiefly the work of this Society that has raised the lid a little and exposed us to this danger. The culture of Europe has for a brief period rested upon the twin supports of dogmatic affirmation and dogmatic denial, of orthodox religion and scientific materialism. But both of these supports are crumbling, both alike sapped by the tide of free enquiry. And it is the supreme need of our time that these two pillars of dogmatism shall be replaced by a single solid column of knowledge on which our culture may securely rest. It is the policy of sitting on the lid of the box that is risky; a danger and threat to our civilisation.

I have said that I belong to the extreme right of our Society, and I fear that I may shock and hurt some of our members of the left by the following remark, which nevertheless, I feel I am bound to make. It is conceivable to me that we may ultimately find the box to have been empty from the first, as empty as some of our dogmatic critics assert it to be. Even then I should maintain that the work of our Society in boldly exploring its recesses and showing its emptiness to the world had been of the very greatest value. But I do not anticipate this result, though I do not dread it. As regards our positive conclusions and their value I will say only this, I believe that telepathy is very nearly established for all time among the facts recognised by Science, mainly by the work of this Society. If and when that result shall have been achieved, its importance for Science and Philosophy will far outweigh the sum of the achievements of all the psychological laboratories of the universities of two continents.

As regards the other main lines of enquiry of our Society, I confidently hold that nothing hitherto established by Science or Philosophy can be shown to imply that these enquiries must have a purely negative result. Our conclusions must be founded eventually upon just such collection and critical sifting of the empirical evidence as our Society has resolutely pursued for nearly forty years. During these forty years a whole generation of devoted workers has passed away. But what are forty years in the great procession of knowledge! Even though it were clear that four hundred years will be needed for the attainment of definite conclusions, we ought not to shrink from the task, or falter by the way. The supreme importance of the problems before which we stand would justify an indefinitely great expenditure of time and energy upon them. For the interests of our culture and civilisation demand that the present chaos of conflicting opinions and prejudices shall be replaced by clear and definite knowledge.

After these few remarks in the nature of a confession of my attitude towards our works, I propose to devote the remainder of my time to formulating a speculative suggestion, which may have value as a working hypothesis for some branches of our work. The suggestion is not a new one; what I have to say is merely an attempt to develop a little an old idea in the light of modern knowledge.[1] Some years ago I published a book, *Body and Mind*, in which I maintained that, however we conceive the body, we are compelled to conceive our conscious mental life as the activity of a unitary being endowed with the faculties of knowing, feeling and striving, the ego, soul, or self. It has been made a reproach to me that the long argument of that book came to an end just when it began to be really interesting. My present purpose is to outline another step of the argument, to add one more chapter to the book. In the years that have passed since its publication, I have been much concerned both practically and theoretically with cases of nervous disorder. Now these cases of functional nervous disorder have been widely held to make untenable that conception of the unitary ego to which the argument of my book had pointed. In such cases we often seem to find evidences of the division of the self into two or more parts, each of which seems to be endowed with the fundamental faculties of mind, conscious knowing, feeling and striving, a striving that expresses itself in part in the control of bodily movements. To many thinkers the facts of this order seem to shew that the stream of consciousness is, like any other stream, a composite structure, something that is composed of separable parts; for, they say, if it is capable of being broken into parts, it must consist of such parts, and must be conceived as formed by the coming together of such parts. Thus they arrive at the notion of consciousness as a sort of stuff which may be variously combined, broken up and recombined, much as a stream of water or, let us say, of treacle, may be split into minor streams and recombined. Some then speak of a cosmic reservoir of this stuff, some of which is somehow filtered through a screen in tiny trickling streams to form the consciousness of you and me and each of us. Others speak of a mind-dust, ultimate elements or atoms of consciousness, which may be brought together in greater or lesser masses or streams to form what each of us calls his consciousness.

If I am asked—has my more intimate study of these cases of divided personalities led me to accept this way of regarding consciousness; has this way forced itself upon me as an inevitable conclusion from the facts?—I reply— not in the least. The argument for the unity of the ego seems to me as strong and conclusive as ever. And that other way of regarding consciousness, as a stuff which can be divided into smaller or united into larger streams, seems to me just as impossible and false as ever it did. Do I then deny the facts on which the critics of the ego rely? No—I accept these facts as established. I believe we are compelled to recognise that sometimes, and not infrequently, a single human organism or person is the seat of more than one stream of conscious knowing, feeling and striving, more than one train of mental activity; and that these trains may be not only distinct, but may be in acute opposition and conflict one with another, just as really as I may be in conflict with you, a conflict of purposes, of efforts towards different ends.

If my former conclusion holds good, it follows that each of such distinct streams of purposive effort is the activity of a unitary self or ego. Are we then to fly to the ancient theory of possession, whenever we observe evidence of such multiplicity of distinct mental activities within a single organism? By no means. The obvious and, I believe, inevitable inference from the facts is that I who consciously address you am only one among several selves or egos which my organism, my person, comprises. I am only the dominant member of a society, an association of similar members. There are many purposive activities within my organism of which I am not aware, which are not my activities but those of my associates. I am conscious at any moment only of those processes within the organism, and of those impressions from without, which it is most necessary that I should take cognisance of. And I consciously control and adjust only a few of the executive processes of my organism, those only which are of primary importance for my purposes. But I and my associates are all members of one body; and, so long as the whole organism is healthy, we work harmoniously together, for we are a well-organised society, the members of which strive for a common good, the good of the whole society. My subordinates serve me faithfully in the main, provided always that I continue to be resolute and strong. But, when I relax my control, in states of sleep, hypnosis, relaxation and abstraction, my subordinates, or some of them, continue to work and then are apt to manifest their activities in the forms we have learnt to call sensory and motor automatisms. And if I am weak and irresolute, if I do not face the problems of life and take the necessary decisions for dealing with them, then conflict arises within our system, one or more of my subordinates gets out of hand, I lose my control, and division of the personality into conflicting systems replaces the normal and harmonious co-operation of all members in one system. And in extreme cases such a revolted subordinate, escaped from the control of the dominant member or monad, may continue his career of insubordination indefinitely, acquiring increased influence over other members of the society and becoming a serious rival to the normal ruler or dominant. Such a rebellious member was the famous Sally Beauchamp, and such was, I suggest, the childish phase of the Doris Fischer case. All such automatisms imply literally a dis-association of the society or association.

We may, I think, see a close analogy between the organisation of such a society of selves and that of an army. At headquarters sits the general or commander-in-chief. Through a radiating system of telephone wires he constantly receives reports which inform him of the general condition and activities of each part; and chiefly his attention at any moment is given to the reports from areas of greatest activity. But he is not made acquainted with every detail of the life and activity of the army; the reports which reach him have passed upwards through a hierarchy of officers of successively higher rank; at each stage they have been condensed and epitomised; and from those parts of the whole organisation where everything is going on smoothly in routine fashion no report is made. Thus his information is always highly general; it is the cream skimmed from the whole mass of facts. His powers of attention and assimilation permit him only such epitomised and highly condensed information. In the same way, the orders that he gives are general only. He decides and gives orders only on the larger movements.

The working of them out in detail is effected by the descending series of members of the hierarchy; his orders are concerned only with new adjustments and movements of the whole or its parts; and to those parts which are executing routine actions, he issues no orders; to do so would diminish rather than increase their efficiency; it would be a needless and unwarranted interference with his experienced subordinates, who exercise at their discretion an authority delegated by him.

Especially if any disorder or disharmony of the parts of the system arises, his authority is required to restore order; he continues to suffer pain or distress which distracts his attention from all other duties until the disorder is rectified.

This analogy gives us, I suggest, a true picture of the life of the human organism. One great difference obtains between the two systems of our analogy. In the army the general's touch with all parts of the organism is effected through a material system of written and printed orders and telephone wires and dispatch riders. In the organism on the other hand communication between the members seems to be direct, that is to say it seems to be of the nature of reciprocal telepathic rapport, in large part at least. But still the dominant monad is in direct rapport, not with every member of the system, but only with those immediately beneath him in the hierarchy; and the same seems to be true of every member of the system. Thus my consciousness is not a 'collective consciousness,' it is not a fusion of the minor consciousnesses of the subordinate members of my organism. By our fundamental postulate such fusion is impossible. It is rather a condensed essence of all their separate and distinct consciousnesses; it reflects what in them is most essential, whatever is most necessary for me to know; and this is presented to me in a conveniently condensed and elaborated form. That this is really true we see on considering any complex act of perception, as when I perceive visually a complex field of objects. Between the impressions on my sense organ and the completed perception there intervenes a large amount of synthetic activity of truly mental nature; this is the work of my subordinates. And only certain features of the whole field in which I am most interested come fully to my consciousness in elaborated detail; much of the rest of the field remains outside my consciousness, but nevertheless plays a part in determining the total reaction of my organism, subconsciously as we say, *i.e.* through the work of my subordinates.

And in executing any complex bodily action, I make the decision or choice of action and issue a general order, but of the details of its execution I remain for the most part unconscious, although these details are guided by mentally elaborated impressions on my sense organs, again the work of my subordinates.

Let us see how this conception throws light upon certain forms of automatism so frequent and widespread as to fall within the bounds of the normal. In sleep I, the dominant member of my system, become passive and inert; I cease to send out controlling messages. My subordinates, released from my controlling purposes, may continue to be alert and to think their own thoughts; and these are more or less reflected in my passive self as dream-images and dream-thoughts. Since the modes of activity of these subordinates are more primitive, nearer to the purely organic and instinctive, than my own (for we must suppose that the mental functions are delegated to them in an order corresponding to their positions in the hierarchy, the most primitive to those lowest in the scale, the less primitive to those nearer to myself) the dream shews those archaic primitive and intuitive qualities which have been so well pointed out by Dr. C. G. Jung. And they come to my consciousness as something wholly foreign to myself, in the shaping of which my purposes and my thinking have had no share.

In hypothesis also I am passive and my subordinates work independently of my control. They may receive and understand, retain and execute suggestions of which I remain unconscious. And, if they carry out these suggestions in the posthypnotic period, I may be surprised to find myself performing actions of which I have no intention and no prevision; and, if I attempt to inhibit or prevent such actions, I may be aware of a real difficulty in doing so, *i.e.* a difficulty in controlling and subduing the efforts of my subordinates.

Frequently I form an intention and initiate a train of action for its execution and then I may turn my attention to other topics, while my faithful subordinates continue to work towards the end prescribed. To take a very simple instance, I form the intention to go to a certain place and start out; then, though I may be wholly occupied with thoughts of other things, my purpose is duly achieved by my organism, *i.e.* my subordinates. Or, a more complex instance, I may set out to play a piece of music, and, having begun, may engage in conversation on other topics, while the execution of my purpose nevertheless continues to unroll itself through processes which involve a great amount of mental activity, including the appreciation at every step of the complex musical sounds which my fingers call from the instrument.

This view of the nature of a person thus renders intelligible many facts of our normal mental life which on any other view remain paradoxical; and it solves the difficulty of reconciling the facts of automatism and divided personality with the fundamental principle of the unitary ego or self as the ground of the unity of consciousness. And we can apply it successfully to solve another great difficulty, namely the apparent dependence of memory on the integrity of the brain. The facts which seem to imply this dependence have, ever since they began to be discovered, formed a principal support of materialism. The facts are that destruction of this or that part of the brain seems to deprive me of certain memories or memory functions. And the assumption of materialism, reached by an inference from these facts, is that destruction of the whole of my brain would deprive me of all memories.

Now the view I am putting before you assumes that each monad of my system retains the memory of its own activities. Hence I myself retain no memory of a multitude of the mental activities by which the life of my whole organism has been governed; namely of all those that belong to my subordinates. Nevertheless these or many of them are normally at my disposal. By suitable direction of my attention I can secure their reflection in my consciousness as dreamlike images of the past. And in hypnosis there seems to be no limit to the extent to which this process may be carried, remote events and details to which my attention was never directed being reflected to my dreaming, passively receptive self.

We may fairly assume that, when a part of my brain is destroyed, some grave disorder of my functional relations with some of my subordinates must ensue, so that I can no longer command their memories, and these are for all practical purposes lost to me. But in spite of such loss of some part of the memories which normally are at my service, I retain the memories of those experiences which were most truly my own, and those powers of thought and feeling and command which I have developed by my own efforts in pursuit of the ends which I have chosen of my own volition.

If this is true of the destruction of any one part of my brain, we may infer that it would be true also in the event of the destruction of all its parts. Whether there would then remain to me any capacity for sensory experience and sensorial imagination seems to me an obscure question that must be left open at the present time. I am inclined to think that sensorial perception and imagination are essentially the expression of the interaction of the monads. If that be true, then, unless and until I should enter upon relations with some other society, become a working member of some other system, I should enjoy only imageless thought.

This way of regarding the effects of brain-injuries upon memory seems to be compatible with all the facts. And there is one class of facts which it seems impossible to interpret in terms of any other hypothesis. I refer to the effects upon sense-perception, produced by destruction of certain parts of the sensory cortex of the brain, as recently demonstrated by the brilliant researches of Dr. Henry Head.[2] These researches seem to have shewn that, when certain sensory areas are destroyed, leaving intact the basal ganglia of the brain, the patient does not lose altogether the capacities of sensory experience with which the destroyed areas are concerned. Rather he retains the capacity for the corresponding qualities of sensation; but these sensory experiences are now of a crude undiscriminating kind. The change may be roughly expressed by saying that impressions on the sense organs which normally initiate delicate intellectualised perceptions, evoke in such patients only crude sensations. On the view I am putting before you, we may interpret such facts as follows. The sense impressions are normally transmitted through a hierarchy of monads, undergoing further elaboration at each level, until they are reflected to the dominant in a highly elaborated form, conveying delicate spatial, temporal, and other meanings. The injury to the brain throws the higher members of this hierarchy out of action. In consequence the lower members must now report directly to the dominant; just as, if, in an army, the superior officers of a division are thrown out of action, reports to headquarters must be sent forward by subordinate officers of the division, who, lacking the special experience of their incapacitated superiors, will report crudely and inadequately, so that their reports will reach headquarters lacking the intellectual elaboration and condensation which normally characterise them. That seems to be a quite satisfactory interpretation of the facts of this order, and I can conceive of no alternative; and I find in this strong confirmation of the hypothesis.

You will observe that I take the spatial relations of the parts of the brain to be significant of some real and important relations. But I do not mean to bind myself to the view that the material world and its spatial relations as perceived by us is exactly what it appears to be. Nor do I apply to the monads any metaphysical adjectives, such as timeless or eternal or immortal or indestructible or indivisible; to do so would be to go beyond the warrant of the facts, it would gratuitously involve us in difficulties, and it is quite unnecessary. For the purposes of science we may with advantage leave the metaphysical questions on one side; we need not enquire whether what we call the body is merely the appearance to us of the system of monads, *i.e.* we need not attempt to choose between a dualistic and a monistic, or a pluralistic metaphysic. It is for the metaphysicians to adapt their speculations to the results of scientific research as these are brought to light and formulated in far-reaching hypotheses.

The hypothesis which I sketch in vaguest outline brings before our minds a host of new questions to which we cannot at present return any definite answers. But this does not in any sense detract from its value or raise any presumption against it. Any such far-reaching hypothesis must have this result, which is indeed evidence of its value as a guide to research. Among such questions three stand out very prominently for my mind.

First, Plato described the soul as a charioteer, controlling with more or less success a team of powerful unruly creatures, the passions, which draw him along in reckless fury. This has usually been regarded as a literary metaphor. May we, in the light of the view I am putting before you, take this description to be literally true? In other words—is each of the great primary instinctive tendencies of our nature the peculiar function of some one subordinate monad? It is a possibility that deserves consideration.

Secondly, what is the relation of the dominant monad to heredity and evolution? Is he not only the ruler of his society, but also the patriarch and progenitor? I do not see how we can avoid the assumption that the monads are propagated by a process analogous to budding. And this process must be of two kinds. On the one hand a throwing off of a bud which contains all the potentialities and powers of the progenitor and is capable of becoming the progenitor of a new society and hence of governing the whole development of a new individual organism. On the other hand, a process of budding off subordinates to which only subordinate powers are delegated. And, since the development of the individual mirrors that of the race, we must suppose that these functions are delegated in an order which recapitulates that delegation of functions which must have been the essential process in the specialisation and differentiation of racial types. Such specialisation and differentiation of functions within the organism can only have been combined with continued effective integration of the organism through such extensive delegation of functions combined with continued dominance of the parent monad.

Lastly, there is the question of the bearing of this view upon the great problem which for so many members of the Society for Psychical Research is or should be its predominating interest, the problem of life after death. Well, adoption of our hypothesis would necessitate a development of our view of the life after death of the body, one directly in line with the development which that view has already undergone in the slow process of cultural evolution. Primitive man conceived the dead as having still not only the bodily form and organs but also the dress and ornaments and weapons which they bore in this life. Then these external adjuncts of personality were given up, and men were content to conceive the dead as having the naked bodily form and organs only.

By a further and comparatively recent step, the conception of the dead was purged of the material embodiment, and men learned to think of them as spirits devoid of bodily form; but they continue to expect that the departed soul should retain every mental function and the memory of every mental activity manifested throughout the life of the organism. But now, I suggest, we have to make a further step and purge our conception still further. I, if I survive the dissolution of my bodily organism, shall, by our hypothesis, retain only those functions which I have not delegated but have developed by active exercise and those memories which are most truly mine, the memories of my own activities. And after all is not this truly a gain, an advance of our conception? Does it not represent that purification from dross and from the lower elements of which so many seers have spoken?

Further, it would seem to follow that, just as in this life I live effectively and fully only by actively participating in the life of an intimately organised society of like members, so hereafter can I hope to live richly and satisfactorily only by entering into and playing an active part as a member of some other society which will demand my faithful co-operation and service. For we are essentially social beings; outside of and apart from such intimate communion, our selves would have no meaning and no value, and perhaps could not be said to live or be conscious in any intelligible sense of those words.

I venture to think that these considerations may afford some guidance, if they are kept in mind when we confront the baffling problems, the perplexities and disappointments which seem to be the lot of those bent upon the major quest of Psychical Research.

NOTES

[1] It is the notion of 'monads' which came down to us from Leibnitz. In recent years it has been developed as the basis of a pluralistic metaphysic by Prof. James Ward (in his *Pluralism and Theism*) and by his disciple Mr. C. A. Richardson (in his *Spiritual Pluralism*). R. H. Lotze may be claimed as its chief exponent in the nineteenth century: and Mr. Gerald Balfour (in his presidential address) has urged its claims upon the attention of this Society.

[3] Reported in a series of papers in recent volumes of *Brain*.

4. The Bearing of the Results of "Psychic Research" on the Psycho-Physical Problem*

During the last thirty years the Society for Psychical Research has investigated in a strictly scientific manner certain obscure phenomena, the occurrence of which has been accepted by the popular mind in all ages and in all countries, but which have been rejected by the official world of modern science as merely superstitious survivals from the dark ages, reinforced by contemporary errors of observation due to the influence of these traditional superstitions.

At the present day, no one undertaking to review the psycho-physical problem can ignore the results of these investigations without laying himself open to the charge of culpable ignorance or unscientific prejudice.

The principal aim of the Society for Psychical Research has been to obtain, if possible, empirical evidence that human personality may and does survive in some sense and degree the death of the body. A considerable mass of evidence pointing in this direction has been accumulated. Its nature is such that many of those who have devoted attention to the work and have had a full and first-hand acquaintance with the investigations and their results, have become convinced that survival is a fact. And among these persons so convinced are several who, in respect to their competence to form a sane and critical judgment on this difficult question, cannot be rated inferior to any other persons.

Nevertheless, in my judgment, the evidence is not of such a nature that it can be stated in a form which should produce conviction in the mind of

---

* Originally published as Chap. XXV of William McDougall's *Body and Mind*. London: Methuen & Co., Ltd., 1923.

any impartial inquirer. Again and again the evidential character of the observations has fallen just short of perfection; the objections that stand between us and the acceptance of the conclusion seem to tremble and sway; but still they are not cast down, the critical blow has not been struck; and, perhaps, they will remain erect in spite of all efforts. This being the state of affairs, I shall not adduce any of this evidence,[1] but will merely point out that one of the advantages of the animistic solution of the psycho-physical problem is that its acceptance keeps our minds open for the impartial consideration of evidence of this sort; and that it is possible and seems even probable that Animism may receive direct and unquestionable verification through these investigations:[2] whereas Parallelism (including under that term all forms of the anti-animistic hypotheses) closes our minds to this possibility, and is liable at any moment to be finally refuted by improvement of the quality of this empirical evidence for survival.

For if, as was argued in Chapter XIV [*Body and Mind*], Animism is the only solution of the psycho-physical problem compatible with a belief in any continuance of personality after death, the empirical proof of such continuance would be the verification of Animism; it would be proof that the differences between the living human organism and the corpse are due to the presence or operation within the former of some factor or principle which is different from the body and capable of existing independently of it.

But though, in my judgment, this verification of Animism has not been furnished by "psychical research," a very important positive result has been achieved by it, namely, it has established the occurrence of phenomena that are incompatible with the mechanistic assumption. I refer especially to the phenomena of telepathy.[3]

I cannot attempt to present here the evidence for the reality of telepathy. It must suffice to say that it is of such a nature as to compel the assent of any competent person who studies it impartially. Now, so long as we consider only the evidence of telepathy between persons at no great distance from one another, it is possible to make the facts appear compatible with the mechanistic assumption by uttering the "blessed" word "brainwaves."[4] But the strain upon the mechanistic assumption becomes insupportable by it when we consider the following facts: minute studies of automatic writings, and especially those recently reported[5] under the head of "Cross-Correspondences," have shown that such writings frequently reveal knowledge of facts which could not have been acquired by the writer by normal means, and could not have been telepathically communicated from any living person in the neighbourhood of the writer. In short, the evidence is such that the keenest adverse critics[6] of the view which sees in these writings the expression of the surviving personalities of deceased persons, are driven to postulate as the only possible alternative explanation of some of them the direct communication of complex and subtle thoughts between persons separated by hundreds and even thousands of miles, thoughts of which neither is conscious or has been conscious at any time, so far as can be ascertained. There is good evidence also that in some cases three persons widely separated in space have taken part in expressing by automatic writing a single thought. Unless, then, we are prepared to adopt the supposition of a senseless and motiveless conspiracy of fraud among a number of persons who have shown themselves to be perfectly upright and earnest in every other relation,[7] we must recognize that we stand before the dilemma—survival or telepathy of this far-reaching kind. The acceptance of either horn of the dilemma is fatal to the mechanistic scheme of things. For, even if the hypothesis of "brain-waves" be regarded as affording a possible explanation of simple telepathic communication at short range, it becomes wholly incredible if it is suggested as an explanation of the co-operation of widely separated "automatic" writers in the expression of one thought. This, then, is the principal importance I attach to the results hitherto achieved by "psychical research," namely, I regard the research as having established the occurrence of phenomena which cannot be reconciled with the mechanistic scheme of things; and I adduce the results here in order to add them to the great mass of evidence to the same effect set forth in the foregoing chapters.

Besides the evidence that leads to this dilemma, so fatal to the mechanistic dogma, "psychical research" has established the reality of other phenomena very difficult to reconcile with it. Of these I will cite here only two classes. First, it has been shown that under certain conditions (especially in the hypnotic and post-hypnotic states) the mind may exert an influence over the organic processes of the body far greater than any that had been generally recognized by physiologists. Especially noteworthy are the production of blisters, erythemata, and ecchymoses, of the skin (the so-called stigmata) in positions and of definite shapes determined by verbal suggestions, and the rapid healing of wounds or burns with almost complete suppression of inflammation; and with these may be put the complete suppression or prevention of pain, even pain of such severity as normally accompanies a major surgical operation.[8]

Now it is true that the production of these and similar effects involves only an extension or intensification of powers normally exercised by the mind over the bodily processes. But to say that, is not to deprive the facts of the significance that I would attribute to them. Rather, these instances of hypernormal mental control over bodily processes serve merely to place in a clearer light, to bring home more forcibly to us, the impossibility of explaining these processes on mechanical principles, the impossibility of exhibiting these psycho-physical processes as purely chemico-physical or mechanical processes. By the free use of speculation I have myself carried the hypothetical account of the nervous changes involved in hypnosis as far, perhaps, as any other physiologist.[9] But it must be frankly recognized that even though my account, or any other yet proposed, be accepted as approximately true, the processes are by no means explained; the chief part of the facts remains refractory to explanation by mechanical hypotheses. Let us consider for a moment one of the simplest and most familiar instances of such control; the production of local anæsthesia or the allied process of the suppression of local neuralgic pain. I touch the left eye of a subject in hypnosis[10] as he sits with closed eyes, and tell him that he can see nothing with that eye. On opening his eyes he is then blind of the left eye,[11] and remains so until its vision is restored by a new suggestion to that effect. Or a subject who has been racked for days, or weeks, with intense neuralgic pain becomes completely free of the pain almost instantaneously upon mere verbal suggestion to that effect during hypnosis. Now it seems highly probable that in every such case the sensory path or centre of the brain concerned in the production of the sensation which is, as it were, cut out of the subject's consciousness, becomes functionally dissociated from the rest of the brain, *i.e.*, circumscribed or isolated. But how is this dissociation or circumscription effected? The subject himself knows nothing of the anatomy of his brain; and, even if his brain could be so enlarged that all the members of the International Congress of Physiologists could walk about inside his nerve fibres and hold a conference in one of his "ganglion cells," their united knowledge and the resources of all their laboratories would not suffice to enable them to effect such an operation as the isolation of the sensory centres of the left eye from those of the right eye, and from the rest of the brain. If it be suggested that the anæsthesia of the left eye is produced by some paralysis of the optic nerve, comparable to the application of a ligature to it (and this of course would be within the competence of the physiologist), the case is brought no nearer to the possibility of a mechanistic explanation; for it is utterly impossible to conceive that the neural impulses initiated in the auditory nerve by the sound of the words, "Your left eye is blind," should find their way to the fibres of the left optic nerve; nor, if arrived there, could they in any conceivable fashion paralyse the conductivity of the nerve.

These processes in short remain no less mysterious and no less refractory to mechanistic explanations than the processes of growth and repair by which complex organisms develop from the germ-cells and maintain or restore the integrity of their organs. The similarity to normal processes of growth and repair of these processes of control of organic function initiated by verbal suggestion, i.e. by mental influences (though carried out in detail by processes of which the subject remains wholly unconscious), goes far to justify the assimilation of the processes of these two types, and to justify the belief that the normal processes of growth and repair are in some sense controlled by mind, or by a teleological principle of which our conscious intelligence is but one mode of manifestation among others.

Hypnotic experiments of another class seem to me to call for special mention in the present connexion, namely those which have revealed in several subjects an astonishing power of appreciating time or duration.[12] The essence of the experiments was that the subject, having been instructed during hypnosis to make some simple written record at some future moment (generally stated in thousands of minutes), carried out the instruction in a great majority of cases with hardly appreciable error.[13] Many interesting problems are raised by these experiments; but, leaving on one side the evidence of subconscious calculations of considerable complexity, I wish to insist only on the main point, the awareness of the arrival of the prescribed moment. It is usual to seek to explain simpler cases of appreciation of the passage of time by some vague suggestion of a subconscious counting of some physiological rhythm. But in these cases, even if the ordinary means of learning the time (*e.g.* a reliable watch) had been used by the subject at the moment of the reception of the suggestion, this explanation would remain very farfetched and improbable; for we know of no bodily rhythm sufficiently constant to serve as the basis of so accurate an appreciation of duration as would have enabled the subject to carry out the suggestion with the high degree of accuracy shown. And in some cases the subject had no normal means of learning the time of day for considerable periods before and after the reception of the suggestion, and yet the accuracy of the result was not diminished. What then can be made of these cases? They are too numerous, too carefully studied and reported by competent observers, to be set aside as merely instances of mal-observation. The most commonplace hypothesis that seems adequate to account for them is one of subconscious telepathy. But, whatever the true explanation may be, they must, I think, be added to the class of phenomena manifestly irreconcilable with the mechanistic dogma.

NOTES

[1] For full accounts of the work the reader must turn to the Proceedings of the S. P. R. He will find excellent samples and discussions of the evidence in Sir O. Lodge's "Survival of Man," and in the late Mr. Podmore's "The Newer Spiritualism." The former accepts, the latter rejects the evidence for survival.

[2] Some of my readers may object that empirical evidence of the survival of personality is in principle impossible. This was the opinion forcibly expressed by Kant in his "Träume eines Geister-sehers," and never abandoned by him. The question is important, and a brief discussion of it here may serve to reinforce what was said on an earlier page in criticism of Kant's arbitrary restriction of empirical science to mechanistic conceptions.

The unjustified assumption implied by the objection is that conceptions based upon empirical evidence must be conceptions of objects capable in principle of being perceived through the senses. It has already been pointed out that many of the most valuable conceptions of physical science do not conform to this requirement. In order to bring home to our minds the invalidity of the assumption, let us imagine the following case. After the death of an intimate friend you seal up a pencil and a writing-block in a glass vessel. Then, whenever mentally or verbally you address questions to your deceased friend as though he were beside you, the pencil stands up and writes upon the paper, giving intelligent replies to your questions. In this way you conduct elaborate and oft-renewed conversations, in which the writing seems always perfectly to express the personality of your friend, even to revealing many facts which, as you are able afterwards to discover, must have been known to him but to no other person, facts such as the contents of a private writing-desk, or a sealed personal journal. If this occurred, it would constitute an empirical proof of the continued existence of the personality of your friend in some manner not directly perceptible by the senses, in spite of the complete dissolution of his bodily organism. You would infer his continued existence from the phenomena, though you would remain unable to imagine the mode of his existence; and to refuse to do so would be irrational and absurd. No one asserts that such phenomena have been observed; but to assert that it is impossible that they should occur is to beg the question in dispute and to argue in a circle; for the denial of its possibility could only be based on *a priori* grounds. But nothing is impossible save the self-contradictory. Now, although the phenomena we have imagined have not been observed, something similar, something constituting evidence of a similar nature, does occur. Pencils do produce what seem to be messages written by deceased persons; but in the observed cases (I leave out of account the alleged cases of "direct writing") the pencil is held and moved by the hand and arm of a living person, who, however, remains ignorant of its doings and of the thought expressed in the writing. This fact, that the pencil is moved by the hand of a living person, complicates immensely the task of evaluating the significance of the writing, but does not in principle affect the validity of the inference that may be drawn from it.

[3] "The communication of mind with mind by means other than the recognized channels of sense." The evidence is reviewed in *Encycl. Brit.* 11th Ed. Art. "Telepathy."

[4] The explanation of telepathy at close quarters by the hypothesis of "brainwaves" transmitted through the ether cannot be absolutely rejected. But to my mind the difficulties are so great that the hypothesis is incredible. It is usual to support this hypothesis by pointing to the facts of wireless telegraphy.

[5] Proceedings of the S.P.R. from 1907 onwards.

[6] This was the alternative hypothesis adopted by the late Mr. F. Podmore, whose acquaintance with the facts was intimate and extensive, and who during many years had built up for himself a reputation as the keenest critic of the advanced wing of the S.P.R. (See his posthumous work, "The Newer Spiritualism.")

[7] I may add that my personal knowledge of leading members of this group of workers renders this supposition ridiculous to my mind.

[8] For the evidences of such effects I refer the reader to Dr. Milne Bramwell's "Hypnotism, its History, Theory, and Practice," London, 1903.

[9] "The State of the Brain during Hypnosis," *Brain*, vol. 31, and Art. "Hypnotism" in *Ency. Brit.*, 11th Ed. [These articles are reprinted in this volume, pp. 262ff, pp. 221ff.]

[10] This and similar effects can be obtained in a considerable proportion of subjects, but the reader must not be misled into supposing that they can be readily produced in every subject.

[11] Any critically disposed reader unfamiliar with experiments of this kind, will be inclined to assume that the subject feigns blindness of the left eye, out of complaisance or obedience to the operator. But that the blindness of the left eye is genuine and involuntary may easily be shown by the following procedure. The lateral parts of the normal field of view are fields of monocular vision, the middle part only being a field of binocular vision;

the ordinary working man is ignorant of the boundaries between the monocular and the binocular parts of the field, and if, while his eyes are directed to a spot before him, an object is brought slowly forward from behind his head, it passes at a given moment from the monocular to the binocular part of his field of view, without affording him any indication of the fact. Now if this experiment be made with a subject whose left eye has been rendered anæsthetic by suggestion, an object being brought slowly forward on his left side and the subject being instructed to indicate the moment at which it becomes perceptible to him, he will signal his perception of the object at the moment that it crosses the boundary between the monocular and the binocular parts of his normal field of view, *i.e.* the moment at which it enters the field of the right eye.

[12] The principal instances are those carefully studied and reported by the late Prof. Delbœuf, by Dr. Milne Bramwell (*op. cit.*), and by Dr. T. W. Mitchell, "A Case of Post-Hypnotic Appreciation of Time" (Proc. S. P. R., vol. xxi.). At the time of going to press I am engaged in studying a subject who seems to exhibit this power in a very striking manner, as well as the production of blisters and extravasations of blood from the skin in response to verbal suggestion.

[13] The time-errors were frequently less than one minute, seldom more than five.

5. *Psychical Research as a University Study**

This course of lectures on Psychical Research is, I believe, the first of its kind to be given in any university, whether of this or of any other country; and I venture to think that this innovation will prove to be yet another leaf added to the laurels of Clark University, already so distinguished by its impartial and courageous spirit of research.

Other lecturers, persons distinguished in the most various lines of activity, but all of them qualified by special study of the field of Psychical Research, will deal with special parts or aspects of the field and from the most diverse points of view. For it is the intention of those who have designed the course that it should represent with perfect impartiality every point of view from which this most difficult and controversial field may be approached; the only stipulation being that each lecturer shall present his facts, his evidences, and his reasoning upon them in a truly critical spirit and with all the impartiality and openness of mind attainable by him.

This course being so great an innovation, it is fitting that this lecture should be devoted to the justification of the inclusion of Psychical Research among University Studies; for there can be no doubt that Clark University, while it will be praised by many for its courage and its pioneer spirit in thus opening its doors to a study hitherto denied University recognition, will also be severely criticized by others. It will be said by those adverse critics that the University is encouraging superstition and countenancing charlatanry; that it runs the risk of leading its students into a slough of despair, of entangling

* Clark University Press, Worcester, Mass. Lecture Series Symposium, 1926, pp. 149-162.

70

them in a quagmire where no sure footing is to be found, where will-o'-the-wisps gleam fitfully on every hand, provoking hopes that are destined to disappointment and emotions that blind us to the dangers of this obscure region; dangers ranging from mere waste of time to disturbance of intellectual balance and loss of critical judgment; dangers which he who enters by the gate we seek to open must inevitably encounter.

Let me begin, then, by frankly admitting that such criticism is not wholly without substance and foundation. The field of Psychical Research has pitfalls and morasses unknown in other fields of science. The student entering this field cannot avoid contact with vast currents of traditional sentiment, which sentiments, in nearly all cases, he either shares or repudiates with an intensity of feeling that renders calm and critical judgment well nigh impossible. It is as though the student were invited to embark with Coleridge's Ancient Mariner; to exclaim, with him, "We were the first that ever burst into that Silent Sea"; to witness, with him, strange and even horrible phenomena that seem to defy all the ascertained laws of nature, a phantasmagoria that can have no reality and no origin other than the phantasy of minds disordered by the conflict of strong emotions and blinded by glittering hopes long held before the imagination of mankind, hopes long deferred and now threatened with total extinction by the triumphant progress of scientific enquiry.

Let it be admitted, then, that this is no field for the casual amateur; for the man who merely wishes to take a rapid glance at the phenomena and thereupon form his own conclusions; for the person who approaches it in the hope of finding solace for some personal bereavement; for the dilettante who merely seeks a new and sensational hobby. It is a field of research which at every step demands in the highest degree the scientific spirit and all round scientific training and knowledge; a field which gives the widest scope for the virtues of the scientific intellect and character and which, just because it makes these demands and affords this scope, is of the greatest value as an intellectual discipline.

Here the mind long disciplined in other branches of science may find the supreme test of its powers and its training, tests of impartial observation, of relevant selection, of sagacious induction and deduction, of resolute discounting of emotional bias and personal influence. Here, better than in any other field, it may learn to recognize its own limitations, limitations of knowledge, of power, of principle; and to recognize also the limitations of science and philosophy themselves, their inadequacy to give final answers to problems which mankind has long answered with ready-made formulae, handed down from the dim dawn of human reflection, and before which it now halts with burning desire for certainty or unsatisfied longing for more light.

The difficulty, the obscurity, the dangers of a field of research are no sufficient grounds for excluding it from our Universities. Has not the teaching of all science in our schools and Universities been vigorously opposed on just such grounds, on the ground that such teaching might lead young people into intellectual and moral error, or raise in their souls insoluble problems and conflicts that would destroy their peace of mind? That question has been decisively answered. Our Western civilization has definitely repudiated the old way of authority, has committed itself irrevocably to live by knowledge, such knowledge as the methods of science can attain. It cannot return to live by instinct and traditional beliefs; it has gone so far along the path of knowledge and of self-direction in the light of knowledge that it cannot stop or turn back without disaster. The inclusion of Psychical Research in the scientific studies of our Universities is the inevitable last step in this advance from a social state founded on instinct and tradition to one that relies upon knowledge and reason.

But it may be answered by our opponents—The introduction of Science to our Universities was justified, in spite of its risks, because Science offers a mass of well–established truths, truths which are indispensable to the life of the modern state. Psychical Research has rightly been excluded because it furnishes no such body of established truth; it has solved no problems, has attained to no sure conclusions.

Let us admit that this contention also is not without substance and force. But to accept it as a sufficient argument would be disastrous. It would imply a false and fatally narrow view of the functions of our Universities. It is on just such grounds that the movement against the teaching of evolution takes its stand. It is said that evolutionary biology must not be studied by young people, because evolution is not an established fact, but merely a theory, or a mass of unverified hypotheses. Yet all enlightened opinion rejects this reasoning, rightly holding that the teaching of established truth is only one of, and perhaps not the most important of, the functions of a modern University. Such teaching may perhaps be the sole or main function of Technical Schools. Our Universities have other, higher, more important functions.

We may, I think, distinguish three main functions of the University, as follows: First, the function of educating the young people within its gates; secondly, the function of research, of extending the bounds of knowledge; thirdly, a function which, as the life of the modern State assumes an accelerating complexity, becomes more and more important, namely, the function of exerting a controlling influence in the formation of public opinion on all vital matters. Consider each of these three great functions in relation to our question: Should Psychical Research find a place in our Universities?

First, then, the educational function. Under this head we may properly distinguish two very different, though inseparable, subfunctions; namely, first, the imparting of knowledge; secondly, intellectual and moral discipline. It is only as regards the former of these that Psychical Research is open to the indictment of its opponents. Let us admit, for the purpose of the argument, that it has not achieved any conclusions that may be taught as firmly established truths. That admission denies it a role only in what we may roughly estimate as one-sixth of the total field of activity of the modern University, a fraction of the field which is its lowest or least important part.

As regards the other educational functions, intellectual training and moral discipline, it may well be claimed for Psychical Research that it ranks very high, perhaps highest of all possible subjects of University Study. For consider—In what does such discipline consist? First, in attacking problems patiently and resolutely, in spite of failures and disappointments, in spite of uncertainty that any solution may be attainable. Surely, in this respect Psychical Research may claim a foremost place! No other field of study makes such large demands on the patience and resolution of the student. Secondly, the discipline of observing exactly and recording faithfully phenomena presented to our senses. There is a lower form of such discipline to which the young student of science is extensively subjected; namely, the task of recording as exactly as possible all he can observe within some very limited field; as when he has to weigh exactly some chemical substance, or when he is set down before a microscope and required to draw what is there presented to his view. Psychical Research offers little scope for discipline of just this kind; but this is a lower form of observation, one which does not of itself lead to discovery. There is a higher form of observation which requires selective sagacity; it is conducted with a problem in view and under the guidance of some hypothesis which is to be tested. It requires the observer to distinguish the relevant from the irrelevant, to look for the relevant, to concentrate upon it, and to devise experiments which shall isolate or accentuate the relevant. For discipline in this higher kind of directed observation, Psychical Research offers unlimited opportunities and makes upon the observer demands of the highest order. Then as regards the reasoning processes by aid of which general conclusions are drawn from the phenomena observed. Here the demands upon the thinker in the field of Psychical Research are very great and the discipline consequently severe. The physicist or chemist observes the reactions of a single sample of some substance under particular conditions, and is forthwith in a position to state a general conclusion with high probability. The biologist observes some particular feature in fifty or one hundred specimens of some species and, without great risk, makes a generalization as probably true of all members of the species.

But the Psychical Researcher is dealing with the most complex and highly individualized of all known objects, namely human beings; before he can summarize his observations in any generalized statement, he must exercise infinite caution, observe unlimited precautions, be ready to allow for an immense range of possible disturbing factors of unknown nature and magnitude. And, when he proceeds to apply statistical treatment to his data of observation, he finds himself facing problems of unrivalled delicacy. For he can never, like other scientists, be content with the comfortable assumption that each of his unit facts is exactly or even approximately equivalent to every other one of the same general order.

If, by reason of the complexity and delicacy of its problems, Psychical Research rivals all other branches of science, it far surpasses them all in respect of the demands it makes on character and, consequently, in respect of the character-discipline which it affords. It requires perfectly controlled temper, and a large and understanding tolerance of human weaknesses of every kind, intellectual and moral alike; an infinite patience in face of renewed disappointments; a moral courage which faces not merely the risk and even the probability of failure, but also the risk of loss of reputation for judgment, balance, and sanity itself. And, the most insidious of all dangers, the danger of emotional bias in favour of one or other solution of the problem in hand, is apt to be infinitely greater for the Psychical Researcher than for the worker in any other field of science; for, not only is he swayed by strong sentiments within his own breast, but also he knows that both the scientific world and the general public will react with strong emotional bias to any conclusion he may announce, just because such conclusions must have intimate bearing on the great controversy between Science and Religion, a controversy which, in spite of the soothing reassurances which great scientists and religious leaders now utter in unison, is still acute and may well become again even more embittered and violent than it has been in the past.

As regards the second function of the University, the extension of knowledge, Psychical Research may boldly claim its place within the fold; on this ground any opposition to it can only arise from narrow dogmatic ignorance, that higher kind of ignorance which so often goes with a wealth of scientific knowledge, the ignorance which permits a man to lay down dogmatically the boundaries of our knowledge and to exclaim "*ignorabimus.*" This cry— "we shall not, cannot know!"—is apt to masquerade as scientific humility, while, in reality, it expresses an unscientific arrogance and philosophic incompetence. For the man who utters it arrogates to himself a knowledge of the limits of human knowledge and capacity that is wholly unwarranted and illusory. To cry *ignorabimus* in face of the problems of Psychical Research, and to refuse on that ground to support or countenance its labour, is disingenuous camouflage; for the assertion that we shall not and cannot know the answers to these problems implies a knowledge which we certainly have not yet attained and which, if in principle it be attainable, lies in the distant future when the methods of Psychical Research shall have been systematically developed and worked for all they may be worth. The history of Science is full of warnings against such dogmatic agnosticism, the agnosticism which does not content itself with the frank and humble avowal that we do not know, but which presumes to assert that we cannot know.

Let us suppose that, after forty years of tentative skirmishing in the wilderness, Psychical Research, in part as the consequence of this course of lectures, should be received within the scientific fold and systematically cultivated in our Universities; and suppose that, after a hundred years of such cultivation, its representatives, surveying the results of all the work done, should find themselves compelled to utter a purely negative verdict, to assert that Psychical Research had attained to no positive answers to any of the problems it had set out to solve. What then? We should still have to repeat —There is the gate to which we have no key; there is the veil through which we may not see. But, also, we should still have to add—And there the Master-knot of Human Fate! And, though Science might then turn aside, baffled and discouraged, it would at least have given some respectable foundation for the cry *Ignorabimus* and have made some real contribution to our knowledge of the limitations of human knowledge.

But, some hearer will object, this question of the limits of human knowledge is one not for Science but for Philosophy; and in all our Universities Philosophy has long had a well-recognized place and its numerous representatives; it is for the philosophers to answer the questions which Science leaves unsolved. Such an objection would imply an old-fashioned and quite mistaken view of the scope and functions of Philosophy.

Philosophy may rightly claim to teach us how to think, how to live, and how to die. It may answer the question—Given the present state of the world and of our knowledge of it, what ought I to do? But it is wholly incompetent to answer the questions—What may I hope? What may I expect? A cosmogony that is to be more than a fanciful speculation must be a scientific cosmogony; and, as science progresses, our cosmogony must change with it. Every cosmogony that professes to be philosophical rather than scientific is a hollow pretense. Only Science working by the methods of Science can presume to answer the question—What is? Philosophy must learn that its proper field is defined by the question—What ought to be?

And here I will ask leave to revert to the disciplinary, the educational, function of Psychical Research with special reference to students of Philosophy. In my opinion, formed through considerable contact with such students, their chief lack is knowledge of Science; and of all forms of Science, that which can most enlighten them in literature can go far to induce in them that which so many of them need, namely, a clear recognition of the limitations of the scope of Philosophy and a corresponding humility in themselves as philosophers. For here they will find that questions which philosophers through all the ages have answered in their peculiar and utterly diverse fashions are capable of being approached by the methods of Science; and the mere act of following in imagination such lines of approach can hardly fail to bring home to the student the fact that the methods of Philosophy, divorced from Science, are of no avail. He will be brought to realize that Philosophy, whether it aims to sketch the main features of the Universe or seeks to instruct us regarding the values and the duties of mankind, must, in both cases, proceed from the fullest possible knowledge of what Science has achieved, or lay itself open to those charges of futility and ignorant presumption which so often have been launched against it.

What, then, are the essential questions on which we may expect new light from Psychical Research? They may all be resumed in one, namely—Does Mind transcend matter? Or more fully stated—Is all that we call mental, intellectual or spiritual activity, is all understanding and reason, all moral effort, volition, and personality, merely the outcome and expression of a higher synthesis of physical structures and processes and, therefore, subject to the same general laws and interpretable by the same general principles as those which Physical Science arrives at from the study of the inanimate world? Or are mental activities, are all or some of the essential functions of personality, in some degree independent of the physical basis with which they are so intricately interwoven? Have they their own peculiar nature, interpretable only in terms of principles quite other than those whose validity has been proved by the victory of man over his physical environment?

It is the old problem of materialism *versus* spiritualism or idealism, of mechanism *versus* vitalism in biology; or, as I would prefer to formulate it, the problem of animism *versus* mechanistic-monism. This has been the central problem of Philosophy for more than two thousand years; and always the philosophers have been pretty equally divided into two groups, those who say "Yes" and those who say "No". The course of development of modern Science has on the whole tended strongly to give predominance to the view which denies the transcendence of Mind. Idealistic philosophers have struggled in vain to stem this tide, urging that it is absurd to regard as subject to the laws formulated for the interpretation of physical phenomena, the mind, which conceives the physical world and which has itself in some degree created those phenomena.

But this and all similar reasoning remains inconclusive and must ever remain so. We are up against a question of empirical fact; and the answer to the question can be brought only by the methods of empirical Science. Many of the greater physicists have inclined to think that their own science points towards a positive answer to this question of transcendence; and it is possible that the progress of physical science and of biology may in the course of time lead us to a decisive answer to this central problem. But, if so, the answer will be achieved only very slowly by very indirect methods of attack. The essence of Psychical Research is the proposal to attack the problem directly. If Mind in any manner and degree transcends the physical world and its laws, surely it may somehow and somewhere be possible to obtain direct evidence of the fact by the methods of science, by observation of phenomena and by reasoning from them! That is the proposition on which Psychical Research is founded. Psychical Research proposes, then, to go out to seek such phenomena, namely phenomena pointing directly to the transcendence of Mind, and, if possible, to provoke them experimentally. Phenomena of this kind have been reported in every age; and in every age antecedent to our own age, dominated as it is by the principles of scientific evidence, their obvious implication has been accepted. Psychical Research proposes to marshal all such sporadically and spontaneously occurring phenomena, to examine them critically, to classify them, to discover if possible the laws of their occurrence and to add to them experimentally induced phenomena of similar types.

Consider now the third great function of our Universities, the guidance of public opinion. It is perhaps from this point of view that the admission of Psychical Research to the Universities is most urgently needed. Here is a most obscure question vitally affecting the intellectual outlook and the moral life of men in general. Surely it is for the Universities to find, if possible, the light that we need! What ground can be found for their neglect or repudiation of the task? Several such grounds are implied, though rarely formulated explicitly.

First it may be said, the task is one for the philosophers and theologians, who are well represented in the Universities. But philosophers and theologians have wrestled with it for long ages; and there is no faintest reason to believe that by their methods alone they can achieve in the future any greater success than they have attained in the past. Let us glance at the grounds they offer us for accepting a positive answer in face of the general tendency of science to insist on the negative answer. They may all be reduced to two. First, the moral ground; to believe in the transcendence of Mind is a moral need of mankind in general. Such belief, it is said, is essential to the maintenance and progress of our civilization. Our civilization has been built up on a foundation of and under the sway of such belief; and, if that foundation and that influence should be taken away, our civilization must

surely decline; even though it be possible for exceptional individuals to continue to attain high moral excellence in an attitude of stoic agnosticism. This
argument is respectable; it has weight and substance. Given a balance of
evidence and the impossibility of assured knowledge, we would be justified
in accepting that view which seems the more conducive to human welfare.
This argument, which perhaps William James was the first to state and defend explicitly, is, I suppose, implied by those who ask us to continue to
accept the transcendence of Mind as an article of faith. But this moral argument in no sense justifies a refusal to countenance or support Psychical
Research, which is nothing less than an endeavour to replace faith by knowledge in this matter. If, from time to time, religious leaders exhort their flocks
to eschew Psychical Research and pour scorn upon it and all its works, we
cannot wholly acquit them of a preference for ignorance over against knowledge. It would seem that they fear the result of Psychical Research; they
fear either a negative outcome of the great enquiry, or a positive outcome
which shall disturb the minds of their flocks by bringing knowledge not
strictly in accord with traditional beliefs. Therefore they ask us to remain
content to accept these beliefs on authority. But it is too late to advocate
that policy with any hope of success. As I said before, it is obvious that we
have left the age of authority behind and that our civilization is irrevocably
committed to the attempt to live by knowledge, rather than by instinct and
authority. Consider now the second main ground offered for acceptance of
the positive answer. If we ask whence does ecclesiastical authority derive
the views it seeks to impose, the answer is that they are founded upon alleged
historical events of a remote age, events of just such a nature as Psychical
Research is concerned to investigate at first hand as contemporary events.
However we regard the evidence of those remote events, we can hardly claim
that the lapse of some two thousand years has made the evidence of them
less disputable; and in any case it is clear that mankind in general is ceasing
to find that evidence sufficient. More and more we are inclined to say—You
ask us to accept the transcendence of mind because we have certain records
of events which, if the records be above suspicion, would seem to justify
and establish that belief; and yet you would forbid us to examine, in a candid
and critical spirit, similar events that are reported as occurring among
friends and neighbours. Truly, he who repudiates Psychical Research in the
interests of religion and of religious authority cannot easily be absolved from
the charge of a timid obscurantism.

But it is not only in respect of this high problem of transcendence that
public opinion needs from the Universities guidance of a kind which they
can give only if they cultivate Psychical Research. That after all is a problem for the intellectual few; although the views of those few may have far-

reaching influence upon the lives of the many. The great public does not much concern itself with the question—Are we truly in some degree rational beings capable of moral choice and creative endeavour? In the main they continue to regard themselves as such beings, in spite of all statements of scientists and philosophers to the contrary. But they are much concerned to know what kind and degree of influence Mind can exert upon bodily processes, what truth there is in the claims of many sects and schools of mental healers. They do keenly desire to know whether there is a kernel of truth in the widely accepted claims of communication with departed friends; whether each of us, as science tells us, is forever shut off from all his fellows by the distorting and inadequate means of communication provided by sense-organs and muscular system; whether there is not some common stock of memory and experience upon which men may draw in ways not recognized by Science; whether at death each of us is wholly exterminated; whether ghost stories are founded only on illusion and other forms of error.

There is in all lands an immense amount of eager questioning about such matters; immense amounts of time and energy are given to ineffective efforts to obtain more light on such questions. And unfortunately there is a multitude of persons who for the sake of filthy lucre take advantage of these eager desires, these strong emotional needs, and of the prevailing lack of sure knowledge, to falsify, obscure and fabricate the evidence.

It is perhaps this last aspect of the present situation which most urgently calls for action of the Universities. In spite of the immense and growing prestige of Science and its steady and scornful negative to all such questioning, the whole civilized world increasingly becomes the scene of a confused welter of amateur investigation, of conflicting opinions, of bitter controversies, of sects and schools and parties, each confidently asserting its own views and scornfully accusing the others of error, and of woeful blindness or wilful deception.

The negations of the scientific world are of little or no effect upon this chaos of conflicting beliefs and ardent desires. And so long as Science stands apart, coldly refusing to take a hand in the game, refusing to take seriously the questions asked, refusing to bring to bear upon the many phenomena that keep alive these conflicts, these hopes, and these beliefs, its powerful, highly organized apparatus of investigation, its negations will continue to exert but little influence toward stilling the tempest.

Let me state the demand upon our Universities at its simplest and lowest. Let us suppose that we are firmly convinced that no positive knowledge is attainable, that the outcome of a sustained, organized, and co-operative attack upon the problems of Psychical Research, such as the Universities alone are capable of making, must lead to purely negative conclusions; I submit

that, nevertheless, we ought to recognize such enquiry as a task which the
present state of chaos in the public mind urgently requires of the Universities
that they undertake and steadfastly pursue.

The situation, its needs and its demands on the Universities may be illustrated on a small clear-cut scale by one particular problem which has long
been recognized as crucial in Psychical Research, namely the problem of
telepathy. Does telepathy occur? That is to say—Do we, do minds, communicate with one another in any manner and degree otherwise than through
the sense-organs and through the bodily organs of expression and the physical
media which science recognizes?

Science asserts that no such communication occurs or can occur. Yet in
all ages antecedent to our own, belief in such communication has been universal. And in our own sceptical age and community, such belief is still
very general. It is held by all intelligent Christians; for it is implied in the
practice of prayer and communion. A very large proportion of intelligent
educated persons believe they have observed or experienced instances of such
communication. In that highly educated, scientific and sceptical class, the
medical men, it is I think true to say that about one in three believes that
he has first-hand knowledge of indisputable instances of it. A careful, highly
critical statistical survey of such sporadic instances, made by persons of the
highest qualifications, has resulted in a strongly positive verdict. A number
of carefully conducted attempts to obtain evidence of it under experimental
laboratory conditions have given equally positive results. A number of men
of great distinction and of the highest intellectual and moral qualifications
have announced themselves as convinced, after due enquiry, of its occurrence.
Yet, in spite of all this, Science, especially Science as represented in the
Universities, refuses to regard the question of its occurrence as one to be
taken seriously, as one deserving of investigation. And why? Simply because we cannot at present see how such communication can take place.

Now, to deny that phenomena of a certain kind may occur on the ground
that we cannot understand how they may be brought about, is very unsatisfactory even in the sphere of physical science. It is still more unsatisfactory
and positively misleading in the biological sciences. And in relation to any
events in which the human mind or personality plays a part, it is reprehensible and utterly inadmissible as a ground of denial or refusal of investigation.

What more suitable task for a research department of a University can be
conceived than the task of investigating such a problem? The individual
man of science may and does offer two valid excuses for ignoring this and
other problems of Psychical Research. He may say—That is not my line,
I have other things to do. Or he may say—I have tried and have had purely

negative results. But our Universities as a group of national institutions cannot excuse themselves in this way. The signs of the times call aloud to them that they shall follow the courageous lead of Clark University, shall frankly acknowledge their responsibility and welcome Psychical Research to an honoured place within their gates. Nowhere else may we hope to find the calm critical temper of scientific enquiry sufficiently developed and sustained; to no other institutions or associations can we hopefully entrust the task of shedding the cold clear light of science upon this obscure and much troubled field of vague hopes and vaguer speculations.

In conclusion, greatly daring, I will venture to say a few words in reply to a question which I feel sure many of my hearers wish to put to me, the question, namely—In your opinion has Psychical Research hitherto achieved any positive results? I am not the sort of person who holds a great number of clear-cut positive and negative beliefs. I am rather a person of the kind that deals in probabilities and degrees of probability, recognizing that our best formulations are but relatively true, that human mind and speech are incapable of formulating absolute truths. Therefore I can attempt in all frankness only qualified answers. In my view the evidence for telepathy is very strong; and I foretell with considerable confidence that it will become stronger and stronger, the more we investigate and gather and sift the evidence. In my opinion there has been gathered a very weighty mass of evidence indicating that human personality does not always at death wholly cease to be a source of influence upon the living. I am inclined to regard as part of this evidence the occurrence of ghostly apparitions; for it seems to me that, in many of these experiences, there is something involved that we do not at all understand, some causal factor or influence other than disorder within the mental processes of the percipient. I hold that a case has been made out for clairvoyance of such strength that further investigation is imperatively needed; and I would say the same of many of the alleged supernormal physical phenomena of mediumship. I am not convinced of the supernormality of any of these in any instance. But I do feel very strongly that the evidence for them is such that the scientific world is not justified in merely pooh-poohing it, but rather is called upon to seek out and investigate alleged cases with the utmost care and impartiality.

To some of you this confession will seem to make extravagant claims for Psychical Research; to others it will seem that I am quite unduly sceptical. Such wide differences of view will continue to divide us until the Universities shall have brought order, system, and co-operative effort into the domain of Psychical Research.

6.   Extra-Sensory Perception*

The work reported in this volume is the first fruit of the policy of naturaliza-
tion of "psychical research" within the universities. It goes far to justify that
policy; to show, first, that a university may provide conditions that will
greatly facilitate and promote this most difficult branch of science; secondly,
that the university may benefit from such liberal extension of its field of
studies. On the former head I will say nothing; it is for the instructed public
to judge of the value of this work. On the second head, I may properly testify
here that to the best of my judgment, the group of students who have taken
part in this work have reaped in a high degree the chief benefits which scientific research has to offer, namely, discipline in careful experiment and
observation, and in logical thinking, practice in faithful cooperation, and the
gratification of pushing back the bounds of knowledge, in this case in a field
of peculiar difficulty and significance. There has been no hysteria, no undue
excitement, among this group of students, nor has this work unduly pre-
occupied their minds to the detriment of other activities.

Though it would be unseemly for me to pronounce upon the value of this
work, I may properly say a few words to help the reader to form his estimate
of it. On reading any report of observations in the field of psychic research,
invariably there rises in my mind the question—What manner of man is this
who so reports? And I find that my estimate of the validity and value of the
report depends very largely upon the answer to that question. A report may
appear to be above serious criticism; and yet a brief acquaintance with its
author may suffice to deprive it (for me, at least) of all claim to serious con-

* Originally published as the Foreword to J. B. Rhine's *Extra-Sensory Perception*.
Boston: Bruce Humphries, Inc., 1935.

sideration or, on the other hand, may convince me that its statements must (provisionally at least) be accepted at their full face value. I do not stop to explain or to justify this attitude of mine. I believe it is well justified and to be very general among all who are interested in this field. Therefore I may assume that readers of this report who have no personal acquaintance with the author will welcome a few words from me about him and some of his collaborators, while the author, recognizing the purity of my motive, will pardon my intrusion on his privacy.

In introducing Dr. Joseph Banks Rhine to the reader, I must premise that almost all I have to say of him is true also of Dr. Louisa E. Rhine, his wife. Both have taken their doctorates in biology at the University of Chicago, both had begun promising careers as university teachers of biology, and both have resigned these. When Dr. J. B. Rhine burnt his boats, gave up his career in biology and came over to psychology and psychical research, it was with the full consent, endorsement, and parallel action of his wife—a unique and remarkable event in the history of this subject. For the Rhines are no monied amateurs. They are working scientists without worldly resources other than their earnings. When the facts became known to me I was filled with admiration and misgiving. Their action seemed to me magnificently rash. I had always plumed myself on indifference to worldly considerations; but here was a young couple who made me seem small, made me seem to myself a cautious, nay, a timid worldling. Nor was this action prompted by some overwhelming emotional and personal interest, such as the desire to make contact with some lost loved one. The motivation was, so far as I could and still can judge, the desire to work in the field that seemed to contain most promise of discoveries conducive to human welfare. Indeed in this age when we erect monuments to the boll-weevil, send up prayers for drought, pest and plague, and are chiefly concerned to make one ear of wheat grow where two grew before, it is difficult to retain enthusiasm for botanical research, unless one is a scientist of the peculiarly inhuman type.

The action filled me, I say, not only with admiration but also with misgiving; for it appeared that I was in some measure unwittingly responsible. The Rhines, in pondering the question—What is most worth doing? To what cause can we give ourselves?—had come upon my *Body and Mind* and upon others of my writings, especially my plea for *Psychical Research as a University Study*, and had determined to join forces with me at Harvard. Accordingly, Dr. Rhine arrived on my doorstep in Cambridge, Mass. one morning in June 1926, at the moment when I had completed the bestowal of my family and worldly possessions in two taxi cabs, with a view to begin a journey round the world, a journey which, owing to unforeseen alteration of my course, terminated in North Carolina. Nothing daunted, the Rhines spent the year at Harvard studying psychology and philosophy and in making acquaintance with Dr. W. F. Prince and the Boston S. P. R. And in the fall of 1927 they turned up at Duke University, as determined as ever to work in the field of psychic research, and, if possible, within the walls of a university. It was then I began to realize what manner of man I had to deal with. I found J. B. Rhine to be a ruthless seeker after truth, almost, I may say, a fanatical devotee of science, a radical believer in the adequacy of its methods and in their unlimited possibilities. He is one of those whole-hearted scientists for whom philosophy and theology are but preliminary skirmishings beyond the frontiers of scientific knowledge; one of those who will not admit a sphere of valuation in which philosophy must always retain her relative independence and prerogatives and responsibilities, no matter how greatly the province of science may be extended. When he comes into my room and finds me reading a book on metaphysics or religion, he scratches his head and (though he is too polite to utter his misgivings) wonders whether, after all, I, in my latter years, am becoming a renegade.

He has devoted much thought and study to the history of science and to the problem of scientific method. And he manifests in every relation the scrupulous honesty and regard for truth that befit such a student. Yet, though a fanatic devotee of science, he is very human in the best sense. He has again and again shown that he is ever ready to share his resources of every kind with those who are in need; a multitude of students, both men and women, bring their troubles to him, knowing that they will receive tactful sympathy and sound advice. And this power to inspire and attract the confidence of young people has been of no little value from the point of view of the researches reported in this volume. For it has overcome the initial difficulty of inducing students to participate in and to give time and effort to research of a kind which is looked at askance by the world in general and by the scientific world especially. The manifest sincerity and integrity of Dr. Rhine's personality, his striking combination of humane sympathy with the most single-minded devotion to truth have induced in his collaborators a serene confidence in the worthwhileness of the effort, and have set a tone which, to the best of my judgment, pervades the group and contributes an important, perhaps an indispensable, condition of the striking successes here reported.

I cannot pretend to be intimately acquainted with all of those who have participated in the experiments. But I have some acquaintance with all of them and my impressions are entirely favorable. Four of those who have taken a prominent part have worked for some years in our department as senior and graduate students, and of them I can speak, with entire confidence, as students of the highest class, in respect of general training and ability, of scientific devotion and of personal integrity.

A question that must rise in the mind of many a reader of this report may be formulated as follows:—Granting that Dr. Rhine is all that is here claimed for him, is it not possible that his collaborators have deceived or tricked him, perhaps with the benevolent desire to reward with positive results so earnest a seeker? My reply is that, if the experiments involved only some two or three collaborators and that during a brief period only, neither Dr. Rhine nor I could perhaps adduce any completely convincing objection to such interpretation; but in view of the considerable number of participants, often unknown to each other, and of the prolonged period of participation (extending in some cases through several years) it becomes wildly improbable that any such conspiracy of deception can have been successfully maintained throughout and under the constant variation of conditions, without any trace or indication of it coming to light. To which it may be added that the experimenters have been at special pains from the beginning to exclude by the conditions maintained, any possibility of deception, conscious or unconscious.

Finally, I would testify that I have "sat in" at the experimentation on a number of occasions, and have in some instances personally conducted the experiments, and have failed to discover either any indication of lack of good faith or any serious flaw in the procedures followed.

7.   In Memory of William James*

At the end of August of this year [1910] the telegraphic cables carried
to every part of the civilised world the news of the death of William James,
and in every country many hundreds of men and women felt that one of the
great lights was gone, one of the great forces withdrawn. It was no occasion
for bitter regret; for James was approaching the usual term of man's active
life, and, though there had been good reason to anticipate further additions
to his intellectual output, he had already made a rich and splendid contribution to the thought of our age; he had achieved a world-wide fame and
was regarded with intense admiration and affection by a host of readers
and a large band of personal friends. We had rather to be glad in the knowledge that his death was preceded by no severely disabling and prolonged
malady, and that he enjoyed until the last days the active exercise of his
great powers.

It is fitting that at this, the first meeting of the Society since his death,
we should record our sense of his services to the Society; and that we should
spend a little time in bringing before our minds the nature and extent of
those services, and in making clear to ourselves the attitude towards the work
and aims of the Society of one whose opinion in regard to that work and
those aims was entitled to carry more weight than the opinion of any person
now living.

I could wish that the honour of voicing our tribute to William James had
fallen to one who could claim old-standing friendship with him, one who

* From *Proc. S.P.R.*, Vol. 25 (1911), pp. 11-29.

could give you some intimate glimpses of his noble and strenuous character and of the growth and working of his clear-shining intellect. My own personal acquaintance with James (I hope I may say friendship, for he won my heart at our first meeting) was of few years' standing only. But for nearly twenty years I have been an enthusiastic reader of all his works, and for nearly the same period have known him to be the largest influence affecting my intellectual life.

I must, then, be content to try to put together an outline sketch of James' work and influence in relation to our Society.

James was happy in that his life was in a quite exceptional degree a unified system of activities. Beginning with a thorough study of the biological and medical sciences, he actively pursued these until near his fortieth year as assistant professor of physiology at Harvard. He was then appointed to a chair of psychology in the same University and devoted himself chiefly to that subject for more than twenty years. The appearance in 1891 of his great book, the *Principles of Psychology*, secured for him a world-wide reputation as the greatest psychologist of his age, perhaps (as Prof. Dewey has lately said) the greatest of any age. From that time onward his productive activity turned more and more towards the problems of general philosophy, and since 1902, when he became professor of philosophy at Harvard, it was devoted almost wholly to those problems. This may well be regarded as an ideal course of intellectual activity: would that all our philosophers could approach their tasks with the same expert knowledge of the natural sciences and of psychology!

During the period of his philosophic activity James made himself the acknowledged leader of a school of thought (the pragmatic and radical empiricist school) which, whatever fate be in store for it, has been a most active ferment in the philosophical world; to it has been largely due that great revival of philosophical activity which marks the opening years of the twentieth century.

James' active interest in "Psychical Research," which extended through the last thirty years of his life, was not something apart from and disconnected from the main system of his activity; rather it was for him an integral part of the whole, a part most intimately connected with the rest. It was the expression of the same tendencies of mind which shaped all his philosophical work; to it he brought, or rather, to it he was brought by, just those peculiar qualities of mind that made him so original and successful in the more strictly academic fields of philosophy and psychology.

In any attempt to define these special qualities, the first place must be assigned to his direct vision of, and to his keen sense of the importance of, the concrete realities of human life. Always he comes back to empirical realities, to the immediate experience of men in general as the ground and test of all theoretical constructions. This was the keynote of all his efforts, of all that was most original in his psychology (*e.g.* his description of the stream of thought with which the *Principles* sets out), of his pragmatism, of his radical empiricism, of his pluralism, of his epoch-making study of the religious consciousness, and of his keen interest in "Psychical Research."

It was this keen sense of reality which, in spite of his large tolerance, led him to occasional expressions of impatience directed against what he called vicious intellectualism, and against the rationalistic construction of theories of the universe that are totally indifferent to the actual nature of the world we know. It was this which forbade him to attempt to impose system and order where none can be discerned, forbade him to aim at constructing a finished picture of the universe, and led him to prefer a "thick" to a "thin" philosophy; meaning by the "thin" highly abstract and purely logical procedures such as those which lead to the conception of the Absolute as the only reality; and by the "thick" a way of thinking that involves constant reference to, and faithful regard for, the largest possible mass of empirical fact. "A large acquaintance with particulars," he said, "often makes us wiser than the possession of abstract formulae, however deep."

Another striking characteristic was his wonderful open-mindedness. He was always ready and anxious to find the possible grain of truth in every belief, the possible gleam of insight in every human utterance, whether in a philosophical system of the kind least attractive to him, in the wildest assertions of religious exaltation, or in the crude expressions of less gifted, and especially younger, colleagues. He had the keen eye of the great scientist for the significance of the exceptional, the seemingly irregular and unintelligible phenomenon. I well remember a Fellow of the Royal Society saying to me: "I'm not interested in anything until I can understand it." James' attitude was just the opposite of that. He was most interested in whatever was most difficult to understand, most problematic. I venture to say that this is the truly scientific attitude characteristic of all great discoverers. The smaller minds are not interested in, they cannot apperceive or become aware of, phenomena that will not fit into their particular system of pigeon-holes, and will not wear any one of their stereotyped labels.

This large openness of mind, together with his native kindliness, rendered him wonderfully appreciative of the work of other men; also it prevented his thought from crystallising in any rigid forms, and allowed his intellect to go on growing till the last. To his generous appreciativeness many a younger and obscure colleague in the fields of philosophy and psychology could bear grateful witness. It was finely displayed when, two years ago, James introduced the ideas of Prof. Bergson to an Oxford audience. Instead of regarding his younger and less widely famous colleague as a rival to be jealously criticised, he gave a glowingly eulogistic account of his teaching, admitted that it had worked a revolution in his own mind, and ranked himself as a disciple. The same fine trait was strikingly displayed again in the last published work of his pen, the article on a Pluralistic Mystic in a recent number of the *Hibbert Journal.*

Thirdly, it was characteristic of James that he took his philosophy very seriously. For him it was no merely academic game in which each player plays for his own hand, striving to devise some system peculiar to himself; rather, in his view, the advance of philosophy was a matter of the greatest practical importance for the welfare of mankind. Constantly he had in view human needs and aspirations, human limitations and human possibilities. In all his writings there is manifested (and more and more clearly if they are considered in the order of their production) his earnest wish to come to agreement with others, to achieve a view of the world that shall be acceptable to all men; his strong desire to bring increase of philosophic understanding rather than merely to develop and establish his own circle of ideas. The same earnestness was shewn by the continuance of his strenuous activity after his retirement from his chair at Harvard at an age which he might well have claimed the right to rest on his laurels.

If to these three distinctive qualities of his mind we add a penetrating and versatile intellect, a strong sense of humour, and great powers of expression, we have, I think, the main psychological keys to the understanding of his intellectual achievements. That the style is the man was eminently true of James; his lively and forcible style, which made everything he wrote a delight to his readers, reveals everywhere the qualities we have noted, the keen eye for empirical fact and the faithful acceptance of it as the foundation and test of all theoretical constructions and of all beliefs; the openmindedness; the interest in and generous appreciation of the ideas of other men; the earnest desire to harmonise all human knowledge in one continuously advancing body of pragmatic truth.

Such in barest outline was the man. Let us now record with gratitude his services to the cause of "Psychical Research." Most obvious to the world at large and of inestimable benefit to this Society was the fact of his open and active espousal of its cause, his lending his name and prestige at a time when to be a prominent member of the Society was to incur risk of ridicule, or worse. The Society has been fortunate in counting among its members, especially among its presidents and vice-presidents, a number of names of the highest intellectual distinction; but, with the single exception of that of our revered first President, no name probably has been, or could have been, of so much service to the Society as that of William James. For his claims to be heard with respect on all branches of our work were unique. No other man of our time has made an equal mark in science, philosophy, and religion; no one has moved with so much mastery in all these three great fields of thought.

But James was not content to serve as our figure-head, and to lend us moral support and the prestige of his name. He has done much hard spade-work for the Society. He was one of the founders of the American Society, and one of its most active leaders from its inception in 1884 until its union with our parent Society in 1890. He was the discoverer of Mrs. Piper, and the first carefully to investigate and report upon her trances; and, after Dr. Hodgson went to America to take up her case, James supported that prince of investigators with active help and warm friendship. To the *Proceedings* of the American Society he contributed papers on hypnotism and automatic writing based on personal investigation. He was a Corresponding Member of the English Society from 1884-1889, a Vice-President from 1890-1910, and President during the years 1894-5. Besides his presidential address, he contributed a number of papers to our *Proceedings* and undertook a large amount of work in connexion with the census of hallucinations.

James wrote also at least three weighty expositions of the work and aims of the Society in three of the leading popular magazines of the United States;[1] and he brought together parts of these in an essay published in the very widely read volume entitled "The Will to Believe." That essay must, I think, be regarded as the most powerful and convincing of all apologies for this Society.

But James' moral support of, and his active participation in the work of, the Society were neither the whole nor the chief part of his services to "Psychical Research." If James had never been a member of our Society, if even he had never heard of it and its work, we should still have to recognise him as a great influence, perhaps the greatest individual influence of our time, making for the progress and extension of our enterprise. For the main tendency and aim of all his widely influential teaching was identical with what I take to be the deepest lying aim which the Society pursues along its highly special line of inquiry—namely, the reconciliation of science and religion on empirical grounds.

That the reconciliation of science with religion is the essential task of philosophy has long been widely recognised. But no such reconciliation has yet been achieved. James found himself in a world in which almost all influential thinkers accepted one or other of two types of philosophy. On the one hand was the naturalistic school, which held fast to the world of empirical fact, and to the principle that the laws of mechanism hold undisputed sway throughout the universe; its utmost concession to religion being such recognition of an Unknowable power behind all things as Herbert Spencer taught. On the other hand were the transcendental idealists, who, having capitulated to empirical science as regards all the phenomenal world, claimed to have learnt from Kant and Hegel how to preserve a quasi-religious sphere of thought by constructing a purely logical scheme of reality that bore no relation whatever to the world of empirical fact, one which would remain equally valid no matter what might be the nature of our human experience of the world in which we live our daily lives—a time-less, space-less, cause-less, unchanging, infinite whole.

However widely different were the tempers and teachings of these two dominant schools of the Unknowable and the Absolute, they agreed in one point of fundamental importance, namely, they acknowledged the absolute sway of mechanical principles in the empirical world; that is to say, both alike were thoroughly mechanistic. To both these schools James resolutely opposed himself. He doubted whether the human mind would ever achieve the ideal of philosophy, a system of knowledge complete and harmonious in all its parts; he was very certain that no such system has been, or can yet be, constructed. "The actual universe," he said, "is a thing wide open, but rationalism makes systems, and systems must be closed."[2] He protested and rebelled against all closed systems; he saw on every hand the raw edges of our knowledge; but that did not lead him merely to seek more facts; he was a genuine and original philosopher in that he persistently sought better ways of understanding the facts we have. He firmly believed that human knowledge is but at the beginning of its course; and he believed that, if only because human knowledge is growing, the universe, of which that knowledge is a part, is growing also. "Reality," he said, ". . . is still in the making, and waits part of its complexion from the future . . . the universe is still pursuing its adventures."[3]

The only reality recognised by Rationalism of either type he found intolerably unreal. He could not away with the optimism of the Absolutist rationalism which condones the miseries of man as necessary parts of the Absolute's perfection; he recognised the looseness of the reasoning by which Absolutism seeks to establish itself, and affirmed the absurdity of the claim of that reasoning to compel our assent to its conclusions. He boldly asserted that the only view of the universe acceptable to him was one that regards it as capable of becoming something better than it is, and as one in which the moral efforts of men may contribute towards that result. His philosophic aim was to conceive the universe in accordance with these demands, and to shape a philosophy capable of development, consciously incomplete, looking to the empirical sciences for aid, and requiring for its completion the co-operative efforts of many generations of thinkers; a philosophy which shall

work in the scientific spirit rather than in that of rationalistic dogma, regarding its most cherished conceptions as but hypotheses to be constantly
tested and evaluated by the pragmatic method, that is to say, with regard
to their significance and value as guides to human life.

James, therefore, rejected as unproven and improbable the assumption
common to both the dominant schools, the assumption of the absolute sway
of mechanical causation in the empirical world; and in standing out thus
against the mechanistic dogma, he was, of course, striking a powerful blow
for "Psychical Research." For of all the considerations that lead men to
ignore and deny the aims of "Psychical Research," to affirm the impossibility
of the happenings we record, the mechanistic dogma is by far the most
influential; "these things," they say, "cannot happen, for they are incompatible with our mechanical first principles."

James' brilliant attack on the two most prevalent philosophies has swept
away this dogma from the minds of many, and has shaken its hold on the
minds of many more; it has shewn that these are not the only possible
philosophies for a self-respecting man of modern culture; it has taught all
who have felt its force to keep open minds, to recognise the uncertainty of
all philosophic conclusions, to respect empirical fact, and to recognise that
in our present state of ignorance it is absurd to pretend to say that this or
that *cannot* happen.

Every part of James' work contributed towards this effect, so favourable
to "Psychical Research"; for it was all of a piece. His pragmatism was
primarily an extension of the scientific attitude of mind towards the problems and theories of philosophy. As the instrumental theory of truth it became a powerful lever for the uprooting of the dogmas of both naturalism
and absolutism. His radical empiricism was the natural supplement of his
pragmatism, and his pluralism the natural, if not the inevitable, outcome
of their conjunction. Together they made strongly for the rescue of human
personality from the position of indignity and insignificance to which it had
been reduced by both the prevalent systems. They made plausible, or at
least possible, a belief in some survival after death, the belief in a personal
God and in a real communion between God and man, and even the belief
in the objective efficacy of prayer and of moral effort.

James treated psychology as one of the natural sciences; but he consistently refused to reduce all consciousness to the level of an epiphenomenon
or silent spectator; he insisted always on the real efficiency of our consciousness, our feelings, our efforts, our thoughts as teleological co-determinants of
our bodily movements. He discovered an unsuspected wealth of detail in the
stream of consciousness; and he restored to that stream its unity, rejecting
root and branch the mechanical descriptions and explanations of association-

ism. He restored effort, activity, desire, in short, the will, to its rightful place. He was the first academic psychologist to make adequate recognition of the importance of modern medical studies of hysteria and of the reality and theoretical importance of hypnotism, automatic speech and writing, and states of dissociation in general.

Above all he was the first to grasp firmly the thorny subject of the psychology of the religious consciousness; boldly to admit the pathological character or affinities of many of its manifestations, and yet to affirm their value and to find in them empirical evidence of the truth of religion. His *Varieties of Religious Experience* was immensely successful. Psychology had been regarded as the natural enemy of religion. All that was changed at once, and the few years that have elapsed since the appearance of that book have seen the birth of several journals wholly devoted to religious psychology, and the publication of a dense stream of books and pamphlets on the same subject, mostly written by religious-minded persons, many of them by theologians and eminent divines.

In all these ways, then, James' philosophical activity ran parallel in a larger orbit with the work of the S.P.R. It was a philosophy which justified our methods and our aims, and rendered possible at least the hope of finding in the general scheme of things an intelligible place for the facts we aim at.

In these three ways, then, James rendered immense service to "Psychical Research." Let us ask—What did the Society do for him? What in his view has it achieved, and what was the importance for his thought of that achievement?

James distinguished broadly what he called the mechanical and the personal views of nature—"science," he said, "essentially only stands for a method and for no fixed belief; yet as habitually taken, both by its votaries and outsiders, it is identified with a certain fixed belief—the belief that the hidden order of nature is mechanical exclusively, and that non-mechanical categories are irrational ways of conceiving and explaining even such things as human life." To this "mechanical rationalism," as he called it, James' whole drift and striving were opposed; for him the personal view of nature was the true one; and there can be no doubt that he was greatly strengthened in this belief by his knowledge of the results of "Psychical Research."

As early as 1890 he proclaimed Mrs. Piper as his 'one white crow,' meaning that her case had made it impossible to accept the principle that our knowledge comes to us only by the channels of sense. And, needless to say, his conviction of the supernormal origin of her trance-knowledge was but strengthened by his later acquaintance with that remarkable woman. This case, together with other evidence, convinced him that our minds can and do communicate in some way that cannot be reconciled with the mechanical categories; or, in other words, that telepathy is a fact of nature, and that it is not explicable on physical principles.

To have found adequate empirical evidence of this transcendence of the mechanical categories was of crucial importance for James' system of thought. If, as he held, the proof is conclusive, mechanistic rationalism is finally shattered by it, and the personal view of nature established, and it was this he had in view when he wrote that our Society has restored the continuity of history.[4]

In his lectures at Oxford, two years ago, James announced his firm conviction that "most of the phenomena of psychic research are rooted in reality," and it was obvious, I think, to those who knew him, that the results of "Psychical Research" had played a greater part in shaping the thought of those lectures than he judged it expedient explicitly to affirm before an audience so ignorant of the facts.

In a recent number of the American Magazine, James' undertook to state the principal effect upon his opinions of "twenty-five years of dabbling in 'Psychics.'" The following are the main points of his confession. "I am baffled as to spirit-return, and as to many other special problems." He held the spiritistic hypothesis unproven; and it was not consistent with his view of personality; nevertheless, with his invariable largeness, he kept an open mind in that direction. As regards "Physical phenomena," he wrote: "I find myself believing that there is 'something in' these never-ending reports of physical phenomena, although I haven't yet the least positive notion of the something. It becomes to my mind simply a very worthy problem for investigation." The main ground of this opinion was the accumulation of evidence to form what he called a faggot, and the constancy of type of the phenomena.

He affirmed the frequency of automatic writing, and its constancy to type.

He affirmed "the presence, in the midst of all the humbug, of really supernormal knowledge. . . . In really strong mediums this knowledge seems to be abundant, though it is usually spotty, capricious and unconnected."

He inclined "to picture the situation as an interaction between slumbering faculties in the automatist's mind and a cosmic environment of *other consciousness* of some sort which is able to work upon them. If there were in the universe a lot of diffuse soul-stuff, unable of itself to get into consistent personal form, or to take permanent possession of an organism, yet always craving to do so, it might get its head into the air, parasitically, so to speak, by profiting by weak spots in the armor of human minds, and slipping in and stirring up there the sleeping tendency to personate. It would induce habits in the subconscious region of the mind it used thus, and would seek above all things to prolong its social opportunities by making itself agreeable and plausible. It would drag stray scraps of truth with it from the wider environment, but would betray its mental inferiority by knowing little how to weave them into any important or significant story."

He added his conviction that "the phenomenon is actuated by will of some sort anyhow," meaning that the messages of "automatic speech and writing" are not, as the term seems to imply, the products of merely mechanical neural processes, but express desire, intention and design.

He concluded by asserting the enormous complexity of the phenomena and the necessity for suspension of judgment and prolonged and patient inquiry. "That is why I personally am as yet neither a convinced believer in parasitic demons, nor a spiritist, nor a scientist, but still remain a psychical researcher waiting for more facts before concluding."

"Hardly, as yet, has the surface of the facts called 'psychic' begun to be scratched for scientific purposes. It is through following these facts, I am persuaded, that the greatest scientific conquests of the coming generation will be achieved."

These few extracts will suffice to indicate the nature of the effect in James' mind produced by the work of this Society; they show that this effect was of very great, in fact, of crucial importance. They show also that his attitude towards the work of the Society was truly scientific in the higher sense of that word, and that, while he remained thoroughly critical and chary of forming positive conclusions, he confidently regarded the results hitherto achieved as but a small and imperfect sample of a splendid harvest of knowledge still to be reaped by "Psychical Research." To my mind his attitude seems wholly admirable, a model to be held up for all of us to copy as nearly as our powers will permit.

While, then, James rendered great services to our Society, the work of the Society powerfully influenced his thought. The relations between him and the Society were fruitful and reciprocally advantageous in a high degree. By this action and reaction between his philosophical principles and the results of "psychical research," James' thought was led to a definite issue upon the problem, which is at once the central problem of all philosophy, and the immediate and special problem for the illumination of which this Society exists, namely, the problem of the nature of human personalities and their position in the universe.

In his *Principles of Psychology,* James took up decidedly the antimechanical view of the human organism, criticising most effectively and destructively those various formulations of the relation of mind to body, which deny all real efficiency in the physical world of our consciousness, our thought, feeling, and will, the epiphenomenalism of Huxley and most naturalists, and the various forms of psycho-physical parallelism. Classing all these together under the head automaton-theory, he wrote "My conclusion is that to urge the automaton theory upon us, as it is now urged, on purely *a priori* and *quasi*-metaphysical grounds, is an unwarrantable impertinence in the present state of psychology."[5] And he affirmed that "it is to my mind quite inconceivable that consciousness should have *nothing to do* with a business which it so faithfully attends";[6] meaning the processes of the brain.

Throughout he never wavered in his opposition to the mechanical philosophy, whether in the form of mechanical materialism or the mechanistic rationalism of the transcendental idealists or absolutists.

Now throughout the history of thought the great rival to all the mechanistic theories has been the soul-theory, the animistic theory that man's body is animated by a soul, an immaterial thinking being, which is the ground of his individuality, and is capable of surviving the death of his body, and preserving all or something of his personality beyond the grave.

It might have been expected that James' rejection of all the mechanistic doctrines would have led him to embrace the soul-theory. But he never did accept it. In the *Principles* he presented the soul-theory forcibly and sympathetically, and confessed "that to posit a soul influenced in some mysterious way by the brain-states and responding to them by conscious affections of its own, seems to me the line of least logical resistance, so far as we yet have attained."[7] But, though treating the theory with respect, and asserting that "it is at any rate less positively objectionable than either mind-stuff or a material monad creed,"[8] he insisted that "it does not strictly explain anything,"[9] that the conception of the soul is not required by psychology, and that the passing thought of each moment of consciousness is the only subject logically required for the intelligible description of our mental life.

In the *Principles*, then, James, refusing to accept the soul-theory, left open the question of the nature and ground of personality; and in his later writings we find him more decidedly opposed to the soul-theory. In his Oxford lectures of two years ago he returned to the question and said—"Souls have worn out both themselves and their welcome, that is the plain truth. Philosophy ought to get the manifolds of experience unified on principles less empty. Like the word 'cause,' the word 'soul' is but a theoretic stopgap—it marks a place and claims it for future explanation to occupy."[10] And he complained that the conception of the soul has no pragmatic significance; which for him was equivalent to saying that it is useless, and therefore invalid.[11]

This is not the occasion for any examination of James' reasoning. We have rather to seek to grasp as clearly as possible what his own view was: and this is worth doing because his view was unfamiliar, distinctive, and by no means easy to seize. James' frequent and sympathetic references to Myers' conception of the Subliminal Self may easily lead the casual reader to suppose that he accepted Myers' hypothesis or one very similar to it. But that would be an error. We must recognise clearly that Myers' doctrine was a development and extension of the soul-theory and that James rejected that theory.

Yet it is equally clear that James believed and taught that the mind of man is not wholly destroyed at death, that in some sense and in some degree it survives the death of his body.

In the *Principles* James criticised very forcibly and decisively rejected the view that individual human consciousness can be regarded as compounded of lesser consciousnesses, sensations, or units of feeling, or fragments of consciousness of any kind. And he recognised that the only logical alternative to this doctrine of mind-stuff (of atoms of consciousness capable of being compounded into larger and larger wholes of consciousness) seems to be the soul-theory; but yet, as we have seen, he rejected that theory and left open the problem for further investigation.

In his *Ingersoll Lecture on Human Immortality*,[12] he adopted a peculiar theory of the function of the bodily organism or of the brain in our mental life, one which he called "the theory of separation" or "the transmission theory." By these names he implied the notion that there exists a great sea of consciousness or thought; that the consciousness of each one of us is but a ray of this universal consciousness; and that the brain of each man is a translucent or half-transparent spot in the veil of nature through which a ray of the universal consciousness intermittently struggles to illumine for brief moments the material world. According to this view, then, the bodily organism is the principle of individuality; mind or consciousness is essentially one; and our individual consciousnesses, so-called, are but distorted beams filtered out from the universal consciousness by our brains; and, when those brains decay, the beams cease to be thus transmitted. It is clear that this "transmission theory" escapes materialism, but it is equally clear that it does not provide for any survival of human personality after the death of the body.

James returned to the transmission theory in his lecture on the "Energies of Men," developing it from the point of view that in our moral and intellectual efforts each of us draws spiritual energy from that larger whole of which, according to the hypothesis, his mind is but a fragmentary manifestation; and, in accordance with his invariable tendency, he adduced in a striking and original way new empirical evidences of the reality of such influx of the greater tides of life through the channels of human personality.[13]

But his later utterances show that he was not satisfied with the position defended in the Ingersoll lecture. It was obvious to him that it was hardly consistent with his rejection of the notion of the compounding of consciousness. For the reabsorption of individual consciousness in the universal sea implies such compounding. Accordingly he returned to the problem in his Oxford lectures. He told us how he had wrestled long and long with this notion of the compounding of consciousness, and how, approaching it now from the side of over-individual consciousness, rather than, as in the *Principles*, from the side of composition of individual human consciousness from lesser parts, he had reversed his opinion, thrown over his own brilliant demonstration of the absurdity of the notion, and made it the keystone of his philosophic scheme of the universe. After this revolution, it was possible to modify the doctrine of the Ingersoll lecture in a way that made it less intangible, less a matter of metaphor and vague suggestion merely. He modified it in the direction of assimilating it to Fechner's panpsychic view of the universe. "The drift," he said, "of all the evidence we have, seems to me to sweep us very strongly towards the belief in some form of superhuman life with which we may, unknown to ourselves, be co-conscious. We may be in the universe, as dogs and cats are in our libraries, seeing the books and hearing the conversation, but having no inkling of the meaning of it all. . . . The analogies with ordinary psychology and with the facts of pathology, with those of psychical research, so called, and with those of religious experience, establish, when taken together, a decidedly *formidable* probability in favour of a general view of the world almost identical with Fechner's."[14] And Fechner's view or vision of the world was one of a hierarchy of consciousnesses, each member of the hierarchy being at once both a consciousness for itself and a part of a more widely inclusive consciousness of a higher level or order. James expressed his conception of the relation of the individual human consciousness to the more inclusive consciousness as clearly perhaps as it is capable of being expressed in the following words: "Out of my experience, such as it is (and it is limited enough) one fixed conclusion dogmatically emerges, and that is this, that we with our lives are like islands in the sea, or like trees in the forest. The maple and the pine may whisper to each other with their leaves, and Conanicut and Newport hear each other's foghorns. But the trees also commingle their roots in the darkness underground, and the islands also hang together through the ocean's bottom. Just so there is a continuum of cosmic consciousness, against which our individuality builds but accidental fences, and into which our several minds plunge as into a mother-sea or reservoir. Our 'normal' consciousness is circumscribed for adaptation to our external earthly environment, but the fence is weak in spots, and fitful influences from beyond break in, showing the otherwise unverifiable common connection. Not only psychic research, but metaphysical philosophy and speculative biology are led in their own ways to look with favour on some such 'panpsychic' view of the universe as this."[15]

He refused to identify this wide mother-sea of consciousness with the absolute mind of idealistic monism, basing his refusal chiefly on moral grounds. Even the widest consciousness of all he regarded as less than the whole universe. "However much may be collected, however much may report itself as present at any effective centre of consciousness or action, something else is self-governed and absent and unreduced to unity."[16] This is the essential character of his pluralistic universe. To what more inclusive forms our individual consciousnesses belong he did not pretend to say; but that they do so belong was his main thesis; and he believed that the mystic's experience of union and absorption of the self in a higher power is what it claims to be; and it is after that model that he would have us conceive the life beyond the grave. It is clear that this view implies no personal immortality; the life of the individual man is but a temporary and partial separation and circumscription of a part of a larger whole, into which it is reabsorbed at death, and the body remains the individualising principle. But he held that this view, besides being more consonant than any other with all the empirical evidence, is pragmatically justified on moral grounds; because, as organs of the larger whole, we play a part in determining its development and welfare; "our thoughts determine our acts, and our acts redetermine the previous nature of the world";[17] and so we may, in a very real sense, hold ourselves to be co-workers with God, helping Him to make the universe something nobler than it yet is.

More than any other man of our time, James was qualified by his openness of mind, his courage and originality, his powerful intellect, his wide knowledge of empirical fact and philosophical speculation, and his prolonged and earnest wrestling with the fundamental problems, to express conclusions that must command a deeply respectful hearing. To many members of this Society it must be a disappointment that such a leader should have reached a conclusion adverse to the survival of human personality. But it is much that his final position is one which affirms the real efficiency and abiding value of the moral and intellectual efforts of mankind. And our Society may well renew its courage and its conviction of the value of its work, in recognising that that work played no small part in enabling James to reach and maintain that position. And let us bear in mind the deliberate expression of his mature judgment. "Hardly, as yet, has the surface of the facts called 'psychic' begun to be scratched for scientific purposes. It is through following these, I am persuaded, that the greatest scientific conquests of the coming generation will be achieved."

That such a leader in the world of thought has published to the world this high estimate of the importance of the Society's work, and has generously avowed the large influence of that work upon his constructive efforts, must

permanently strengthen the Society and must support us in the conviction
that we have set our hands to no mean task.

NOTES

[1] *Scribner's Magazine*, March, 1890; *The Forum*, July, 1892; *The American Magazine*, 1908.

[2] *Pragmatism: a New Name for some old ways of thinking*, London, 1907, p. 27.

[3] *Pragmatism*, p. 257.

[4] "Religious thinking, ethical thinking, poetical thinking, teleological, emotional, sentimental thinking, what one might call the personal view of life to distinguish it from the impersonal and mechanical, and the romantic view of life to distinguish it from the rationalistic view, have been, and even still are, outside of well-drilled scientific circles, the dominant forms of thought. But for mechanical rationalism, personality is an insubstantial illusion. The chronic belief of mankind, that events may happen for the sake of their personal significance, is an abomination. . . . But the S.P.R.'s *Proceedings* have, it seems to me, conclusively proved one thing to the candid reader; and that is that the verdict of pure insanity, of gratuitous preference for error, of superstition without excuse, which the scientists of our day are led by their intellectual training to pronounce upon the entire thought of the past, is a most shallow verdict. The personal and romantic view of life has other roots besides wanton exuberance of imagination and perversity of heart. It is perennially fed by *facts of experience*. . . . It is the intolerance of science for such phenomena as we are studying, her peremptory denial either of their existence or of their significance (except as proofs of man's absolute innate folly), that has set science so apart from the common sympathies of the race. I confess that it is on this, its humanizing mission, that the Society's best claim to the gratitude of our generation seems to me to depend. It has restored continuity to history. It has shown some reasonable basis for the most superstitious aberrations of the foretime. It has bridged the chasm, healed the hideous rift that science, taken in a certain narrow way, has shot into the human world" (Essay on "Psychical Research" in the vol. *Will to Believe*, pp. 324-326).

[5] *Principles*, vol. i. p. 138.

[6] *Op. cit.* p. 182

[7] *Ibid.* p. 136.

[8] *Op. cit.* p. 371.

[9] Vol. i. p. 181.

[10] *A Pluralistic Universe*, p. 210.

[11] *Ibid.*

[12] Boston, 1898.

[13] *Philosophical Review*, 1907.

[14] *A Pluralistic Universe*, p. 309.

[15] *The American Magazine*, "The Confidences of a Psychical Researcher," 1908.

[16] *A Pluralistic Universe*, p. 322.

[17] *Op. cit.* p. 318.

PART II

1.   *Abnormal Psychology**

Abnormal psychology offers a vast and fascinating and, just at the present time, a very fruitful field of research. It can probably claim a much larger number of serious students than any of the other departments, and it excites much more popular interest than any of them. The ordinary man is so accustomed to the ordinary behaviour of normal men and to his own habitual modes of thinking, that he cannot see behind them any problems to be solved. The notion of any one trying to find out more about the human mind than he himself knows, generally fills him with impatient scorn, even though he may be prepared to tolerate those who spend their lives in classifying beetles or minutely describing the skeletons of microscopic animalcules. But, when one meets a man who gravely and persistently asserts that his conduct is constantly governed by the voice of an invisible being, or that he sees beside him a human figure which none other can see, or that he is the emperor of the world; or when one hears of a man who repeatedly inflicts painful mutilations upon his own body, or who refuses to move hand or foot for months at a time; then even the dullest man is startled into curiosity, and feels himself in presence of a fact that calls for explanation and understanding.

Abnormal psychology comprises a number of sub-departments, which in the main have been pursued independently by different bodies of workers; happily, in recent years these groups have come more closely together and are now giving mutual aid. We may broadly distinguish two groups of these

* Originally published as Chap. VII in *Psychology, The Study of Behaviour* by William McDougall. Oxford University Press, 1959, pp. 130-154.

sub-departments, namely, those that are concerned with minds in definitely morbid or pathological states, and those concerned with distinctly unusual or abnormal states of mind which cannot fairly be classed as morbid. The former group consists of two sub-departments: the study of mental diseases proper and that of the psycho-neuroses. The separation of these studies is largely conventional and professional rather than scientific, and there is manifest at the present time a strong tendency to abolish it.

Until the present century the study of mental diseases had in the main been pursued in strange detachment from the other branches of psychology, and it had thrown but little light on the major problems of the science. This was mainly due to the prevalence among the physicians for mental diseases of a tendency to seek to understand and explain all the morbid conditions of mind in terms of structural disorder or disease of the brain only. Some mental diseases are primarily diseases of the brain, and in cases of certain types gross inflammatory or degenerative changes of the brain tissues are regularly found upon *post-mortem* examination. But this fact does not justify the assumption that all mental disease is of this nature; and of late years there has appeared a strong tendency to seek for mental or functional causes of the abnormal course of mental process in insane patients. This tendency has been greatly stimulated by the modern developments of the other department of mental pathology. In this second department the disease which provides the largest number of patients and the most interesting material for the student of psychology is hysteria.

A generation ago the attitude of the medical profession towards hysteria and allied abnormal conditions was, with very few exceptions, wholly unscientific, being based merely on popular psychology. It was vaguely recognized that the extraordinary behaviour of the hysterical patient implied some kind of mental abnormality, and that no gross disease of the nervous system was implied by it. But the tendency then prevalent may be crudely described by saying that the abnormal behaviour of the hysteric was attributed to 'pure cussedness'; the treatment accorded was 'firmness', strong electric shocks, cold douches, and other decorous substitutes for a sound birching. To a small group of French physicians belongs in the main the credit of having put the study of hysteria and allied conditions on a scientific basis, by showing that the patients must be regarded as suffering from a disorder of mental origin and must be treated in the main through the mind. They succeeded in showing that in many such cases, perhaps in all, the essence of the disorder is some division of the mind into parts which, instead of co-operating in normal fashion, function more or less independently of one another and even enter into some sort of rivalry. It was shown that, while in the majority of cases the division takes the form of the separation of some minor functions only, in others there occurs something like a separation of functions into two rival systems that compete with one another for the control of behaviour, sometimes the one, sometimes the other predominating; and it was shown that more rarely such rival systems seem to maintain their activities simultaneously, the behaviour of the patient seeming to express at any one moment the purposes of two minds. In this way was introduced the notion of the division or splitting of the personality, resulting in alternating or in coexistent dual personalities. Of these two conceptions that of alternating personalities is the clearer and more intelligible. Under it are generally classed rare cases of the type which in former ages was explained as due to 'possession' of the body of the patient by a 'demon' or by the spirit of some deceased person.

In a typical well-marked case of this sort, the patient's normal life suddenly gives way to a period in which he behaves in a manner altogether 'unlike himself'. He wanders perhaps to some distant place, and there takes up some new mode of life under a new name, behaving sufficiently like a normal person to avoid the attention of the police or of the medical profession. After weeks, months, or years of the new mode of life, he suddenly changes again, perhaps waking up one morning to find that his surroundings are wholly strange to him, and that he remembers nothing of his past life from the moment at which he left home; in short, he becomes himself again, after being to all intents and purposes a different person. Thereafter he may relapse at longer or shorter intervals into the secondary state, 'coming to himself' again after each period of secondary existence. In the greater number of such cases, each of the two alternating personalities has no direct knowledge of the other or of his doings, the period of the dominance of the one being a complete blank for the memory of the other; and the two personalities commonly differ widely in respect to temperament.

It is attempted to render such cases intelligible by pointing out that most of us experience from time to time changes similar in kind, though much less in degree; for example, one passes into a mood in which all one's thinking has an unusual emotional tone, say, a tone of melancholy; and so long as this tone prevails, one dwells upon gloomy memories, forgetting the brighter phases of one's past life, one's thinking reaches pessimistic conclusions, and one's behaviour reveals this inward gloom. Now, it is said, imagine this condition to be accentuated and recurrent, and you have an approximation to alternation of personalities; the border-line being crossed when the emotional tones of the alternating periods become so widely different that in each period the memories only of the periods of congruent tone are recoverable.

The cases of dual personality of the concurrent type are rarely so extreme.

The existence of a secondary personality is inferred from certain features of the behaviour of the bodily organism which seem to bear no relation to the thinking of the subject, so far as he can reveal it to us; for example, the patient has an anæsthetic or insensitive arm and hand, and this can be induced to write intelligible answers to questions whispered in his ear, while the subject, who afterwards denies all knowledge of both question and answer, maintains an animated conversation with a third person. Or the anæsthetic hand may be pricked a given number of times, and, though the subject remains, so far as can be ascertained, unaware that the hand has been touched, the hand itself may be induced to write down the number of the pricks.

In such cases, according to the commonly received view, the impressions made on the anæsthetic limb fail to affect the thinking of the subject, but evoke instead a feeble trickle of mental activity, which flows on as an independent subsidiary stream alongside the main stream; since this main stream is, as it were, deprived of the influence of these sense-impressions, the lesser stream is said to have been split off from the greater. The facts are interpreted after the analogy of a river which overflows its banks at one spot, and thus sends off a small divergent stream which follows for a time a separate course.

In the rarest and most interesting of all these strange cases of dual personality, the phenomena of the alternating and the concurrent types are presented by the same organism. During the dominance of the normal personality, a secondary personality reveals itself occasionally in the production of movements of which the normal personality remains unconscious or for which he denies all responsibility, and which yet express intelligent appreciation of the circumstances of the moment; and later, when the secondary personality is dominant, he claims to remember the incident and to have willed the 'automatic' movements.

In face of such puzzling cases, some of which have been studied with the most admirable patience and acumen by the French physicians, and also more recently by some American doctors, any hypothesis must be put forward tentatively. The view that they all imply or result from some kind of division of the mental functions into two systems which carry on their activities independently of one another—this view finds support in many facts (though others cannot easily be reconciled with it), and is widely accepted. But this view is really nothing more than a hypothetical description of the condition, and needs to be supplemented by some hypothesis which will explain the production of the condition. Such an hypothesis is that of Pierre Janet, to whose pioneer studies so much of our present knowledge of these states is due. He assumes that the unity of the mind, as normally revealed in the direction of its activity towards one topic at any one moment, is conditioned by the exercise of a synthetic power or energy which is one of the fundamental functions or faculties of mind; and he supposes that, in the patients who exhibit these curious modes of behaviour, this synthetic energy is for one reason or another defective; hence, he says, the mind cannot perform so completely as the normal mind its unifying function, and its activities, instead of being harmonized in one stream which, however broad and deep, is nevertheless a single complex activity, fall apart into two or even more streams, with the result that the patient's field of consciousness or stream of mental activity is narrowed and that indications of subconscious activities appear.

In recent years our knowledge of this group of pathological states of mind has been further enriched by the work of Sigmund Freud of Vienna, who also has sought to carry further the theoretical explanation of them by means of a system of ingenious hypotheses. At the present time these hypotheses are by no means generally accepted, but are the subject of a most lively and heated controversy; nevertheless, they are so well supported by the good results obtained by many physicians who have applied them in the treatment of patients, and their interest from the point of view of the major problems of psychology is so great, that some indication of their nature must be given here.

The French conception of hysteria tends to be intellectualistic; i.e. it takes but little account of the function of will or conation in mental life. In the teaching of Freud a leading role is assigned to conation. The fundamental fact from which the theory starts out is that our organized conative tendencies are apt to come into conflict with one another, producing what we called moral struggles. Every case of what is commonly called temptation involves such a conflict of conative tendencies; when, in such a conflict, we conquer our temptation, our highly organized self-consciousness brings into operation a strongly organized system of conative tendencies which support the more moral or social tendency in its conflict with the immoral or socially disapproved tendency, and thus secure the defeat of the latter. Now, we know that such a defeated tendency, or conquered temptation, is not always destroyed or wholly abolished by such a victory of one's moral nature in open conflict; we know that in some cases it recurs and requires to be thrust down again and again. But in many cases we succeed, either at once or after repeated conflicts, in banishing this temptation from consciousness. We commonly feel then that we have done with it and wholly cast it out or destroyed it. Now, it is possible or even probable that, when we stoutly face a temptation, frankly recognizing it for what it is, an expression of a lower possibility of our nature, a conative tendency opposed to our moral sentiments, and when we thus conquer it, the tendency is destroyed. But it seems (and this is the essential novelty in Freud's teaching) that many natures, especially perhaps women brought up in a strictly conventional manner, react in a different way to their temptations; they are so horrified at the first dim awareness of the nature of their temptation that they never frankly recognize it, never bring it out into the light in order to confront it in open conflict. The tendency is apt then to be repressed and yet to live and work in the mind in a subterraneous fashion; it becomes, as it were, a parasitic growth seeking constantly to force its way to consciousness, or, in other words, to determine the conscious thinking of the subject. But the subject's moral nature, being radically opposed to it, maintains a rigid censorship, again in a subconscious fashion; and so there goes on a perpetual subterranean or subconscious conflict. In states of diminished mental alertness, as in dreaming or mere day-dreaming, this repression, maintained by the organized system of tendencies which constitute the moral nature, is liable to partial remission; it becomes less effective, and then the repressed tendency finds its chance to determine the subject's conscious thinking. Even in such states, it commonly fails to express itself directly and clearly in the course of the subject's thinking, but rather finds expression only in symbolical fashion. Thus, in the dreams of such a person, the repressed tendency is apt to manifest itself in a flight of imagery which, when described by the dreamer, may seem to have no relation to the repressed tendency, and which is not recognized by the dreamer as so related, but which in reality symbolizes the course of events subconsciously desired by him. In this way, it is held, the tendency achieves a certain measure of the satisfaction which in the waking state is wholly denied to it by the rigid censorship of the moral nature.

Such analysis and interpretation of dreams occupies a very important position in Freud's system of psychopathology; for it was a main point of departure from which the whole system was developed; and it discovers an analogy between the dream-experiences of normal persons and the processes which are assumed to underlie and express themselves in the symptoms of hysteria. It has, therefore, been much criticized; but there can be little doubt that, though some of its most enthusiastic exponents have gone too far in asserting that every dream is determined by the subconscious working of a repressed tendency, such interpretation does in some cases hit the mark and reveal a wealth of subconscious mental activity of which the dream is the expression in consciousness.

It may be objected—How is it possible to establish any such interpretation?—How can it be more than guesswork? To this the reply is that the interpretation is achieved by an intricate process of delicate analysis; and, through this process opens the door to many possibilities of error, yet on the whole the analysis of a very large number of dreams, by various observers who have used this method, has revealed a certain lawfulness and consistency of mode of operation which forbid us to set aside the interpretations as purely arbitrary; and further, they are borne out by the analogous processes revealed as issuing in the symptoms of hysterical patients.

The symptoms of the hysteric take the form not only of perverted modes of thinking, such as the baseless conviction of having performed some reprehensible action, or other troublesome obsessions; but also very commonly that of the performance of seemingly senseless actions, of paralysis of various organs, legs, arms, organs of speech, and so forth; and of anæsthesia or complete insensitiveness of parts of the skin or of other sense-organs. Now, according to the doctrine of Freud, these symptoms also are, like the perverted course of thinking and like the thinking of the dreamer, symbolical expressions of repressed tendencies. We have to suppose that in the normal person the mental forces which maintain the repression suffice to prevent any expression of the tendency save in dreams, or in reverie, or in occasional bodily movements which seem to be senseless and accidental; but that in certain persons, whose mental energy is depressed either by violent emotional shock, by long-continued excess of work, or by the persistent subconscious conflict between the repressed tendency and the moral nature, the repressing forces fail to accomplish their task in an adequate manner; so that the tendency succeeds in asserting itself more fully, though still in a symbolical or indirect manner only. The symptoms of the hysterical patient thus appear as so many disguises, adopted by a repressed tendency in order to evade the censorship of the moral nature and to obtain a partial satisfaction through playing some part in the determination of conscious thought and of behaviour.

A relatively simple type of such indirect expression of a repressed tendency, which may serve to illustrate the principle, is the recurrent hallucinatory perception of some object. The object thus falsely perceived is found in some cases to be one with which the patient happened to be employed at the moment of some emotional crisis in the course of the moral conflict that resulted in repression; such an object has no intrinsic connexion with the tendency, and the occasion of the perception of it may have escaped the conscious memory of the patient; and, just for this reason it would seem, it is seized upon by the repressed tendency as a means of evading the censorship and securing a secret satisfaction. In a classical instance of this type recorded by Freud, the patient complained of perceiving almost constantly a strong odour of burnt pudding. Of this hallucination she could suggest no explanation; yet it was ultimately found that, at a moment of emotional crisis in the history of a repressed love attraction, she had been occupied with a burnt pudding.

Now, as of the interpretation of dreams, the reader properly and naturally asks—What proof can be given of the correctness of such interpretation of symptoms? The answer is twofold: first, when by a long and delicate process of analysis the physician has discovered a repressed tendency and its probable connexion with such a symptom, the patient frequently remembers the circumstances which determined the form of the symptom and recognizes the significance attributed to it; secondly, it appears that in many cases, when the patient has been led to recognize frankly the nature of the tendency which has been repressed, to face it courageously, and to bring the whole history of it under the free criticism of his intellectual and moral nature, all the symptoms rapidly disappear and the patient is restored to health.

A useful confirmation of the reality of the subconscious operation of conative tendencies has been provided by the application of a very simple experimental procedure to both normal and abnormal subjects. If a list of words is called aloud to any subject, he having been instructed to reply to each one by calling aloud some other word with the least possible delay, he will reply to most of the words after a delay whose duration is not more than one or two seconds; but in any considerable list of words so applied; there are usually a few to which his reaction is longer delayed or in some other respect abnormal. And it is found, in nearly all such cases, that the word in question has some emotional significance, or that the object denoted is connected in the mind of the subject with some strong conative tendency, often one or more or less repressed.

Enough, perhaps, has been said to suggest the nature of this new system of ideas, and to indicate their value and significance. It is sometimes asked —What has psychology done to enable us to benefit in any way our fellowmen? Much might be said in reply to this question, but perhaps the most striking answer would be to point to a number of men and women, who, after being for many years a painful burden to themselves and their friends, and after having been subjected without benefit to many forms of medical treatment, have been restored to health and happiness and usefulness by the application of psychological knowledge and psychological theory. This new doctrine and the practice based upon it are of importance not only in the one province of medicine in which they have been worked out; their interest and importance go far beyond those limits. They are leading to a great extension of the psychological attitude towards mental diseases of all kinds; and they are opening vistas of great extensions of our knowledge of the workings of the normal mind; especially they are revealing a realm of subconscious mental activity the existence of which had been vaguely conjectured, but which had remained unexplored and altogether problematical. For both the continued repression of the reprehensible tendencies, and the processes by which they partially evade control, are distinctly purposive activities; and the latter seem to involve in some cases complex and subtle operations. And, if the interpretation of dreams according to this new method is not altogether fanciful, some complex dreams are not, as hitherto generally assumed, merely fortuitous and purposeless streams of pictorial fancies; rather, they are full at every point of significance, are in fact highly elaborated trains of symbolical imagery produced by ingeniously selective and constructive thinking, which, while remaining subconscious, is guided and sustained by a hidden purpose or design.

If the symptoms of the hysteric, and the imagery that fills the consciousness of the dreamer, are the products of elaborate though subconscious mental activity, we may fairly suppose that the waking thoughts of the normal man may be in part the expression of similar subconscious activities; and Freud and his followers have actively carried their principles into many fields of normal psychology, and have fruitfully applied them to throw light upon the genesis of works of art and literature. In this way morbid psychology is being brought into fruitful relations both with normal psychology and with the study of mental states and processes that are abnormal without being morbid.

These latter constitute a wide field of study which can only be negatively defined by saying that it comprises all states and processes that are neither normal nor morbid. It may be roughly divided into two parts, that of the subnormal and that of the supernormal. The former comprises such states as idiocy and weakmindedness, and alcoholic and other intoxications in so far as they involve impairment of mental processes. These are not without their own special interest, but they cannot compete in this respect with the supernormal manifestations; for in dealing with this division we are constantly confronted by the problem of the future evolution of the human mind, and we seem to get glimpses of immense possibilities, of modes of mental operation and communication indefinitely transcending the recognized limits of the usual and the normal. The principal topics of this field may be grouped under the following heads:—

(1) Subconscious operations producing results similar to those of normal thinking; (2) supernormal manifestations in the domains of intellect and character, including the production of works of genius, religious conversion, and mystical experiences; (3) supernormal influence of the mind over the body; (4) supernormal processes of communication between mind and mind.

The phenomena falling under all these heads are connected by the fact that all of them seem to imply more or less extensive subconscious operations; and it has been attempted to bring them all under one explanation by the hypothesis that each of us has a twofold mental constitution and a double mental life; namely, the normal life of conscious thought conditioned by one of the two constitutions, and the subconscious mental life conditioned by a second more or less independent mind or department of the mind. Various names, such as the 'subliminal self', the 'subconscious mind', the 'secondary self', and so forth, have been applied to this hypothetical department of the mind. Now, it cannot be too strongly laid down, in view of the popularity of these catchwords, that, as commonly used, they are little or nothing more than words that serve to cloak our ignorance and to disguise from ourselves the need for further investigation. For the ordinary procedure is to postulate a 'subconscious mind', and then merely to assign to its agency all the varied phenomena of a supernormal character, its nature remaining completely undefined and its capacities for the production of marvels being regarded as without limit in any direction.

It is, of course, a legitimate enterprise to attempt to work out an hypothesis of this sort; but we must recognize that none has yet been devised which can claim to be a satisfactory working hypothesis by which the facts can be brought into intelligible order. We must recognize also that the relations of subconscious operations to conscious thinking are in many cases so intimate, so much of the nature of participation in the working out of a single purpose, that any such division of the mind into two unlike parts, such as is commonly implied by names of the kind mentioned above, appears wholly unwarranted. We shall, therefore, do well to consider the supernormal phenomena under some such provisional classification as that suggested above, without committing ourselves to any hypothesis which attributes them all to any one special agency or entity.

(1) The evidence of subconscious operations producing results similar to those of normal thinking is abundant. It is obtainable experimentally in unlimited quantities by hypnotic and post-hypnotic suggestion. Hypnosis is an artificially induced condition of partial quiescence of the mind, allied to sleep. After a long period of unscientific dogmatic denial, the scientific world at last recognizes that this condition can be induced in the great majority of normal persons, and that it is in itself perfectly harmless. It is now recognized also that hypnotism (the study of hypnosis) opens many problems of the greatest interest and provides methods for investigating them. By means of it, many of the peculiarities of mental process characteristic of hysteria and other pathological states, and many of the supernormal phenomena, can be experimentally produced and studied; and it provides effective methods of treating many disorders in the production or maintenance of which a nervous or a mental factor plays a part.

In the present connexion the facts of post-hypnotic suggestion claim our attention. Any good subject may be told, while in the hypnotic state, to perform some simple action at some definite time or upon some signal being given; and, if then awakened before the appointed moment, he will carry out the suggestion, although he cannot remember in the interval or immediately after performing the action, even if closely questioned, what suggestion was given him. And the signal may be of such a nature that its appreciation involves mental activity of considerable complexity; for example, the subject may be told that he will open and shut the door when the observer touches his own face with his left hand for the eleventh time. In such a case (and the experiment may be varied and complicated indefinitely with the best subjects) the subject in some sense watches the operator, notes and counts the significant movements, and carries out the suggestion; and yet he truthfully denies that he was aware of the nature of the command given, or of the fact that the observer had touched his face even once; and in some cases the subject cannot even remember his execution of the suggested action immediately after its performance. Here, then, is indisputable and abundant evidence that a train of purposive mental activity, which controls to some extent the behaviour of the subject, may go on while he is consciously thinking of other matters.

Another and equally striking kind of evidence of the same fact is afforded by 'automatic' writing, an accomplishment which a certain number of normal persons are capable of acquiring. In an ordinary case of this kind the subject may sit reading or talking, while his hand, holding a pencil upon a writing-block, writes more or less coherent and intelligible passages of prose or verse, of which he remains ignorant until, like any other person, he reads the script. In various closely analogous ways other automatic movements may reveal guidance which is indisputably intelligent and yet independent of the conscious thinking of the subject; popular methods of inducing such movements are table-tilting with the fingertips, planchette writing, and the 'ouija' game. In some cases these movements reveal knowledge of facts which cannot be recalled to conscious memory; and in others they reveal deliberate intention and ingenious design of which the subject remains unconscious. It should be added that the 'automatic script' commonly consists chiefly of detached sentences or mere fragments of sentences; yet in some cases it consists of long connected passages not without literary merit.

(2) Another type of evidence of the same class consists in the solution of problems, or the production of written matter of literary merit, during sleep or while the mind is occupied with other matters. The special interest of these cases is that they form a transition to the processes of the second class, namely, the production of works of genius, religious conversion,

and mystical experience. For there is a natural tendency to set such processes apart by themselves and to accentuate their differences from normal mental process. But it is more conducive to an understanding of them to seek and to accentuate the points of resemblance, rather than those of difference. From this point of view we do well to begin the consideration of such facts by insisting on the large proportion of subconscious mental activity which is involved in our everyday thinking. Whoever has made on the spur of the moment a witty remark will probably be prepared on reflection to acknowledge that the words sprang to his lips without any deliberate search for them, and that the mental process, the assimilation of two seemingly unlike things, or relations, or what not, accomplished itself in secret, the result only coming to consciousness as the words issued from his lips; and he may subsequently have found, somewhat to his surprise, that there was more in his remark than he at first realized.

This is the kind of normal activity which we may set at the lower end of a continuous scale, at the upper end of which we may place the achievement of the greatest works of genius. At every level of this scale we seem to see at work the same factors or contributing conditions, but in very different proportions. In the first place it is to be noted that the subconscious activity which is revealed by the achievement expresses in some sense the previous mental development of the subject, his interests, knowledge, and character. The dull pedant does not suddenly coruscate in flashes of wit; the calculating prodigy does not solve problems in the higher branches of mathematics without previous study of those branches; the person who has neither learnt to enjoy, nor been trained in the technique of, a particular art does not suddenly produce a masterpiece. Sudden conversions and mystical experiences may seem in some cases to be exceptions to this rule; but it is doubtful whether on closer examination any such exception could be substantiated. It will usually be found that the religious convert or mystic, no matter how little his previous life may have shown the influence of religion, has been at some period of his life subjected to religious influences; in the common phrase, the good seed has been sown and has ripened in secret.

Again, the subconscious activity usually expresses the influence of some conscious volition or conation. The problem which is solved during sleep is usually one with which the sleeper has striven while awake. Even the sudden outburst of wit implies a certain conative attitude. The sudden formulation of a great scientific hypothesis is preceded by much thinking directed to the problem. The compositions of the musician or the poet express his will to compose, often his explicit intention at the moment, but in any case a general attitude of his will. Even the automatic writer can to some extent voluntarily set himself to produce the automatic script. And religious conversion or ecstasy is usually preceded by a longing or striving for some change of life, some new mode of consciousness, though it may be little more than a vague discontent with life as hitherto known and lived. These considerations justify us in seeking to exhibit even the more extreme and extensive forms of subconscious activity as continuous with normal mental activities, rather than as processes of an altogether different order, wholly attributable to some second mind, whether a 'subconscious mind' of the subject or some mind external to and altogether independent of his normal mind.

(3) The supernormal control of the mind over the bodily processes is a topic that has been brought into the forefront of popular interest of late years. Systems of mental healing, or at least methods of treating bodily disease that rely little or not at all on physical or chemical agencies, are enjoying a great vogue; and even the medical men of this country are becoming aware that there is 'something in' hypnotism, and that the methods of suggestion and persuasion and even the claims of the 'Christian Scientists' are deserving of some unbiased attention.

In all this disputed region, in which the plain man of science feels himself to be walking on a quagmire, surrounded with mists, the effects of hypnotic suggestion provide the one sure evidence that mental influences upon bodily processes may go far beyond the normal or ordinarily recognized. And this evidence forbids us to shut our eyes to the possibility that some elements of truth and reality are mixed up with the large mass of error and deception that grows up in connexion with every system of mental healing. For it shows us the reality of mental influences upon the nutrition, repair, and regulation of bodily organs, which influences nevertheless completely elude our understanding; and it forces us to recognize that we can set no limit to the extent of such influences. It is characteristic of all or most of the methods of mental healing that, in so far as they are real, they involve mental activities which are largely subconscious.

(4) Passing now to consider supernormal communication of mind with mind, we enter a region of critical importance for our interpretation of the foregoing classes of supernormal phenomena. For if, as has always been maintained by most of the religious systems, minds can communicate with, or in any way influence, one another in some direct fashion which does not involve the use of the organs of sense, then we must be prepared to look outside the mind of the individual for the explanation of some at least of the supernormal manifestations of mental activity. Explanations of this sort have always been accepted by the greater part of mankind: hence the crucial importance of any positive empirical evidence of such direct communication or influence, and hence the need for the most impartial and critical examination of any evidence alleged to be of this nature. The word 'telepathy' has re-

cently come into general use to denote the direct action of mind on mind; the crucial question may therefore be stated in the form—Does telepathy occur? The efforts of the well-known Society for Psychical Research have for more than a generation been largely directed towards establishing an affirmative answer to this question, by means of experiments of many kinds and the collection and critical sifting of facts which seem to demand this hypothesis for their explanation. The evidence accumulated by these efforts is such as would suffice to establish the fact in dispute for all normal minds, were it not that the question is of so momentous importance.

Admitting, then, the necessity of still holding our minds in suspense on this question, let us glance at the prospect opened out by the highly probable, but not perhaps completely verified, assumption that telepathy occurs. If this assumption is accepted, the mind of the individual organism no longer appears as inevitably isolated from all other minds, or as communicating with them only by the medium of the bodily organs of expression and sense-perception; and it is open to us to seek to explain mental processes and effects that seem otherwise inexplicable as due to the direct influence of other minds. Two distinct lines of explanation are then open to us. First, we may seek to explain certain supernormal mental processes by invoking the influence of some of those minds of which we have positive knowledge, namely, the minds of our contemporary fellow-men; we might, for example, suppose that religious conversions, or some of the supernormal effects of mind on body, are brought about by the influence of some one stronger mind, or by the concentration of several or many minds, upon the one. But this supposition would fail to explain some of the facts and alleged facts, notably the inspirations of genius that exceed the powers of all other existing persons, and cases in which persons seem to display knowledge that was in the possession of no person living at the time.

In this way, many of those who regard some of these supernormal manifestations as inexplicable, unless the direct influence of mind on mind is assumed, are led to see in them evidence of the influence of disembodied minds. The study of abnormal psychology has thus become a field in which it is sought to find empirical evidence for two of the most ancient and widely held beliefs of the human race; namely, the belief in the survival of human personalities after bodily death, and the belief in the communion of human with divine mind.

Evidence in support of the former belief is sought chiefly in automatic speech or writing, which seems in so many cases to express the personalities of deceased human beings. So faithfully are such personalities thus portrayed that many hundreds of cultured men and women have become convinced that these 'automatic messages' are what they so often seem and claim to be, namely, messages formulated in the still surviving minds of deceased persons, and somehow expressed through the medium of the automatic writer. Those whose first impulse is to dismiss this conception with a sneer should try to abstain from this course, until they have first-hand acquaintance with instances of this strange phenomenon. On the other hand, a hasty acceptance of this interpretation of the facts is equally to be deprecated. For the evaluation of the evidence is a most delicate and difficult work, requiring complete freedom from bias; yet the number of persons who are capable of maintaining the attitude of impartial inquiry in the face of this evidence seems to be but a minute fraction of the cultivated world.

Empirical support for the belief in communion with the divine mind is sought along two lines chiefly. First, it is argued that the process of religious conversion is often one which cannot be accounted for in terms of the known properties of the human mind in general and of the mental peculiarities of the persons concerned. Secondly, it is pointed out that in all ages the specifically religious experiences of men, even of men brought up under the influence of the most diverse traditions, have certain features in common which mark them as the work of a common influence and point to their determination from a common source. Hence, it is argued, it is reasonable to believe that this religious experience, of which the fullest or completest type is the mystical sense of the absorption of the self in a larger whole, is what it appears to be to those who best know it; namely, an actual union or communion of the human mind with the divine mind. This reasoning has been urged in modern times by a number of writers, but by none so forcibly as by the late William James in his celebrated treatise, *The Varieties of Religious Experience*. The influence of that work has been very great; and to it is largely due the fact that psychology, which until very recently was commonly regarded with hostile suspicion by the leaders of religious thought, as well as by the rank and file, seems now in a fair way to become the chosen handmaid of theology and even its principal support. For, since the publication of that book, there has sprung up what may almost be called a new branch of literature in the shape of several journals and a stream of articles and books devoted to the psychology of religious experience and written for the most part by theologians.

It will be seen from this brief review of the field of abnormal psychology that in most of its branches we are compelled to recognize the reality of subconscious mental operations; and that though the results both in behaviour and in consciousness of such operations are often similar to those of normal mental process, yet in many cases these results go beyond the normal.

More than one attempt has been made to devise an hypothesis which will bring all these supernormal effects under one explanation. Of such attempts the most interesting, perhaps, is that of William James. He suggested that we may regard all minds as connected in some immediate fashion which permits of their reciprocal influence and of the conjunction of their powers; or, to put the notion in another way, that all mind, human and infra-human as well as superhuman mind, is one, and that our individual minds are but partial manifestations of the one mind, conditioned by the peculiarities of our bodily organisms. All the supernormal effects of mental action, including the extremer instances of control of bodily processes, the expression of knowledge not acquired by any normal means, the supreme achievements of genius, religious conversion, and the ecstatic sense of absorption of the self in a larger all-comprehensive whole, which seems to be the extreme form of the specifically religious experience—all these effects might then be attributed to a partial or temporary suspension of the conditions which commonly isolate the individual mind.

No open-minded student of psychology will refuse to recognize the legitimacy and the fascination of such speculations. But the chief work of abnormal psychology must continue to be impartial observation and critical sifting of the empirical data, on the basis of which alone such speculations can be tested or verified.

2.   *Automatisms**

Prince's Theory of Hallucination

When a dissociated system manifests itself in bodily movements during the persistence of waking consciousness and normal control of the rest of the organism, it is usual to speak of the movements as automatisms. Such automatic movements range from simple twitches of some muscle-group, to which it may be difficult to attribute any significance, to regard as in any sense an evidence of mental or psychic activity, up to such highly elaborate movements as those of automatic speech and writing. When such movements produce sentences; long, coherent, and intelligible utterances; and even well-ordered and more or less logically constructed romances or poems or philosophic treatises, we cannot refuse to regard them as expressing mental activity.

When, half a century ago, such phenomena began to be seriously studied, men of science were generally inclined to argue in the following fashion: These elaborate movements, expressing intelligence and purpose, go on automatically, *i.e.,* without the consciousness of the person whose limbs produce them; they are therefore expressions of *unconscious cerebration.* We may therefore conclude that the various parts of the brain can function equally well with, or without, the accompaniment of consciousness. Cerebral activity is therefore a purely mechanical process which may, or may not (for reasons not known), be accompanied by the *epiphenomenon* called "consciousness." This was the line taken by T. H. Huxley and W. B. Carpenter. Others chose to assume that all "automatic" actions are executed through the spinal cord

---

* Originally published as Chap. XIII in McDougall's *An Outline of Abnormal Psychology.* London: Methuen & Co., Ltd., 1926.

alone, the brain taking no part in the production of them. This was, for example, the view taken by the physiologists Heidenhain and McKendrick, who sought to explain along this line all the movements produced by hypnotic and post-hypnotic suggestion.

Increased knowledge of the facts compels us to reverse this argument and to believe that the so-called automatisms are expressions of mental activity as truly as any other actions; and, although we must admit that it is impossible to prove by any absolutely compelling reasoning that any person other than oneself is conscious, or consciously thinks and acts, we must recognise that all the grounds which justify us in believing a man's normal conduct to be the expression of conscious thinking justify us equally in believing that automatic actions express conscious thinking. So long as we have only objective evidence of this, in the intelligence, purpose, design, or intention expressed by the automatic actions, doubt or suspension of judgment on this question may seem to be well justified. But in many cases it has been found possible to obtain introspective and retrospective evidence of the truth of the view that the so-called automatic action expresses conscious thinking; that is to say, it has been possible to get into touch with a part, or fragment, or aspect, of the personality which produces and controls the "automatic" movements and to obtain from it an introspective or retrospective account of the thinking and feeling expressed in the action.

In those cases in which (as in somnambulism) the normal personality seems to be asleep during the execution of the "automatic" actions, this interpretation of them as expressions of conscious thinking (possibly, in many cases, thinking of a restricted kind) seems acceptable enough to most students of the phenomena. It is when the "automatic" actions are executed during the waking state that this interpretation of them meets with resistance on the part of many students. They have become accustomed to believe that the stream of conscious thinking is a single stream; and they cannot easily rid themselves of this prejudice.[1] Under the influence of this prejudice it has become usual to separate, as phenomena of two distinct classes, the "automatic" actions of sleep and trance states, on the one hand, from those of waking states on the other. But there is no valid ground for such separation. Automatic actions of exactly the same kind may go on in both states. That most elaborate form of "automatic" action, automatic writing, goes on in some subjects equally well and in similar forms in both states; and the same is true of simpler forms of automatism.

Moreover, in our study of hypnosis we have found experimental evidence of the truth of the view I am urging. For we found that, after the execution of some post-hypnotic automatic action, it is possible in some cases to obtain (on rehypnotisation) a retrospective account of the thinking expressed by the action.[2] Further, reflection on common experience should prepare us to accept this view; for, although it may seem that concentrated thinking commonly has, as it were, a single moving focus, and though during such activity we may seem to be aware only of the objects to which our thinking is directed; yet in many cases we may become introspectively aware that a second stream of thinking, some reverie, or fantasy, or recollection, goes on alongside the main stream. Under exceptional circumstances, this duality of the stream of thinking becomes more extreme.[3] And, as after dreaming, we often feel sure that such reveries or recollections, irrelevant to the task on which we are consciously concentrated, have complicated our mental state, although we may be unable to remember them in detail.

All these considerations point strongly to the view that in all automatic actions we have to do with expressions of a subsidiary stream of conscious mental activity, which we may best describe by the term "co-conscious activity," following Dr. Morton Prince, who has given currency to the expression and done more than any other psychologist to establish the reality of such co-conscious thinking.

I do not wish to force this view upon the reader. I merely put it before him at this stage of our discussion as a well-founded view and as, in my opinion, the only one that can be consistently applied to the interpretation of a multitude of facts of abnormal psychology.[4]

AUTOMATIC WRITING

Students who have no first-hand acquaintance with the phenomena of automatic writing may well feel sceptical of the claim that it is produced without any knowledge of its contents on the part of the subject. Such natural scepticism cannot stand in face of the abundance of carefully studied cases of such writing. Such writing is produced sometimes during a trance, or sleep-like condition, that comes on spontaneously, as in the case of the famous Mrs. Piper and other trance "mediums." In other cases it is produced during a fully waking condition, the hand being completely anæsthetic during the writing and the subject unaware that it is making any movements, so long as it is screened from his vision. Other subjects are aware that the hand is moving; though they may converse, or read, or otherwise concentrate their attention, during the writing, and remain entirely unaware of the nature of what is being written until they read it after its completion. Others again become aware of the words as the hand forms them, but do not know what words or sentences are about to be written, have no foresight of what is coming, and no sense of intending, planning, or imagining the substance of the story.

Many persons who have never written automatically can readily be induced or trained to do so by post-hypnotic suggestion; and many can develop the power spontaneously by simply holding a pencil upon a writing-pad while they immerse themselves in some interesting piece of reading. Of those who cannot produce automatic writing with a pencil, many can produce automatically spelled and intelligible sentences by the aid of some such device as the "ouija"-board, or the "planchette"; especially if two or three subjects co-operate by laying their fingers on the same apparatus.[5]

In many such cases it is possible to obtain some retrospective account of the thinking that governed the writing, if the subject is afterwards hypnotised.

That poems or other literary works of merit have often been produced automatically is well known. R. L. Stevenson's description of the "Brownies" at work in his brain is famous; and his story of "Dr. Jekyll and Mr. Hyde" would seem to indicate that he was familiar in his own person with some of the extreme manifestations of dual personality.

There is no reason to doubt S. T. Coleridge's statement that "Kubla Khan" was composed during sleep. A somewhat different and equally striking case is the following, the facts of which I had from the lips of the author himself:

Case 10. A man in his early prime, who followed the calling of a stockbroker, lived a normally active social and athletic existence. His tastes were those of an average member of his class; he had no special literary interests; poetry he had always regarded with indifference as a thing rather for women than for men. He had the habit of lying in a half-waking state for some little time before rising each morning. He noticed that, thus half-awake, lines of what seemed to be verse would come into his mind. He was sufficiently interested to jot them down on paper, and found that they made connected and coherent verses, which seemed to him as good as other verses he had seen in print. He therefore sent some of the verses, thus subconsciously produced, to the editor of a magazine. To his astonishment they were accepted. At the time when he told me of these facts, a number of his poems, produced in this way, had been published in leading magazines, and—paid for. Such of these poems as I read seemed to me of considerable merit, in a bold romantic style. An interesting feature of the production was that often the lines of a poem would come into his consciousness as complete but detached lines in irregular order; these lines could then be sorted out in the fully waking condition, and arranged, without other change, to make the complete poem. This fact shows very clearly that the verses were designed and constructed before the several lines came to consciousness.

THE FUGUE

"Fugue" is the name given to those instances in which a person suddenly disappears from his accustomed haunts and reappears at some distant place, astonished and puzzled to find himself there, and unable to give any account of himself in the period between his disappearance and his reappearance.[6]

Case 11. A colour-sergeant of long service was carrying a despatch from one part of the front to another, riding a motor-bicycle. He suddenly found himself, a few hours later, pushing his bicycle through the streets of a seaport town some hundred miles from the front. He was utterly bewildered and, in order to avoid suspicion of desertion, he surrendered himself to the military police. He remained unable to give any account of his long journey from a spot near the front to the seaport.[7] After some stay in various hospitals he came under my care. He had no symptoms beyond his amnesia for this short period of some hours' duration, and a certain depression and lack of self-confidence, such as naturally resulted from the circumstances in a man of his good record and responsible position. Waking conversation having failed to overcome the amnesia, I tried hypnosis and at once the amnesia yielded; the dissociative barrier was overcome, and he continued in the waking state to be able to recollect and describe the whole incident: how a shell exploded near him, throwing him down; how he remounted his cycle and set off for the seaport; how he found his way by studying the sign-posts and asking questions, etc. It was clear that, though his actions had been conscious, intelligent, and purposive, yet his conscious activity was of a restricted kind; he seemed to have had no thought about the consequences of his action, but to have been driven on by the single strong impulse of fear, taking the form of a desire to get far away from the danger-zone.

It is probable that in such a case the actual fugue realises some fantasy previously generated by a repressed desire for such escape from the scene. In the foregoing case I did not succeed in obtaining evidence of such preceding fantasy and repression. In the following case, which I take from Janet's best-known work,[8] the influence of preceding fantasies in shaping the fugue is well illustrated.

Case 12. Rou was a poor boy who lived with his mother in a city where he was employed in the humdrum tasks of a small store. He had for years been in the habit of frequenting taverns, where he associated with sailors and listened avidly to their stories of adventure on the high seas. He longed for a life of such adventure and dreamed of tropic isles and fairy seas. We are given no detailed account of fantasies of this time; but we may safely infer from the account that they occurred and were largely occupied with such scenes and adventures. One day (when in all probability Rou had been drinking with his acquaintances, as his habit was—and we have seen that alcohol favours dissociation) he disappeared. Subsequent investigation showed that he had worked his way towards the coast, at first on canal barges, enduring many hardships, later in the service of a travelling tinker. One day, some months after Rou had left home, his master procured some wine, it being a feast day, and proposed a little festivity. Again we are not positively told whether alcohol was taken before the change; but only that, at the mention of the date, Rou cried out: "It is my mother's birthday!" and therewith was himself again, except that he could not recollect any event since the day of his departure from home.[9]

Such are typical fugues; they are prepared for by day-dreams motivated by repressed tendencies; then occurs (generally, perhaps always, at the moment of some emotional shock) a dissociation of the system of mental dispositions concerned in and built up through the fantasies; and forthwith the repressed tendency, working through the dissociated system, finds expression in action.

SOMNAMBULISM

The relation of fugues to somnambulisms is very close. The difference seems to consist mainly in that the fugue expresses a larger part of the total personality; so large a part that the patient is able to conduct himself in a manner sufficiently near the normal to avoid being detected as a person in a distinctly abnormal state.

Compare with the fugue the following simple case of somnambulism:

Case 13. A soldier, a big vigorous man, was in hospital after being rendered briefly unconscious or dazed by shell-explosion. He showed no symptoms, and I was about to return him to duty when other inmates of his ward complained of his walking in his sleep. I found that, several times nearly every night, he would get up, walk over to the bedside of the only sergeant in the ward, and stand there until led back to his bed. He could throw no light on this peculiarity. In hypnosis he at once relived and described the scene of his accident. A shell had exploded, killing and wounding several comrades; he rushed off to the sergeant to report; and, as he did so, a second shell exploded, dazing him. In the somnambulism he was reliving this scene, the memory of which was dissociated; just as Irene re-enacted the scene of her mother's death.

HYSTERICAL FITS

It would be easy to arrange a series of cases ranging by small transitions from an elaborate fugue, through anticipatory and recollective somnambulisms, to typical "hysterical fits." The following case will illustrate the transition from the somnambulism to the fit.

Case 14. A game young soldier had fought very gallantly until wounded in one foot. When convalescing from the wound he began a long series of "attacks," each of which closely resembled the rest. Sometimes the "attack" came on in his sleep, sometimes during waking. He would suddenly fall to the ground, seem to be utterly unaware of his surroundings, and would re-enact, in the most dramatic way, a scene lived through in the trenches but forgotten; in this scene he took a very active part in repelling an attempt of the enemy to rush the trench; he worked a machine-gun, shouting in the utmost excitement to his comrades. As the excitement subsided the dramatic actions gave place to mere spasmodic movements and contortions, which in turn would subside and leave him sleeping quietly.

In the more usual "hysterical fit," only the latter part of such a complete fit as that of the last one is enacted. The patient falls suddenly, seems to lose all consciousness of his surroundings, writhes on the floor with movements which may, or may not, express or suggest some definite form of bodily and mental activity, and after a time sleeps, or suddenly or gradually "comes to himself" with no recollection of what he has been doing or thinking.

In such cases among soldiers the leading rôle was played by fear. In many such cases a sudden loud sound of any sort sufficed to occasion such a fit; and in many of them it was easy to show, by hypnotic exploration, that, even though the movements might be very impressive, the patient was reliving in recollection a scene of the battle-field the memory of which was dissociated. And it was generally easy also, in such cases, to bring the "fits" to an end by breaking down the dissociation, that is, by insuring, through suggestion during the return to the waking state, that the patient should continue to recollect the hitherto forgotten incident.[10]

It was said on an earlier page that a purely dissociative disability often, or generally, produces remarkably little disturbance of the equanimity of the patient; in fact, in many such cases, the patient seems to find a secret satisfaction in the possession of his disability, and to be otherwise in good health, cheerful, and active. Perhaps this lack of concern over the disability should be ascribed in part to ignorance of the automatisms displayed.

In these cases the formula for the neurological interpretation suggested on page 229 [of *An Outline of Abnormal Psychology*] seems entirely adequate. We have to conceive the fear-disposition at the base of the brain (in the Thalamus) and the system of dispositions (in the cortex) concerned in the memory of the fearful event as reciprocally connected by ascending and descending paths; and the cortical system as isolated from all other parts by a dissociative barrier; the two then form a reciprocating couple. The cortical system is incapable of being directly excited through association-paths of the cortex; but any impression that excites fear may bring it into action by way of the ascending path from the fear-centre; and it then plays down upon the fear-centre, increasing its excitement. And, because the cortical system is isolated, the fearful scene of the past is lived through again as though actually present; it is lived, not as the normal man might remember it, with clear consciousness that it is an incident of the past set against the background of present safety, but, as in a dream in which we accept as real and present all that we imagine and recollect.[11]

The vividness, the strong emotional tone, and the sense of actual presence of all that recurs to consciousness in such fits are clearly manifested when such patients relive and recount in hypnosis such forgotten scenes. They may throw themselves about with vivid gestures and violent symptoms of the appropriate emotions. This is the so-called *Abreaction*, some discussion of the alleged therapeutic value of which the reader may find in Chapter XXIX [*An Outline of Abnormal Psychology*].

The recital of such forgotten scenes in hypnosis presents another point of interest; namely, the duality of attitude of the patient; he commonly continues to be in *rapport* with the physician, replying to his questions and responding more or less to his suggestions, even while he visualises the scene as one in which he is taking part, rather than as a mere memory. He lives two parts at once; his rôle as spectator of and actor in the recollected scene, and his rôle as patient responding to the physician.

In the cases of the pure neurasthenic type there are no dissociative disabilities, no complete amnesia, no paralysis or anæsthesia, no fugues, fits, or somnambulisms, but merely the symptoms of continuing conflict.

But the two kinds of disorder are not incapable of being combined in the same patient, as has been indicated in Chapter XII. It seems worth while to discuss a few cases in which this combination was strikingly presented. They will serve to illustrate further the complicated relations between repression and dissociation.

NOTES

[1] Let him who finds this prejudice working strongly in him ask himself on what foundations it rests, or how he can justify it.

[2] Cf. Chapter XXXI [*An Outline of Abnormal Psychology*].

[3] Prof. G. M. Stratton has recently described a striking instance of such duality of the conscious stream, in his article in "Problems of Personality," N. Y., 1925. The subject, an aviator, describes at length his experience during an accident in the air. I cite a few lines: "It was at this time that a dual personality came into play. I had a rapid survey of my life, not as though I were looking at scenes of my past, but as though I were doing and living them again. Yet I was conscious at the same time of having to manage my ship. For as I started down in the tailspin I realised that I had a certain amount of time, and I went carefully over the different controls, etc."

[4] Of course, if the reader is a behaviourist and not interested in "consciousness," he will not be interested in this problem. But then he had better keep away from the field of abnormal psychology, and confine his attention to the conditioned reflexes of animals and infants.

[5] It is a curious fact, the explanation of which is by no means clear, that a group of three or four persons may thus succeed in producing automatic writing, and that the omission of any one member of the group may put a stop to the process.

[6] The word is sometimes used in a wider sense to include wanderings of a seemingly aimless kind for which the subject (generally a psychopath) can assign no adequate reason or motive, but of which nevertheless he can give some description.

[7] Similar cases were common enough during the war; and it is highly probable that a certain number were punished with the extreme penalty.

[8] "The Major Symptoms of Hysteria."

[9] It should be added that this was only one, though the most prolonged, of several similar fugues achieved by this subject.

[10] Cf. Chapter XXIX, section on *Abreaction* [*An Outline of Abnormal Psychology*].

[11] Compare here the statement by Dr. Stratton's subject, cf. note 3.

3. *Hallucination**

Hallucination [is] a psychological term which has been the subject of much controversy, and to which, although there is now fair agreement as to its denotation, it is still impossible to give a precise and entirely satisfactory definition. Hallucinations constitute one of the two great classes of all false sense-perceptions, the other class consisting of the "illusions," and the difficulty of definition is clearly to mark the boundary between the two classes. *Illusion* may be defined as the misinterpretation of sense-impression, while *hallucination*, in its typical instances, is the experiencing of a sensory presentation, *i.e.* a presentation having the sensory vividness that distinguishes perceptions from representative imagery, at a time when no stimulus is acting on the corresponding sense-organ. There is, however, good reason to think that in many cases, possibly in all cases, some stimulation of the sense-organ, coming either from without or from within the body, plays a part in the genesis of the hallucination. This being so, we must be content to leave the boundary between illusions and hallucinations ill-defined, and to regard as illusions *those false perceptions in which impressions made on the sense-organ play a leading part in determining the character of the percept,* and as hallucinations *those in which any such impression is lacking, or plays but a subsidiary part and bears no obvious relation to the character of the false percept.*

As in the case of illusion, hallucination may or may not involve delusion, or belief in the reality of the object falsely perceived. Among the sane the hallucinatory object is frequently recognized at once as unreal or at least

* Article by William McDougall for the *Encyclopædia Britannica*, 11th ed. (1911), Vol. 12, pp. 858-863.

as but quasi-real; and it is only the insane, or persons in abnormal states, such as hypnosis, who, when an hallucination persists or recurs, fail to recognize that it corresponds to no physical impression from, or object in, the outer world. Hallucinations of all the senses occur, but the most commonly reported are the auditory and the visual, while those of the other senses seem to be comparatively rare. This apparent difference of frequency is no doubt largely due to the more striking character of visual and auditory hallucinations, and to the relative difficulty of ascertaining, in the case of perceptions of the lower senses, *e.g.* of taste and smell, that no impression adequate to the genesis of the percept has been made upon the sense-organ; but, in so far as it is real, it is probably due in part to the more constant use of the higher senses and the greater strain consequently thrown upon them, in part also to their more intimate connexion with the life of ideas.

The hallucinatory perception may involve two or more senses, *e.g.*, the subject may seem to see a human being, to hear his voice and to feel the touch of his hand. This is rarely the case in spontaneous hallucination, but in hypnotic hallucination the subject is apt to develop the object suggested to him, as present to one of his senses, and to perceive it also through other senses.

Among visual hallucinations the human figure, and among auditory hallucinations human voices, are the objects most commonly perceived. The figure seen always appears localized more or less definitely in the outer world. In many cases it appears related to the objects truly seen in just the same way as a real object; *e.g.* it is no longer seen if the eyes are closed or turned away, it does not move with the movements of the eyes, and it may hide objects lying behind it, or be hidden by objects coming between the place that it appears to occupy and the eye of the percipient. Visual hallucinations are most often experienced when the eyes are open and the surrounding space is well or even brightly illuminated. Less frequently the visual hallucination takes the form of a self-luminous figure in a dark place or appears in a luminous globe or mist which shuts out from view the real objects of the part of the field of view in which it appears.

Auditory hallucinations, especially voices, seem to fall into two distinct classes—(1) those which are heard as coming from without, and are more or less definitely localized in outer space, (2) those which seem to be within the head or, in some cases, within the chest, and to have less definite auditory quality. It seems probable that the latter are hallucinations involving principally kinaesthetic sensations, sensations of movement of the organs of speech.

Hallucinations occur under a great variety of bodily and mental conditions, which may conveniently be classified as follows.

I. Conditions which imply normal waking consciousness and no distinct departure from bodily and mental sanity.

a. It would seem that a considerable number of perfectly healthy persons occasionally experience, while in a fully waking state, hallucinations for which no cause can be assigned. The census of hallucinations conducted by the Society for Psychical Research showed that about 10% of all sane persons can remember having experienced at least one hallucination while they believed themselves to be fully awake and in normal health. These sporadic hallucinations of waking healthy persons are far more frequently visual than auditory, and they usually take the form of some familiar person in ordinary attire. The figure in many cases is seen, on turning the gaze in some new direction, fully developed and lifelike, and its hallucinatory character may be revealed only by its noiseless movements, or by its fading away *in situ.* A special interest attaches to hallucinations of this type, owing to the occasional coincidence of the death of the person with his hallucinatory appearance. The question raised by these coincidences will be discussed in a separate paragraph below.

b. A few persons, otherwise normal in mind and body, seem to experience repeatedly some particular kind of hallucination. The voice (δαιμόνιον) so frequently heard by Socrates, warning or advising him, is the most celebrated example of this type.

II. Conditions more or less unusual or abnormal but not implying distinct departure from health.

a. A kind of hallucination to which perhaps every normal person is liable is that known technically as "recurrent sensation." This kind is experienced only when some sense-organ has been continuously or repeatedly subjected to some one kind of impression or stimulation for a considerable period; *e.g.* the microscopist, after examining for some hours one particular kind of object or structure, may suddenly perceive the object faithfully reproduced in form and colour, and lying, as it were, upon any surface to which his gaze is directed. Perhaps the commonest experience of this type is the recurrence of the sensations of movement at intervals in the period following a sea voyage or long railway journey.

b. A considerable proportion of healthy sane persons can induce hallucinations of vision by gazing fixedly at a polished surface or into some dark translucent mass; or of hearing, by applying a large shell or similar object to the ear. These methods of inducing hallucinations, especially the former, have long been practised in many countries as modes of divination, various objects being used, *e.g.* a drop of ink in the palm of the hand, or a polished finger-nail. The object now most commonly used is a polished sphere of clear glass or crystal (see CRYSTAL-GAZING). Hence such hallucinations go by the name of *crystal visions*. The crystal vision often appears as a picture of some distant or unknown scene lying, as it were, in the crystal; and in the picture figures may come and go, and move to and fro, in a perfectly natural manner. In other cases, written or printed words or sentences appear. The percipient, seer or scryer, commonly seems to be in a fully waking state as he observes the objects thus presented. He is usually able to describe and discuss the appearances, successively discriminating details by attentive observation, just as when observing an objective scene; and he usually has no power of controlling them, and no sense of having produced them by his own activity. In some cases these visions have brought back to the mind of the scryer facts or incidents which he could not voluntarily recollect. In other cases they are asserted by credible witnesses to have given to the scryer information, about events distant in time or place, that had not come to his knowledge by normal means. These cases have been claimed as evidence of telepathic communication or even of clairvoyance. But at present the number of well-attested cases of this sort is too small to justify acceptance of this conclusion by those who have only secondhand knowledge of them.

c. Prolonged deprivation of food predisposes to hallucinations, and it would seem that, under this condition, a large proportion of otherwise healthy persons become liable to them, especially to auditory hallucinations.

d. Certain drugs, notably opium, Indian hemp, and mescal predispose to hallucinations, each tending to produce a peculiar type. Thus Indian hemp and mescal, especially the latter, produce in many cases visual hallucinations in the form of a brilliant play of colours, sometimes a mere succession of patches of brilliant colour, sometimes in architectural or other definite spatial arrangement.

e. The states of transition from sleep to waking, and from waking to sleep, seem to be peculiarly favourable to the appearance of hallucinations. The recurrent sensations mentioned above are especially prone to appear at such times, and a considerable proportion of the sporadic hallucinations of persons in good health are reported to have been experienced under these conditions. The name "hypnagogic" hallucinations, first applied by Alfred Maury, is commonly given to those experienced in these transition states.

f. The presentations, predominantly visual, that constitute the principal content of most dreams, are generally described as hallucinatory, but the propriety of so classing them is very questionable. The present writer is confident that his own dream-presentations lack the sensory vividness which is the essential mark of the percept, whether normal or hallucinatory, and which is the principal, though not the only, character in which it differs from the representation or memory-image. It is true that the dream-presentation, like the percept, differs from the representative imagery of waking life in that it is relatively independent of volition; but that seems to be merely because the will is in abeyance or very ineffective during sleep. The wide currency of the doctrine that classes dream-images with hallucinations seems to be due to this independence of volitional control, and to the fact that during sleep the representative imagery appears without that rich setting of undiscriminated or marginal sensation which always accompanies waking imagery, and which by contrast accentuates for introspective reflection the lack of sensory vividness of such imagery.

g. Many of the subjects who pass into the deeper stages of hypnosis (see HYPNOTISM) show themselves, while in that condition, extremely liable to hallucination, perceiving whatever object is suggested to them as present, and failing to perceive any object of which it is asserted by the operator that it is no longer present. The reality of these positive and negative hallucinations of the hypnotized subject has been recently questioned, it being maintained that the subject merely gives verbal assent to the suggestions of the operator. But that the hypnotized subject does really experience hallucinations seems to be proved by the cases in which it is possible to make the hallucination, positive or negative, persist for some time after the termination of hypnosis, and by the fact that in some of these cases the subject, who in the post-hypnotic state seems in every other respect normal and wide awake, may find it difficult to distinguish between the hallucinatory and real objects. Further proof is afforded by experiments such as those by which Alfred Binet showed that a visual hallucination may behave for its percipient in many respects like a real object, *e.g.* that it may appear reflected in a mirror, displaced by a prism and coloured when a coloured glass is placed before the patient's eyes. It was by means of experiments of this kind that Binet showed that hypnotic hallucinations may approximate to the type of the illusion, *i.e.* that some real object affecting the sense-organ (in the case of a visual hallucination some detail of the surface upon which it is projected) may provide a nucleus of peripherally excited sensation around which the false percept is built up. An object playing a part of this sort in the genesis of an hallucination is known as a *"point de repère."* It has been maintained that all hallucinations involve some such *point de repère* or objective nucleus; but there are good reasons for rejecting this view.

h. In states of ecstasy, or intense emotional concentration of attention upon some one ideal object, the object contemplated seems at times to take on sensory vividness, and so to acquire the character of an hallucination. In these cases the state of mind of the subject is probably similar in many respects to that of the deeply hypnotized subject, and these two classes of hallucination may be regarded as very closely allied.

III. Hallucinations which occur as symptoms of both bodily and mental diseases.

a. Dr H. Head has the credit of having shown for the first time, in the year 1901, that many patients, suffering from more or less painful visceral diseases, disorders of heart, lungs, abdominal viscera, &c., are liable to experience hallucinations of a peculiar kind. These "visceral" hallucinations, which are constantly accompanied by headache of the reflected visceral type, are most commonly visual, more rarely auditory. In all Dr Head's cases the visual hallucination took the form of a shrouded human figure, colourless and vague, often incomplete, generally seen by the patient standing by his bed when he wakes in a dimly lit room. The auditory "visceral" hallucination was in no instance vocal, but took such forms as sounds of tapping, scratching or rumbling, and were heard only in the absence of objective noises. In a few cases the "visceral" hallucination was bisensory, *i.e.* both auditory and visual.

In all these respects the "visceral" hallucination differs markedly from the commoner types of the sporadic hallucination of healthy persons.

b. Hallucinations are constant symptoms of certain general disorders in which the nervous system is involved, notably of the *delirium tremens,* which results from chronic alcohol poisoning, and of the delirium of the acute specific fevers. The hallucinations of these states are generally of a distressing or even terrifying character. Especially is this the rule with those of *delirium tremens,* and in the hallucinations of this disease certain kinds of objects, *e.g.* rats and snakes, occur with curious frequency.

c. Hallucinations occasionally occur as symptoms of certain nervous diseases that are not usually classed with the insanities, notably in cases of epilepsy and severe forms of hysteria. In the former disorder, the sensory aura that so often precedes the epileptic convulsion may take the form of an hallucinatory object, which in some cases is very constant in character. Unilateral hallucinations, an especially interesting class, occur in severe cases of hysteria, and are usually accompanied by hemi-anaesthesia of the body on the side on which the hallucinatory object is perceived.

d. Hallucinations occur in a large, but not accurately definable, proportion of all cases of mental disease proper. Two classes are recognized: (1) those that are intimately connected with the dominant emotional state or with some dominant delusion; (2) those that occur sporadically and have no such obvious relation to the other symptoms of disease. Hallucinations of the former class tend to accentuate, and in turn to be confirmed by, the congruent emotional or delusional state; but whether these are to be regarded as primary symptoms and as the cause of the hallucinations, or *vice versa,* it is generally impossible to say. Patients who suffer delusions of persecution are very apt to develop later in the course of their disease hallucinations of the voices of their persecutors; while in other cases hallucinatory voices, which are at first recognized as such, come to be regarded as real and in these cases seem to be factors of primary importance in the genesis of further delusions. Hallucinations occur in almost every variety of mental disease, but are commonest in the forms characterized by a cloudy dream-like condition of consciousness, and in extreme cases of this sort the patient (as in the delirium of chronic alcohol-poisoning) seems to move waking through a world consisting largely of the images of his own creation, set upon a background of real objects.

In some cases hallucinations are frequently experienced for long periods in the absence of any other symptom of mental disorder, but these no doubt usually imply some morbid condition of the brain.

Physiology of Hallucination. There has been much discussion as to the nature of the neural process in hallucination. It is generally and rightly assumed that the hallucinatory perception of any object has for its immediate neural correlate a state of excitement which, as regards its characters and its distribution in the elements of the brain, is entirely similar to the neural correlate of the normal perception of the same object. The hallucination is a perception, though a false perception. In the perception of an object and in the representation of it, introspective analysis discovers a number of presentative elements. In the case of the representation these elements are memory images only (except perhaps in so far as actual kinaesthetic sensations enter into its composition); whereas, in the case of the percept, some of these elements are sensations, sensations which differ from images in having the attribute of sensory vividness; and the sensory vividness of these elements lends to the whole complex the sensory vividness or reality, the possession of which character by the percept constitutes its principal difference from the representation. Normally, sensory vividness attaches only to those presentative elements which are excited through stimulations of the sense-organs. The normal percept, then, owes its character of sensory reality to the fact that a certain number of its presentative elements are sensations peripherally excited by impressions made upon a sense-organ. The problem is, then, to account for the fact that the hallucination contains presentative elements that have sensory vividness, that are sensations, although they are not excited by impressions from the external world falling upon a sense-organ. Most of the discussions of this subject suffer from the neglect of this preliminary definition of the problem. Many authors, notably W. Wundt and his disciples, have been content to assume that the sensation differs from the memory-image only in having a higher degree of intensity; from which they infer that its neural correlate in the brain cortex also differs from that of the image only in having a higher degree of intensity. For them an hallucination is therefore merely a representation whose neural correlate involves an intensity of excitement of certain brain-elements such as is normally produced only by peripheral stimulation of sensory nerves in the sense-organs. But this view, so attractively simple, ignores an insuperable objection. Sensory vividness is not to be identified with superior intensity; for while the least intense sensation has it, the memory image of the most intense sensation lacks it completely. And, since intensity of sensation is a function of the intensity of the underlying neural excitement, we may not assume that sensory vividness is also the expression in consciousness of that intensity of excitement. If Wundt's view were true a progressive diminution of the intensity of a sensory stimulus should bring the sensation to a point in the scale of diminishing intensity at which it ceases to be sensation, ceases to have sensory vividness and becomes an image merely. But this is not the case; with diminishing intensity of stimulation, the sensation declines to a minimal intensity and then disappears from consciousness. This objection applies not only to Wundt's view of hallucinations, but also to H. Taine's explanation of them by the aid of his doctrine of "reductives," for this too identifies sensory vividness with intensity. (H. Taine, *De l'intelligence*, tome i. p. 108.)

Another widely current explanation is based on the view that the representation and the percept have their anatomical bases in different element-groups or "centres" of the brain, the "centre" of the representation being assigned to a higher level of the brain than that of the percept (the latter being sometimes assigned to the basal ganglia of the brain, the former to the cortex). It is then assumed that while the lower perceptual centre is normally excited only through the sense-organ, it may occasionally be excited by impulses playing down upon it from the corresponding centre of representation, when hallucination results.

This view also is far from satisfactory, because the great additions recently made to our knowledge of the brain tend very strongly to show that both sensations and memory-images have their anatomical bases in the same sensory areas of the cerebral cortex; and many considerations converge to show that their anatomical bases must be, in part at least, identical.

The views based on the assumptions of complete identity, and of complete separateness, of the anatomical bases of the percept and of the representation are then alike untenable; and the alternative—that their anatomical bases are in part identical, in part different, which is indicated by this conclusion —renders possible a far more satisfactory doctrine. We have good reason to believe that the neural correlate of sensation is the transmission of the nervous impulse through a sensori-motor arc of the cortex, made up of a chain of neurones; and the view suggests itself that the neural correlate of the corresponding memory-image is the transmission of the impulse through a part only of this chain of cortical elements, either the efferent motor part of this chain or the afferent sensory part of it. Professor W. James's theory of hallucinations is based on the latter assumption. He suggests that the sensory vividness of sensation and of the percept is due to the discharge of the excitement of the chain of elements in the forward or motor direction; and that, in the case of the image and of the representation, the discharge takes place, not in this direction through the efferent channel of the centre, but laterally into other centres of the cortex. Hallucination may then be conceived as caused by obstruction, or abnormally increased resistance, of the paths connecting such a cortical centre with others, so that, when it becomes excited in any way, the tension or potential of its charge rises, until discharge takes place in the motor direction through the efferent limbs of the sensori-motor arcs which constitute the centre.

It is a serious objection to this view that, as James himself, in common with most modern authors, maintains, every idea has its motor tendency which commonly, perhaps always, finds expression in some change of tension of muscles, and in many cases issues in actual movements. Now if we accept James's theory of hallucination, we should expect to find that whenever a representation issues in bodily action it should assume the sensory vividness of an hallucination; and this, of course, is not the case.

The alternative form of the view that assumes partial identity of the anatomical bases of the percept and the representation of an object, would regard the neural correlate of the sensation as the transmission of the nervous impulse throughout the length of the sensori-motor arc of the cortex, from sensory inlet to motor outlet; and that of the image as its transmission through the efferent part of this arc only; that is to say, in the case of the image, it would regard the excitement of the arc as being initiated at some point between its afferent inlet and its motor outlet, and as spreading, in accordance with the law of forward conduction, towards the motor outlet only, so that only the part of the arc distal or efferent to this point becomes excited.

This view of the neural basis of sensory vividness, which correlates the difference between the sensation and the image with the only known difference between their physiological conditions, namely the peripheral initiation of the one and the central initiation of the other, enables us to formulate a satisfactory theory of the physiology of hallucinations.

The anatomical basis of the perception and of the representation of any object is a functional system of nervous elements, comprising a number of sensori-motor arcs, whose excitement by impulses ascending to them by the

sensory paths from the sense-organs determines sensations, and whose excitement in their efferent parts only determines the corresponding images.
In the case of perception, some of these arcs are excited by impulses ascending from the sense-organs, others only by the spread of the excitement
through the system from these peripherally excited arcs; while, in the case
of the representation, all alike are excited by impulses that reach the system
from other parts of the cortex and spread throughout its efferent parts only
to its motor outlets.

If then impulses enter this system by any of the afferent limbs of its sensori-motor arcs, the presentation that accompanies its excitement will have
sensory vividness and will be a true perception, an illusion, or an hallucination, according as these impulses have followed the normal course from the
sense-organ, or have been diverted, to a lesser or greater degree, from their
normal paths. If any such neural system becomes abnormally excitable, or
becomes excited in any way with abnormal intensity, it is thereby rendered
a path of exceptionally low-resistance capable of diverting to itself, from
their normal path, any streams of impulses ascending from the sense-organ;
which ascending impulses, entering the system by its afferent inlets, excite
sensations that impart to the presentation the character of sensory vividness;
the presentation thus acquires the character of a percept in spite of the absence of the appropriate impression on the sense-organ, and we call it an
hallucination.

This view renders intelligible the *modus operandi* of many of the predisposing causes of hallucination; *e.g.* the pre-occupation with certain repre-
sentations of the ecstatic, or of the sufferer from delusions of persecution; the
intense expectation of a particular sense impression, the generally increased
excitability of the cortex in states of delirium; in all these conditions the
abnormally intense excitement of the cortical systems may be supposed to
give them an undue directive and attractive influence upon the streams of impulses ascending from the sense-organs, so that sensory impulses may be
diverted from their normal paths. Again, it renders intelligible the part played
by chronic irritation of a sense-organ, as when chronic irritation of the internal ear leads on to hallucinations of hearing; perhaps also the chronic
irritation of sensory nerves that must accompany the states of visceral disease, shown by Head to be so frequently accompanied by a liability to
hallucinations; for any such chronic irritation supplies a stream of disor-
derly impulses rising constantly from the sense-organ, for the reception of
which the brain has no appropriate system, and which, therefore, readily
enters any organized cortical system that at any moment constitutes a path
of low-resistance. A similar explanation applies to the influence of fixed gazing upon a crystal, or the placing of a shell over the ear, in inducing visual

and auditory hallucinations. The "recurrent sensations" experienced after prolonged occupation with some one kind of sensory object may be regarded as due to an abnormal excitability of the cortical system concerned, resulting from its unduly prolonged exercise. The hypothesis renders intelligible also the liability to hallucination of persons in the hysterical and hypnotic states, in whose brains the cortical neural systems are in a state of partial dissociation, which renders possible an unduly intense and prolonged excitement of some one system at the expense of all other systems (cf. HYPNOTISM).

Coincidental Hallucinations. It would seem that, in well-nigh all countries and in all ages, apparitions of persons known to be in distant places have been occasionally observed. Such appearances have usually been regarded as due to the presence, before the bodily eye of the seer, of the ghost, wraith, double or soul of the person who thus appears; and, since the soul has been very commonly supposed to leave the body, permanently at death and temporarily during sleep, trance or any period of unconsciousness, however induced, it was natural to regard such an appearance as evidence that the person whose wraith was thus seen was in some such condition. Such apparitions have probably played a part, second only to that of dreams, in generating the almost universal belief in the separability of soul and body.

In many parts of the world traditional belief has connected such apparitions more especially with the death of the person so appearing, the apparition being regarded as an indication that the person so appearing has recently died, is dying or is about to die. Since death is so much less common an event than sleep, trance, or other form of temporary unconsciousness, the wide extension of this belief suggests that such apparitions may coincide in time with death, with disproportionate frequency. The belief in the significance of such apparitions still survives in civilized communities, and stories of apparitions coinciding with the death of the person appearing are occasionally reported in the newspapers, or related as having recently occurred. The Society for Psychical Research has sought to find grounds for an answer to the question "Is there any sufficient justification for the belief in a causal relation between the apparition of a person at a place distant from his body and his death or other exceptional and momentous event in his experience?" The problem was attacked in a thoroughly scientific spirit, an extensive inquiry was made, and the results were presented and fully discussed in two large volumes, *Phantasms of the Living*, published in the year 1886, bearing on the title-page the names of Edmund Gurney, F. W. H. Myers and F. Podmore. Of the three collaborators Gurney took the largest share in the planning of the work, in the collection of evidence, and in the elaboration and discussion of it.

Gurney set out with the presumption that apparitions, whether coincidental or not, are hallucinations in the sense defined above; that *they are false per-ceptions* and are not excited by any object or process of the external world acting upon the sense-organs of the percipient in normal fashion; that they do not imply the presence, in the place apparently occupied by them, of any wraith or any form of existence emanating from, or specially connected with, the person whose phantasm appears. This initial assumption was abundantly justified by an examination of a large number of cases for it, which showed that, in all important respects, most of these apparitions of persons at a dis-tance, whether coincidental or not, were similar to other forms of hallu-cination.

The acceptance of this conclusion does not, however, imply a negative answer to the question formulated above. The Society for Psychical Research had accumulated an impressive and, to almost all those who had first-hand acquaintance with it, a convincing mass of experimental evidence of the reality of telepathy (*q.v.*), the influence of mind on mind otherwise than through the recognized channels of sense. The successful experiments had for the most part been made between persons in close proximity, in the same room or in adjoining rooms; but they seemed to show that the state of con-sciousness of one person may induce directly (*i.e.* without the mediation of the organs of expression and sense-perception) a similar state of conscious-ness in another person, especially if the former, usually called the "agent," strongly desired or "willed" that this effect should be produced on the other person, the "percipient."

The question formulated above thus resolved itself for Gurney into the more definite form, "Can we find any good reason for believing that coin-cidental hallucinations are sometimes veridical, that the state of mind of a person at some great crisis of his experience may telepathically induce in the mind of some distant relative or friend an hallucinatory perception of him-self?" It was at once obvious that, if coincidental apparitions can be proved to occur, this question can only be answered by a statistical inquiry; for each such coincidental hallucination, considered alone, may always be re-garded as most educated persons of the present time have regarded them, namely, as merely accidental coincidences. That the coincidences are not merely accidental can only be proved by showing that they occur more fre-quently than the doctrine of chances would justify us in expecting. Now, the death of any person is a unique event, and the probability of its occurrence upon any particular day may be very simply calculated from the mortality statistics, if we assume that nothing is known of the individual's vitality. On the other hand, hallucinatory perceptions of persons, occurring to sane and healthy individuals in the fully waking state, are comparatively rare occur-rences, whose frequency we may hope to determine by a statistical inquiry.

If, then, we can obtain figures expressing the frequency of such hallucinations, we can deduce, by the help of the laws of chance, the proportion of such hallucinations that may be expected to coincide with (or, for the purposes of the inquiry, to fall within twelve hours of) the death of the person whose apparition appears, if no causal relation obtains between the coinciding events. If, then, it appears that the proportion of such coincidental hallucinations is greater than the laws of probability will account for, a certain presumption of a causal relation between the coinciding events is thereby established; and the greater the excess of such coincidences, the stronger does this presumption become. Gurney attempted a census of hallucinations in order to obtain data for this statistical treatment, and the results of it, embodied in *Phantasms of the Living*, were considered by the authors of that work to justify the belief that some coincidental hallucinations are veridical. In the year 1889 the Society for Psychical Research appointed a committee, under the chairmanship of the late Henry Sidgwick, to make a second census of hallucinations on a more extensive and systematic plan than the first, in order that the important conclusion reached by the authors of *Phantasms of the Living* might be put to the severer test rendered possible by a larger and more carefully collected mass of data. Seventeen thousand adults returned answers to the question, "Have you ever, when believing yourself to be completely awake, had a vivid impression of seeing or being touched by a living being or inanimate object, or of hearing a voice; which impression, so far as you could discover, was not due to any external physical cause?" Rather more than two thousand persons answered affirmatively, and to each of these were addressed careful inquiries concerning their hallucinatory experiences. In this way it was found that of the total number, 381 apparitions of persons living at the moment (or not more than twelve hours dead) had been recognized by the percipients, and that, of these, 80 were alleged to have been experienced within twelve hours of the death of the person whose apparition had appeared. A careful review of all the facts, conditions and probabilities, led the committee to estimate that the former number should be enlarged to 1300 in order to make ample allowance for forgetfulness and for all other causes that might have tended to prevent the registration of apparitions of this class. On the other hand, a severe criticism of the alleged death-coincidences led them to reduce the number, admitted by them for the purposes of their calculation, to 30. The making of these adjustments gives us about 1 in 43 as the proportion of coincidental death-apparitions to the total number of recognized apparitions among the 17,000 persons reached by the census. Now the death-rate being just over 19 per thousand, the probability that any person taken at random will die on a given day is about 1 in 19,000; or, more strictly speaking, the average probability that any person will die within any given period of twenty-four hours duration is about 1 in 19,000. Hence the probability that any other particular event, having no causal relation to his death, but occurring during his lifetime (or not later than twelve hours after his death) will fall within the same twenty-four hours as his death is 1 in 19,000; *i.e.* if an apparition of any individual is seen and recognized by any other person, the probability of its being experienced within twelve hours of that individual's death is 1 in 19,000, if no causal relation obtains between the two events. Therefore, of all recognized apparitions of living persons, 1 only in 19,000 may be expected to be a death-coincidence of this sort. But the census shows that of 1300 recognized apparitions of living persons 30 are death-coincidences and that is equivalent to 440 in 19,000. Hence, of recognized hallucinations, those coinciding with death are 440 times more numerous than we should expect, if no causal relation obtained; therefore, if neither the data nor the reasoning can be destructively criticized, we are compelled to believe that some causal relation obtains; and, since good evidence of telepathic communication has been experimentally obtained, the least improbable explanation of these death-apparitions is that the dying person exerts upon his distant friend some telepathic influence which generates an hallucinatory perception of himself.

These death-coincidences constitute the main feature of the argument in favour of telepathic communication between distant persons, but the census of hallucinations afforded other data from which a variety of arguments, tending to support this conclusion, were drawn by the committee; of these the most important are the cases in which the hallucinatory percept embodied details that were connected with the person perceived and which could not have become known to the percipient by any normal means. The committee could not find in the results of the census any evidence sufficient to justify a belief that hallucinations may be due to telepathic influence exerted by personalities surviving the death of the body.

The critical handling of the cases by the committee seems to be above reproach. Those who do not accept their conclusion based on the death-coincidences must direct their criticism to the question of the reliability of the reports of these cases. It is to be noted that, although only those cases are reckoned in which the percipient had no cause to expect the death of the person whose apparition he experienced, and although, in nearly all the accepted cases, some record or communication of the hallucination was made before hearing of the death, yet in very few cases was any contemporary written record of the event forthcoming for the inspection of the committee.

4. *Hallucinations**

Hallucination is "seeing things that are not there"; or, in more technical terms, to hallucinate is to think of remote objects with sensory vividness.

Hallucination may or may not be accompanied by delusion, by belief in the physical reality and presence of the object hallucinated. The more vivid and persistent the hallucination, the more apt is the subject to believe in the reality and presence of the object. Probably most normal persons have occasionally hallucinated; but persistent hallucination is one of the most common symptoms of mental disorder.

We cannot draw any sharp line between hallucination and illusion, or false interpretation of sense-impressions, because we can never be sure that some sense-impression does not play a part in the genesis of hallucination; but in practice we speak of illusion when the rôle of the sense-impressions is obvious, of hallucination when it is doubtful or of secondary importance. For example, obscure sounds due to internal stimulation of the auditory nerve seem to conduce to auditory hallucination; but we do not on that account describe hallucination of voices, in a case complicated by tinnitus, as illusion.

In some healthy persons hallucinations may readily be induced. In most good hypnotic subjects, verbal suggestion may induce hallucinations of any kind during hypnosis and, in some subjects, in the post-hypnotic state. In others, visual hallucinations may be induced by "crystal-gazing" or by putting a shell over the ear. In crystal-gazing, the successful subject generally seems to pass into a hypnoid condition; and it is, in the main, persons who are

* Originally published as Chap. XXI in William McDougall's *An Outline of Abnormal Psychology.* London: Methuen & Co., Ltd., 1926.

readily hypnotised, and who can by a little practice acquire the art of auto-matic writing, who readily see "crystal-visions." For the induction of crystal-visions it is usual to ask the subject to gaze intently into a highly refracting sphere of glass or quartz; but any polished surface may serve almost equally well. The appearance of visions in the crystal is generally preceded by a clouding of it, as though it were filled with white mist. After a few moments the mist clears and the subject sees pictures which, in some cases, are of the most various kinds, in others, are of some one scene repeated upon suc-cessive occasions. In the more usual cases, the picture in the crystal resembles a small-scale coloured cinematographic show; figures come and go and move and dissolve, on various backgrounds, the whole being naturally coloured. Sometimes the scenes are fantastic; in other cases they are so realistic that the subject is inclined to feel that he is peeping through some strange telescope into some distant scene of real life.[1]

Dr. Morton Prince has done pioneer work in showing that crystal-visions, together with automatic writing, may be of great assistance in exploring subconscious mental activities. On the basis of observations made with the assistance of these methods, he has put forward a very interesting theory of the genesis of hallucinations.

Before considering this theory, let us notice that hallucinating, being only a special form of imagining, shows the same fundamental varieties; there are reproductive, constructive, and creative hallucinations.

Reproductive hallucination is perhaps the most frequent variety, and lends itself most readily to a simple theoretical interpretation. Sometimes a person in good health who has for any reason repeatedly perceived some object or impression, or very similar objects, may seem to perceive the same object again when it is no longer present. One of the simplest and commonest of such hallucinations is the perception of motion of the earth after a journey by ship or railway-train. Very similar is the following. After occupying myself intently for some thirteen hours with stained sections of muscle-tissue under the microscope, I was surprised to find, in the evening as I sat read-ing, that whenever I turned my eyes from my book, I saw projected upon the walls or furniture the coloured patterns with which I had been busy. Oft-repeated sounds are not infrequently repeated in similar hallucinatory fashion; and such auditory hallucinations are more difficult to distinguish from actual perceptions. Such hallucinations have been called, somewhat unsuitably, "recurrent sensations."

During the War, a common form of hallucination was the hearing of shells screaming overhead long after the soldier was far removed from the fighting line. In some cases the sights and sounds of the battle-field con-tinued to recur and to fill the consciousness of the soldier for days after his removal from the field. One such case, admitted to my wards some days after removal from the front, was wholly concerned with shells exploding overhead. One could secure his attention, but the next moment he would point to the ceiling with a terrified glance and dodge under the bedclothes; and he would repeat this again and again so long as he was not covered over completely. Closely allied was the hallucination (examples of which are mentioned in other chapters) of the cry of agony uttered by an enemy at the moment of receiving a bayonet thrust. Very similar was the hallucination of Case 36, who saw repeatedly the corpse beside his bed. In these last cases we come nearer to the type of hallucination common in delusional insanity, where the hallucination expresses a repressed affect, commonly of the nature of self-reproach or remorse.

In many simple instances of reproductive hallucination, it is not possible to assert that any repressed affect plays an essential rôle; still less that there was operative any dissociated system; though it is possible that there were such factors. The essential condition of such simple reproductive hallucination seems to be the very strong affect evoked by the reproduced impression, repetition of the impression conducing as a secondary factor. And I think we may add that any repression of the affective memory favours the hallucinatory reproduction.

Such reproductive hallucinations are thus closely allied to reproductive dreams, notably the battle-dreams of soldiers. And in this connection it is noteworthy that many normal persons are especially prone to hallucinate in the transition state between sleeping and waking, the so-called hypnogogic and hypnopompic states. At those times especially we are apt to misinterpret sense-impressions in illusions that stand near to hallucinations. Closely allied with these are the illusions and hallucinations of anticipation, which occur more especially when we anticipate some sense-impression with strong affect, with eager desire or strong aversion—as in the traditional seeing of a ghost in any ill-defined object of the moonlit graveyard.

PRINCE'S THEORY OF HALLUCINATION

Dr. Prince's observations have led him to formulate "a theory of visual hallucinations, namely, that in certain instances at least they were the emergence into awareness of imagery belonging to subconscious thought—the same sort of imagery that occurs in conscious thought. Auditory hallucinations, similarly, are the emergence of subconscious verbal 'images,' *i.e.*, sounds of words used in subconscious inarticulate thoughts or internal speech." That is to say, Prince finds evidence that in certain instances of hallucination there are two streams of thinking running side by side, as it

were, in the same organism; that these two streams of conscious activity
are not entirely without influence upon one another, but that some of the
imagery of the one stream may be thrust into the other stream as hallucinatory images.

The evidence in support of this view is obtained in several ways. First,
by retrospection in hypnosis. The subject experiences post-hypnotically an
hallucination suggested in hypnosis. On inducing hypnosis again the secondary subconscious personality, B (or phase of personality), which received and executed the suggestion again comes into *rapport* with the experi-
menter and asserts that, at the moment when the primary personality, A,
hallucinated, he (B) was thinking of that object. Such post-hypnotic hallucinations seem to be closely parallel to post-hypnotic forced movements. Just
as the secondary personality, B, can force A to execute movements with some
sense of impulsion, but without understanding of the goal or ground or purpose of the movements, so B can influence A in such a way that the stream
of A's thinking is interrupted by an hallucinatory image of the object of
which B is thinking.

When confronted with the evidence of such influence of the subconscious
phase upon the thinking of the primary phase of personality, we are prone
to think of the images as concrete entities, in the same way that we think
of material objects, and to think of the image formed by the secondary
personality as being thrust bodily across from the one stream of consciousness to the other. But that would be to conceive the process erroneously.
When A hallucinates the object X of which B is thinking, B does not necessarily lose the image of X; rather, both personalities think of X simultaneously. The process may be likened rather to one of reflection from one mirror
to another. When a mirror B receives an optical image and reflects it onto
mirror A, the presence of the image in A does not imply that the image of X
has left B to pass into A; it implies rather that the image X is still formed
in B. But this physical simile also is very imperfect. We can find a true
simile for the process of induction of hallucination (as indicated by Prince's
observations) only by postulating the reality of the much-disputed telepathic
communication. If I thought of a number or a playing-card, and you at the
same moment (seated in a distant place) thought of the same number or
card: and if this occurred regularly without exception through one hundred
successive experiments, we should have to believe that, somehow, my thinking of the number or card induced you to think of the same number or card
at the same moment. We could not describe the process by saying that my
thinking, my image, passed over into your head and became yours; my
thinking remains mine and yours remains yours, but we think of and image
the same object at the same moment, and there is some causal relation be-

tween my thinking and yours. Just so, in the production of hallucination of the object X post-hypnotically in the primary personality A, the thinking of X by the secondary personality B seems to induce A to hallucinate X. There is no bodily transportation of B's image of X out of the stream of B's consciousness into A's. Nor can the process be described by saying that the image of X becomes common to A and B. When you and I think at the same moment in visual terms of the full moon we saw last night, we think in similar ways of the same object; but it would not be true to say that we both have the same thought, or the same image, although that is the misleading way in which we commonly describe such coincidences. If we wish to avoid confusion and error in psychology, we must use language with some precision; and in such cases we must say that two persons are thinking of the same thing in similar ways. And so with the primary and secondary personalities of the hypnotic subject; when both think of the same object, that is not one thinking but rather two simultaneous thinkings.

I insist upon this point tediously, because it is of great theoretical importance. If we allow ourselves to speak and think of images as entities that exist in their own right, that pass into and out of consciousness, and from the consciousness of one person into the consciousness of another, then we become involved in all the fallacies that have encumbered psychology for centuries in consequence of treating "ideas" as such entities, of taking literally the familiar modes of speech which describe two men as having "the same idea," or one man as getting his "ideas" out of another man's head. I insist upon this point also because Prince's language is sometimes ambiguous in respect of it, and might easily mislead the unwary reader.

Prince finds similar evidence in a number of instances of spontaneous hallucination occurring in cases of well-marked double personality. He writes: "I might analyse a large number of spontaneous hallucinations wherein you would find the same evidence for subconscious processes showing intelligent constructive imagination, reasoning, volition, and purposive effort, and expressing themselves in automatisms which either solve a disturbing problem or carry to fruition a subconscious purpose."[2] And he brings forward similar evidence in respect of some dreams, namely, evidence that the dream-images remembered by the dreamer are partial reflections of the conscious thinking of a secondary personality.

Prince finds the strongest evidence in favour of this view in a case of dual personality who readily produced automatic writing and also visual hallucinations. The plan of the experiment was to obtain automatic writing during the occurrence of the hallucinations; for, if the hallucinations are due to the influence of a secondary personality, it would seem probable that automatic writing may express the thinking of that same secondary personality. Prince succeeded in obtaining simultaneously from his subject continued automatic writing and verbal descriptions of a series of visual hallucinations. In a number of such experiments, it was found, on comparing the writing with the parallel series of hallucinations, that the latter formed, as it were, a series of pictures illustrating the story written automatically by the hand. For the primary personality who reported and described them, these pictures had as little meaning or intelligible connection with one another as have the pictures illustrating a story-book for one who turns over the leaves without reading the story. Confirmation of and a further light on this relation between the two personalities was obtained by hypnotising the subject after the conclusion of the experiment. The personality which had played the subconscious rôle, which had produced the automatic writing and induced the other personality to hallucinate scenes from the stories written, then came into *rapport* with Dr. Prince and was asked to give some retrospective account of the whole process, and, as Prince writes, "very positive introspective testimony as to the source of the imagery of the hallucinations and the relation of those images to the subconscious process was thus elicited. Its credibility must be judged according to the value assigned to the method."

For the details of these experiments I must refer the reader to Prince's article.[3]

As regards the credibility of the evidence, I will only say that, knowing as I do Dr. Prince's skill and care and large experience in such work, I see no reason to reject either the evidence or Prince's interpretation of it. It is, of course, impossible to prove conclusively that any personality other than oneself thinks consciously; but, when a personality behaves as though he were consciously and purposively thinking, and when, further, he gives us an introspective or retrospective account of his thinking, it is pedantic to doubt the reality of his experience. And this is true whether the personality in question is a normal personality, or a secondary personality which for the most part lives subconsciously and perhaps intermittently only, coming into direct *rapport* with the interrogator only occasionally in hypnosis or in some other occasional fashion.

If we accept Prince's view of the genesis of hallucinations in the cases he has studied, the question arises whether we have to regard all hallucination as originating in the same way, namely, as a partial reflection in the primary consciousness of a subconscious stream of thinking. This is a very difficult question which, at present, no one can answer with any reasonable confidence. I am inclined to suppose that in all cases in which the hallucination is not merely reproductive, but is the product of an elaborating process of which the subject remains unaware, the theory of reflection from the consciousness of a subordinate personality is in order; but that, where we have to deal with hallucinations that merely reproduce scenes lived through with great intensity of affect, there is no sufficient ground for invoking the theory. The reader who is not familiar with cases of multiple personality will hardly appreciate the strength of the case for Dr. Prince's theory and its theoretical importance until he shall have read Chapters XXX to XXXIV [in *An Outline of Abnormal Psychology*], in which such cases are described and discussed.

NOTES

[1] In a few cases such crystal-visions have seemed to be veridical; these raise the problem of telepathy. Cf. Chapter XXXII. [This chapter from *An Outline of Abnormal Psychology* is reprinted in this volume. See "Trance Personalities," p. 171. *Ed.*]

[2] "The Unconscious." The evidence is discussed in Chaps. VI and VII [*An Outline of Abnormal Psychology*].

[3] "An Experimental Study of the Mechanism of Hallucinations," *Brit. J. of Psychol.* (Med. Section), Vol. II.

5. Trance*

Trance is a term used very loosely in popular speech to denote any kind of sleeplike state that seems to present obvious differences from normal sleep; in medical and scientific literature the meaning is but little better defined. In its original usage the word no doubt implied that the soul of the entranced person was temporarily withdrawn or passed away from the body, in accordance with the belief almost universally held by uncultured peoples in the possibility of such withdrawal. But the word is now commonly applied to a variety of sleeplike states without the implication of this theory; ordinary sleep-walking, extreme cases of melancholic lethargy and of anergic stupor, the deeper stages of hypnosis (see HYPNOTISM), the state into which many of the mediums of modern spiritualistic seances seem to fall almost at will; all these are commonly spoken of as trance, or trance-like, states. There are no well-marked and characteristic physical symptoms of the trance state, though in many cases the pulse and respiration are slowed, and the reflexes diminished or abolished. The common feature which more than any other determines the application of the name seems to be a relative or complete temporary indifference to impressions made on the sense-organs, while yet the entranced person gives evidence in one way or another, either by the expression of his features, his attitudes and movements, his speech, or by subsequent relation of his experiences, that his condition is not one of simple quiescence or arrest of mental life, such as characterizes the state of normal deep sleep and the coma produced by defective cerebral circula-

* Article written for the *Encyclopædia Britannica*, 11th ed. (1911), Vol. 27, pp. 167-169.

tion by toxic substances in the blood or by mechanical violence done to the brain.

If we refuse the name trance to ordinary sleep-walking, to normal dreaming, to catalepsy, to the hypnotic state and to stupor, there remain two different states that seem to have equal claims to the name; these may be called the ecstatic trance and the trance of mediumship respectively.

The ecstatic trance is usually characterized by an outward appearance of rapt, generally joyful, contemplation, the subject seems to lose touch for the time being with the world of things and persons about him, owing to the extreme concentration of his attention upon some image or train of imagery, which in most cases seems to assume an hallucinatory character (see HALLU-CINATION). In most cases, though not in all, the subject remembers in returning to his normal state the nature of his ecstatic vision or other experience, of which a curiously frequent character is the radiance or sense of brilliant luminosity.

In the mediumistic trance the subject generally seems to fall into a profound sleep and to retain, on returning to his normal condition, no memory of any experience during the period of the trance. But in spite of the seeming unconsciousness of the subject, his movements, generally of speech or writing, express, either spontaneously or in response to verbal interrogation, intelligence and sometimes even great intellectual and emotional activity. In many cases the parts of the body not directly concerned in these expressions remain in a completely lethargic condition, the eyes being closed, the muscles of neck, trunk and limbs relaxed, and the breathing stertorous.

Trances of these two types seem to have occurred sporadically (occasionally almost epidemically) amongst almost all peoples in all ages. And everywhere popular thought has interpreted them in the same ways. In the ecstatic trance the soul is held to have transcended the bounds of space or time, and to have enjoyed a vision of some earthly event distant in space or time, or of some supernatural sphere or being. The mediumistic trance, on the other hand, popular thought interprets as due to the withdrawal of soul from the body and the taking of its place, the taking possession of the body, by some other soul or spirit; for not infrequently the speech or writing produced by the organs of the entranced subject seems to be, or actually claims to be, the expression of a personality quite other than that of the sleeper. It is noteworthy that in almost all past ages the possessing spirit has been regarded in the great majority of cases as an evil and non-human spirit; whereas in modern times the possessing spirit has usually been regarded as, and often claims to be, the soul or spirit of some deceased human being. Modern science, in accordance with its materialistic and positive tendencies, has rejected these popular interpretations. It inclines to see in the ecstatic trance a case of hallucination induced by prolonged and intense occupation with some emotionally exciting idea, the whole mind becoming so concentrated upon some image in which the idea is bodied forth as to bring all other mental functions into abeyance. The mediumistic trance it regards as a state similar to deep hypnosis, and seeks to explain it by the application of the notion of cerebral or mental dissociation in one or other of its many current forms; this assimilation finds strong support in the many points of resemblance between the deeper stages of hypnosis and the mediumistic trance, and in the fact that the artificially and deliberately induced state may be connected with the spontaneously occurring trance state by a series of states which form an insensible gradation between them. A striking feature of the mediumistic trance is the frequent occurrence of "automatic" speech and writing; and this feature especially may be regarded as warranting the application of the theory of mental dissociation for its explanation, for such automatic speech and writing are occasionally produced by a considerable number of apparently healthy persons while in a waking condition which presents little or no other symptom of abnormality. In these cases the subject hears his own words, or sees the movement of his hand and his own hand writing, as he hears or sees those of another person, having no sense of initiating or controlling the movements and no anticipatory awareness of the thoughts expressed by the movements. When, as in the majority of cases, such movements merely give fragmentary expression to ideas or facts that have been assimilated by the subject at some earlier date, though perhaps seemingly completely forgotten by him, the theory of mental dissociation affords a plausible and moderately satisfactory explanation of the movements; it regards them as due to the control of ideas or memories which somehow have become detached or loosened from the main system of ideas and tendencies that make up the normal personality, and which operate in more or less complete detachment; and the application of the theory is in many cases further justified by the fact that the "dissociated" ideas and memories seem in some cases to become taken up again by, or reincorporated with, the normal personality.

But in recent years a new interest has been given to the study of the mediumistic trance by careful investigations (made with a competence that commands respect) which tend to re-establish the old savage theory of possession, just when it seemed to have become merely an anthropological curiosity. These investigations have been conducted for the most part by members of the Society for Psychical Research, and their most striking results have been obtained by the prolonged study of the automatic speech and writing of the American medium, Mrs. Piper. In this case the medium passes into a trance state apparently at will, and during the trance the organs of speech or the hand usually express what purport to be messages from the spirits of deceased relatives or friends of those who are present. A number of competent and highly critical observers have arrived at the conviction that these messages often comprise statements of facts that could not have come to the knowledge of the medium in any normal fashion; and those who are reluctant to accept the hypothesis of "possession" find that they can reject it only at the cost of assuming the operation of telepathy (*q.v.*) in an astonishing and unparalleled fashion. During 1907-1908 the investigation was directed to the obtaining of communications which should not be explicable by the most extended use of the hypothesis of telepathic communication from the minds of living persons. The plan adopted was to seek for "cross-correspondences" between the communications of the Piper "controls" and the automatic writings of several other persons which claimed to be directed by the same disembodied spirits; *i.e.* it was sought to find in the automatic writings of two or more individuals passages each of which in itself would be fragmentary and unintelligible, but which, taken in connexion with similar fragments contemporaneously produced by another and distant writer, should form a significant whole; for it is argued that such passages would constitute irrefutable evidence of the operation of a third intelligence or personality distinct from that of either medium. The results published up to 1909 seem to show that this attempt met with striking success; and they constitute a body of evidence in favour of the hypothesis of possession which no impartial and unprejudiced mind can lightly set aside. Nevertheless, so long as it is possible to believe, as so many of the most competent workers in this field believe, that dissociated fragments of a personality may become synthesized to form a secondary and as it were parasitic personality capable of assuming temporary control of the organs of expression, and so long as we can set no limits to the scope of telepathic communication between embodied minds, it would seem wellnigh impossible, even by the aid of this novel and ingenious plan of investigation, to achieve completely convincing evidence in favour of the hypothesis of "possession."

LITERATURE.—F. Podmore, *Modern Spiritualism* (London, 1902); F. W. H. Myers, *Human Personality and its Survival of Bodily Death* (London, 1903); Morton Prince, *The Dissociation of a Personality* (London, 1906). See also various articles in *Grenzfragen des Nervenund Seelenlebens*, edited by L. Loewenfeld and H. Kurella (Wiesbaden, 1900), especially the article "Somnambulismus und Spiritismus"; also articles in *Proceedings of the Society for Psychical Research*, especially pts. liii., lv. and lvii., and in the *Journ. of Abnormal Psychology*, edited by Morton Prince (Boston, 1906-1909); also literature cited under AUTOMATISM; HYPNOTISM; MEDIUM; TELEPATHY and POSSESSION.

6.   The Case of Sally Beauchamp*

≈≈≈≈≈≈≈≈≈≈≈≈≈≈≈≈≈≈≈≈≈≈≈≈≈≈≈≈≈≈≈≈≈

In his book on *The Dissociation of a Personality*,[1] Dr. Morton Prince gives us a clearly written, detailed account of the remarkable case of Miss Beauchamp, of which he has previously published brief and incomplete descriptions.[2] The case seems to be in many ways the most extraordinary and, from the point of view of the S.P.R., if not also from every point of view, the most important of all the cases of multiple personality that have been carefully studied and described. A summary statement of the principal features of the case must precede any discussion of it, though nothing short of the reading of the whole book can give an adequate impression of its very strange character and of the care and thoroughness with which it has been studied by Dr. Prince. "Miss Beauchamp, the subject of this study, is a person in whom several personalities have become developed; that is to say, she may change her personality from time to time, often from hour to hour, and with each change her character becomes transformed and her memories altered. In addition to the real, original or normal self, the self that was born and which she was intended by nature to be, she may be any one of three different persons. I say three different, because, although making use of the same body, each, nevertheless, has a distinctly different character; a difference manifested by different trains of thought, by different views, beliefs, ideals, and temperament, and by different acquisitions, tastes, habits, experiences, and memories. Each varies in these respects from the other two, and from the original Miss B. Two of these personalities have no knowl-

* From *Proc. S.P.R.*, Vol. 19 (1907), pp. 410-431.

edge of each other and of the third, excepting such information as may be obtained by inference or second hand, so that in the memory of each of these two there are blanks which correspond to the times when the others are in the flesh. Of a sudden one or other wakes up to find herself, she knows not where, and ignorant of what she has said or done a moment before. Only one of the three has knowledge (*i.e.* apparently immediate knowledge) of the lives of the others, and this one presents such a bizarre character, so far removed from the others in individuality, that the transformation from one of the other personalities to herself is one of the most striking and dramatic features of the case. The personalities come and go in kaleidoscopic succession, many changes often being made in the course of twenty-four hours."

To these three abnormal phases or personalities Dr. Prince gives the names Bi., Biii. (or Sally), and Biv. in the order of their discovery, Bii. being merely Bi. in the hypnotic state.

When the patient first came under Dr. Prince's care she was a serious, refined, and reserved college-student showing neurasthenic symptoms, due apparently to the influence of a series of moral shocks and of excessive study upon a constitution congenitally somewhat unstable. This was the personality that became known as Bi., and which seems to have been dominant for some years previous to this time, although a history of occasional trance-like states of brief duration suggests that during these years Bi. may have occasionally been supplanted by Biii. or iv. or some other abnormal phase. Other remedies having failed, treatment by hynotic suggestion was undertaken. The patient passed easily into a well-marked hypnosis of a not unusual kind, in which she was passive, but could converse intelligently and knew of her waking life, although on waking she remembered nothing of the hypnotic period. Very soon, however, traces of what proved to be a very different personality appeared. This was Biii. or Sally, by far the most interesting member of this strange group. At times during hypnosis the patient spoke of the waking Miss B. as "she," and claimed to be a different person, "Because 'she' does not know the same things that I do." Dr. Prince assures us that, being led to suspect the development of an abnormal personality, he now made every effort to suppress this tendency, but in vain. Biii. continued to alternate with Bii. in the hypnotic periods, and soon claimed the name Sally Beauchamp. Although Biii. seemed to know all about Bi. and Bii. (*e.g.* could remember their conversation), they knew nothing of her, and were kept in ignorance of her for some time, and eventually only learnt of her indirectly. "One of the most interesting features when the change to Biii. took place was the sudden alteration of character, which was almost dramatic. It was amazing to see the sad, anxious, passive Bii. suddenly become transformed into a new personality, stuttering abnominably, and exhibiting a lively vivacity, boldness, and saucy deviltry, difficult to describe. No longer sad, but gay and reckless, she resented any attempt to control her." BIII. soon began to provide indications that she continued to have a conscious existence while BI. was dominant. It has already been said that BIII. shewed extensive knowledge of BI.'s life and thoughts, and now sometimes BI. executed certain actions quite involuntarily, *e.g.* threw down the book she was reading, much to her own annoyance, and BIII. claimed to have produced these actions, because Dr. Prince had told her that BI. must not read too much. (p. 37.) "It is worth while noting how sharply differentiated were the volitions of the two personalities at this early date. Later, I personally witnessed similar phenomena on numerous occasions." This, in fact, was an early stage of a prolonged struggle for mastery between the two personalities BI. and BIII. "From almost the very first her (BIII.'s) language implied a concomitant existence for herself, a double mental life for Miss Beauchamp. She always spoke as if she had her own thoughts and perceptions and will *during the time while Miss Beauchamp was in existence.*" BIII., *i.e.* Sally, being questioned as to her knowledge of what BI. had read, "her answer implied co-existence and parallelism of thought, for she explained certain lapses of knowledge by asserting that ordinarily, as she herself was not fond of books, she did not pay attention while Miss B. was reading; but that when she did so, which was only when interested, she could understand and remember the text; that she liked different books from those BI. liked, and that she understood some things BI. did not, and *vice versa.*"

It became apparent also that while BI. had good command of the French language and of shorthand, Sally knew neither. (p. 47.) Nevertheless, Sally "claimed, in her own peculiar language, to be always present as a subconsciousness." Dr. Prince, who rejects as grossly fallacious the doctrine that an independent subconsciousness is a normal feature of human personality, or that the hypnotic self usually persists as such a subconsciousness during waking life, was very sceptical of the truth of this claim of Sally's, but was soon compelled by overwhelmingly strong evidence to admit it. BI. began to be troubled by an increasing variety of uncontrollable involuntary impulses. Among other things she told lies, and talked disrespectful nonsense to her friends, much to her own distress. A series of experiments in crystal-gazing seemed to prove, "first, the distinctiveness of the two co-existent conscious selves, as far at least as concerns the separateness of the simultaneous perceptions; and second, the greater completeness of the memories of Sally *for a certain class of facts.*" (p. 85.)

About two months after Sally's appearance as a phase of hypnotic personality and a sub- or co-consciousness, she made a great step towards a fuller control of the organism. Both Bii. and Sally in hypnosis had frequently rubbed their eyes, and this Sally declared was due to her efforts to get her eyes open, a thing not hitherto allowed to either hypnotic phase. At last Sally succeeded in rubbing and opening Bi.'s eyes, whereupon Bi. disappeared and 'Sally' came, mistress of herself, and, for the first time, able to see." (p. 95.)

From this time on Sally frequently had possession of the whole organism for considerable periods, during which Bi. seemed to be entirely unconscious, and she began to play all sorts of tricks for the annoyance of Bi. when she should have her turn of conscious life, among other things writing abusive letters to Bi., and leaving them to be found and read by her on returning to consciousness. In this way Bi. learnt of the existence of Sally, and concluded she was possessed of devils.

When Bi. was fatigued and in poor health Sally dominated and excluded her frequently, and the better Bi.'s health the more difficult did Sally find it to get the upper hand—she felt herself "squeezed," as she said, and for periods of some months of exceptionally good health Bi. was free from Sally's interventions. But on the whole Sally gained upon Bi., and succeeded in supplanting Bi. in the control of the body with increasing frequency. During one period Bi. fell into a delirium, and then Sally alternated with her at short intervals, appearing perfectly sane. This was but one instance of the fact that Sally's health and spirits were always much better than Bi.'s. Sally, in fact, did not know fatigue and lassitude, so frequent with Bi.

This absence of all fatigue in Sally must be connected with the fact that she, *i.e.* the patient, during the weeks of Sally's dominance had "a peculiar form of anaesthesia. With her eyes closed she can feel nothing. The tactile, pain, thermic, and muscular senses are involved. You may stroke, prick, or burn any part of her skin, and she does not feel it. You may place a limb in any posture without her being able to recognise the position which has been assumed. But let her open her eyes and look at what you are doing, let her join the visual sense with the tactile or other senses, and the lost sensations at once return. . . . The same is true of auditory perceptions. If Sally hears a sound associated with an object, she can feel the object." "Sensation may also be restored by suggestion. But the restoration is only temporary, lasting for a few hours or for the day." "Sally's anaesthesia extends to the somatic feelings. She is never hungry or thirsty." (p. 149.)

After about a year of this sort of life appeared a third distinct personality, Biv., "who seemed quite as much a real person as did the Miss Beauchamp whom we all knew (*i.e.* Bi.)." Biv. knew nothing of recent events in the patient's life, nothing of Bi. and of Sally, and did not recognise Dr.

Prince or other friends of the patient. She seemed a normally intelligent person suddenly set among scenes and persons hitherto unknown to her. She soon set herself to find out all she could of her environment, concealing her ignorance as far as possible with considerable skill. In character and temperament she was quite unlike both BI. and Sally, being less reserved than BI., and far more combative and determined, and having nothing of Sally's childish and impish delight in fun, in breaches of decorum, and practical jokes. BIV. now alternated frequently with BI. and Sally. Sally's relation to BIV. was curiously different from her relation to BI. Sally was aware not only of all BI.'s actions, but also apparently of all her thoughts and emotions; but as regards BIV., Sally knew only her actions, and nothing directly of her conscious states, but like any other constant spectator, could infer much of BIV.'s mental processes from her actions and expressions.

As BIV. began to realise her strange relations to BI. and to Sally, she conceived a violent dislike of Sally, which was reciprocated, and for BI. she had contemptuous indifference. Unlike Sally, BIV. shared most of BI.'s accomplishments, *e.g.* a knowledge of the French language. Dr. Prince was soon able to discover that BIV.'s memory was a blank as regards the life of the patient during the six years preceding her appearance, a period initiated by a moral shock. Events antecedent to that incident she remembered in normal fashion. The amnesia was, however, not quite complete. BIV. had momentary dream-like memories of incidents in the life of BI., and by inducing her to fix her mind upon these visions and to describe them Dr. Prince was able to obtain an account of the episodes that seemed to have been the immediate cause of the patient's strange condition, and to arrive at the following conclusions: "Putting together all the facts thus far learned which bear upon the development of BI. and BIV., we are able to make the following historical summary, for which the evidence is conclusive: Miss Beauchamp was distinct as a unity, a single consciousness, up to the summer of 1893. At that time there occurred a psychical catastrophe, which produced a disintegration of consciousness, by which her personality changed and she developed into BI. BI. retained all the memories of her youth, as well as of the accident which led to her development; and also, of course, of her whole life (that is, exclusive of Sally's entrances) during the six years succeeding the accident of 1893, that is, up to June 7, 1899. She also retained a memory of those periodical times when she had been in existence since the latter date. She differs from her original state in certain bodily characteristics known as neurasthenia, and in certain mental characteristics—instability and suggestibility—and, above all, in certain alterations of character. BI. therefore remained the sole personality in existence for six years—to June 7, 1899—when owing to some cause thus far unknown, a hitherto unobserved personality was awakened, which in associations of memory reverted to a past period of life, namely, that which antedated and ended with the aforesaid catastrophe of 1893."

"This personality (Biv.) apparently belonged to that earlier period, and remembered the events of her life up to a certain hour, namely, that just preceding the incident which caused the psychical shock, at which time her memory ceased. From that eventful moment this new personality had absolutely no memory of anything that occurred during the following six years, ending June 7, 1899. Since this last date she knows and remembers only the events that have happened during those interrupted periods when she herself has been in existence. Since her appearance she has been constantly alternating with Bi. and with Biii." (p. 224.)

It is to be noted that in this passage Dr. Prince ignores the evidence of Sally's (Biii.'s) existence before she made herself known to him, and writes only of Bi. and Biv.

The further discovery was shortly made that the appearance of Biv. was due to a communication to Bi., which strongly revived the memory of the event of six years ago with all its agitating emotions. Dr. Prince then set himself to find out whether Biv. could properly be regarded as the original Miss B., and for some time was strongly of that opinion, and therefore did all he could to suppress Sally and Bi., but without success, although the situation was explained fully to Biv., and her co-operation invited and willingly given. The next important step was the discovery that Biv. hypnotised seemed in all respects identical with Bi. hypnotised; either one on being hypnotised remembered all the experiences of both, and spoke of both as "I" and "myself." This hypnotic phase common to Bi. and Biv. was henceforth known as Bii. Bii. had no direct knowledge of, or memory of, Sally's experience. An attempt was made to waken up Bii., and make her retain in the waking state the character and complete memory (save for the Sally periods) of Bii. The attempt failed repeatedly, for Bii. on awaking became Biv. Then began a contest for predominance between Biv. and Sally, Biv. being determined to suppress Sally, and Sally resisting with all her resources. They exchanged quarrelsome notes, and Sally seemed to be able partially to control Biv.'s movements, either forcing "automatic" movement, such as writing, or suppressing her voluntary movements, as when she made her dumb (p. 284); she also produced certain forms of systematised anæsthesia and of hallucination, and seems actually to have hypnotised Biv. by writing her a note suggesting sleep. (p. 320.)

Next it was found that Bi. and Biv. seemed to become one in sleep, for both remembered the same dreams; and further, that Sally seemed to be awake while Bi. and Biv. slept, and to be directly aware of their dreams.

Sally was now induced to write her autobiography, and produced a most interesting document, partly written while she herself was in control or possession of the body, partly by way of automatic writing while Biv. was in possession.

Repeated attempts to give permanence to Bii., who seemed to be a synthesis of Bi. and Biv., were frustrated by the active opposition of both Biv. and Sally—by Biv. because she disliked and despised the meek character of Bi., by Sally because she felt that the success of this operation would mean that she would be suppressed or permanently "squeezed," as she described her state when incapable of securing control of the body and banishing her rivals.

For two years the patient continued this strange existence without any important new development. Then somehow, in a way which is apparently not understood by Dr. Prince, but is briefly described as an ingenious artifice (p. 436), Sally became aware of Biv.'s thoughts and feelings much as she had always known Bi.'s, and now carried on her contest with Biv. at a greater advantage. Being aware of Biv.'s determination to suppress her, Sally countered her efforts by inducing in Biv. terrifying hallucinations, and by a great variety of annoying tricks, going so far as to scratch and bruise severely their common body. (p. 456.) In this way Biv.'s resolution was broken down by Sally and her plans frustrated. But Sally herself was now somewhat discouraged and depressed, and in this mood accepted Biv.'s proposal of a *modus vivendi*. Their plan was to set out on a holiday trip to Europe and to remain there, each agreeing to allow the other control of the body for half the time, and to suppress Bi. completely. Their plan was discovered and frustrated by Dr. Prince.

After some more months of troubled existence, a restoration of the normal Miss B. seems to have been effected by wakening Bii., the hypnotised state of Bi. and Biv. which combined the memories and characteristics of both Bi. and Biv. Dr. Prince had often before attempted to bring about this result by wakening Bii., but always without success, and the ultimate success seems to have been due to Sally, for it was not achieved until she had confessed that it was she who had prevented the success of the earlier attempts, and had promised not to interfere any longer. It is not made clear that Sally had any new motive for this more accommodating behaviour, and one is left with the impression that she had grown a little tired of her games. Whatever this new attitude of Sally may have been due to, it seems to have rendered possible the desired result. Bii. on being wakened appeared as a normal person, who in character was a fusion of Bi. and Biv., and consequently superior to both, who remembered the experiences of both Bi. and Biv., as also the patient's life of the period previous to the disintegrating shock, and who seemed to enjoy much better health than either BI. or BIV. This personality Dr. Prince regards as the real Miss Beauchamp. She has suffered a few relapses into BI., BIV., and BIII., but has remained continuously unchanged for periods as long as six months. Sally in these periods gives no sign of her existence; to use her own expression, she seems to have gone back whence she came!

Although this brief summary necessarily omits many interesting features of this strange case, enough has been said to shew that it surpasses all previously recorded cases in many respects. So strange and wildly improbable does the story seem, that any one may well hesitate to accept it, and indeed it would be incredible were it not that in recent years similar, though less extreme, cases have been reported by a number of independent observers, whose care, capacity, and good faith are above suspicion. These analogous cases, taken in conjunction with the author's high standing in his profession and with the internal evidence of his strictly scientific attitude, his caution, patience, sincerity, and deep interest in the case, warrant us in accepting the facts as observed and reported by him. Dr. Prince does not give us in this volume a full discussion of the theoretical interpretation of this case, but promises to do so in a later volume, and since his earlier work on *The Nature of Mind and Human Automatism* shews him to be well qualified for the task, this supplementary volume should be one of great interest. In the meantime I am bidden to discuss it, and, summoning all my resolution, proceed to make the attempt.

In face of this strange case, it is necessary to admit fully our complete ignorance of the conditions of psychical individuality. The field is completely open to speculation. Hitherto neither science nor philosophy has been able to establish any certain conclusions.

If for the moment we put aside Sally, the case appears comparatively simple, and comparable in almost all important respects to several other well-known cases, namely, the cases of Mr. Hanna, of Ansel Bourne, of Mary Reynolds, of Léonie B., Félida X., and others. It appears to be a case of disintegration of a personality, or psychical individual, into two alternating personalities, each of which is conscious and controls the body for a period during which the other seems to have a merely potential existence. This view, that alternating personalities are the products of the disintegration of the normal personality, is very generally accepted. Some authors, *e.g.* Prof. Pierre Janet, are content to state the view in terms of psychical process only; they assume that any state of consciousness of a normal person is literally a synthesis of a great number of elementary psychical elements or entities, sensations, images, and feelings, and that in these abnormal states these become synthesised in two (or more) groups or complex systems instead of one. This does not constitute in any sense an explanation of these cases; it is merely a hypothetical description. For any explanatory hypothesis must set out from some definite view or assumption as to the conditions of unity of the consciousness of the normal individual.

In respect to this great problem there are two, and strictly speaking, only two rival views. (1) The one assumes that structural and functional continuity of the elements of the brain is the condition of the unity of consciousness or of the psychical individuality of normal persons. This is the assumption explicitly made by many modern authors, most clearly and explicitly perhaps by Ed. von Hartmann, the philosopher of the Unconscious, and by G. T. Fechner, the father of psycho-physics, and implicitly by many others. All who accept materialism or the epiphenomenalism of Huxley and Tyndall, or the doctrine of psycho-physical parallelism, or the dual-aspect theory of mind and body, including H. Spencer, Bain, Stout, Paulsen, Münsterberg, Wundt, Ebbinghaus, and the majority of psychologists of the present time— all, in fact, who adopt one or other form of the monistic view of mind and body are logically committed to this assumption.

(2) The other doctrine, radically opposed to the former, is dualistic and maintains that whatever view we may take of matter, even if we regard it as essentially of the same nature as mind, we must assume that each normal human mind or personality results from the functional association of, and interaction between, the body and a unitary psychic being, the ego or soul, or psyche, and that the latter is the ground of psychical individuality, of the unity of normal individual consciousness. This is not merely a popular view, but has been maintained in recent years by a number of psychologists of the first rank, *e.g.* by Lotze, Ward, Bradley, Stumpf, Külpe and James. Unfortunately most of those who adopt this view have been very reticent as to the nature and the scope of the functions of the psychic being.

Two principal varieties of this view may be distinguished. According to the one, all that we mean by memory or retention of experience and knowledge, is conditioned by the persistence in the nervous system of modifications of its structure, induced during each experience that leaves its mark upon the mind. Our conscious mental life is then, according to this view, the reaction of the psychic being upon the brain processes, according to its own nature and faculties; but the constitution of the nervous system and sense organs, and the processes excited in them, determine the character of the content of consciousness, and provide the occasions for the exercise by the psychic being of its intrinsic powers, powers of feeling, of judgment, of reasoning, of volition. This form of the dualistic doctrine thus separates the forms of mental activity from the content of the mind, the systems of ideas and beliefs acquired through experience, assigning the former to the psychic being, the latter to the nervous system.

According to the other form of the dualistic doctrine, it is the psychic being that retains those impressions in virtue of which each experience plays its part in determining future experience, or, in more popular language, the psychic being is regarded as capable of memory independently of traces left in the nervous system. This view, then, ascribes both form and content of mental process to the psychic being, and regards the nervous system as merely an apparatus, through the mediation of which the things of the physical world are enabled to act upon the psychic being, and through which the psychic being in turn is able to act upon them—as a merely receptive and executive mechanism, in fact.

This latter view alone is compatible with any belief in the continued existence of the personality after the death of the body, using personality to mean the mental individual as developed by his intercourse with his physical and social environment. For the developed personality is the product of a long process of growth, of accumulation of habit and effects of experience of all kinds; and if the retention of these effects is, or is dependent upon, persistent modifications of the structure of the nervous system, this retention can persist only so long as the nervous system is intact. The former variety of the dualistic doctrine is therefore compatible only with a belief in impersonal immortality.

Let us for convenience of discussion denote by the letter C this last view of the relation of mind and body, let us denote the other variety of the dualistic view by the letter B, and the monistic view by the letter A, and further, let us call the kind of psychic being assumed by the doctrine of B, the "psyche," and that assumed by doctrine C, the soul; for the latter alone corresponds to the conception of the soul generally entertained and usually implied by the word.

Cases of multiple personality derive their great importance from the fact that it seems probable they may throw light upon this great problem, and in this respect the case under review is second to none.

It must be admitted that in so far as cases of multiple personality are capable of being regarded as resulting from division of the normal personality, they lend themselves readily to explanation in terms of the monistic hypothesis, A. We may suppose that in such cases the elements of the nervous system, which normally constitute a single functional group, have become divided into two or more such groups, and that the functioning of each group is then accompanied by its own stream of consciousness, a synthesis of the elementary psychical processes accompanying the elementary nervous processes of that group. This is the explanation of these cases most generally accepted. There are cases which seem clearly to involve this kind of functional splitting of the nervous system and a corresponding splitting of the conscious personality. These are the cases of hysterical anaesthesia so well studied by Janet. There seems good reason to suppose that in these cases certain sensori-motor areas of the brain (*e.g.* the area with which an anaesthetic limb is directly connected by afferent and efferent projection fibres), together with more or less of the regions of higher function, become functionally dissociated from the rest of the brain, and that the functioning of such a dissociated group of nervous elements is accompanied by its independent stream of consciousness.

Many of the anaesthesias and paralyses produced by hypnotic suggestion fall readily into the same class.

But it is, I think, very doubtfully legitimate to extend this kind of explanation to all cases of multiple personality and to regard them all as of this one type. It is true that we seem to be able to set all these cases in a series ranging from the simple types of the kind just mentioned to the most complex, such as Miss Beauchamp; and it is this seeming ease with which they may be thus arranged in a series of progressive complexity that gives the extension of this type of explanation to all cases its best claim for acceptance. It is, however, very possible that this appearance is deceptive, and that we really have to deal with cases of two radically different types, of which the simpler alone fall under the above type of explanation, while for the explanation of the others some very different hypothesis must be found.

Still putting aside Sally, the case of Miss Beauchamp may fairly be claimed as a case of multiple personality resulting from division of the normal personality, and it is of the relatively intelligible type in which the resultant personalities are alternately and never simultaneously conscious. There was a sharply cut division of all mental content acquired after a given date between the alternating personalities Bi. and Biv., and yet the mental content acquired before that date was common to both of them. Further, they appear to have become eventually recombined or synthesised, so that the two systems of mental content, the two memory-continua, were fused to a single one. That Bi. and Biv. were the products of a division of the personality of Miss B. we seem justified in believing. But if we accept this view we are not thereby logically compelled to accept doctrine *A*.

If we assume *B* to be the true doctrine, then we must believe that there was a functional splitting of the patient's nervous system, for the mental content was divided between Bi. and Biv., and we may suppose either that Miss B.'s "psyche" was in interaction with the two parts of the nervous system alternately, or that a second "psyche" entered into functional relations with one part, while Miss B.'s "psyche" maintained its relations with the other part. Of these alternatives the latter seems the less improbable. If we are to discuss these strange cases with any hope of profit, we must give rein to speculation, and, as was said above, there are no established facts that set certain limits to hypothesis. Now if we accept doctrine *B*, it must be admitted that we know nothing of the conditions which determine the functional association of any "psyche" with any nervous system. It may be that, as Mr. H. G. Wells has suggested in one of his weird stories, disembodied souls are crowding thickly about us, each striving to occupy some nervous system and so to become restored to a full life of sense and motion and human fellowship. Or it may be that with each organism is associated an indefinitely large number of psychic beings, each capable, on fitting opportunity, of playing its part as the dominant "psyche" in interaction with the whole nervous system; although, in the case of the normally constituted brain, only one such can play this part, while all the rest remain suppressed and latent, or playing subordinate parts in association with subordinate nervous centres. And we may suppose that, as soon as the brain becomes functionally split, a second "psyche" finds its opportunity and has its faculties, its capacities for sensation, for feeling, emotion, judgment and volition called into play by the influence of that part of the nervous system which has fallen out of touch with the originally dominant "psyche." It may be, *e.g.*, that the personality BIV. resulted from this kind of change, that Miss B.'s original "psyche" was for a period of seven years thrown out of touch with all those nervous dispositions that became newly organised under the influence of "psyche" BIV., but was later brought into functional relation with these, with the consequent exclusion of BIV., or its repression to its original subordinate status and restricted activity. The extremely different characters of BI. and of BIV., and the determined antagonism of BIV. to BI., the strong opposition of her will to every attempt to restore BI. to her normal condition seem to countenance this view.

On the other hand, if we regard, as apparently we must, this case (Sally excluded) and other cases of multiple personality as cases of divided personality, it is extremely difficult, if not impossible, to reconcile this view with doctrine *C*, and the conception of a soul in the full sense of the words as the bearer of both form and content of the mind, as being in itself the full personality independently of any nervous system. This task was, of course, attempted by the late F. W. H. Myers in his work on *Human Personality*, but, as I have argued at length elsewhere,[3] his attempt cannot be regarded as so successful as to compel our acceptance of his doctrine or to render unnecessary the search for a more satisfactory explanation, and, as I shall point out below, Myers' doctrine gives us no help when we attempt to solve the perplexing problem of Sally.

When we turn to consider the personality BIII., or Sally, our difficulties increase. Dr. Prince in many passages (*e.g.* p. 18, p. 234) confidently assumes that Sally also is the product of the division of the original Miss B., and that the restoration of the normal personality involves the reabsorption or synthesis of Sally with Bi. and Biv. No doubt Dr. Prince will seek to justify this view in the promised volume of theoretical discussions, but the confidence with which he puts forward this opinion in the present volume is difficult to understand or to justify. No argument is adduced in favour of it, and no single fact recorded implies (so far as I can see) that Sally arose by a splitting-off from the original personality, or that she became reabsorbed or synthesised with the personalities Bi. and Biv. in the process of restoration of Miss B. to her original self. The evidence, in fact, points all the other way. If we may accept unreservedly Dr. Prince's description of Sally, then I think we may say with confidence that Sally was not merely a split-off part of Miss B., and that still less can she be accounted for by the monistic doctrine *A* and the assumption that the nervous system of Miss B. became dissociated to form three principal functional systems of elements.

That Sally was a personality capable of being fully conscious, capable of ideas, of reasoning, of emotion and of strong volition *simultaneously* with the conscious existence of Bi. seems established by Dr. Prince's careful studies, and seems to be fully accepted by Dr. Prince himself. Such a consciousness of a hidden personality existing contemporaneously with that of another personality which is in control of the bodily organs, Dr. Prince calls a sub-consciousness, and this is, I think, the most appropriate usage of this term which has been used so loosely and with so many different meanings by different authors. Sally claimed, and supported with strong evidence the claim, that she had existed as a sub-consciousness (in this sense of the word) from the earliest years of Miss B.'s life; *i.e.* long before the date of the psychic shock which changed Miss B. into Bi.; and there seems no good reason to deny the validity of this claim, although, of course, the evidence of Sally's existence as a personality during these early years is less good than that for her continued existence as a sub-consciousness in the period of Dr. Prince's observation of the case.

Again, there is no evidence to shew that when Bi. and Biv. became synthesised to form the apparently normal Miss B. Sally was in any sense or degree included in this synthesis; the evidence rather shews that she was not; the restored personality Miss B. seems to have had no memory of Sally's experiences, as she had of those of both Bi. and Biv. (see pp. 272 and 525), and no direct awareness of Sally's existence. Again, Sally cannot be regarded as merely a group of ideas and memories dissociated from the original personality, "some sort of a dissociated group of conscious states," if only because of the fullness of her personality, the very distinctive and strong traits of character and emotional disposition, her developed self-consciousness and strong will, her acute intelligence and comprehensive memory. I would refer the reader to the following passages for statements bearing on the mental capacities of Sally (p. 238) : "Sally became for the moment serious and earnest, showing great intelligence and perspicacity in her analysis of the psychological and other facts. She discussed them with intelligence and interest, went over the history of the past year, explained many facts which were obscure, and recalled others which I had overlooked. Reference to my notebook showed that Sally's memory was correct." Notice that these correct memories were not merely evoked by appropriate questioning by Dr. Prince, they were appositely and spontaneously brought forward by Sally in order to bear out the comprehensive scheme or ideal construction which she evolved to account for the peculiarities of the case. On pp. 267, 268, again Sally is revealed as keenly reasoning and reflecting upon the case, and giving Dr. Prince valuable suggestions, often in long and carefully reasoned letters, such as no child and no person not of more than average intellectual power could produce. On p. 278 Sally's description of her early life seems to shew her to have had a separate mental life from the time that Miss B. learnt to walk, with very different emotions and some scorn for the personality controlling the body, to whom she felt herself superior in energy of character. This is further borne out by Sally's autobiography (chap. xxiii), a very remarkable account of childish experiences, revealing an intelligence and memory which would be exceptional in any autobiographical account by an adult of the years of childhood. In fact, as regards fullness and accuracy of memory and voluntary and appropriate recollection, Sally seems to have been superior to any normal individual, for her memory comprised not only almost all the waking experiences of the original Miss B. and of BI., and of her own periods of dominance over the body, but also all BI.'s dream life and her own periods of subconscious existence, and, later, BIV.'s experiences also. As regards Sally's volition, many examples of her determined and successful opposition to BI., BIV., and to Dr. Prince might be quoted. (See especially pp. 284 and 285.) She would render BI. or BIV. dumb, or force them while dominant to speak, write, or act in ways quite opposed to their intentions and wishes, and she seemed at times to be capable of shifting the scenes almost at will, causing herself or one or other of her rivals to control the body. It must be noted that these effects exerted by Sally were by no means due to the working of mere blind impulses, but in most cases were apparently truly volitional, the outcome of well-reasoned, self-conscious deliberation in resolute pursuance of a well-conceived purpose. So acute was Sally, and so well informed, so resolute in the pursuit of her ends, that for more than two years she was able to defy and bring to nought the combined efforts of Dr. Prince, BI., and BIV. to suppress her, and, as was said above, the eventual restoration of Miss B. by the reunion of BI. and BIV. seems to have become possible only because Sally, for some unknown reason, ceased to offer active opposition to Dr. Prince's efforts to bring about this change. Beside all this evidence of the fullness of Sally's mental life and of the independence and completeness of her personality, we must put the following facts: (1) That Bɪɪ. (the hypnotic state of the complete Miss B. comprising Bɪ. and Bɪv.), while recognising both Bɪ. and Bɪv. and herself as essentially the same person, repudiated with horror the suggestion that Sally might be identified in any way with herself. (p. 448.) (2) That when Bɪ. and Bɪv. became synthesised to form the person whom Dr. Prince, seemingly with good reason, regards as the real, original and complete Miss B., Sally continued to exist as a subconsciousness, aware of all Miss B.'s thoughts; and that this restored Miss B. could remember the events of all periods save those in which Sally had controlled the body to the exclusion of the other personalities. (p. 516.) The relation of Sally to the personality regarded by Dr. Prince himself as the complete Miss B. is thus different in every respect from the relation of Bɪ. and Bɪv. to Miss B. For neither of these was aware of or could remember Miss B.'s experiences, while she remembers theirs. But we are told of Sally that when, after the restoration of Miss B. she "appeared again as an alternating personality, her language implied a persistent existence as a subconsciousness like that of her early youth, and as described in the autobiography" (p. 524), *i.e.* she had become aware of and could remember Miss B.'s experiences.

In face of all these facts it is, I think, impossible to agree with Dr. Prince in regarding Sally as a group of states of consciousness dissociated or split off from the normal personality. Dr. Prince's own statements are incompatible with this view, and further, they are inconsistent with one another, as when he tells us that the synthesis of Bɪ. and Bɪv. restored the complete Miss B., and yet in other passages speaks of the production of Sally by dissociation, and also of "the synthesising of Bɪv.'s consciousness with that of the subconsciousness (Sally)" without, however, offering us a particle of evidence that either one of these latter processes ever took place.

Dr. Prince seems, in fact, to have set out with the conviction that every case of multiple personality is to be regarded as resulting from dissociation of a normal personality, and to have allowed this prejudice to limit the range of his search for hypotheses, and to blind him to the unmistakable implications of his own descriptions. In short, to assert, as Dr. Prince does, that Sally is a split-off fragment of Miss B. *is to maintain that the part may be greater than the whole.*

If, then, Sally is not merely a fragment of Miss B., the product of mental disintegration, she is not to be explained in terms of the monistic doctrine *A*, for that doctrine can only give account of multiple personalities resulting from disintegration. What, then, is she? Can she be explained in terms of either form, *B* or *C*, of the dualistic doctrine? We may state the alternatives more fully thus: If one of the essential conditions of Sally's conscious life is a psychic being or entity distinct from that of the normal Miss B., must we ascribe both form and content of her mind to this psychic being (doctrine *C*), or can we suppose that the content of her mind (her systems of ideas and memories) is determined by some part of Miss B.'s brain that has become dissociated from the rest and entered into functional relations with this second and superfluous psychic being?

The latter alternative seems hardly tenable, for two reasons chiefly: (1) We can hardly suppose that there could be in Miss B.'s brain sufficient nervous matter to serve as the physical basis for the very full memories of Sally, in addition to those of BI. and BIV., for since Sally can remember so much of Miss B.'s experiences as well as BI.'s and her own, the content of her mind must be regarded as at least as abundant as that of all the other personalities together; the whole content of the mind is as it were duplicated. If, then, the content of Sally's mind has a physical basis in the brain of Miss B., that brain has to serve as the physical basis for at least two minds fully furnished with memories of all sorts. This would seem to imply that of the brain of a normal individual but one-half the nervous substance may be concerned in mental processes, the other half lying dormant; this implication, whether in the form that one hemisphere alone normally functions or in any other form, seems in the last degree improbable. For it is impossible to understand how this great mass of extremely expensive, but superfluous, nervous tissue could have been evolved as a normal feature of the human brain. (2) More important perhaps is the consideration of the peculiar relation of Sally to BI. and to Miss B. Sally seems to have become aware of all BI.'s and Miss B.'s perceptions, ideas, feelings in an immediate fashion. But it was not that these states of consciousness were simply duplicated, forming two similar and parallel streams. Sally was aware of these states of Miss B.'s consciousness as Miss B.'s; she did not regard them as her own, but knew them for Miss B.'s; she did not simply have the same perceptions, ideas, and feelings as Miss B. or BI., but she knew of them in an intimate fashion, and had her own thoughts and feelings and volitions in regard to them. How was this knowledge acquired by, or conveyed to, Sally? There seems no alternative to the view suggested by our President in his recent address to the Society, namely, that the process is telepathic, *i.e.* an immediate influencing of one mind by another, a telepathic communication between Sally and BI. or Miss B.

There are three ways in which the telepathic communication between separate persons may be conceived. (1) It may be a purely physical interaction, an influence exerted by one brain upon another through some physical medium. This is the natural view for those who adopt doctrine *A*. (2) It may be a psycho-physical interaction, an influence directly exerted by the brain of one person upon the psychic being of another. This is the view of telepathy which would be naturally taken by those who hold by doctrine *B*. If direct interaction between "psyche" and body of each person is the rule, it must be admitted that we know nothing of the conditions of the alliance of any "psyche" with any body, and therefore nothing which necessitates the assumption commonly made, that this psycho-physical interaction is of an exclusive character. Why should not my brain, under certain unknown favourable conditions, act upon your "psyche," or any other, as well as upon my own? (3) The third view, adopted by the President in his address, is that the telepathic interaction is purely psychical, an immediate action of one soul upon another. This is the view of telepathic action which is most naturally taken by those who hold doctrine *C*.

I submit that the relation of Sally to the other personalities can only be explained by applying the telepathic hypothesis in the third form distinguished above.

Adopting for the moment doctrine *B* and the second form of the telepathic hypothesis, we may suppose that the neural processes of the one brain affect the "psyche" of Sally as well as that of Miss B., each responding according to its own nature. But there are insuperable difficulties in the way of any such attempt to explain Sally and Miss B. as two psychic beings having in common one brain which is the physical basis of the memories of both. If this were the case, all memories should be common to both Sally and Miss B., but this is not so. Miss B. knows nothing of Sally's experiences, and Sally seems to know only those of Miss B. in which she takes an interest, *e.g.* she knows nothing of Miss B.'s highly specialised learning, such as her command of the French language. It would seem, in fact, that the retained traces of Sally's experience, or her memory in the widest sense of the word, is independent of Miss B.'s, and that she becomes aware of Miss B.'s mental processes only through the exertion of an attentive and selective activity. We seem driven therefore to accept the third form of the telepathic hypothesis, which implies immediate interaction between souls in the full sense of the word, psychic beings whose constitutions determine both form and content of the mind in so far as content is not determined by present sensory impressions, but by past experience, souls which are capable of retention independently of the physical basis.

My conclusion is, then, that if we accept Dr. Prince's description of Sally Beauchamp, we can only account for her by adopting that view of the relation of mind and body which I have called in this review the *C* doctrine—the view that the normal personality consists of body and soul in interaction, the soul being not dependent upon the brain or other physical basis for its memory, but having the faculty of retaining and remembering among its other faculties. I confess that this conclusion, involving the rejection of the physical basis of memory, is inconsistent with a very large mass of evidence which I have hitherto considered as almost, if not quite, proving the dependence of all memory and, therefore, of all developed personality on the persistence of the physical basis, of the physical changes produced in the brain in the course of each moment of experience.[4] This great mass of evidence is not to be lightly set aside in view of any one case, but if a number of cases of the type of Sally Beauchamp, as described by Dr. Prince, were to be described by other equally careful and credible observers, I think the weight of their testimony would be irresistible. This conclusion would give very strong support to the spiritistic explanation of such cases as Mrs. Piper, and would go far to justify the belief in the survival of human personality after the death of the body. It is for this reason that Sally Beauchamp seems to me of so great interest to this Society.

On summing up my discussion of this case, I am compelled to admit the unsatisfactory character of my conclusions, for I have argued that the disintegration of Miss B. into BI. and BIV., and especially the restoration of Miss B. by the synthesis of BI. and BIV. is incompatible with the dualistic doctrine in the second form *C*, which assumes the soul in the full sense of the word; but on the other hand, I have argued that this doctrine alone is adequate to account for Sally. It is, of course, impossible to accept both these opposed doctrines, and one has to recognise three possible flaws in the argument. (1) The premises may be false, *i.e.* the facts of the case may have been incorrectly reported. (2) The argument may have been illogically conducted. (3) The conceptions used may have been hopelessly inadequate to the realities. The third possibility, as in the case of most philosophical argument, probably represents the actual state of affairs. Recognising this probability, one is bound to look round for any other conception that has been formulated to deal with facts of this order, and Myers' conception of the subliminal self naturally claims consideration.

I will conclude, then, by asking—Does Myers' doctrine of the subliminal self help us to understand this case? I cannot see that it does. Myers' doctrine is, of course, a variety of the *C* doctrine, the doctrine of the soul, not merely in the full sense of the word, but in a greatly extended sense.

I take the essence of this doctrine to be that the soul has a far richer store of faculties, memories, and ideas than it is capable of manifesting in the mental processes of normal waking life, and that the restricted character of these manifestations is due to the imperfections of the nervous system. How can we apply this conception to explain the manifestation through the one body of the two personalities, Miss B. and Sally, each having her full complement of faculties, memories, and ideas? If we ascribe this duality to the soul, we are assuming two souls, and that we can do equally well without making the additional vast assumptions of the doctrine of the "subliminal self." If we ascribe the duality to the body, to a functional division of the nervous system, we ascribe to it an importance and an extent of influence upon the mental life which is compatible only with the monistic doctrine *A*, and not at all with a thoroughgoing dualistic doctrine. For one who holds by the conception of the soul in the full sense in which it is implied by the doctrine of the subliminal self, to suppose that the soul can simultaneously will in two opposed senses, because its instrument, the nervous, is functionally divided, would be as reasonable as to expect a man to be able to walk in two opposite directions at one moment, because he has two legs. I venture to think that the phrase "the subliminal self" may prove detrimental to the efficiency of our Society if we do not sternly resist the tendency to use it as a mere cloak for our ignorance whenever we are confronted by the inexplicable events with which we have to attempt to grapple. This remarkable case is just of that baffling kind which tempts us to soothe our perplexities, "to lay our intellects to rest on a pillow of obscure ideas," by the utterance of that seductive phrase the "subliminal self."

NOTES

[1] *The Dissociation of a Personality: A Biographical Study in Abnormal Psychology*. By Morton Prince, M.D., Professor of Diseases of the Nervous System in Tufts College Medical School, Physician for Diseases of the Nervous System, Boston City Hospital. (Longmans, Green & Co., 1906.)

[2] "The Problem of Multiple Personality," a paper read to the International Congress of Psychology at Paris in 1900, and "The Misses Beauchamp," *Proceedings S.P.R.*, Vol. XV. Part 40.

[3] *Mind*, October, 1903, vol. xii.

[4] I believe that the great weight of this evidence is not appreciated by many members of this Society. It was almost completely ignored by the author of *Human Personality*.

7.   *Trance Personalities**

"It goes without saying that, in order to occupy oneself with the supra-normal, it is necessary to admit theoretically the possibility thereof, or, what comes to the same thing, to be sceptical of the infallibility and the perfection of science as it now exists. If I consider it *a priori* absolutely impossible that an individual should know, long before the arrival of any telegram, of the accident which has just killed his brother on the other side of the world, or that another person can voluntarily move an object at a distance without the use of a thread in a manner inexplicable by the known laws of mechanics and physiology, it is clear that I shall raise my shoulders at every recital of telepathy, and shall not stir a step to take part in a séance with the most celebrated of mediums. Excellent means these for enlarging one's horizon and discovering novelties, to recline upon a completed science and a fore-gone conclusion, entirely convinced that the universe comes to an end at the opposite wall, and that nothing can exist or occur outside that system of daily routine which we have become accustomed to regard as marking the limits of the Real! That philosophy of the ostrich—illustrated formerly by the grotesque pedants at whom Galileo knew not whether to laugh or weep, who refused to put an eye to his telescope for fear of seeing things that had no official right to exist . . . that philosophy is still entertained by many brains petrified by intemperate reading of works of popularised science and by unintelligent attendance at university lectures, those two great intellectual dangers of our time."

* Originally published as Chap. XXXII in William McDougall's *An Outline of Ab-normal Psychology*. London: Methuen & Co., Ltd., 1926.

I open this chapter with the foregoing plea for the open mind. They are the words of the late Prof. Th. Flournoy, philosopher and medically trained psychologist, the investigator of the remarkable case of Hélène Smith, which I am about to present. I cite also after him two other similar pleas which are none the less effective for being of older date. "What shall we think of occultism and spiritism? The theory of these is obscure, the principles vague, uncertain, and somewhat visionary; but there are embarrassing facts, affirmed by serious men who have observed them or have learned them from others like themselves; to accept them all, or to deny them all, seems equally inconvenient, and I venture to say that in this matter, as in all extraordinary matters that go beyond the common rules there is a position to be found between the credulous and the strong-minded." And the second runs: "We are so far from knowledge of all natural agencies and of their diverse modes of action, that it would not be philosophic to deny any phenomena simply because they are inexplicable in the present state of our knowledge. But we ought to examine them with an attention the more painstaking, the more difficult it may seem to accept them as real." The former of these two pleas was made by La Bruyère, the second by the great exponent of the mechanical view of the universe, Laplace. Flournoy proposes to call the principle enunciated by La Bruyère "the principle of Hamlet," and formulates it concisely in the words—"all things are possible." The other he would call "the principle of Laplace" and state briefly in the form—"the weight of the evidence should be proportional to the strangeness of the alleged facts." Armed with these two principles, we may, says Flournoy, move among the alleged evidences of the supernormal without danger of making fools of ourselves, either by too great credulity or by too great incredulity.

In this chapter I propose to discuss a type of multiple personality which is less rare than the type described in the foregoing chapter [*An Outline of Abnormal Psychology*], but of which nevertheless the true interpretation and classification remain equally obscure and much more debated. These are the personalities manifested in the trances of persons regarded by the spiritists as "mediums." We may use the word "medium" without committing ourselves to accept its literal meaning, without accepting the view that such a person is really a medium of communication between the living and the dead. I would, however, enter a protest against the attitude of most men of science towards the problem raised by these cases, the attitude of dogmatic negation, the dogmatic negation of every interpretation that does not seem to conform readily with the general principles of science as at present formulated. Some of the acutest intellects of our time have paid much attention to this problem, and, failing to reconcile the evidence with the principles of science, have regarded it as demanding a continued suspension of judgment and as pointing to the possibility of a great extension of our knowledge of man's nature and a revision of the view of his place in the universe implied by the current formulations of science. Of the names of such men, I will mention only four—Henry Sidgwick, William James, Henri Bergson, and Hans Driesch.[1] When such men have studied the evidence over many years and have pronounced themselves convinced that it is of a nature which demands further careful study, it is surely a little presumptuous for young scientists who have never deigned to pay any attention to it to dismiss it with indifference or contempt. I shall not attempt to present or discuss in these pages the evidence in question. Any such attempt would require a large volume. But no survey of the field of abnormal psychology can properly ignore the manifestations of the mediumistic trance.

The common feature of these secondary personalities of the trance mediums is that they claim to be manifestations of personalities formerly living and now surviving in some disembodied condition. There are transitional cases, such as Sleeping Margaret,[2] in which the secondary personality makes this claim in a hesitating manner, and makes little or no endeavour to support it. But in the common run of such cases the trance personality seems to appear more or less full-blown, and to claim from the outset identity with some departed spirit. Another distinguishing mark of secondary personalities of this class is that their appearance commonly involves no appreciable change of the normal personality, no amnesia, no departure from health, except during the actual manifestation of the secondary personality. And, though they manifest themselves most commonly during a trance, or deep sleep-like condition of the normal personality, that is not always the case. In some instances they are manifested only by automatic writing, or, more rarely, by automatic speech. A further difference, consonant with the last, is that a secondary personality of this type, though it may, in some cases, claim to know something, much or little, of the inner life of the normal personality, does not usually share the memories of that personality or in any sense claim them as its own. Further, unlike the other types, it does not admit itself to be tied to the body of the medium or to share in its vicissitudes, but rather to be entirely independent of it, except in so far as the body is useful as a medium or instrument of communication.

There is, however, no sharp line to be drawn between the types we are comparing. The secondary personality in Case 57 [*An Outline of Abnormal Psychology*, p. 495] stoutly claimed to be the surviving spirit of a Spanish gipsy of the seventeenth century, sustained the rôle with very fair consistency, and was accepted as such by the primary personality and by many of her friends.

Among the many cases of the trance-medium type, one stands out pre-eminent by reason of the richness and variety of the phenomena presented, of the thoroughness and competence with which it was studied, and of the success attending the endeavour to throw the light of science upon its complexities; I mean the case of Hélène Smith, most admirably studied and reported by Th. Flournoy, late professor of psychology at Geneva.[3] The case combines almost all the features of interest discovered by other mediums, with the exception of the alleged supernormal physical phenomena; from every point of view it must rank as a classical case, and is deserving of our most respectful consideration.

Case 60. Hélène Smith was a young woman who filled with success a responsible position in a large house of business. In normal life she was in every respect a capable and altogether admirable person. Having become a participator in the séances of a private circle of spiritists, she very soon showed mediumistic powers, which rapidly developed and were manifested through a long period to a circle of admiring and deeply interested friends, many of whom were persons of much intelligence and cultivation. "Her mediumship has presented from the first a complex type . . .: visions in the waking state, accompanied by automatic speech and writing and auditory hallucinations. From the point of view of their content, these messages have for the most part referred to past events, of which the persons present were usually ignorant, but the reality of which was always verified by recourse to historical works or the traditions of the families concerned. To these phenomena of retrocognition or of supernormal memory were added occasionally, according to the circumstances, moral exhortations dictated automatically, more frequently in verse than in prose, and addressed to the persons present; medical consultations with prescriptions that were generally happily chosen; communications from relatives or friends recently deceased; lastly revelations as piquant as they were unverifiable upon the former lives [*i.e.*, previous incarnations] of the members of the circle, who, almost without exception, convinced spiritists as they were, learned with some astonishment that they were the reincarnation of Coligny, of Vergniaud, of the Princess Lamballe, or of other historical personages. It should be added that all these messages seemed to be more or less connected with the mysterious presence of a 'spirit' responding to the name of Leopold, who claimed to be the guide and protector of the medium."

At first the automatisms occurred in the waking state; but soon, as is not unusual in such cases, the medium fell into trance before or during the manifestations, and, on recovering her normal consciousness, had no recollection of the events of the trance period. This semi-voluntary falling into trance as soon as the conditions are set for a séance is in itself an interesting phenomenon common to many such cases. Flournoy discovered that during the automatisms of the waking state the medium (henceforward H) was subject to a variety of disturbances of sensory and motor functions. At the first trance Leopold appeared and took charge of the proceedings; and from this time onward the somewhat fragmentary communications of earlier sittings became elaborated into long-continued romantic dramas.

In addition to revelations of the life and personality of Leopold, these communications took the form for the most part of three dramatic stories; thus "we have to do with four subconscious creations of vast extent, which have evolved side by side through several years, manifesting in irregular alternations in the course of different séances, and often also in the same séance. They have, no doubt, a common origin in the depths of H and they have not developed without influencing one another and establishing certain points of contact in the course of time."

It appeared that H had twice lived upon the earth before her present incarnation. Once five hundred years ago as an Arab chief's daughter, who (Simandini by name) became the favourite wife of a Hindu prince. This prince, Sivrouka, reigned over a kingdom of Kanara, and constructed, in 1401, the fortress of Tchandraguiri. This romance was developed with a wealth of detail; and the astonishing features of it were, first, that research in old and little-known books on Indian history confirmed some of the details, such as the names of places and persons described; secondly, that Simandini uttered (in the trance automatisms) many Hindu words and phrases, sometimes appropriately used, sometimes mingled with other words which the experts failed to identify, and wrote also similar phrases in Arabic script. Further, the entranced medium would act the rôle of Simandini, putting other members of the circle into the vacant places of the drama. "All this various mimicry and this exotic speech have so strongly the marks of originality, of ease, of naturalness, that one asks with stupefaction, whence comes to this daughter of Lake Leman, without artistic training and without special knowledge of the Orient, a perfection of art which the best of actresses might attain only at the cost of prolonged studies or by residence on the banks of the Ganges."

Flournoy confesses that he has not been able to resolve the mystery, especially the Hindu language and the historical statements about the kingdom of Kanara, statements which after much research were verified in an old and rare book, to which, so far as could be ascertained, H had never had access. Nevertheless, he was able to show that this knowledge of the ancient kingdom showed distinct traces of its derivation by one unknown route or another from the one book in which its history is recorded, and that the few words of Arabic script were written in a manner which indicated that they reproduced visual images of the words retained without understanding of them. And he concludes that the whole Hindu drama was a subconsciously elaborated fantasy, incorporating very skilfully fragments of knowledge picked up in haphazard fashion. "I do not think that this is to do too much honour to the subliminal faculties—in view of all that we know of their promptitude, their delicacy, their perspicacity, sometimes so astonishingly fine and exquisite."

The second drama of reincarnation presented by H was that of Queen Marie Antoinette. This royal cycle also was developed with a wealth of imaginative detail, and but little of historical fact; and, since sources for such knowledge as was revealed were easily accessible, this knowledge presented no such difficult problem as that of the Hindu drama. Flournoy writes: "One sees in these examples the mixture of preparation, of repetition, and of improvisation, implied by the varied incidents. . . . It is probable that if one could witness, or if Mlle. Smith could remember, all the spontaneous automatisms which have contributed to the royal romance, night-dreams, hypnogogic visions, subconscious fantasies during waking, etc., one would be the spectator of endless imaginary conversations with the marquis, with Philippe, with Cagliostro, and all the fictitious personages who have appeared occasionally in the somnambulic scenes of Marie Antoinette. It was by such labours, submerged and ignored, and perhaps never interrupted, that were prepared and slowly elaborated the personality of the Queen of France, who burst forth and displayed herself with so much magnificence in the evenings spent with Philippe of Orleans and the Marquis de Mirabeau." And he points out that the whole drama was of just that compensatory nature which we have learned to expect in fantasies. H was a girl of refinement who secretly aspired to social distinctions and, like many such children, had conceived that perhaps she was in reality the child of some unknown magnates; and her very restricted mode of life and occupation had favoured the flowering of such fantasies. "They express the experience of the bitter irony of things, of the fruitless revolt, of the fatality ruling human life. They whisper that all that is happy and brilliant in life is but an illusion, soon dispelled. The daily negation of desires and of dreams by implacable and brutal reality could find in the hypnoid imagination no more adequate compensation, no symbol more emotionally satisfying, than the royal lady, whose existence seemed made for the heights of happiness and glory and ended on the scaffold."

The third drama consisted in the manifestation, through the medium, of a young man, the deceased son of a member of the circle, who claimed to have been translated to the planet Mars and who revealed with a wealth of detail the strange customs, the environment, and the language of the inhabitants of that planet. Here the interest of the investigator was centred in the language of the Martians rather than in the florid and fanciful descriptions of the flora, persons, customs, and habitations of the planet. A key that rendered possible a translation of the language having been obtained from the Martian visitor, a careful study of the abundant material showed that the language was essentially composed of European roots, and chiefly French. "I submit that the Martian language is a natural language in the sense that it has been automatically incubated without the conscious participation of Mlle. Smith, in the emotional state or by the secondary self which is the source of all the rest of this cycle." And Flournoy proceeds to display "the traits which seem to show that the inventor of all this subliminal language has never known any idiom other than the French, that she is much more alive to verbal forms than to the logical relations of ideas, and that she possesses in an eminent degree that infantile or puerile quality which I have already demonstrated in the author of the Martian romance." Of the latter he writes: "All the traits that I have demonstrated in the author of the Martian romance, and many others, may be resumed under one heading—the profoundly infantile quality. Only the candour and the imperturbable naïveté of childhood, which has no doubts because it has no knowledge, could launch itself seriously upon an enterprise such as the ostensibly exact and authentic drawings of all the features of an unknown world, or could attain an imaginary success by simply changing and colouring in Oriental travesties and bizarre puerilities the familiar environment of this earth. Never would an adult person, of moderate cultivation and some experience of life, waste her time in elaborating such fancies— Mlle. Smith less than most others, intelligent and mature as she is in her normal state." In other words, Flournoy shows abundant reasons for believing that the Martian romance was constructed by some infantile subconscious personality within the organisation of the medium, a personality not unlike Sally Beauchamp or Margaret (of the Fischer case), but one of a more romantic trend and one which never "came out" to dominate the whole organism in the waking state.

It remains only to tell the story of Leopold, a personality who, more closely than any of the other manifestations of this case, conforms to the type of the mediumistic trance personality or "control," the possessing or controlling and invading spirit of a deceased person.

Leopold played consistently the rôle of a discreet adviser and benevolent guardian to H. He manifested himself in visual hallucinations, in automatic speech and writing, and in various other automatisms, most commonly during trance, but also at other times. He disclosed the claim that beneath the pseudonym of Leopold was hidden the personality of the famous Cagliostro. Of him Flournoy writes: "One could not conceive of a being more independent, and more different from Mlle. Smith herself, having a character more personal, an individuality more marked, and an existence more positive."

Nevertheless Flournoy arrived at an adverse verdict upon this claim. He shows how, in all probability, the personality of this guardian spirit took shape in the depth of H's organism.

At ten years of age H had been protected from the attack of a savage dog by a stranger of imposing and romantic appearance. Flournoy traces to this incident the birth of Leopold. On several subsequent occasions when H was in various ways threatened, she hallucinated this figure. But it was not until the immersion in spiritistic séances had gone far that Leopold began to play a more prominent rôle. One of the spiritist circles frequented by the budding medium was of a very mixed character, and some of its junior members permitted themselves to attempt liberties not consonant with H's high standards of propriety. Flournoy finds reason to believe that these circumstances engendered in H a conflict between, on the one hand, her natural enjoyment of her rôle as the admired of all observers and her desire to continue it and, on the other hand, her equally natural reserve and modesty. Out of this conflict Leopold emerged, embodying (if so material a word may be used) or integrating the tendencies making for discretion and reserve. Under his influence H withdrew from that particular circle. Thus, says Flournoy, Leopold represents "the quintessence and the flourishing of the most hidden springs of the psychophysiologic organism. He sprang forth from that mysterious depth in which are immersed the ultimate roots of our individual being, roots by which we are connected with the species itself and perhaps with the absolute, and whence sound obscurely our instincts of physical and moral conservation, our sentiments related to the sexes, the modesty of soul and senses, all that which is most obscure, most intimate, and least rational in the individual." And Flournoy was able to trace the influences which seem to have played a determining part in casting this personality in the rôle of Cagliostro, that long-deceased Italian who in this reappearance knew nothing of the Italian language and displayed only a very sketchy acquaintance with the history of his former life.

Flournoy cites various incidents of which he writes: "These examples suffice to allow us to see how, from a purely psychological point of view, one may conceive the formation of this secondary personality. It is made up of normal pre-existing tendencies of a very intimate nature, which took form in the infancy and youth of Mlle. Smith, to synthesise themselves separately from the rest of the ordinary consciousness on the occasion of certain emotional shocks, and which, thanks to the favourable influence of the spiritistic exercises, have succeeded in assuming the form of a personality under the mask (of suggestive origin) of Leopold-Cagliostro."

Flournoy shows that there is no absolute separation between the mental organisation of Leopold and that of the normal H. "It is rather an interlacing, the limits of which are vague and difficult to define. Leopold knows and foresees and recalls much of which the normal personality knows absolutely nothing, owing simply to amnesia on her part or to her having always been ignorant of it. On the other hand, he by no means commands all the memories of H; he knows nothing of a large part of her daily life; even some striking incidents escape him entirely . . . the two personalities are not coextensive; each surpasses the other in certain points, so that one cannot say which, on the whole, is the more extensive."

Flournoy finds it impossible to affirm with confidence that the two personalities ever coexisted, were ever coconscious. He thinks it possible that the appearances pointing to such coconscious existence may really imply merely a rapid alternation of the two conscious personalities. But it is possible that, if he were able to review the facts of this case in the light of such more recent studies as those reported in the foregoing chapter, he would relinquish this natural prejudice against the recognition of coconscious personalities within the one organism.

Flournoy thus repudiates decidedly the spiritistic hypothesis of "possession," holding that the facts of the case of Hélène Smith do not call for it. At the same time he admits that some knowledge was displayed the acquisition of which by normal means would seem to have been well-nigh impossible; and he recognises that the assumption of the reality of telepathic communication would go far to account for these otherwise inexplicable facts. He sums up his conclusions in the following wise words. "The fact of the primitive nature and the different ages of the diverse hypnoidal lucubrations of Mlle. Smith seems to me to constitute the most interesting feature of her mediumship. It tends to show that the secondary personalities are probably at their origin . . . phenomena of reversion of the ordinary actual personality, survivals or momentary returns of inferior phases, which have been left behind for a longer or shorter time and which normally would have been absorbed in the development of the individual in place of springing forth in strange proliferations. Just as teratology illustrates and explains embryology, and as both of them contribute to illuminate anatomy, so one may hope that the study of the facts of mediumship will contribute to furnish us one day with a true and fertile view of normal mental development, which in return will enable us better to understand the appearance of these curious phenomena, and that the whole of psychology will gain a better and more exact conception of human personality."

I have cited Flournoy's account of this case at some length not only because it combines so many interesting features and was studied and reported in a manner that is beyond criticism, but also because it is historically interesting in that it shows that Flournoy had anticipated much that is now becoming common doctrine, and the credit for which is commonly assigned to later writers. We see how Flournoy, writing in the nineteenth century, made use of the conceptions of conflict, repression, and regression, and how, unlike so many of his contemporaries, he saw that such cases cannot be understood in terms of any purely associationist or intellectualist psychology, but only in terms of one which takes account of the instinctive tendencies of our nature and recognises that the normal unitary personality is the product of a process by which these diverse tendencies are integrated into one harmonious system.

OTHER TRANCE PERSONALITIES

I do not propose to describe any other cases of this type, but will add merely a few words concerning some of the most famous cases.

Of all such cases, those of Mrs. Piper and Mrs. Leonard are perhaps the most deserving of attention, by reason of the care with which they have been studied and the extensive evidence of supernormal knowledge furnished by them. These two cases are in many respects very similar. Mrs. Piper's trances have recurred through many years, and, though certain changes in the personalities and in the modes of communication have occurred, such changes have been less striking than the continuity and constancy of the manifestations. There are certain "controls," personalities who, like Leopold in the Hélène Smith case, play the part of master of ceremonies and of mediator between the investigator and other personalities. But sometimes these other personalities, some of whom claim to be identical with deceased persons wellknown to the investigator, seem to manifest themselves directly in the automatic speech or writing of the medium. In some of these instances the speech or writing seems to reveal traits that impress the observer as highly characteristic of the personality impersonated. But the chief interest and the most difficult problem presented is the fact that the "automatic" speech or writing seems to contain, among much that may seem irrelevant, statements of fact that, so far as careful investigation can ascertain, could not have come to the knowledge of the medium in any normal fashion, any fashion recognised by science, or, in other words, through the senses of the medium.

In face of the evidence of such supernormally acquired knowledge in these two cases (and the same is true in less degree of other cases) all, or almost all, of those who have competently and open-mindedly considered the evidence acknowledge themselves in the presence of a dilemma: either the personalities are what they claim to be, or they are secondary personalities of the mediums who have the faculty of acquiring knowledge in ways not recognised by science.

In view of other evidence for the reality of telepathy, the direct communication of mind with mind without the use of sense-perception, the least extravagant hypothesis for the interpretation of the facts is the hypothesis that such subconscious or secondary personalities have wide-reaching powers of telepathic reception. It is only fair to add that some very competent students of such cases hold strongly the opinion that the telepathic hypothesis will not cover the facts. Some claim that it is necessary to postulate at least far-reaching "clairvoyance" in addition to telepathy. It is obvious that, if both telepathy and "clairvoyance" be postulated, the possibility of finding in such cases evidence that will suffice to establish the claim of identity with, or communication with, deceased personalities, becomes very remote.

NOTES

[1] Cf. especially Prof. Driesch's recent work, "The Crisis in Psychology."

[2] P. 502 [*An Outline of Abnormal Psychology*].

[3] "Des Indes à la Planète Mars," Geneva, 1899. The study of Flournoy was supplemented by those of several of his colleagues, and no less than seven books have been devoted to this famous case.

8.   The Case of Margery

∿∿∿∿∿∿∿∿∿∿∿∿∿∿∿∿∿∿∿∿∿∿∿∿∿∿∿∿∿

A.   The "Margery Mediumship" *

It might have been hoped that the adverse verdict of the *Scientific American* Committee, followed as it was by Mr. Hoagland's article in the *Atlantic Monthly* for November, 1925, would have satisfied all but a few resolute believers that the claims made on behalf of this medium have no solid foundation. But it seems clear that no such result has been attained: Margery, it would seem, has recently been fêted by the American Society for Psychical Research, and photographed in the newspapers as the recipient of a silver cup from a group of English scientists; and her many partisans, some of whom are persons of excellent standing, continue to make public large claims on her behalf, claims which, if they were well founded, should establish her as perhaps the most remarkable medium[1] of all time, by reason of the great variety of her alleged supernormal physical phenomena. Recently an influential group of the Margery partisans has distributed very widely a pamphlet of 109 pages.[2] In that pamphlet the most far-reaching claims are renewed; but, as its title implies, the pamphlet is mainly concerned to impugn the good faith and the competence of those members of Harvard University who, after devoting some time to the study of the case, have returned verdicts unfavourable to the claim of supernormality of the phenomena. As I have personally investigated the case, taking part in many sittings in the years 1923, '24, and '25; as the onus of the *Scientific American's* Committee fell chiefly on me; and as I have been instrumental, directly and indirectly, in

---

* Originally published in *Psyche*, Vol. 7, No. 2 (1926), pp. 15-30.

interesting other members of Harvard University in it, and have been in touch with most of them during and since their investigations, I feel that my position both qualifies me to review the evidence and lays some obligation upon me to reply to the pamphlet.

It would be futile to attempt to lay before the public the detailed accounts of all or even of a few of the phenomena. Such an account would be of little service, even if it were widely read, as it could hardly hope to be. In such a matter the general public necessarily forms its opinion at second hand; and its opinion as to the validity of the claims of the medium must in the main depend on its opinion as to the relative competence, good faith, and absence of vitiating bias on the part of the opposed parties—that which asserts and that which denies that the case for supernormality has been established, the Pros and the Cons.

It is very easy to write detailed descriptions of sittings with mediums which shall contain no false statement and which will induce the average reader to declare—Either this *is* genuine mediumship, or the reporter is a liar or utterly incompetent. Yet such a description may, in virtue of omission of important details, details either unobserved or unreported, give a totally misleading impression. The Margery partisans claim that the case must stand or fall by the evidence contained in notes of sittings dictated during or immediately after each sitting. No incident or observation not at once recorded in the presence of the medium and her possible collaborators is, according to their arbitrary rules of evidence, to be taken into account. Now it must be freely admitted that, if this rule of evidence be acceptable, the Pros have an excellent case. It is reminiscent of some of the technicalities of the law by insistence on which the clever criminal lawyer in America so often and so flagrantly succeeds in freeing his guilty client. Such ruling cannot be accepted by any honest and unbiased critic of the evidence. Let me give a concrete illustration. At one dark sitting a luminous disc was lifted three times from the table when all hands and feet were adequately controlled. The head of the medium was also supposed to be controlled. I was entirely baffled by the first and second of these movements. Fortunately during the third movement I detected what was to me convincing evidence that the medium's head had escaped from control and that the disc was lifted by her mouth. I was under no moral obligation to report this observation in the presence of the medium. I did not do so, and signed the notes of the sitting which contained no mention of this crucial observation; without it the notes seem to report a supernormal phenomenon, an instance of telekinesis three times repeated; with it they amount to nothing in the way of evidence. I could cite many instances of this sort.

It is clear that, if the observer were compelled to report every observation in the presence of the medium, he would have little chance of arriving at a decisive opinion or of detecting trickery; he would never be given the opportunity to repeat or confirm his observation of suspicious incidents. The observer, if he were bound in this way, would have to rely upon a single crucial demonstration of trickery, a thing which, if he abides by his promise to keep intact the circle of clasped hands and otherwise abstain from interference with the phenomena, he has very little chance of achieving.

Here I would point out that there are three distinct procedures that may be followed by any investigator of such physical mediumship. First, he may, on the first or an early occasion on which he feels sure, or strongly suspects, that trickery is in progress, venture a sudden *coup*, such as seizing a furtive limb. I have done it myself in other cases with success. It is the method natural to any one already convinced of the fraudulent nature of the mediumship and impatient, for one reason or another, of prolonged investigation. But it is a hazardous procedure, and, even when it fully convinces the observer himself, it may often fail to convince others who, in the darkness and confusion of the moment, fail to follow the rapid course of events. He who adopts this method is apt to find himself in the situation that his statement of what he did and what happened is flatly and indignantly denied by the medium, whose partisans then accept her verdict rather than his. And, even if he succeeds in effecting a convincing demonstration of trickery in this one instance, he will have produced little effect; the partisans will pooh-pooh it, probably alleging that all genuine mediums occasionally use subconscious trickery, and that, besides, no one can be quite sure of what really happened; the investigator, they will say, had probably decided to prove trickery at all costs, even the cost of truth and honour.

A second method is to devise an absolutely fool-proof or trick-proof test; such, for example, as the displacement of objects within a sealed bottle; or the movement of a weighted scale in a sealed chamber. This is the method that recommends itself to those who are already convinced of the occasional occurrence of supernormal physical phenomena and seek a convincing demonstration of it. It is the method that was followed, under the direction of Dr. D. Comstock, during a large part of the sittings with Margery of the *Scientific American's* Committee. I acquiesced in this somewhat reluctantly, foreseeing that it meant so much lost time—a forecast that was amply justified by the sequel of events, for nothing definite came of these experiments.

The third method is that which in this case, as in all others that have made out a strong prima facie case for supernormal powers, commends itself to me; and it is that to which I strictly adhered in the Margery case, except in so far as I took some part in attempting the second method out of deference to my colleagues. This third method consists in accepting all the medium's conditions, faithfully abiding by them, in the hope that thus, if genuine supernormal phenomena occur, one may attain a conviction of their reality; and that also, if trickery is used, close observation on repeated occasions will discover the fact and something of the *modus operandi.*

Within the limits of this third method, we may again distinguish two varieties. The one is to concentrate upon some particular phenomenon, such as an apparent instance of telekinesis; and, when it occurs, to argue from the conditions believed to have obtained that it could, or could not, have been produced by normal methods; if the latter seems to be the conclusion of the argument, the instance is then proclaimed as an established instance of supernormal happenings. I may, I think without injustice, allege that this was the method favoured by Mr. E. J. Dingwall, the expert of the English Society for Psychical Research, in his dealings with the Margery case in January, 1925. To my mind this is a very questionable method. I prefer the second variety, which may be described as follows: Observe with the utmost care everything that occurs in the séance room, as well as outside it, so far as this is possible; then collate all the recorded observations, including those that may seem at first sight to have little or no relevance. Pile up in this way through many sittings a mass of evidence; take everything into account; weigh the probabilities and try gradually to reach a sure conclusion. Things may occur that seem at the time to throw no light, to be quite irrelevant, but which later become significant. Mr. Dingwall's method seems to be to brush aside such incidents with the remark: "In these cases queer irrelevant things always happen; don't let us be led away by these from the central phenomenon, concentrate on that." Such a prescription seems to me a decidedly dangerous guide for the participator in dark séances. It is precisely by reckoning on the natural tendency to follow this prescription that the conjuror chiefly relies to attain his effects.

If, when the second variety of the third method has been applied throughout a varied series of sittings, the observer has failed to detect any indications of trickery or bad faith on the part of the medium or of any member of the circle, he may justly feel that he is hot on the scent of a real marvel, something new to be added to the achievements of science. If on the other hand evidences of trickery accumulate—what then? Should the serious inquirer stop short as soon as he is fairly well convinced of a single instance of trickery? He may and, I think, should go on until he has acquired similar conviction in respect of a number of phenomena. Each such case then strengthens his confidence in his former conclusion; the several phenomena, thus separately suspect, rightly co-operate in his mind to strengthen his confidence in his conclusion that trickery is used and extensively used. Must he still persevere until he shall have obtained similar good evidence of trickery in respect of every phenomenon produced? In the Margery case that would be an impossible task; for the medium has proved remarkably fertile in the production of novelties; a conscientious observer might pursue his investigations for many years without ever attaining good evidence of trickery in respect of all types of phenomena produced. At some point he is justified in stopping and saying: "I have abundant evidence that trickery is extensively used; so extensively that, if there be any residue of really supernormal phenomena, I cannot hope to prove it amongst so much that is spurious." He cannot hope to prove the negative, to prove that this medium never did and never can produce a supernormal phenomenon. If you tell me that you can leap over a twenty-foot wall, and I watch you try and fail twenty times, I am justified in concluding that you cannot do it, though I cannot absolutely prove the thing to be impossible for you, nor prove that you have never done it. And so it is with Margery. That is the point I had reached in February of 1925 when I returned my adverse verdict to the *Scientific American.* Margery might be, for all I could prove, a great medium; but she had failed to convince me of it; on the contrary, I had become convinced that deliberate trickery had been used in the production of a considerable proportion of the phenomena. At that time much public interest in the case had been excited, and I was known to be a member of the committee of the *Scientific American,* which was pressing for a verdict. Therefore, although I was willing and anxious to prolong my observation of the case, I published my general conclusion with some indications of the supporting evidence (in the Boston *Transcript* of Feb. 18th, 1925) well knowing that this action would terminate my opportunities for observation. In the spring of that year appeared Mr. Malcolm Bird's book *Margery* and several other manifestoes of the Pros. Mr. Bird's pronouncedly *ex parte* account of the case provoked me to make a more detailed statement of the grounds of my adverse opinion in an article published in the *Journal of the American Society for Psychical Research* in June 1925.

Meanwhile, throughout the early months of 1925, a group (consisting of Mr. H. Hoagland, a graduate student of the psychological department of Harvard, and of four young instructors of the same University) was attending Margery sittings and becoming deeply interested in the case.

In May of 1925, Mr. Hoagland reported to me that all or most of the members of this group had become convinced of the supernormality of Margery's phenomena, and that he himself was inclining in the same direction, though reserving his judgement. I invited the group to a conference and found that they seemed to be, as Mr. Hoagland had reported, pretty thoroughly convinced that they were observing supernormal phenomena of the most remarkable kinds; they were decidedly resentful of my sceptical attitude which implied that the phenomena were produced by trickery, either conscious and deliberate or possibly subconscious. I urged the group to persevere in its investigation, keeping their minds open as far as possible and refining their methods of control; and I offered them, with this object in view, the use of a room in the Harvard psychological laboratory. This advice and this offer were accepted, and throughout the following weeks the group (assisted by the advice and occasional presence at the sittings of several professors of the scientific departments of Harvard) held a series of sittings in a room of the laboratory. I left Cambridge about the middle of June; and before my departure Mr. Hoagland reported to me that the new series of sittings was confirming the group in their favourable view of the phenomena, and that he himself was so well impressed that he proposed to offer a study of the Margery mediumship as a thesis in support of his candidacy for the Ph.D. degree; in this design I encouraged him, merely stipulating that he should make his investigations thorough and conclusive.

Early in July I was informed, by letter and by a visit to me in the country from Messrs. Hoagland and Code, of the dramatic and somewhat unsatisfactory conclusion of their investigations, as reported in Mr. Hoagland's article in the *Atlantic Monthly*. For the benefit of those who have not read Mr. Hoagland's article, the essence of it may be concisely stated as follows. During the last two or three sittings of the group, about the end of June, the members discovered, or believe and allege that they discovered, clear evidence that Margery was making use of means which enabled her to evade their control, which control they had up to that time believed to be adequate. In the light of this new insight into the methods of the medium, they alleged that they were able to explain to their own satisfaction, as the products of normal processes, all the phenomena they had observed up to that time, and which they had regarded, or been strongly inclined to regard, as produced in some supernormal manner. Mr. Code appeared to be very confident of the truth of his view, namely, that, though all the Margery phenomena were produced by the tricky use of normal means, yet all the tricky conduct involved was subconsciously directed, the medium in her normal waking personality remaining entirely innocent and ignorant of the means used. Although I had myself suggested this possibility in my *Transcript* article, I was not able to reconcile it with many facts which indicated very clearly that Margery had prepared in a perfectly waking state the apparatus required for the production of some of the phenomena.

The publication of Mr. Hoagland's article provoked a storm of indignant protest from the Pros. And, in the course of publishing their protests and their renewed affirmations of the supernormal nature of the phenomena, they have not scrupled to impute, to all or most of those who have expressed adverse opinions, the concealment of and denial, from the most unworthy motives, of their supposed true opinions; that is to say the Pros have repeatedly insinuated or alleged that the Cons are privately convinced of the truly supernormal nature of Margery's phenomena, and that, from fear of ridicule or of being thrown out of their academic posts or from other similar despicable motives, they have entered into a conspiracy to deny what they know to be true, at the cost of blackening the reputation of the medium and her friends and supporters. This charge of the Pros involves also the imputation that Harvard University is so grossly intolerant of freedom of research and opinion that it would discharge from its rolls any of its teaching staff who might be known to express acceptance of any inexplicable phenomena, any phenomena not explicable by the principles of science at present in vogue.

The Cons, on the other hand, have carefully abstained from all such reproaches and imputations, except in so far as the expression of their adverse opinion inevitably implies the view that Margery, or other habitual members of her circle, have consciously or subconsciously made use of trickery.

It is, then, for the public to judge between the claims of the two groups, the Pros and the Cons. The Pros group comprises a large number of persons of excellent standing, intelligence, and education, especially Dr. Mark W. Richardson, a physician of excellent reputation, who has actively espoused the cause of Margery and whose name heads the list of authors of *Margery, Harvard, Veritas*. The Cons believe that Dr. Richardson and most, perhaps all, of the Pro group are honestly deceived; and they are able to point to many instances of the past in which numbers of equally reputable and capable persons have long entertained similar errors in regard to mediums afterwards shown to be thoroughly and indisputably fraudulent.

It is necessary for the guidance of the public to set forth the leading facts about the Cons. If it should appear that all or most of them have given evidence of minds resolutely closed to acceptance of any supernormal phenomena, that would justify the public in attaching relatively little weight to their opinions. If on the other hand it should appear that all or most of them have approached the investigation with open minds and in a sincere spirit of inquiry, their adverse opinions must carry great weight. It is easy to show that, with a single possible exception, all the leading Cons answer to the latter description. The possible exception is Houdini. I do not question the sincerity of his motives and intentions; but it must be admitted that he has by his actions and utterances clearly shown his conviction that supernormal phenomena do not and cannot occur and that the sole function of the psychic researcher is to discover the fraudulent means used to produce alleged supernormal phenomena. He is entitled to his opinion; and it is based, in part at least, on extensive experience.

Of the other Cons Dr. W. F. Prince, the research officer of the Boston S.P.R. deserves to be mentioned first. He has had large experience in investigation of supernormal phenomena; and no one I think has ever seriously charged him with lack of courage or with unreadiness to admit the reality of supernormal phenomena when the evidence seems good. He has published accounts of a number of his own investigations which have led him to believe in the occasional occurrence of such phenomena; notable among these is his recent book, *The Psychic in the House.*

Next comes Mr. H. Hoagland, the author of the *Atlantic Monthly* article. He is a man of twenty-eight years, well trained in the physical sciences as well as in biology and psychology. He approached the Margery case in a somewhat sceptical spirit, but open-mindedly prepared to accept any conclusions to which the evidence might lead him. And as a matter of fact he did become for a time very favourably disposed towards the acceptance of the Margery phenomena; an attitude which was radically changed only when he discovered, as he believed, unmistakable evidence of trickery during his last few sittings. All of the other four members of his group, the so-called Harvard group, are young men of some intellectual distinction, and of sufficient ability and education to become instructors in Harvard University. They are men of literary rather than strictly scientific training; and all of them were, I believe, favourably disposed by their general outlook to the acceptance of supernormal phenomena. Mr. Foster Damon had made a very thorough study of the history and literature of the field. Mr. Grant Code is an expert amateur conjuror. Mr. Hillyer and Mr. Marshall have alert inquiring minds. And, as has been said, all of them were for a considerable time (with the partial exception of Mr. Hoagland) ready warmly to defend the favourable interpretation of Margery and her mediumship. The professors who incidentally assisted at some of the Harvard sittings need perhaps hardly be mentioned; since their opportunities of observation were few. It should, however, be noted that they were sufficiently open-minded to give some time to the investigation, and that their contact with members of the Harvard group of investigators seems to have satisfied all of them of the good faith of the group and of the soundness of their adverse conclusions.

Lastly, there is myself. For more than twenty years I have been a member of the council of the English S.P.R. and have filled the presidential chair of that society, and also, to my cost, and from a strong sense of duty alone, the presidential chair of the American S.P.R. I have, during more than these twenty years, appeared in print again and again as one of the few active supporters of psychical research among men of science of established reputation. I may add that I am and have long been, not only open-minded towards the occurrence of supernormal phenomena, but actually a little biased in their favour; because I have realized that the establishment of their occurrence would be a heavy blow against the materialistic and mechanistic dogmas which so largely rule the scientific world and against which I have fought with my pen ever since my first attack upon them published in 1897. I have taken part in a considerable number of investigations of alleged supernormal phenomena; but hitherto have failed to find convincing evidence in any case, but have found rather much evidence of fraud and trickery. I have recently expressed my attitude as honestly as possible in an article in the *Forum* (April, 1926) in which I call upon men of science to give full and open-minded support to psychical research.

Perhaps it should be added that Dr. Daniel Comstock, a physicist of high standing, who has convinced himself by careful study of other cases of the reality of certain supernormal phenomena, gave much time and effort to the study of the Margery case, but failed to obtain such evidence as he felt would justify the pronouncement of a favourable verdict in this case.

The Cons thus constitute a group than which it would be difficult to conceive one better disposed towards the phenomena, yet of a nature to carry weight with the public if they should pass a favourable verdict. Their unfavourable verdict, then, must *a fortiori* carry much weight. The Pros suggest that all these men have given long hours of tedious labour, in most cases repeatedly throughout many months, in the endeavour to secure irrefutable evidence of supernormal phenomena, and then, having become convinced that they have found what they have arduously sought, have with one consent turned about and denied with slanderous lies what they knew to be the truth. The imputation is preposterous.

No less preposterous and slanderous is the imputation made by the Pros against Harvard University. Harvard needs not any defence from me in this respect. Her honourable record as a defender of freedom of opinion and research is above reproach and is well known to the world. I will add that, when in the summer of 1925 Houdini wrote to President Lowell drawing his attention to the fact that investigation of the Margery case was or had been conducted in the psychological laboratory and fervently warned him that the reputation of the University was thereby endangered, Mr. Lowell merely forwarded the letter to me without comment, in order that I might be aware of its contents. I will add this also: if, tomorrow or at any time, Margery or any other medium shall convince me of the reality of any supernormal phenomenon, I will cheerfully make public announcement of the fact; and I am convinced that by so doing I shall neither endanger my position in Harvard nor lose in any degree the esteem of my colleagues in that institution. No doubt I should thereby confirm in their opinion of me certain learned young men in the cruder institutions of learning in America who, because I do not share their metaphysical prejudices in favour of dogmatic materialism, have long regarded me as suspect in the scientific sense. But that consequence I am prepared to accept with equanimity.

Having thus reviewed the opposing parties, I wish to add some account of an alleged supernormal phenomenon which occupies as it were a key position in the whole strange story, namely the appearance of the so-called 'ectoplasm'. It is alleged that certain mediums have the power to cause, or serve as the medium by aid of which some intelligent and purposive agency causes, a mass of tissue to issue from the body of the medium and to take various forms, sometimes the form of a limb or face, sometimes that of ill-defined rods. And these ectoplasmic protuberances, remaining continuous with the body of the medium by some strand of tissue, are alleged to project themselves in various directions; to move actively and spontaneously independently of all action of the medium's normal muscular system; and to exert, in so moving, considerable force intelligently and purposively directed. It is commonly alleged by those who accept the reality of the ectoplasm that, in it and its strange power of movement, we are to find the explanation of the various forms of telekinesis, the movements of objects produced mysteriously by other than normal means.

Such telekinetic phenomena form a very large and important proportion of all the alleged physical phenomena of mediumship. This is true of the Margery case; and the ectoplasmic theory is offered by her partisans as affording the explanation of her many telekinetic phenomena. Let us glance for a moment at some of these. In the dark the séance table is moved, partially or wholly lifted, or violently overturned; smaller or larger objects are lifted from the table, waved to and fro, or passed from the table to the floor and back again, or thrown across the room with some precision of aim; and, it is claimed, they are sometimes swung up above the medium's head and there mysteriously suspended.

Among the most striking of such telekinetic phenomena witnessed by me was the sliding of a piano-stool across the floor of a room, while the medium and all other persons visible were seated in an adjoining room at a distance from the stool of some twenty feet. This took place twice in a fair red light.* It is clear that, if this was accomplished by the agency of an ectoplasmic rod, it must have been invisible in fair red light and have returned, almost immediately after accomplishing its astonishing task, into the body of the medium who sat fully clothed among the group of observers. It is true that, on each

* [A reference to the practice of using only red lamps or bulbs for lighting during séances. Normal white light supposedly represents a hazard to the medium's health under séance conditions, but infra-red light rays are usually considered harmless. *Ed.*]

of these two occasions, the stool slid across the floor in a straight line towards and nearly up to the edge of an open register. And it is true that the conditions imposed forbade any examination of the room immediately before or after the occurrence, facts which inevitably suggest to all but resolute believers that the stool was pulled across the floor by a fine thread and that the power was supplied not by or through ectoplasm, but rather by a very human hand beneath the register. But I mention the instance as illustrating the extent of the telekinetic powers attributed to Margery's ectoplasm by her admirers.

It was therefore with keen curiosity that I joined the small circle of observers constituted by Mr. Dingwall on his arrival in January, 1925. For 'Walter', the control, had promised that he would make the long-talked-of ectoplasm visible to this select group. For many months we had been as it were stepping over the invisible ectoplasm, carefully getting out of its way, and avoiding all interference with its movements, and especially avoiding breaking its continuity with the medium. For Walter had insisted on these precautions; and he had dwelt on the awful consequences to the medium, if the ectoplasm should be ruptured or rudely handled in any way.

At the first full-dress sitting the 'ectoplasm' duly appeared. We were in total darkness, but for a few pieces of cardboard smeared with luminous paint and laid upon the table. After an interval of waiting, something moved on the table at the medium's edge of it. I condense the reports of several sittings at which the 'ectoplasm' appeared on the table, as follows. The Ec. moved in a somewhat spasmodic fashion, like an inspired jelly fish flopping about the table. It raised, or seemed to raise, the luminously painted ring of cardboard; it cautiously crept over the border of a larger sheet of luminous cardboard, so that we saw part of it vaguely silhouetted; it caused, or seemed to cause, violent movements of small objects on the table, e.g. on one occasion a cork lying near the medium's edge of the table was suddenly projected against the necktie of the sitter opposite, as though an expert finger and thumb had flipped it.

On several occasions we were allowed to see the Ec. for two or even three seconds in dim red light; and, most gruesome of all, we were several times allowed to palpate it very gently and to explore with our finger tips a few inches along the clammy cord which seemed to pass down between the thighs of the medium.

It should be explained that the medium wore on these occasions a single ample warm bath-robe. We were allowed to satisfy ourselves that the Ec. emerged by the channel of normal parturition; and it was explained that its emergence was a process closely allied to normal parturition. Finally, it was photographed by flashlight on several occasions.

Let us now inquire what grounds were there for regarding this 'ectoplasm' as a supernormally produced phenomenon.

First, its movements. If these were not impressed upon it by the muscular action of one or other of the persons at the table, they implied not only intrinsic power of movement, but also the power of intelligently and purposively directing its own movements. I must assert, very categorically, that the movements afforded no conclusive evidence of this kind. Careful analysis of all instances shows that every movement of the ectoplasm may well have been impressed upon it by normal muscular action. The evidence in detail would be tedious. In general, the ectoplasm moved pretty freely when the Medium's right hand was controlled only by C. (the medium's husband) and by a luminous band on the large loose sleeve of the bath-robe (which band did curiously move coincidently with every movement of the ectoplasm).

On the single occasion on which continuous adequate control of both hands of M. was permitted, Ec. made no movement beyond a very slight retreating movement; this might easily have been communicated to it by the cord which passed down between M's thighs. And on this occasion the left hand of M. was frankly used to lift it from M's lap to the table. Here then is the outstanding fact, namely, that Ec. moved freely whenever conditions were such as to permit M. to impart movement to it. It moved not at all when this possibility was ruled out. We were invited to believe that Ec. issued also from other orifices of M's body, especially the meatus of the ear. But there was no supporting evidence of this. Here, as in many other instances, a vast amount of suggestion was used of a kind likely to induce such belief. And here, as throughout, it is of the first importance to distinguish between actual observations and suggested beliefs.

The only remaining ground for regarding the Ec. as supernormally produced is the moral improbability of the projection of it upon the table by normal means. We have then a moral improbability over against a biological improbability. And who shall weigh them? Dr. M. Richardson in a letter to me accuses me of having made an "unspeakable insinuation", when I expressed the opinion that the Ec. was nothing but a piece of animal lung surgically manipulated. But we have the fact that, on at least one occasion, M's left hand was used to extract the Ec. and throw it upon the table. May not the same hand have played a still larger rôle, even if only subconsciously, in the preparatory stages? The incident seems to lessen the moral improbability, which Dr. Richardson seems to regard as an absolute bar to any questioning of this phenomenon.

Now this question of moral improbability is central in the whole affair. If we refuse to criticize one phenomenon on the ground of moral improbability, we can draw no line and are committed to accept every one of Margery's phenomena at their face value, with our eyes resolutely and honourably shut. We shall have to accept as genuine the *apport* of the white pigeon; which seems too much for even Mr. Malcolm Bird's strong stomach. We shall have to accept as supernormal the two slidings of the piano-stool across the floor, a phenomenon which bore every conceivable mark of a simple bit of trickery. We shall have to accept the parafin-glove incident, which bore an equally imposing array of similar marks. If Walter can do these astonishing things on one occasion, why does he not do them again, instead of fiddling for months over a tricky little bell-box? There is only one plausible answer—namely, he knows that if he should attempt them again, the trick will be exposed; that is, if any critically minded person should be present.

The weight of moral improbability is, I say, a factor of the first importance in this case. This, rather than any critical weighing of the facts of observation, has been the main factor in inducing so many persons of good capacity and education to accept the Margery phenomena. They reason somewhat as follows. Here are two persons of good social standing who allege the occurrence of an array of marvels and deny that they use normal means to produce them (for it is rightly felt and argued that Margery cannot have produced all these effects by means of trickery without some connivance from her husband). It seems impossible to suggest any adequate motives that could have led these persons into a course of elaborate deception and have sustained them to prosecute it in a manner that can only be called heroic. Further, they say, similar supernormal phenomena have been proved to occur, in the presence of other mediums; then why should they not occur in this case? Why trouble to examine the evidence so sceptically? Even if these phenomena are faked, they are serving to make known a great truth, just as William James's self-confessed faking of the movements of the heart during a lantern demonstration by Prof. Bowditch, served to illustrate to the students an important truth.

There are two parts to this argument. Let me deal first with the latter. The occurrence of the supernormal physical phenomena of mediumship is not established. Only the favourable verdict of organized science can establish the reality of their occurrence; and we are very far from any such state of affairs. It may well be that, in all of the many alleged instances, the observers have been honestly mistaken, as they certainly have been in many of them. The question is of the most crucial and vital importance. If and when the occurrence of such phenomena should be established, science would be revolutionized. No other scientific discovery that has ever been made could rank in the same class with such a result. Hence, since the observations have to be made under peculiarly difficult circumstances, especially the absence of good light, it behoves us to move with the utmost caution in making observations and drawing conclusions. I will not say that moral probabilities and improbabilities should be given no weight. That would be to take up an impossible position. We accept all scientific conclusions on the strength of the moral improbability that men of science have entered into a conspiracy to deceive the rest of the world.

As regards the moral improbability in the case in hand, I confess that it is great; so great, that, in face of it, I have literally sweated with doubt and anxiety and lain awake pondering it for long hours. But the obstinate fact remains that all over and about the Margery phenomena, so far as extensively observed by myself, are marks of trickery and deception. The advocate replies: What of it? Is it not well recognized that nearly all the best accredited mediums occasionally indulge in trickery? I reply: Yes, that seems to be true; but the fact renders the strictest scrutiny of the evidence all the more imperative. It renders it altogether improper to pile up a great number and variety of phenomena each of which may rightly be described as difficult to explain away, and to argue that all these together should rightly exert a cumulative effect inclining us to a favourable verdict. It renders it necessary to demand one or two clear-cut phenomena repeated again and again under satisfactory conditions, conditions that can be varied in such a way as to rule out every conceivable possibility of the production of the phenomena by normal means.

I will add in this connection that some of the oldest and most active workers of the English Society for Psychical Research, who for more than forty years have had intimate knowledge of nearly every case of physical mediumship, remain sceptical about the occurrence of supernormal physical phenomena, even though they are convinced of the reality of supernormal happenings in the mental sphere.

With these considerations in mind, let us return to M's ectoplasm. We have seen that the only ground for accepting it is the moral improbability of its being a faked phenomenon. Now we must consider positive reasons for so regarding it.

First, the inconsistency of the claims made for the 'ectoplasm.' We are asked to believe that it moves stools across the room at twenty feet from the medium, levitates tables and other objects to considerable heights measured not only in inches but in feet, and performs the most delicate manipulations of a highly intelligent kind. Yet, when at last it appears upon the table for our inspection by ear and eye and touch (all grossly handicapped in their exercise by the conditions rigidly imposed by Walter) it appears as a semi-gelatinous membranous mass of vague shape, which, when M's hand is free to move it, flops awkwardly about the table, and, when M's hand is not free to move it, remains inert and motionless.

Further, it must be added that several of the photographs of the ectoplasm taken by flashlight show it as a mass that bears a very striking resemblance to a piece of animal lung cut to present some crude resemblance to a hand. Some of these photographs show what I and several other men of biological and medical training regard as the appearance of the pleural surfaces, also cut alveolar surfaces with sections across bronchial tubes, bloodvessels and, lastly, the wind-pipe or trachea, forming the cord which during the sittings was observed to pass from the mass of ectoplasm on the table to the medium's body, generally between the thighs. Surely one is not over sceptical if one hesitates to accept this ectoplasm as necessitating a complete reversal of all the teachings of science!

NOTES

[1] I use the word 'medium' in a non-committal sense.
[2] Entitled *Harvard, Margery, Veritas.*

B.   Claims of "Margery" Rejected *

The famous Margery case is over so far as the Scientific American Psychic Investigation is concerned. On February 12, 1925, two members of the Psychic Committee released for publication formal statements announcing that they had been unable to obtain convincing evidence of the supernormal production of physical phenomena. Together with the statements issued previously by other committee members, this constitutes a four-to-one vote against the claims of the medium.

"Margery" is not a professional medium. She is, in fact, Mrs. Le Roi G. Crandon, the wife of a well-known surgeon of Boston. In the issue for November, 1924, we published statements from four members of the committee, dealing with her case. After the issuance of these statements, Dr. Prince and Dr. McDougall continued the investigation of the case. The other three members of the committee have had no further sittings.

Joint Statement by Dr. Prince and Dr. McDougall

FEBRUARY 9, 1925.

We, the undersigned members of the committee for psychic investigation appointed by the Scientific American, report as follows on the "Margery" case.

We have shared in the labors of the committee which has devoted a large amount of time and careful observation to this case, affording every facility

* Originally published in the *Scientific American*, Vol. 132 (1925), pp. 229-230.

for the production of phenomena. We have observed phenomena, the method of production of which we cannot in every case claim to have discovered. But we have observed no phenomena of which we can assert that they could not have been produced by normal means, although we have looked for such phenomena patiently and with open minds. It is obvious that we cannot prove that the "medium" never has produced and never can nor will produce supernormal phenomena. But in our opinion we have afforded the "medium" ample opportunities for the demonstration to us of such phenomena and no such demonstration has hitherto been made.

Therefore, we report that, in our judgment, the "medium" is not entitled to the award of the prize offered by the Scientific American for the production of supernormal physical phenomena.

> Walter Franklin Prince (Chairman),
> Wm. McDougall.

Supplementary Statement by Dr. Prince

FEBRUARY 9, 1925.

In November last I guardedly stated that "thus far the experiments have not scientifically and conclusively proved the exercise of supernormal powers" by "Margery."

Since then I have had three sittings: two of these were unworthy of consideration, since, what with the complete darkness and the medium's husband close to her on one side, no proof of genuineness in the phenomena produced was possible. The third was under conditions which I considered satisfactory for the time being, since I had secure control of the medium's hands and feet in near-daylight, with the bell-box on my knees a few inches from those of the medium. Twice when my attention was momentarily abstracted the sound of a bell came from the region of the bell-box, but ceased instantly as I looked down, with no movement of the contact board perceptible. Since the medium volubly promised me repeated experiments under precisely similar circumstances I expected in one or two further sittings to be able to determine whether the sound of a bell actually issued from the bell in the box or from another such as could easily have been concealed between the medium's knees and under her garments.

But all such opportunities have since been denied me, in spite of my repeated efforts to obtain them, nor have I been able to secure any prospect that sittings in a red light would be allowed me. For some weeks Dr. Crandon has refused to allow my presence under any circumstances. The work of the committee having been brought to an end through his own act, the time has come for my final official statement.

No sitting at which I was present was to me convincing, and I am still profoundly unconvinced, after giving respectful attention to all that advocates have had to say. In fact I could write a chapter of indications which, in the absence of contravening proof, seem to tell the story of normal and deceptive production.

Although fully aware of the scorn which the committee would incur by its policy of utmost leniency toward the conditions said by the medium and her husband to be necessary, I fully concurred in that policy. So long as the alleged conditions on which phenomena depend are violated, the claims of the phenomena cannot logically be refuted. We gave the medium a long series of opportunities to establish her claims under the conditions alleged to be necessary, embarrassing and suspicious though they were. In my judgment she has not made out a case.

Walter Franklin Prince.

Supplementary Statement by Dr. McDougall

February 8, 1925.

I think the time has come when, as a member of the committee for psychic investigation appointed by the Scientific American, I should express my opinion on the "Margery" case. I should have preferred to have a few more sittings with this case, before expressing my opinion, but the unfortunate degree of publicity already given to the case forces my hand.

As long ago as November, 1923, when I had enjoyed only a few sittings, I wrote to "Margery's" husband, stating frankly that I was inclined to regard all the phenomena I had observed as produced by normal means, possibly with the admirable design of testing and exposing the gullibility of scientific men who venture to dabble in the field of "Psychic Research." Since that date I have taken part in three series of sittings, eagerly looking for evidence of supernormal phenomena and doing my best to keep my mind open to such evidence. During this period, the inclination described above has grown steadily stronger in the main, in spite of some minor fluctuations, and now has become well-nigh irresistible. I feel sure that, if it were worth while to set down in detail the many observations and inferences which have contributed to bring me to this state of mind, all sensible and unbiased persons who could accept my statements as those of a trustworthy reporter would be inclined to the same conclusion.

Wm. McDougall.

Statement by Mr. Orson D. Munn

FEBRUARY 11, 1925.

The statements of the members of our Psychic Committee, herewith made public, speak for themselves. Comment from the staff of the Scientific American is not really required.

Nevertheless, I may add, for what it may be worth, that we concur entirely in the opinions expressed by Dr. Prince and Dr. McDougall. Speaking for myself, I am of the conviction that no evidence of supernormal phenomena has been produced and that many circumstances of the case create a strong suspicion that all of the reported phenomena have been brought about in quite normal and understandable ways.

The committee has been exceptionally patient. As is apparent from their statements, some of them had reached a tentative unfavorable opinion months ago. In the meantime the case has been tried and retried, most vociferously, in the newspapers and elsewhere. Nevertheless, the majority of the committee kept quiet and remained at work. In the most admirable scientific spirit they declined to be moved by the clamor of either side but continued sittings in a whole-hearted effort to ascertain the truth. It now seems useless to delay the decision longer.

Last November, two members of the committee filed statements declining to recommend the granting of the award to "Margery." Together with the two statements now announced, these constitute a vote of four out of five. The psychic award will not be granted to "Margery." It is only fair to state, however, that this fact has no financial significance. At the beginning of the sittings with her, "Margery" stated that she was not applying for the money award and would not accept it personally, if received.

The Margery case being disposed of so far as the committee and the Scientific American are concerned, the committee will now proceed with the investigation of other persons who have applied for the award and whose cases are awaiting attention. There has been no change whatsoever in the personnel of the committee nor in its plan of procedure.

Orson D. Munn.

C. Further Observations on the "Margery" Case*

EDITORIAL NOTE: Professor McDougall submits the article herewith, in sequence to my discussion, appearing in the April *Journal*, of his published statements on the Margery case. In order that it may abundantly appear that my opinion of the Margery mediumship, so diametrically opposed to his, has in no way interfered with Dr. McDougall's free ex-

* From *Jour. A.S.P.R.*, Vol. 19 (1925), pp. 297-309.

pression in these pages, his manuscript has gone to the printer without having been read in this office; and the only proof-reading it will get will be at the printer's hands. The President and the Research Officer of the Society and the members of the Publication Committee, who collectively discharge the editorial functions of the *Journal*, will read it for the first time in the published form, when copies of this issue of the *Journal* are available. At this moment I do not know whether the present text is mainly an attempt to meet mine of April, or mainly a vehicle for the recording of the various observations, heretofore unrecorded, which Dr. McDougall mentioned in his *Boston Transcript* statement and which I invited him to set down in the columns of the *Journal*. An abstract is therefore not possible; and I judge that an abstract would hardly do the text justice—that it would have to be read in full before any judgment could be formed of its content. I have no desire to keep controversy about the Margery case alive indefinitely in these columns, and I therefore hope that Dr. McDougall says nothing which either Dr. Crandon or I will feel calls for any reply. Such reply, if found necessary, will appear in the *Journal* for July or August.—J. M. B. [*Journal A.S.P.R.*]

Mr. J. M. Bird's long article entitled "Dr. McDougall and the Margery Mediumship" (*Journal Am. S. P. R.*, April, 1925) seems to require some answer from me. Mr. Bird avers that his article is not an attack upon me; therefore I will not make an attack upon him. I will confine myself to my "scientific duty" of reporting further observations in support of my adverse opinion; merely remarking that some of Mr. Bird's statements about matters of which he has no first-hand knowledge are inaccurate and that, if these inaccuracies were corrected, his formidable indictment of myself would be shorn of some of its brightest jewels.

In order to avoid undue length I shall confine myself to sittings of January, 1925, in which I took part with Mr. E. J. Dingwall and Dr. Ellwood Worcester, under the general direction of the former. In these sittings "ectoplasmic" phenomena were the principal features. If these "ectoplasmic" phenomena were genuine, or what they are claimed to be, we need not haggle about the various questionable phenomena of earlier series. If, on the other hand, there is sufficient ground to regard them as produced by natural means for the mystification of the sitters, then that fact would seem to relieve me of any obligation to attempt to explain all the many phenomena of earlier sittings, the causation of which remains doubtful.

The "ectoplasmic" mass appeared on the table on several occasions on which I was present; and I, with the other sitters, was allowed a number of brief inspections of it by red light and to palpate it gently (sometimes only with the back of my hand—a restriction laid only upon me, the only one of the investigators of medical training). Apart from these brief visual and tactual observations, we had to rely upon observation by hearing movements, by seeing the mass outlined against luminous paint, and by seeing the movements that seemed to be imparted by it to several objects marked with luminous paint, and finally upon a series of flashlight photographs of the mass, some taken in my presence, some on other occasions.

MOVEMENTS OF THE "ECTOPLASM"

At several successive sittings early in January, the ectoplasmic mass (which for brevity's sake I shall call E. C.) appeared on the table and made a number of free, often rather violent, movements, ranging from side to side of the table and beyond the middle of its surface from Margery's side. These movements are of crucial importance, because they constitute the only evidence that the E. C. is a supernormal phenomenon.

On all the occasions on which these movements occurred, Margery's (M.) left hand was tactually controlled by Dingwall; and her right hand by F. H. In addition to these tactual controls, the cuff of each loose sleeve of M.'s bathrobe bore an annular stripe of material with luminous paint. Similar stripes were upon her ankles and on the cuffs of F. H. and of Dingwall. The table was transverse to M. Dr. Worcester and I sat "in circle" at the side of the table opposite M. The luminous bands on M.'s cuffs were usually visible to me, but not always so; for M. was restless and made many movements and changes of position. It is important that the reader should understand that I know no means of knowing the position of the luminous band on M.'s right arm. It might readily shift from the wrist to the elbow, or to a still higher position, without my having any indication of the fact. The arrangements were made by Mr. Dingwall under whose general direction all the sittings of this series were made. M. wore also a head–band carrying a small disc of luminous paint about the middle of the forehead, to enable us to locate her head in the darkness.

All the movements of the ectoplasm observed by me (with the exception of those of two sittings which I shall presently describe) were made under these conditions. That is to say, they were made under such conditions that M.'s right hand was practically uncontrolled.[1] Further, careful and oft-repeated observation showed me that, in almost every instance of free movement of the E. C., the luminous band on M.'s right arm made a clearly perceptible and simultaneous movement, just such as might be expected if M.'s right hand were causing the movement of E. C.

After several sittings of this kind, I openly expressed to the circle my entire dissatisfaction with the control of M.'s right hand. During many sittings of 1923 and 1924 I had been allowed to control one hand of M. This I commonly did by allowing her fingers to rest on my open palm with my thumb lightly resting upon them. As soon as the Dingwall series began, it appeared that there had evolved a myth to the effect that my control of M.'s hand was so violent or "fierce" that it caused her considerable pain and therefore I could not be permitted again to control her hand. In view of this state of affairs, I urged that I might be allowed to reach across F. H. (who sat between me and Margery) with my left hand and so control the joined hands of M. and F. H. during some of the movements of E. C. This request was well received and bore fruit in the next sitting (Jan. 9th) in the following way:

M. was very restless during this sitting. She was in "trance;" but unlike earlier "trances" in which she had remained lethargic, the "trances" of this series were accompanied by much movement of head and limbs. We had asked repeatedly that M. should be placed in a comfortable armchair, in place of the uncushioned Windsor chair commonly used. But Walter had rejected the suggestion obstinately. The E. C. appeared early and there were various movements of it and of M. M.'s head-band became displaced and, after several attempts to replace it under Walter's instruction, it had slipped down about M.'s neck where the luminous disc upon it was invisible to me.

There were several luminous objects on the table, including a ring of cardboard about five inches in diameter. On three occasions I was given brief contact (some few seconds) of my left hand with M.'s right hand joined with F. H.'s left hand beneath the end of the table. During each of these contacts, which (for the first time in this series) established control of M.'s right hand, as well as of her left hand (controlled by Dingwall), there were movements of objects on the table. These movements were therefore of great interest and crucial importance; for, as I have pointed out above, the seemingly spontaneous and self-originated movements of E. C. remain the only evidence of its supernormal nature during these sittings. On the first of these three occasions, the movement consisted only in slight movement of the ring towards M. as it lay on the table. During the second and third of these contacts, the ring was raised into the vertical plane above M.'s edge of the table and made several swaying movements parallel to the edge of the table. If these movements had been made during red light, or if M.'s head-band had been visible in its actual position during this time, the movements would have been crucial evidence of supernormality of E. C. During the occurrence of the movements, I was, in fact, deeply impressed by them. But there occurred an incident which suddenly and completely destroyed for me their evidential value. Having become accustomed to regard M.'s head as adequately controlled by the luminous disc on her forehead, I had forgotten for the time being that this disc was no longer visible, and M.'s head therefore uncontrolled. The lateral swaying movements of the ring on the third of these three occasions were terminated by the ring falling to the floor. At the moment the ring fell I saw a small luminous disc moving upward and backward from the position from which the ring fell (a few inches above M.'s edge of the table) towards the position normally occupied by M.'s head, when sitting approximately upright in her chair. I at once jumped to the conclusion that this luminous spot was the disc upon M.'s head-band, admittedly now around her neck, and obscured until this moment, but now (unfortunately for the evidential quality of the phenomena) accidentally exposed to view by M.'s movements. That conclusion remains with me as one of high probability.[2]

The movements made by the ring were just such as would have been imparted to it, if its edge had been seized between M.'s teeth or lips and her head swayed from side to side. In order to make my account of this crucial incident completely fair and as nearly accurate as possible, I must add that I am not sure that the head-band was invisible during the first of these three contacts controlling M.'s right hand. But, during this first contact, the movement of the ring was nothing more than a slight shifting upon the table towards M.'s edge. And, since the E. C. was connected with her thighs or the lower part of her body by a stout cord, and since her left hand (then in contact with Dingwall's right) made rather free movements (as revealed by the wrist-band) during this movement of the ring, no evidential value can be attached to it. I am sure that the head-band was invisible during the second contact and during the third, until the moment at which the ring fell to the floor.

Following this sitting came several in which the E. C. did not appear; they were devoted to the incubation of a new phenomenon, a promised ectoplasmic mouth, from which we were to expect the utterance of an "independent voice." It was during this period, on Jan. 18th that I wrote to Mr. Dingwall the letter reproduced below. The letter expresses clearly my attitude at that time, exhibiting my readiness to seek and accept good evidence of supernormality as well as something of my caution and the grounds for it.

Jan. 18, 1925.

"My Dear Dingwall:

"At last evening's sitting I expressed some difference of opinion with you about the policy you are following in the present conduct of the Margery sittings, and I wish now to say a little more in support of my opinion. You must remember that I have seen far more of this case than you have. I wish to be as frank as possible with the Crandons, but I cannot express to them all my reservations without serious risk *either* of diminishing the prospect of the occurrence of interesting phenomena, *or* of finding myself excluded from the sittings. Such is my opinion, and as I have already given so much time to this case, and since a very serious responsibility rests upon me owing to the widespread publicity of the case, I desire to go through with it to the point where I can render a definite opinion on the phenomena. I must therefore ask you to treat the contents of this letter as *strictly confidential,* and not to be communicated to any one without my consent, least of all to the Crandons.

"It seems to me that 'Walter' is playing a game with you—a game which he has played again and again, namely of this nature; he works at some phenomenon until we are deeply interested and seem to be approximating to a crucial test; then he promises some new and highly interesting phenomenon and by so doing seeks to divert us from the quest we have been pursuing. E.g., last autumn Doctor Worcester and I concentrated, at the suggestion of Walter and Dr. Crandon (it is difficult often to distinguish between them in this respect), upon the bell-box. I accepted the suggestion, thinking we might quickly get a crucial demonstration. The thing dragged on through some eight sittings, some being blanks and others nearly blank, until about the middle of November, when we seemed to have got near to crucial conditions which we hoped to achieve at the next sitting. At the last or penultimate sitting of this series Walter suddenly, and quite gratuitously, promised to produce a psychic photo of my little daughter who died some years ago. I refused to rise to this bait and persisted in demanding the bell-box demonstration. The result was that the series of sittings was terminated. Without any explanation offered, I was not invited to any further sitting until your arrival in early January. I believe Dr. Worcester was treated in the same way.

"During the spring and summer of 1924, Dr. Comstock, to whom I was leaving the conduct and policy of the investigation, was, as it seems to me, the victim of the same 'game.' He was encouraged by Walter to attempt a series of tests with various pieces of apparatus, e.g., the enclosed balance and the sealed glass bottle, Walter promising success repeatedly, if we only gave him the opportunity to practise with the apparatus. Under the influence of these promises, Comstock persevered heroically first with one then with another apparatus. There were plenty of reports of startling successes when we (i.e., Comstock and I) were not present, but never any clear success when we were present.

"In this way the long series of sittings of the spring and early summer were frittered away without clear result; and the present course of sittings seems to me to be repeating the history. We have come very near to observing the ectoplasm under satisfactory conditions; but, just when I hoped we might be about to realize those conditions at the next sitting, this new red herring is drawn across the trail, namely, the production of the voice from an ectoplasmic mouth at a distance from the medium's head. It seems to me, in the light of my previous experiences, only too probable that the remainder of the present series is in danger of being frittered away in inconclusive attempts at this demonstration. Crandon frequently asserts that Walter never fails in what he has promised. I should rather be inclined to invert the proposition and say that Walter always fails.

"I want you to understand that I am genuinely and keenly interested and that my mind is open; but it is open both ways, to both the reality of the *supernormality* and to the *normality* of the phenomena we observe. As I told you at the first, I shall be glad to go over with you my private notes on the case and to point out the many specific reasons which demand and justify the most extreme caution on our part, and also in detail the observations which justify me in saying that I am not yet satisfied of the reality of the ectoplasmic phenomena.

"In my judgment we ought to concentrate on that question until I am satisfied, until I am of the opinion that it is genuine and feel myself able to testify publicly to its reality and genuineness, as I will not hesitate to do when and if I am satisfied. There are, it seems to me, two principal reasons for so concentrating—first, it is in itself, if genuine, a phenomenon of over-whelming interest and importance. My testimony to it would, I venture to think, carry considerable weight, even in the scientific world; whereas a favorable report by you, if not supported and confirmed by me, might fail to do so. Secondly it seems to me that you need my support in your own self-defense. As you have yourself said, it is highly probable or even in-evitable that, when you report the ectoplasmic phenomena to be genuine, you will be accused by the scientific, or by some of them, of being an ac-complice, of being in collusion with Margery. Your best defense against this would be my concordant testimony and support. Further, I shall, no doubt, be expected to render some report to the English S. P. R.; and it will be very unsatisfactory from every point of view, if your report and mine on the same series of sittings are in serious disagreement.

"I told you frankly in open meeting that I regarded the control of the right hand as the weakest point during the ectoplasmic demonstration, and I requested to be allowed to sit either at the medium's right hand or her left during some of these demonstrations. I have not been allowed to occupy either position, nor has the control of the right hand been rendered satisfac-tory. You agreed to my demand for such control and proposed what would have been satisfactory to me, namely, Comstock and Prince as additional controllers of the two hands. But this proposal has been allowed to lapse and, in the pursuit of the independent voice (which, as I say, seems to me a 'red herring') you seem to have forgotten the need for securing demon-stration of the ectoplasm under satisfactory control. Please try to imagine my situation if, on the basis of the observations up to date, I should assert the reality of the ectoplasm and face the cross-questioning of my scientific colleagues on the subject. The most obvious question they would put to me would be—What was the right hand of Margery doing? I should have to reply that it was controlled only by Crandon and by the vision of the luminous bracelet on the loose right sleeve of Margery; that during the phenomena the right hand lay, as well as I could judge, somewhere in M.'s lap, within a few inches of the ectoplasmic mass; that the hand almost invariably made jerking movements coinciding with the more sudden movements of the ectoplasm. You may ask—What of the three occasions upon which I held the fingers of Margery's right hand for a few seconds during which movement of the ectoplasm occurred? Well, if you care to hear why I do not regard those three occasions as satisfactory, I will tell you when we meet.

"I am trying to explain why I urge concentration on obtaining the ectoplasm under conditions that exclude doubt and would enable us to face a cross-examination on the observation successfully. It must be obvious to you that at present I could not.

"Whatever Walter is, there is no doubt in my mind that, for one reason or another, and (again, for one reason or another) with the connivance (perhaps innocent and not realized) of Crandon, he shirks and avoids the crucial conditions.

"In view of all the facts known to me bearing on this case, I think I have been extremely patient and long suffering. If the present series should terminate without my having obtained decisive evidence of the ectoplasm, that will be one more added to a long series of disappointments.

"Sincerely yours,

W. McDougall."

"P. S. You express yourself frankly as satisfied of the reality of the ectoplasm. That is good as far as it goes; but, it seems to me, you are bound to try to carry me along with you. Therefore it is premature to throw aside the question of the evidential nature of the phenomena (as you have seemed inclined to do during the last few sittings) and to proceed at once to the further question of the exact *modus operandi* and process of production of the ectoplasm, regardless of controls."

I added to this letter a second postscript urging that we should press for any one single phenomenon under really satisfactory conditions.

The consequence of this letter was that on Jan. 20th we sat in a new order, and the E. C. appeared again. I was still unable to secure permission to sit at M.'s right, controlling her right hand; but Dr. Worcester was permitted to enjoy that privilege. On former occasions, when, as I have said M.'s right hand was virtually uncontrolled, the E. C. had commonly made its appearance on M.'s left thigh beneath her large warm bathrobe (which, in addition to stockings, was commonly her sole garment during these E. C. sittings) and had been located there by contact of Dingwall's right hand controlling M.'s left hand. The presumption was that the E. C. mass issued from M.'s body by the natural passage, that in fact its appearance was a sort of parturition. On this occasion we were permitted visual verification (by aid of momentary red light) of this presumption. Then Dingwall reported that M.'s left leg was thrown up on the table and that her left hand seized the E. C. and placed it upon the table. The E. C. then lay inert upon the table, in striking contrast with its lively behavior on the several previous occasions, on each of which (M.'s right hand being uncontrolled) it had exhibited many lively and extensive movements. We now pressed for movements of E. C. under these conditions (conditions of satisfactory control now obtained for the first time). We were first allowed visual inspection by brief red light and slight exploration of the E. C. with our fingers. These inspections revealed the E. C. lying upon M.'s edge of the table and a stout cord of similar substance stretched between it and M.'s thighs, between which (enfolded in the bathrobe) it seemed to be firmly held. Then came several attempts to demonstrate to us movements of E. C. These were successful to this extent. During several brief periods of red light (each lasting a very few seconds) the E. C. was observed to move slightly towards M.

The movements were so slight that on only one occasion, in spite of strained attention, was I able to feel sure of the movement. Its extent could not have been as much as one-quarter of an inch, and I should estimate it as about one-eighth of an inch. Since the cord was tautly stretched between the E. C. and M.'s thighs, it is obvious that these movements may well have been produced by some action of M.'s muscles and that, therefore, they are entirely without evidential value.

On the other hand, the failure to display any movements of E. C. (other than these slight movements of retraction) upon this occasion (whereas, on all previous occasions its movements had been many and extensive) gives strong support to the view that its free movements had been actuated by M.'s uncontrolled right hand.

I have now dealt with all the essential facts of movement of the E. C. so far as they occurred in my presence and I do not know of any claims for its independent movement under satisfactory conditions on other occasions.

OTHER EVIDENCE IN SUPPORT OF THE ECTOPLASM

Apart from self-movement of the E. C., another possible line of evidence for its supernormality might have been afforded by careful surgical examination of M. immediately before and after the sitting. Of course, best of all would have been an adequate examination of E. C. in good light; but we were not allowed to hope for this. On several occasions of the appearance of E. C., M. had been searched by an entirely trustworthy lady immediately before the sitting (but not surgically[3]). In the light of my dissatisfaction with the evidence, Dingwall agreed to invite this lady to take part in a sitting and then, if the E.C. should appear, to request examination of M. by her immediately after the conclusion of the sitting. This was the more desirable by reason of the fact that, at the end of each of the E. C. sittings, Walter had instructed us to sit quietly while M. withdrew from the séance room and thereafter to withdraw ourselves from the room with as little disturbance as possible. This plan was followed upon one occasion. The lady remained during the sitting and the consequence was that no E. C. appeared; the only striking phenomenon was the levitation of a small basket with hoop handle and luminous band about it. This had been placed on the floor to the right of M.'s chair. F. H. was at M.'s right. After a long blank period, all hands were ostentatiously gathered together on the table (effectually preventing visual exploration beneath the table for M.'s luminous anklets), and while we maintained this position, the basket was twice momentarily raised to the level of the table-top between M. and F. H. During these levitations I searched vigorously beneath the table with my foot in the endeavor to locate M.'s feet. But my search was fruitless. I could not reach her feet, as I should have done if they had been in their usual place below the table. Further, the two levitations of the basket were, as Dingwall agreed, just such as might, under the conditions obtaining, have been produced by M.'s right foot.

No further opportunity to pursue this line of evidence was afforded.

The only other evidence bearing upon the nature of the E. C. are the photographs. My opinion upon these has already been expressed in my article in the *Boston Transcript*, reproduced in the course of Mr. Bird's article in this Journal (April, 1925). I there stated that the photos seemed to me to reveal the E. C. as the lung, or part of the lung, of some animal, artificially manipulated to give it a crude resemblance to a hand. I add only that in addition to this close resemblance of the E. C. itself to a natural tissue, I observed in the photos that the cord attached to it closely resembles the trachea or windpipe of an animal. It shows annular bands corresponding to the cartilaginous rings of the trachea; and, in one at least of the photos, is visible what seems to be a large artery lying along side of the trachea, with a number of small orifices which seem to be the openings of small lateral arteries cut off flush with the surface of the main artery. I have asked in vain that the complete series of photos should be submitted for examination and report by independent experts.

THE ATTEMPT TO PRODUCE AN ECTOPLASMIC MOUTH

I turn now to the second principal series of phenomena obtained during the Dingwall sittings in which I took part. These were obtained in sittings intervening in the E. C. series. Walter proposed to form on the table an ectoplasmic mouth from which should issue "an independent voice." It was *à propos* of these sittings that my letter to Dingwall of Jan. 18th was written. The attempt went no further than the production upon or near the surface of the table near M.'s edge of it, of certain hissing or puffing sounds which we were invited to believe were the forerunners of the independent voice, in the shape of its first preliminary aspirations. There were occasionally some very dim luminosities about the same region to which I can attach no importance in view of the abundance of luminous paint in and about the séance room.

These sounds, repeated a number of times, left me entirely sceptical, and I did not entirely conceal my scepticism. A special effort to subdue my scepticism was therefore made during the sitting of Jan. 14th. The sounds above the surface of the table having recurred several times, I was directed by Walter to lay the right side of my head on the table, my face turned towards M. This I did, and, while all possible normal sources of the sound, with the exception of M.'s right hand, were adequately controlled, the hissing or puffing sound recurred some seven or eight times. It seemed to come from a point about eight inches in front of my face, i.e., a point at or about M.'s edge of the table. Accompanying each puff of sound, I felt a puff of cool air on my face. I was thus able to verify the objective reality of the phenomenon by the aid of two senses simultaneously. But, again unfortunately for the evidential nature of the phenomenon, a third sense was unexpectedly brought into play; with each puff of air heard, and felt on my face, I also sensed most distinctly the odor of india-rubber. I confess that I had suspected that the sound was the sound of air issuing from the nozzle of some syringe manipulated by M.'s uncontrolled right hand. But I had not consciously anticipated the odor of india rubber. It may suggest that I had subconsciously anticipated it, and that the odor was a hallucinatory consequence of such anticipation. I am, however, in view of all the facts, strongly disposed to believe that the odor was as objectively founded as the sound and the coolness of the puffs.

The foregoing descriptions illustrate a point of primary importance, bearing not only on this case but on many other cases of alleged physical mediumship. Namely, an honestly written report of a sitting, containing only the statements of observations made, may seem to the reader to afford convincing evidence of the supernormality of the phenomena, given the honesty and a reasonable degree of competence of the reporters. But the best observer cannot observe everything that goes on during a dark séance; and the addition of one or two even slight observations to the record may completely transform its character, depriving it of all evidential value and converting it into good evidence against the supernormality of the phenomena. If this is true of a few of the sittings in which I took part and during which I was fortunate (or unfortunate) enough to make some such supplementary but all-important observations that transform the bearing of the report, are we not justified in believing that similar possibilities remained unrealized in some or all of the many sittings which Mr. Bird has so carefully described in his book "Margery"? I can testify that a few such observations were made by myself and others, but have not been reported in Mr. Bird's pages.

I will conclude this too lengthy article by saying that, about a fortnight before the end of Mr. Dingwall's visit, in view of the very unsatisfactory state of affairs, I induced him to join with me in begging for one single clear-cut supernormal phenomenon, however simple, under satisfactory control conditions; and we suggested, as especially suitable, the levitation of the megaphone with luminous stripe upon it, a phenomenon frequently reported in previous sittings and one frequently thrown in as an extra in my presence, but in every such case without the luminous band and under conditions otherwise unsatisfactory. I was ready to sit every day for this purpose. No such demonstration was made, and the failure of this reasonable request was the final and culminating ground of my decision to report the supernormality unproved.

If further investigation of this most puzzling case should require reversal of my opinion, I shall be ready to make such reversal, declaring that up to this time I have been most remarkably unlucky in failing to observe phenomena under satisfying conditions.

NOTES

[1] I wish to say here that I have received only the most kindly and courteous treatment from Dr. and Mrs. Crandon, and I wish to suggest no reflections upon them. But, since I am unwillingly forced into recording my testimony in this matter, while it remains still in many respects obscure, and since it has assumed a grave importance, I am compelled to weigh all the evidence with the assumption that Dr. and Mrs. Crandon may have deliberately combined in a protracted effort to test the capacity of "psychic researchers." I, therefore, cannot accept any control supposedly exerted by F. H. as effective control. It is noteworthy that much of the evidence offered by Mr. Bird in his book "Margery" assumes the validity of such control. I speak, then, of a hand controlled only by F. H. as "uncontrolled."

[2] That this spot of light was not illusory or hallucinatory was sufficiently proved by the fact that, at the moment which I saw it, F. H. cried out "there's another light!"—or words to that effect.

[3] We were given to understand that surgical examination would not be permitted. I have no complaint to make of that. If the ectoplasm were what it is claimed to be, it should be easy to establish its supernormal nature without resort to surgical examination.

D. The Psychic Investigation*

To the Editor of The New York Times:

May I, as a member of The Scientific American's Committee for Psychic Investigation, ask you to correct some inaccuracies contained in an article on the "Margery" case which appeared in your issue of Feb. 12? Your article states that the verdict of the committee "was that 'Margery' has failed to produce any evidence of 'supernormal phenomena'." That statement is not an accurate condensation of the verdict of the committee. The committee reported that "Margery" had failed to convince of the supernormality of any of her phenomena. I think I represent the opinion of the majority of the committee in saying that "Margery" furnished a large amount of evidence, but that the evidence was defective in quality and that it was outbalanced by a large amount of evidence pointing to the production of the phenomena by normal means.

Your article states that Messrs. Prince, Comstock and McDougall "deny that Houdini exposed anything." Mr. Houdini may well take exception to this statement, and, to the best of my knowledge, it is not true. I was not present at the Houdini sittings and do not presume to give an opinion upon the exposure of trickery which Mr. Houdini claims to have effected. But I maintain, and I think that Messrs. Prince and Comstock take the same view, that, even if the whole committee had accepted his claim, that would not have closed the case. Many mediums who have been detected in trickery are nevertheless held by very respectable investigators, who admit the trickery, to have produced genuine supernormal phenomena on other occasions. And "Margery" had produced many puzzling phenomena which Mr. Houdini has not observed.

Wm. McDougall
Harvard University
Feb. 17, 1925

* Originally published as a Letter to the Editor, *The New York Times*, February 21, 1925, p. 10. © 1925 by The New York Times Company. Reprinted by permission.

9.   Fraudulent Mediums Exposed*

~·~

Sir—A professional medium, who claims to have enjoyed a large and lucrative practice upon the credulity of the good people of many cities and large towns, recently arranged to give two "sittings" or "seances," at a private house near Manchester, for a fee of £5 a sitting, his usual charge. The "medium" proposed to "materialise" various spirits, and to make them visible and audible to his clients, who on our part professed a sceptical attitude, and a desire to see for ourselves what the powers of the "medium" might be. The "medium" arrived with his business manager or agent, and later some half-dozen acquaintances also came, who were said to be useful in the establishing of "sympathetic conditions." A pair of curtains were draped across one corner of a room, and before these we, the audience, sat in a semicircle holding one another's hands. We were told by the agent that the "medium" would presently fall into a trance, and that if we should break the chain of clasped hands while he was thus entranced he would suffer severely and perhaps die. A prayer was offered and hymns sung while the "medium" squirmed and seemed to become unconscious. Then he rose to his feet and spoke with a badly feigned foreign accent, and we were assured by his agent that his body was now possessed by the spirit of a dead French physician.

After about thirty minutes, during which this doctor reeled off meaningless strings of phrases and long words, his manner and mode of speech changed, and his agent addressed him by another name. He babbled of

* Letter originally published in *Two Worlds*, July 28, 1899, p. 486. Cf. *Jour. S.P.R.*, Vol. 12 (1906), pp. 275-276, "Exposures of Mr. Craddock."

squaws and wigwams and pale-faced chiefs, and so on for a considerable period. Then he retired behind the curtains, and the dim light was almost extinguished. Presently a phosphorus-covered pasteboard was thrust from behind the curtains, and a tiny feminine voice whispered inanities, while the agent explained that this was the voice of a familiar spirit, and that she would probably become visible. The luminous pasteboard advanced to the accompaniment of slow and sacred music, and beside it a human face became dimly visible for some moments and passed before each of us in turn. Then a bare arm, to my eyes unmistakably masculine and covered by a thin gauze drapery, appeared before the luminous paste-board. There were some attempts to make noises which should favour the belief that the body of the medium was still behind the curtains. The form retired behind the curtains, and the voice of another spirit, taking up the tale, cracked vulgar and profane jokes, and then announced that various spirits, including those of dead relatives, were at hand, wishing to speak to us, and he gave us messages from these spirits. Then a small patch of phosphorescent light moved to and fro before the curtains, and was recognised by the agent as a spirit light. After some three hours of this sort of thing the sitting was brought to a close with another solemn prayer, and the lights having been turned up a little the "medium" gradually recovered from his "trance." But he was so exhausted by his experience that it was necessary for him to stay the night in the house and be nursed by his agent. So all the next day these two were sympathetically treated, until, when the time for the evening sitting arrived, they were filled with confidence and satisfaction.

Almost the same group of sitters assembled again, and the meeting proceeded with similar solemn fooleries as on the previous evening, including a progressive lowering of the lights and increasing fervour in the singing of hymns. Thus was the "medium" encouraged to issue from his curtained retreat in the form of the materialised spirit of an Indian, his face darkened by a mask, and his head covered with a simple white turban. This awe-inspiring vision began to make the tour of our semi-circle, showing to each in turn the face dimly lit by the phosphorescent paste-board. When my turn came I rose and seized the head in my arms and dragged it, together with the violently resisting body of the "medium," into the gaslight of the next room. There was a scene of some confusion while the "medium" and his agent received corporal chastisement. The "medium" was sullen and would not speak except under compulsion. The agent was made to take an oath to the effect that he would never again aid in similar proceedings, and the meeting dispersed. The mask of thin India-rubber sheeting was picked up from the floor of the dark room, and a knotted handkerchief, which had probably served as the turban, was in the "medium's" pocket. In his bag, when unlocked, we found beside other small "properties" useful in "making up," an interesting pocket book in which were the names of a number of people, including our own, and those of several well-known and titled persons, and appended to each were slight notes of their family affairs and relations. Several of these names we know to be those of persons who have attended "seances" given by the "medium."

The above account is published here in the hope that readers of Two Worlds will be deferred by it from taking part in any such "sittings" conducted in the dark by professional mediums who work for pay. The whole proceedings were, to my mind, of a degrading and reprehensible character, and even if I had been led to believe that the "manifestations" were not fraudulent, I should still have felt that such a meeting, with its mixture of the sacred and the coarse and vulgar, and its atmosphere of mixed religion and hysteria, was in the highest degree undesirable and quite incapable of leading to the establishment of truth or of sincere and well-founded conviction. Yet this "medium" has succeeded in finding many respectable and sincere persons who were prepared to pay him as much as £5 per sitting. The name of this person is known to the editor of Two Worlds, who can vouch for the essential accuracy of the above account, and who will forward any letter of enquiry on this subject to me.

M.A., M.B., Cantab.
[Wm. McDougall.]

PART III

1. *Subliminal Self* *

The phrase "subliminal self," which is one that has figured largely of recent years in discussions of the problems of "Psychical Research," owes its wide currency to the writings of F. W. H. Myers, especially to his posthumous work *Human Personality and its survival of Bodily Death*. It is used in a wider, looser sense and a narrower, stricter sense, which two senses are often confused in a way very detrimental to clear thinking. In the stricter usage the phrase implies the peculiar conception of human personality expounded at great length and with a wealth of learning and eloquence by Myers; it stands for an hypothesis which seemed to its author to bring almost all the strange facts he and his associates observed, as well as many alleged facts whose reality still remains in dispute, under one scheme of explanation and to bring them also into intelligible relation with the body of generally accepted scientific principles. But the phrase "Subliminal Self" is now often used by those who do not fully accept Myers's hypothesis, as a convenient heading to which to refer all the facts of many different kinds that seem to imply subconscious or unconscious mental operations. This article is only concerned to expound the meaning of the phrase as it was employed by Myers, and it is much to be wished that it should only be used in this stricter sense.

In the speculations of Schopenhauer and of Eduard von Hartmann, the "Unconscious" played a great part as a metaphysical principle explanatory of the phenomena of the life and mind of both men and animals. But with these exceptions, the philosophers and psychologists of the 19th century

* Article written for the *Encyclopædia Britannica*, 11th ed. (1911), Vol. 25, pp. 1062-1064.

showed themselves in the main reluctant to admit the propriety of any conception of unconscious or subconscious mental states or operations. The predominant tendency was to regard as the issue of "automatic" nervous action or of "unconscious cerebration" whatever bodily movements seemed to take place independently of the consciousness and volition of the subject, even if those movements seemed to be of an intelligent and purposeful character. This attitude towards the subconscious is still maintained by some of the more strictly orthodox scientists; but it is now very widely accepted that we must recognize in some sense the reality of subconsciousness or of subliminal psychical process. The conception of a *limen* (threshold) of consciousness, separating subconscious or subliminal psychical process from supraliminal or conscious psychical process, figured prominently in the works of G. T. Fechner, the father of psycho-physics, and by him was made widely familiar. Fechner sought to prove that a sensory stimulus too feeble to affect consciousness produces nevertheless a psychical effect which remains below the threshold of consciousness, and he tried to show ground for believing in the existence of a vast realm of such subliminal psychical processes. But his arguments, founded though they were on epoch-making experiments, have failed to carry conviction; and it is in the main on other grounds than those adduced by Fechner that the reality of modes of mental operation which may properly be called subconscious or subliminal is now generally admitted. During the last quarter of the 19th and the opening years of the 20th century, there has been accumulated a mass of observations which suffices, in the opinion of many of those best qualified to judge, to establish the reality of processes which express themselves in purposeful actions and which bear all the marks from which we are accustomed to infer conscious cognition and volition, but of which nevertheless the subject or normal personality has no knowledge or awareness other than such as may be shared by any second person observing his actions.

Among the commonest and most striking of such manifestations is the "automatic writing" which a considerable proportion of normal persons are capable of producing. A person who has this power may sit absorbed in reading or in conversation, while his hand produces written words or sentences, of which he knows nothing until he afterwards reads them. The matter so written varies in different cases from illegibly scrawled fragments of words and sentences to long, connected, sometimes eloquent, frequently more or less dramatic, disquisitions. In some cases the "automatically" writing hand can be induced to make intelligible replies to questions whispered or otherwise put to the subject in such a way as not to draw his attention from some other object or topic with which it seems to be fully occupied. In some cases the matter so written states facts previously known to the subject but which he is unable to recollect by any voluntary effort. And in rare cases the matter written seems to imply knowledge or capacities which the subject was not believed to possess either by himself or by his friends. Other actions, including connected speech, may be produced in a similar fashion, and in the last case the subject hears and understands the words uttered from his own mouth in the same way only as those from the mouth of another person. "Table-tilting," "planchette-writing," and the various similar modes of spelling out by the aid of a code intelligible replies to questions, which have long been current in spiritistic circles and which, by those who practise them, are often regarded as the operations of disembodied intelligences, seem to belong to the same class of process. In extreme cases the manifestations of such subconscious or (better) co-conscious operations are so frequent, exhibit so much continuity and express so clearly a train of thought, purpose and memory, that they compel us to infer an organized personality of which they are the expression; such are the cases of double or multiple consciousness or personality. Very similar manifestations of a "co-consciousness" may be produced in a considerable proportion of apparently normal persons by means of post-hypnotic suggestion; as when suggestions are made during hypnosis, which afterwards the subject carries out without being aware of the actions, or of the signals in response to which he acts, and without any awareness or remembrance of the nature of the suggestions made to him. The more sober-minded of the investigators of these phenomena have sought to display all such cases as instances of division of the normal personality, and as explicable by the principle of cerebral dissociation (see HYPNOTISM); the more adventurous, concentrating their attention on the more extreme instances, regard all such manifestations as instances of the possession and control (partial or complete) of the organism of one person by the spirit or soul of another, generally a deceased person. Myers's hypothesis of the subliminal self was a brilliant attempt to follow a middle way in the explanation of these strange cases, to reconcile the two kinds of explanation with one another, and at the same time to bring into line with these other alleged facts of perplexing character, especially veridical hallucinations (*q.v.*), various types of communication at a distance (see TELEPATHY), and all the more striking instances of the operation of suggestion and of hypnosis, including the exaltation of the powers of the senses, of the memory and of control over the organic processes.

Myers conceived the soul of man as capable of existing independently of the body in some super-terrestrial or extra-terrene realm. He regarded our normal mental life as only a very partial expression of the capacities of the soul, so much only as can manifest itself through the human brain. He regarded the brain as still at a comparatively early stage of its evolution as an instrument through which the soul operates in the material world. So much of the life of the soul as fails to find expression in our conscious and organic life through its interactions with this very inadequate material mechanism remains beneath the threshold of consciousness and is said to constitute the subliminal self. The subliminal self as thus conceived would be better described as the subliminal part of the self, a part which surpasses the supraliminal or normal conscious self to an indefinitely great degree as regards its range of psychical faculties. It was further conceived as being in touch with a realm of psychical forces from which it is able to draw supplies of energy which it infuses into the organism, normally in limited quantities, but, in exceptionally favourable circumstances, in great floods, which for the time being raise the mental operations and the powers of the mind over the body to an abnormally high level.

It is a leading feature of this protean conception, that many of the abnormal mental manifestations that have commonly been regarded as symptoms of mental or nervous disease or degeneration are by its aid brought into line with mental processes that are by common consent of an unusually high type, the intuitions of genius, the outbursts of inspired poesy, the emotional fervour or the ecstasy that carries the martyr triumphantly through the severest trials, the enthusiasm that enables the human organism to carry through incredible labours. Myers's hypothesis thus boldly inverts the dominant view, which sees in all departures from the normal symptoms of weakness and degeneracy and which seeks to bring genius and ecstasy down to the level of madness and hysteria; the hypothesis of the subliminal self seeks to level up, rather than to level down, and to display many of these departures from normal mental life as being of the same nature as the operations of genius, as being, in common with these, uprushes of the subliminal self, which temporarily acquires a more complete control of the organism and therefore achieves at such times a more complete expression of its powers. And these rare displays of subliminal capacities are held to foreshadow the further course of mental evolution, to afford us a glimpse of the higher plane on which the mind of man may habitually and normally live, if further evolution of the nervous system shall render it a less inadequate medium for the exercise of the spiritual faculties and for the influx of the psychical energies which at present, owing to its imperfections, are for the most part latent or confined to the subliminal self.

This bold and far-reaching hypothesis has not up to the present time been accepted by any considerable number of professional psychologists, though its author's great literary power has secured for him a respectful hearing. The comparative indifference shown to it by the scientific and philosophical world must be ascribed to considerations of two kinds. In the first place, it is rightly felt that a very large proportion of the alleged facts which it is designed to explain are not yet supported by evidence of such a nature as warrants an unreserved acceptance of them. Secondly, even if further investigations of the type of those carried on by the Society for Psychical Research should prove Myers's belief in the reality of all or most of these facts to have been well-founded, there will remain difficulties and weaknesses intrinsic to the hypothesis, which at present seem very serious. In addition to all the great difficulties that must attach to any conception of human personality as a spiritual entity capable of existing independently of the body, Myers's conception raises many difficulties peculiar to itself, the chief of which may be briefly indicated. First, the conception of the relation of the subliminal to the normal or supraliminal self is in Myers's presentation extremely vacillating and uncertain, and it is probably radically incapable of definition and consistency. Secondly, two alleged supernormal phenomena, to the establishment of which "psychical research" has been devoted most energetically and (in the view of many of the workers) with the greatest success, and which from every point of view are the most important and interesting, are supernormal communications between the living (telepathy) and communication between the dead and the living. Now, if either or both of these modes of communication should eventually prove to be facts of nature, neither will need the hypothesis of the subliminal self for its explanation. Such evidence as we have of the latter kind of communication is almost wholly of the form of messages written or spoken by entranced persons (see TRANCE) which claim to be sent by the souls of the dead to friends still living, and these messages (if they are what they claim to be) imply, and were held by Myers himself to imply, possession or control of the brain of the living medium by the soul of the dead who transmits the message. Both phenomena need, then, for their explanation only the two great assumptions—first, that the soul is an entity capable of disembodied existence; second, that in its psycho-physical interactions any soul is not strictly confined to interaction with one particular brain.

The third great difficulty is of an emotional order. All the laborious research whose results Myers has sought to harmonize by means of his conception of the "subliminal self" has been initiated and sustained by the desire of proving the continued existence of the human personality after the death of the body. But, if Myers's doctrine is true, that which survives the death of the body is not the normal self-conscious personality of a man such as is known and valued by his friends, but a personality of which this normal personality is but a stunted distorted fragment; and it would therefore seem that according to this doctrine death must involve so great a transformation that such slight continuity as obtains must be insufficient to yield the emotional satisfaction demanded. The hypothesis would thus seem to destroy in great measure the value of the belief which it seeks to justify and establish.

See F. W. H. Myers, *Human Personality and its Survival of Bodily Death* (1st ed., London, 1903; 2nd ed., abridged and edited by L. H. Myers, London, 1907); Morton Prince, *The Dissociation of a Personality* (London, 1906); J. Jastrow, *The Subconscious* (London, 1906). See also many papers by various hands in *Proceedings of the Society for Psychical Research*, especially in part xlvi., vol. xviii., and the literature referred to under TRANCE.

2. *Hypnotism**

Hypnotism [is] a term now in general use as covering all that pertains to
the art of inducing the hypnotic state, or hypnosis, and to the study of that
state, its conditions, peculiarities and effects. Hypnosis is a condition, allied
to normal sleep (Gr. πνος), which can be induced in a large majority of
normal persons. Its most characteristic and constant symptom is the increased suggestibility of the subject (see SUGGESTION). Other symptoms
are very varied and differ widely in different subjects and in the same subject at different times. There can be no doubt that the increased suggestibility and all the other symptoms of hypnosis imply some abnormal condition
of the brain of a temporary and harmless nature. It would seem that in all
ages and in almost all countries individuals have occasionally fallen into
abnormal states of mind more or less closely resembling the hypnotic state,
and have thereby excited the superstitious wonder of their fellows. In some
cases the sate has been deliberately induced, in others it has appeared spontaneously, generally under the influence of some emotional excitement. The
most familiar of these allied states is the somnambulism or sleep-walking to
which some persons seem to be hereditarily disposed. Of a rather different
type are the states of ecstasy into which religious enthusiasts have occasionally fallen and which were especially frequent among the peoples of Europe
during the middle ages. While in this condition individuals have appeared
to be insensitive to all impressions made on their sense-organs, even to such
as would excite acute pain in normal persons, have been capable of maintaining rigid postures for long periods of time, have experienced vivid hallu-

* Article written for the *Encyclopædia Britannica,* 11th ed. (1911), Vol. 14, pp. 201-207.

cinations, and have produced, through the power of the imagination, extra-ordinary organic changes in the body, such as the bloody stigmata on the hands and feet in several well-attested instances. It has been proved in recent years that effects of all these kinds may be produced by hypnotic suggestion. Different again, but closely paralleled by some subjects in hypnosis, is the state of *latah* into which a certain proportion of persons of the Malay race are liable to fall. These persons, if their attention is suddenly and forcibly drawn to any other person, will begin to imitate his every action and attitude, and may do so in spite of their best efforts to restrain their imitative movements. Among the half-bred French-Canadians of the forest regions of Canada occur individuals, known as "jumpers," who are liable to fall suddenly into a similar state of abject imitativeness, and the same peculiar behaviour has been observed among some of the remote tribes of Siberia.

The deliberate induction of states identical with, or closely allied to, hypnosis is practised by many barbarous and savage peoples, generally for ceremonial purposes. Thus, certain dervishes of Algiers are said to induce in themselves, by the aid of the sound of drums, monotonous songs and movements, a state in which they are insensitive to pain, and a similar practice of religious devotees is reported from Tibet. Perhaps the most marvellous achievement among well-attested cases of this sort is that of certain *yogis* of Hindustan; by long training and practice they seem to acquire the power of arresting almost completely all their vital functions. An intense effort of abstraction from the impressions of the outer world, a prolonged fixation of the eyes upon the nose or in some other strained position and a power of greatly slowing the respiration, these seem to be important features of their procedure for the attainment of their abnormal states.

In spite of the wide distribution in time and space, and the not very infrequent occurrence, of these instances of states identical with or allied to hypnosis, some three centuries of enthusiastic investigation and of bitter controversy were required to establish the occurrence of the hypnotic state among the facts accepted by the world of European science. Scientific interest in them may be traced back at least as far as the end of the 16th century. Paracelsus had founded the "sympathetic system" of medicine, according to which the stars and other bodies, especially magnets, influence men by means of a subtle emanation or fluid that pervades all space. J. B. van Helmont, a distinguished man of science of the latter part of the 16th century, extended this doctrine by teaching that a similar magnetic fluid radiates from men, and that it can be guided by their wills to influence directly the minds and bodies of others. In the middle of the 17th century there appeared in England several persons who claimed to have the power of curing diseases by stroking with the hand. Notable amongst these was Valentine Greatrakes, of Affane, in the county of Waterford, Ireland, who was born in February 1628, and who attracted great attention in England by his supposed power of curing the king's evil, or scrofula. Many of the most distinguished scientific and theological men of the day, such as Robert Boyle and R. Cudworth, witnessed and attested the cures supposed to be effected by Greatrakes, and thousands of sufferers crowded to him from all parts of the kingdom. About the middle of the 18th century John Joseph Gassner, a Roman Catholic priest in Swabia, took up the notion that the majority of diseases arose from demoniacal possession, and could only be cured by exorcism. His method was undoubtedly similar to that afterwards followed by Mesmer and others, and he had an extraordinary influence over the nervous systems of his patients. Gassner, however, believed his power to be altogether supernatural.

But it was not until the latter part of the 18th century that the doctrine of a magnetic fluid excited great popular interest and became the subject of fierce controversy in the scientific world. F. A. Mesmer (*q.v.*), a physician of Vienna, was largely instrumental in bringing the doctrine into prominence. He developed it by postulating a specialized variety of magnetic fluid which he called *animal magnetism;* and he claimed to be able to cure many diseases by means of this animal magnetism, teaching, also, that it may be imparted to and stored up in inert objects, which are thereby rendered potent to cure disease.

It would seem that Mesmer himself was not acquainted with the artificial somnambulism which for nearly a century was called mesmeric or magnetic sleep, and which is now familiar as hypnosis of a well-marked degree. It was observed and described about the year 1780 by the marquis de Puységur, a disciple of Mesmer, who showed that, while subjects were in this state, not only could some of their diseases be cured, but also their movements could be controlled by the "magnetizer," and that they usually remembered nothing of the events of the period of sleep when restored to normal consciousness. These are three of the most important features of hypnosis, and the modern study of hypnotism may therefore be said to have been initiated at this date by Puységur. For, though it is probable that this state had often been induced by the earlier magnetists, they had not recognized that the peculiar behaviour of their patients resulted from their being plunged into this artificial sleep, but had attributed all the symptoms they observed to the direct physical action of external agents upon the patients.

The success of Mesmer and his disciples, especially great in the fashionable world, led to the appointment in Paris of a royal commission for the investigation of their claims. The commission, which included men of great eminence, notably A. L. Lavoisier and Benjamin Franklin, reported in the year 1784 that it could not accept the evidence for the existence of the magnetic fluid; but it did not express an opinion as to the reality of the cures said to be effected by its means, nor as to the nature of the magnetic sleep. This report and the social upheavals of the following years seem to have abolished the public interest in "animal magnetism" for the space of one generation; after which Alexandre Bertrand, a Parisian physician, revived it by his acute investigations and interpretations of the phenomena. Bertrand was the first to give an explanation of the facts of the kind that is now generally accepted. He exhibited the affinity of the "magnetic sleep" to ordinary somnambulism, and he taught that the peculiar effects are to be regarded as due to the suggestions of the operator working themselves out in the mind and body of the "magnetized" subject, *i.e.* he regarded the influence of the magnetizer as exerted in the first instance on the mind of the subject and only indirectly through the mind upon the body. Shortly after this revival of public interest, namely in the year 1831, a committee of the Academy of Medicine of Paris reported favourably upon "magnetism" as a therapeutic agency, and before many years had elapsed it was extensively practised by the physicians of all European countries, with few exceptions, of which England was the most notable. Most of the practitioners of this period adhered to the doctrine of the magnetic fluid emanating from the operator to his patient, and the acceptance of this doctrine was commonly combined with belief in phrenology, astrology and the influence of metals and magnets, externally applied, in curing disease and in producing a variety of strange sensations and other affections of the mind. These beliefs, claiming to rest upon carefully observed facts, were given a new elaboration and a more imposing claim to be scientifically established by the doctrine of *odylic force* propounded by Baron Karl von Reichenbach. In this mass of ill-based assertion and belief the valuable truths of "animal magnetism" and the psychological explanations of them given by Bertrand were swamped and wellnigh lost sight of. For it was this seemingly inseparable association between the facts of hypnotism and these bizarre practices and baseless beliefs that blinded the larger and more sober part of the scientific world, and led them persistently to assert that all this group of alleged phenomena was a mass of quackery, fraud and superstition. And the fact that magnetism was practised for pecuniary gain, often in a shameless manner, by exponents who claimed to cure by its means every conceivable ill, rendered this attitude on the part of the medical profession inevitable and perhaps excusable, though not justifiable. It was owing to this baleful association that John Elliotson, one of the leading London physicians of that time, who became an ardent advocate of "magnetism" and who founded and edited the *Zoist* in the interests of the subject, was driven out of the profession. This association may perhaps be held, also, to excuse the hostile attitude of the medical profession towards James Esdaile, a surgeon, who, practising in a government hospital in Calcutta among the natives of India, performed many major operations, such as the amputation of limbs, painlessly and with the most excellent results by aid of the "magnetic" sleep. For both Elliotson and Esdaile, though honourable practitioners, accepted the doctrine of the "magnetic" fluid and many of the erroneous beliefs that commonly were bound up with it.

In 1841 James Braid, a surgeon of Manchester, rediscovered independently Bertrand's physiological and psychological explanations of the facts, carried them further, and placed "hypnotism," as he named the study, on a sound basis. Braid showed that subjects in "magnetic" sleep, far from being in a profoundly insensitive condition, are often abnormally susceptible to impressions on the senses, and showed that many of the peculiarities of their behaviour were due to suggestions, made verbally or otherwise, but unintentionally, by the operator or by onlookers.

It seems, on looking back on the history of hypnotism, that at this time it was in a fair way to secure general recognition as a most interesting subject of psychological study and a valuable addition to the resources of the physician. But it was destined once more to be denied its rights by official science and to fall back into disrepute. This was due to the coincidence about the year 1848 of two events of some importance, namely—the discovery of the anaesthetic properties of chloroform and the sudden rise of modern spiritualism. The former afforded a very convenient substitute for the most obvious practical application of hypnotism, the production of anaesthesia during surgical operations; the latter involved it once more in a mass of fraud and superstition, and, for the popular mind, drove it back to the region of the marvellous, the supernatural and the dangerous, made it, in fact, once more a branch of the black art.

From this time onward there took place a gradual differentiation of the "animal magnetism" of the 18th century into two diverging branches, hypnotism and spiritualism, two branches which, however, are not yet entirely separated and, perhaps, never will be. At the same time the original system of "animal magnetism" has lived on in an enfeebled condition and is now very nearly, though not quite, extinct.

In the development of hypnotism since the time of Braid we may distinguish three lines, the physiological, the psychological and the pathological. The last may be dismissed in a few words. Its principal representative was J. M. Charcot, who taught at the Salpêtrière in Paris that hypnosis is essentially a symptom of a morbid condition of hysteria or hystero-epilepsy. This doctrine, which, owing to the great repute enjoyed by Charcot, has done much to retard the application of hypnotism, is now completely discredited. The workers of the physiological party attached special importance to the fixation of the eyes, or to other forms of long continued and monotonous, or violent, sensory stimulation in the induction of hypnosis. They believed that by acting on the senses in these ways they induced a peculiar condition of the nervous system, which consisted in the temporary abolition of the cerebral functions and the consequent reduction of the subject to machine-like unconscious automatism. The leading exponent of this view was R. Heidenhain, professor of physiology at Breslau, whose experimental investigations played a large part in convincing the scientific world of the genuineness of the leading symptoms of hypnosis. The purely psychological doctrine of hypnosis puts aside all physical and physiological influences and effects as of but little or no importance, and seeks a psychological explanation of the induction of hypnosis and of all the phenomena. This dates from 1884, when H. Bernheim, professor of medicine at Nancy, published his work *De la Suggestion* (republished in 1887 with a second part on the therapeutics of hypnotism). Bernheim was led to the study of hypnotism by A. A. Liébeault, who for twenty years had used it very largely and successfully in his general practice among the poor of Nancy. Liébeault rediscovered independently, and Bernheim made known to the world the truths, twice previously discovered and twice lost sight of, that expectation is a most important factor in the induction of hypnosis, that increased suggestibility is its essential symptom, and that in general the operator works upon his patient by mental influences. Although they went too far in the direction of ignoring the peculiarity of the state of the brain in hypnosis and the predisposing effect of monotonous sensory stimulation, and in seeking to identify hypnosis with normal sleep, the views of the Nancy investigators have prevailed, and are now in the main generally accepted. Their methods of verbal suggestion have been adopted by leading physicians in almost all civilized countries and have been proved to be efficacious in the relief of many disorders; and as a method of psychological investigation hypnotism has proved, especially in the hands of the late Ed. Gurney, of Dr. Pierre Janet and of other investigators, capable of throwing much light on the constitution of the mind, has opened up a number of problems of the deepest interest, and has done more than any other of the many branches of modern psychology to show the limitations and comparative barrenness of the old psychology that relied on introspection alone and figured as a department of general philosophy. In England, "always the last to enter into the general movement of the European mind," the prejudice, incredulity and ignorant misrepresentation with which hypnotism has everywhere been received have resisted its progress more stubbornly than elsewhere; but even in England its reality and its value as a therapeutic agent have at last been officially recognized. In 1892, just fifty years after Braid clearly demonstrated the facts and published explanations of them almost identical with those now accepted, a committee of the British Medical Association reported favourably upon hypnotism after a searching investigation; it is now regularly employed by a number of physicians of high standing, and the formation in 1907 of "The Medical Society for the Study of Suggestive Therapeutics" shows that the footing is has gained is likely to be made good.

Induction of Hypnosis. It has now been abundantly proved that hypnosis can be induced in the great majority of normal persons, provided that they willingly submit themselves to the process. Several of the most experienced operators have succeeded in hypnotizing more than 90% of the cases they have attempted, and most of them are agreed that failure to induce hypnosis in any case is due either to lack of skill and tact on the part of the operator, or to some unfavourable mental condition of the subject. It has often been said that some races or peoples are by nature more readily hypnotizable than others; of the French people especially this has been maintained. But there is no sufficient ground for this statement. The differences that undoubtedly obtain between populations of different regions in respect to the ease or difficulty with which a large proportion of all persons can be hypnotized are sufficiently explained by the differences of the attitude of the public towards hypnotism; in France, *e.g.*, and especially in Nancy, hypnotism has been made known to the public chiefly as a recognized auxiliary to the better known methods of medical treatment, whereas in England the medical profession has allowed the public to make acquaintance with hypnotism through the medium of disgusting stage-performances whose only object was to raise a laugh, and has, with few exceptions, joined in the general chorus of condemnation and mistrust. Hence in France patients submit themselves with confidence and goodwill to hypnotic treatment, whereas in England it is still necessary in most cases to remove an ill-based prejudice before the treatment can be undertaken with hope of success. For the confidence and goodwill of the patient are almost essential to success, and even after hypnosis has been induced on several occasions a patient may be so influenced by injudicious friends that he cannot again be hypnotized or, if hypnotized, is much less amenable to the power of suggestion. Various methods of hypnotization are current, but most practitioners combine the methods of Braid and of Bernheim. After asking the patient to resign himself passively into their hands, and after seating him in a comfortable arm-chair, they direct him to fix his eyes upon some small object held generally in such a position that some slight muscular strain is involved in maintaining the fixation; they then suggest to him verbally the idea or expectation of sleep and the sensations that normally accompany the oncoming of sleep, the heaviness of the eyes, the slackness of the limbs and so forth; and when the eyes show signs of fatigue, they either close them by gentle pressure or tell the subject to close them. Many also pass their hands slowly and regularly over the face, with or without contact. The old magnetizers attached great importance to such "passes," believing that by them the "magnetic fluid" was imparted to the patient; but it seems clear that, in so far as they contribute to induce hypnosis, it is in their character merely of gentle, monotonous, sensory stimulations. A well-disposed subject soon falls into a drowsy state and tends to pass into natural sleep; but by speech, by passes, or by manipulating his limbs the operator keeps in touch with him, keeps his waning attention open to the impression he himself makes. Most subjects then find it difficult or impossible to open their eyes or to make any other movement which is forbidden or said to be impossible by the operator, although they may be fully conscious of all that goes on about them and may have the conviction that if they did but make an effort they could break the spell. This is a light stage of hypnosis beyond which some subjects can hardly be induced to pass and beyond which few pass at the first attempt. But on successive occasions, or even on the first occasion, a favourable subject passes into deeper stages of hypnosis. Many attempts have been made to distinguish clearly marked and constantly occurring stages. But it seems now clear that the complex of symptoms displayed varies in all cases with the idiosyncrasies of the subject and with the methods adopted by the operator. In many subjects a waxy rigidity of the limbs appears spontaneously or can be induced by suggestion; the limbs then retain for long periods without fatigue any position given them by the operator. The most susceptible subjects pass into the stage known as artificial somnambulism. In this condition they continue to respond to all suggestions made by the operator, but seem as insensitive to all other impressions as a person in profound sleep or in coma; and on awaking from this condition they are usually oblivious of all that they have heard, said or done during the somnambulistic period. When in this last condition patients are usually more profoundly influenced by suggestions, especially post-hypnotic suggestions, than when in the lighter stages; but the lighter stages suffice for the production of many therapeutic effects. When a patient is completely hypnotized, his movements, his senses, his ideas and, to some extent, even the organic processes over which he has no voluntary control become more or less completely subject to the suggestions of the operator; and usually he is responsive to the operator alone (*rapport*) unless he is instructed by the latter to respond also to the suggestions of other persons. If left to himself the hypnotized subject will usually awake to his normal state after a period which is longer in proportion to the depth of hypnosis; and the deeper stages seem to pass over into normal sleep. The subject can in almost every case be brought quickly back to the normal state by verbal command of the operator.

The Principal Effects produced by Suggestion during Hypnosis. The subject may not only be rendered incapable of contracting any of the muscles of the voluntary system, but may also be made to use them with extraordinarily great or sustained force (though by no means in all cases). He can with difficulty refrain from performing any action commanded by the operator, and usually carries out any simple command without hesitation. Any one of the sense-organs, or any sensory region such as the skin or deep tissues of one limb may be rendered anaesthetic by verbal suggestion, aided perhaps by some gentle manipulation of the part. On this fact depends the surgical application of hypnotism. Sceptical observers are always inclined to doubt the genuineness of the anaesthesia produced by a mere word of command, but the number of surgical operations performed under hypnotic anaesthesia suffices to put its reality beyond all question. A convincing experiment may, however, be made on almost any good subject. Anaesthesia of one eye may be suggested and its reality tested in the following way. Anaesthesia of the left eye may be suggested, and the subject be instructed to fix his gaze on a distant point and to give some signal as soon as he sees the operator's finger in the peripheral field of view. The operator then brings his finger slowly from behind and to the right forwards towards the subject's line of sight. The subject signals as soon as it crosses the normal temporal boundary of the field of view of the right eye. The operator then brings his finger forward from a point behind and to the left of the subject's head. The subject allows it to cross the monocular field of the left eye and signals only when the finger enters the field of vision of the right eye across its nasal boundary. Since few persons, other than physiologists or medical men, are aware of the relations of the boundaries of the monocular and binocular fields of vision, the success of this experiment affords proof that the finger remains invisible to the subject during its passage across the monocular field of the left eye. The abolition of pain, especially of neuralgias, the pain of rheumatic and other inflammations, which is one of the most valuable applications of hypnotism, is an effect closely allied to the production of such anaesthesia.

It has often been stated that in hypnosis the senses may be rendered extraordinarily acute or hyperaesthetic, so that impressions too faint to affect the senses of the normal person may be perceived by the hypnotized subject; but in view of the fact that most observers are ignorant of the normal limits of sensitivity and discrimination, all such statements must be received with caution, until we have more convincing evidence than has yet been brought forward.

Positive and Negative Hallucinations are among the most striking effects of hypnotic suggestion. A good subject may be made to experience an hallucinatory perception of almost any object, the more easily the less unusual and out of harmony with the surroundings is the suggested object. He may, *e.g.*, be given a blank card and asked if he thinks it a good photograph of himself. He may then assent and describe the photograph in some detail, and, what is more astonishing, he may pick out the card as the one bearing the photograph, after it has been mixed with other similar blank cards. This seems to be due to the part played by *points de repère*, insignificant details of surface or texture, which serve as an objective basis around which the hallucinatory image is constructed by the pictorial imagination of the subject. A negative hallucination may be induced by telling the subject that a certain object or person is no longer present, when he ignores in every way that object or person. This is more puzzling than the positive hallucination and will be referred to again in discussing the theory of hypnosis. Both kinds of hallucination tend to be systematically and logically developed; if, *e.g.*, the subject is told that a certain person is no longer visible, he may become insensitive to impressions made on any sense by that person.

Delusions, or false beliefs as to their present situation or past experiences may be induced in many subjects. On being assured that he is some other person, or that he is in some strange situation, the subject may accept the suggestion and adapt his behaviour with great histrionic skill to the induced delusion. It is probable that many, perhaps all, subjects are vaguely aware, as we sometimes are in dreams, that the delusions and hallucinations they experience are of an unreal nature. In the lighter stages of hypnosis a subject usually remembers the events of his waking life, but in the deeper stages he is apt, while remembering the events of previous hypnotic periods, to be incapable of recalling his normal life; but in this respect, as also in respect to the extent to which on awaking he remembers the events of the hypnotic period, the suggestions of the operator usually play a determining part.

Among the organic changes that have been produced by hypnotic suggestion are slowing or acceleration of the cardiac and respiratory rhythms; rise and fall of body-temperature through two or three degrees; local erythema and even inflammation of the skin with vesication or exudation of small drops of blood; evacuation of the bowel and vomiting; modifications of the secretory activity of glands, especially of the sweat-glands.

Post-hypnotic Effects. Most subjects in whom any appreciable degree of hypnosis can be induced show some susceptibility to post-hypnotic suggestion, *i.e.* they may continue to be influenced, when restored to the fully waking state, by suggestions made during hypnosis, more especially if the operator suggests that this shall be the case; as a rule, the deeper the stage of hyp-

nosis reached, the more effective are post-hypnotic suggestions. The therapeutic applications of hypnotism depend in the main upon this post-hypnotic
continuance of the working of suggestions. If a subject is told that on awaking, or on a certain signal, or after the lapse of a given interval of time from
the moment of awaking, he will perform a certain action, he usually feels
some inclination to carry out the suggestion at the appropriate moment. If
he remembers that the action has been suggested to him he may refuse to
perform it, and if it is one repugnant to his moral nature, or merely one that
would make him appear ridiculous, he may persist in his refusal. But if the
action is of a simple and ordinary nature he will usually perform it, remarking that he cannot be comfortable till it is done. If the subject was deeply
hypnotized and remembers nothing of the hypnotic period, he will carry out
the post-hypnotic suggestion in almost every case, no matter how complicated
or absurd it may be, so long as it is not one from which his normal self would
be extremely averse; and he will respond appropriately to the suggested
signals, although he is not conscious of their having been named; he will
often perform the action in a very natural way, and will, if questioned, give
some more or less adequate reason for it. Such actions, determined by post-
hypnotic suggestions of which no conscious memory remains, may be carried
out even after the lapse of many weeks or even months. Inhibitions of movement, anaesthesia, positive and negative hallucinations, and delusions may
also be made to persist for brief periods after the termination of hypnosis;
and organic effects, such as the action of the bowels, the oncoming of sleep
and the cessation of pain, may be determined by post-hypnotic suggestion.
In short, it may be said that in a good subject all the kinds of suggestion
which will take effect during hypnosis will also be effective if given as post-
hypnotic suggestions.

Theory of the Hypnotic State. Very many so called theories of hypnosis
have been propounded, but few of them demand serious consideration. One
author ascribes all the symptoms to cerebral anaemia, another to cerebral
congestion, a third to temporary suppression of the functions of the cerebrum,
a fourth to abnormal cerebral excitability, a fifth to the independent functioning of one hemisphere. Another seeks to explain all the facts by saying
that in hypnosis our normal consciousness disappears and is replaced by a
dream-consciousness; and yet another by the assumption that every human
organism comprises two mental selves or personalities, a normal one and one
which only comes into activity during sleep and hypnosis. Most of these
"theories" would, even if true, carry us but a little way towards a complete
understanding of the facts. There is, however, one theory or principle of explanation which is now gradually taking shape under the hands of a number
of the more penetrating workers in this field, and which does seem to render

intelligible many of the principle facts. This is the theory of *mental dissociation.*

It is clear that a theory of hypnosis must attempt to give some account of the peculiar condition of the brain which is undoubtedly present as an essential feature of the state. It is therefore not enough to say with Bernheim that hypnosis is a state of abnormally increased suggestibility produced by suggestion; nor is it enough, though it is partially true, to say that it is a state of mono-ideism or one of abnormally great concentration of attention. Any theory must be stated in terms of physiological psychology, it must take account of both the psychical and the nervous peculiarities of the hypnotic state; it must exhibit the physiological condition as in some degree similar to that obtaining in normal sleep; but principally it must account for that abnormally great receptivity for ideas, and that abnormally intense and effective operation of ideas so received, which constitute abnormally great suggestibility.

The theory of mental dissociation may be stated in purely mental terms, or primarily in terms of nervous structure and function, and the latter mode of statement is probably the more profitable at the present time. The increased effectiveness of ideas might be due to one of two conditions: (1) it might be that certain tracts of the brain or the whole brain were in a condition of abnormally great excitability; or (2) an idea might operate more effectively in the mind and on the body, not because it, or the underlying brain-process was more intense than normally, but because it worked out its effects free from the interference of contrary or irrelevant ideas that might weaken its force. It is along this second line that the theory of mental dissociation attempts to explain the increased suggestibility of hypnosis. To understand the theory we must bear in mind the nature of mental process in general and of its nervous concomitants. Mental process consists in the interplay, not merely of ideas, but rather of complex dispositions which are the more or less enduring conditions of the rise of ideas to consciousness. Each such disposition seems capable of remaining inactive or quiescent for long periods, and of being excited in various degrees, either by impressions made upon the sense-organs or by the spread of excitement from other dispositions. When its excitement rises above a certain pitch of intensity, the corresponding idea rises to the focus of consciousness. These dispositions are essential factors of all mental process, the essential conditions of all mental retention. They may be called simply mental dispositions, their nature being left undefined; but for our present purpose it is advantageous to regard them as neural dispositions, complex functional groups of nervous elements or neurones. The neurones of each such group must be conceived as being so intimately connected with one another that the excitement of any part of the group at once spreads through the whole group or disposition, so that it always functions as a unit. The whole cerebrum must be conceived as consisting of a great number of such dispositions, inextricably interwoven, but interconnected in orderly fashion with very various degrees of intimacy; groups of dispositions are very intimately connected to form neural systems, so that the excitement of any one member of such a system tends to spread in succession to all the other members. On the other hand, it is a peculiarity of the reciprocal relations of all such dispositions and systems that the excitement of any one to such a degree that the corresponding idea rises to consciousness prevents or inhibits the excitement of others, *i.e.* all of them are in relations of reciprocal inhibition with one another (see MUSCLE AND NERVE). The excitement of dispositions associated together to form a system tends towards some end which, either immediately or remotely, is an action, a bodily movement, in many cases a movement of the organs of speech only. Now we know from many exact experiments that the neural dispositions act and react upon one another to some extent, even when they are excited only in so feeble a degree that the corresponding ideas do not rise to consciousness. In the normal state of the brain, then, when any idea is present to consciousness, the corresponding neural disposition is in a state of dominant excitement, but the intensity of that excitement is moderated, depressed or partially inhibited by the sub-excitement of many rival or competing dispositions of other systems with which it is connected. Suppose now that all the nervous connexions between the multitudinous dispositions of the cerebrum are by some means rendered less effective, that the association-paths are partially blocked or functionally depressed; the result will be that, while the most intimate connexions, those between dispositions of any one system remain functional or permeable, the weaker less intimate connexions, those between dispositions belonging to different systems will be practically abolished for the time being; each system of dispositions will then function more or less as an isolated system, and its activity will no longer be subject to the depressing or inhibiting influence of other systems; therefore each system, on being excited in any way, will tend to its end with more than normal force, being freed from all interferences; that is to say, each idea or system of ideas will tend to work itself out and to realize itself in action immediately, without suffering the opposition of antagonistic ideas which, in the normal state of the brain, might altogether prevent its realization in action.

The theory of mental dissociation assumes that the abnormal state of the brain that obtains during hypnosis is of this kind, a temporary functional depression of all, or of many of the associations or nervous links between the neural dispositions; that is, it regards hypnosis as a state of *relative dissociation*. The lighter the stage of hypnosis the slighter is the degree of dissociation, the deeper the stage the more nearly complete is the dissociation. It is not essential that the theory should explain in what change this stage of dissociation consists, but a view compatible with all that we know of the functions of the central nervous system may be suggested. The connexions between neural dispositions involve synapses or cell-junctions, and these seem to be the places of variable resistance which demarcate the dispositions and systems; and there is good reason to think that their resistances vary with the state of the neurones which they connect, being lowered when these are excited and raised when their excitement ebbs. Now, in the waking state, the varied stimuli, which constantly rain upon all the sense-organs, maintain the whole cerebrum in a state of sub-excitement, keep all the cerebral neurones partially charged with free nervous energy. When the subject lies down to sleep or submits himself to the hypnotizer he arrests as far as possible the flow of his thoughts, and the sensory stimuli are diminished in number and intensity. Under these conditions the general cerebral activity tends to sub-side, the free energy with which the cerebral neurones are charged ebbs away, and the synaptic resistances rise proportionally; then the effect of sensory impressions tends to be confined to the lower nervous level, and the brain tends to come to rest. If this takes place the condition of normal sleep is realized. But in inducing hypnosis the operator, by means of his words and manipulations, keeps one system of ideas and the corresponding neural system in activity, namely, the ideas connected with himself; thus he keeps open one channel of entry to the brain and mind, and through this one open channel he can introduce whatever ideas he pleases; and the ideas so introduced then operate with abnormally great effect because they work in a free field, unchecked by rival ideas and tendencies.

This theory of relative dissociation has two great merits: in the first place it goes far towards enabling us to understand in some degree most of the phenomena of hypnosis; secondly, we have good evidence that dissociation really occurs in deep hypnosis and in some allied states. Any one may readily work out for himself the application of the theory to the explanation of the power of the operator's suggestions to control movement, to induce anaesthesia, hallucinations and delusions, and to exert on the organic processes an influence greater than can be exerted by mental processes in the normal state of the brain. But the positive evidence of the occurrence of dissociation is a matter of great psychological interest and its nature must be briefly indicated. The phenomena of automatic speech and writing afford the best evidence of cerebral dissociation. Many persons can, while in an apparently normal or but very slightly abnormal condition, produce automatic writing, *i.e.* intelligibly written sentences, in some cases long connected passages, of whose import they have no knowledge, their self-conscious intelligence being continuously directed to some other task. The carrying out of post-hypnotic suggestions affords in many cases similar evidence. Thus a subject may be told that after waking he will perform some action when a given signal, such as a cough, is repeated for the fifth time. In the post-hypnotic state he remains unaware of his instructions, is not conscious of noting the signals, and yet carries out the suggestion at the fifth signal, thereby proving that the signals have been in some sense noted and counted. Many interesting varieties of this experiment have been made, some of much greater complexity; but all agreeing in indicating that the suggested action is prepared for and determined by cerebral processes that do not affect the consciousness of the subject, but seem to occur as a system of processes detached from the main stream of cerebral activity; that is to say, they imply the operation of relatively dissociated neural systems.

Many authorities go further than this; they argue that, since actions of the kind described are determined by processes which involve operations, such as counting, that we are accustomed to regard as distinctly mental in character and that normally involve conscious activity, we must believe that in these cases also consciousness or psychical activity is involved, but that it remains as a separate system or stream of consciousness concurrent with the normal or personal consciousness.

In recent years the study of various abnormal mental states, especially the investigations by French physicians of severe forms of hysteria, have brought to light many facts which seem to justify this assumption of a secondary stream of consciousness, a co- or sub-consciousness coexistent with the personal consciousness; although, from the nature of the case, an absolute proof of such co-consciousness can hardly be obtained. The co-consciousness seems to vary in degree of complexity and coherence from a mere succession of fragmentary sensations to an organized stream of mental activity, which may rival in all respects the primary consciousness; and in cases of the latter type it is usual to speak of the presence of a secondary personality. The co-consciousness seems in the simpler cases, *e.g.* in cases of hysterical or hypnotic anaesthesia, to consist of elements split off from the normal primary consciousness, which remains correspondingly poorer; and the assumption is usually made that such a stream of co-consciousness is the psychical correlate of groups and systems of neurones dissociated from the main mass of cerebral neurones. If, in spite of serious objections, we entertain this conception, we find that it helps us to give some account of various hypnotic phenomena that otherwise remain quite inexplicable; some such conception seems to be required more particularly by the facts of negative hallucination and the execution of post-hypnotic suggestions involving such operations as counting and exact discrimination without primary consciousness.

Supernormal Hypnotic Phenomena. The facts hitherto considered, strange and perplexing as many of them are, do not seem to demand for their explanation any principles of action fundamentally different from those operative in the normal human mind. But much of the interest that has centred in hypnotism in recent years has been due to the fact that some of its manifestations seem to go beyond all such principles of explanation, and to suggest the reality of modes of influence and action that science has not hitherto recognized. Of these by far the best attested are the post-hypnotic unconscious reckoning of time and telepathy or "thought-transference" (for the latter see TELEPATHY). The post-hypnotic reckoning and noting of the lapse of time seems in some instances to have been carried out, in the absence of all extraneous aids and with complete unconsciousness on the part of the normal personality, with such extreme precision that the achievement cannot be accounted for by any intensification of any faculty that we at present recognize or understand. Thus, Dr. Milne Bramwell has reported the case of a patient who, when commanded in hypnosis to perform some simple action after the lapse of many thousands of minutes, would carry out the suggestion punctually to the minute, without any means of knowing the exact time of day at which the suggestion was given or the time of day at the moment its performance fell due; more recently a similar case, even more striking in some respects, has been carefully observed and described by Dr. T. W. Mitchell. Other reported phenomena, such as telaesthesia or clairvoyance, and telekinesia, are hardly sufficiently well attested to demand serious consideration in this place.

Medical Applications of Hypnotism. The study and practice of hypnotism is not yet, and probably never will be, regarded as a normal part of the work of the general practitioner. Its successful application demands so much time, tact, and special experience, that it will probably remain, as it is now, and as it is perhaps desirable that it should remain, a specialized branch of medical practice. In England it is only in recent years that it has been possible for a medical man to apply it in his practice without incurring professional odium and some risk of loss of reputation. That, in certain classes of cases, it may effect a cure or bring relief when all other modes of treatment are of no avail is now rapidly becoming recognized; but it is less generally recognized that it may be used with great advantages as a supplement to other modes of treatment in relieving symptoms that are accentuated by nervous irritability or mental disturbance. A third wide field of usefulness lies before it in the cure of undesirable habits of many kinds. Under the first heading may be put insomnia, neuralgia, neurasthenia, hysteria in almost all its many forms; under the second, inflammations such as that of chronic rheumatism, contractures and paralyses resulting from gross lesion of the brain, epilepsy, dyspepsia, menstrual irregularities, sea-sickness; under the third, inebriety, the morphia and other drug habits, nail-biting, *enuresis nocturna,* masturbation, constipation, facial and other twitchings. In pronounced mental diseases hypnotism seems to be almost useless; for in general terms it may be said that it can be applied most effectively where the brain, the instrument through which it works, is sound and vigorous. The widespread prejudice against the use of hypnotism is no doubt largely due to the marvellous and (to most minds) mysterious character of the effects producible by its means; and this prejudice may be expected to diminish as our insight into the mode of its operation deepens. The more purely bodily results achieved by hypnotic suggestion become in some degree intelligible if we regard it as a powerful means of diverting nervous energy from one channel or organ to others so as to give physiological rest to an overworked organ or tissue, or so as to lead to the atrophy of one nervous habit and the replacement of it by a more desirable habit. And in the cure of those disorders which involve a large mental element the essential part played by it is to drive out some habitually recurrent idea and to replace it by some idea, expectation or conviction of healthy tendency.

It seems clear that the various systems of "mind-curing" in the hands of persons lacking all medical training, which are now so frequently the cause of distressing and needless disasters owe their rapid spread to the fact that the medical profession has hitherto neglected to attach sufficient importance to the mental factor in the causation and cure of disease; and it seems clear, too, that a more general and more intelligent appreciation of the possibilities of hypnotic treatment would constitute the best means at the disposal of the profession for combating this growing evil.

The Dangers of Hypnotism. Much has been written on this head of late years, and some of the enthusiastic advocates of hypnotic treatment have done harm to their cause by ignoring or denying in a too thoroughgoing manner the possibility of undesirable results of the spread of the knowledge and practice of hypnotism. Like all powerful agencies, chloroform or morphia, dynamite or strong electric currents, hypnotic suggestion can only be safely used by those who have special knowledge and experience, and, like them, it is liable to abuse. There is little doubt that, if a subject is repeatedly hypnotized and made to entertain all kinds of absurd delusions and to carry out very frequently posthypnotic suggestions, he may be liable to some ill-defined harm; also, that an unprincipled hypnotizer might secure an undue influence over a naturally weak subject.

But there is no ground for the belief that hypnotic treatment, applied with good intentions and reasonable care and judgment, does or can produce deleterious effects, such as weakening of the will or liability to fall spontaneously into hypnosis. All physicians of large experience in hypnotic practice are in agreement in respect to this point. But some difference of opinion exists as to the possibility of deliberately inducing a subject to commit improper or criminal actions during hypnosis or by posthypnotic suggestion. There is, however, no doubt that subjects retain even in deep hypnosis a very considerable power of resistance to any suggestion that is repugnant to their moral nature; and it has been shown that, on some cases in which a subject in hypnosis is made to perform some ostensibly criminal action, such as firing an unloaded pistol at a bystander or putting poison into a cup for him to drink, he is aware, however obscurely, of the unreal nature of the situation. Nevertheless, it must be admitted that a person lacking in moral sentiments might be induced to commit actions from which in the normal state he would abstain, if only from fear of punishment; and it is probable that a skillful and evil-intentioned operator could in some cases so deceive a well-disposed subject as to lead him into wrong-doing. The proper precaution against such dangers is legislative regulation of the practice of hypnotism such as is already enforced in some countries.

3.   *Hypnosis**

Hypnosis is a state allied to sleep; it may be called an artificial sleep in-duced by the personal influence of the hypnotist or hypnotiser. The inter-esting history of the struggle to obtain scientific recognition of hypnosis and of the striking phenomena presented by the hypnotised person, is well known and need not be repeated here.[1] It may suffice to say that the controversy was initiated by the work of Mesmer in Vienna in the third quarter of the eighteenth century, and was continued until, towards the end of the nine-teenth century, the reality of the hypnotic state and its claims to scientific attention were generally admitted. Mesmer had professed to produce his effects by imparting a mysterious effluence or fluid to his patient, a fluid which came to be known as "animal magnetism." Bertrand, and later Braid, who introduced the term "hypnotism," about 1845, showed clearly that the effects produced are to be explained in the main psychologically rather than by postulating any mysterious physical or physiological fluids.

The leaders of the Nancy school, Liébault and Bernheim, carried Braid's tendency to excess; they declared that hypnotism is the use of suggestion, nothing else and nothing more. The Salpêtrière school, on the other hand, led by Charcot, declared that hypnosis was a peculiar disease, or a symptom of a disease, that it could only be induced in neurotic patients, that, in fact, susceptibility to hypnosis is a symptom of hysteria. Prof. Pierre Janet and a few others still maintain this view, in spite of the fact that scores of ex-perienced physicians have declared against it, and have reported that they find it possible to hypnotise a very large proportion of perfectly normal

---

* Originally published as Chap. IV in William McDougall's *An Outline of Abnormal Psychology.* London: Methuen & Co., Ltd., 1926.

healthy persons (many have claimed ninety per cent or higher). I have no hesitation in accepting the latter view. I have found that strong, well-balanced, healthy men are, in many cases, easy subjects, provided they are perfectly willing to be hypnotised.

HYPNOSIS ALLIED TO SLEEP

Some authors refuse to regard hypnosis as allied to sleep, on the ground that some subjects in hypnosis are lively, walk and talk, and observe the world about them with all their senses. Yet the affinity between sleep and hypnosis, as it most commonly appears, is very close, and the more active phases are to be regarded as anomalies induced by training of the subject. In this connection we must remember that in sleep also complete quiescence is by no means a rule without exceptions; most of us dream more than we suppose, and some of us walk and talk in our sleep occasionally. If one merely induces deep hypnosis and leaves the patient alone, the resemblance of hypnosis to normal sleep is very close. He then lies inert in a condition distinguishable from sleep only in one way, namely, in that he continues for some time to be responsive to the operator in a quite peculiar manner indicated by the word *rapport*. But, if the patient is left to himself, this peculiarity passes away gradually, and the condition becomes indistinguishable from normal sleep; the patient will then continue to sleep for some little time and waken spontaneously as from normal sleep. While the *rapport* continues, the patient, though responsive (and even extremely sensitive in some, though not in all, cases) to every word or touch or other impression from the operator, seems to remain as little receptive of other sense-impressions as the normal sleeper. We may say, then, that a typical deep hypnosis is sleep modified by the *rapport* between patient and operator.

One essential problem of hypnosis is, then, the nature of this *rapport*; and this problem is one of extreme interest. Hypnotism is undoubtedly the most important, the most fruitful and far-reaching, method of experimental psychology. It provides the possibility of inducing in a normal subject, in a temporary and entirely controllable way, almost all the phenomena of functional disorder; and thus enables us to study them experimentally.

Before taking up the problem of *rapport* the more striking phenomena must be concisely reviewed.

INDUCTION OF HYPNOSIS

There is no one method or rule of procedure for the induction of hypnosis. The various methods fall, however, under two heads, the method of domination and the method of co-operation. The former consists essentially in adopting a domineering, commanding tone, and in assuming the possession of a mysterious and tremendous power which one is about to exercise on the patient; in short, the essence of this method is to throw the patient into an attitude of submissive awe towards the operator. The other method consists in explaining as clearly as possible to the patient the nature of the operation, and of the results to be expected, taking him into one's confidence and eliciting his voluntary co-operation. Both methods have their proper occasions. For the purposes of the showman, and for dealing with patients of certain types, the domineering method is, no doubt, the more effective. It is possible that with the majority of patients it may be more effective in producing immediate results; but it has its drawbacks. By the use of it we run a risk of undermining the patient's morale, of creating in him an enduring attitude of dependence; whereas, if we use the method of co-operation, making him feel that he must take an intelligent and voluntary part in the process, rather than merely resign himself into our hands like a mass of soft clay, we avoid that risk.

The habitual use by physicians of one or other of the two methods accounts, I think, for some of the discrepancies of results obtained, especially for the wide discrepancies of statements as to the susceptibility to hypnosis. Janet, following Charcot, and followed in turn by Dr. William Brown and others, asserts that only neurotic subjects are susceptible to hypnotism; and these observers report that, in proportion as they succeed in curing the neurosis, the patient ceases to be susceptible. The majority of physicians who have used hypnosis extensively do not accept these generalisations. They find that a large proportion of perfectly normal persons are susceptible in various degrees, and that their patients are no less susceptible after the cure of their functional troubles than while still subject to them.

The explanation of the discrepancy is, I suggest, to be found in the different effects produced by the two methods. The normal man does not like to be dominated; he resents a domineering manner and every attempt "to put anything over on him" by moral domination. And if a normal man does not desire and voluntarily consent to be hypnotised, any attempt to induce hypnosis has very small prospect of success. I have sometimes made the following experiment with subjects whom I have repeatedly, easily, and deeply hypnotised. I say to the subject: "On this occasion do exactly as usual, with this difference only—make up your mind that you will remain wide-awake in spite of all that I say to you." I then find it impossible to induce hypnosis. I will not assert that hypnosis can in no case be induced against the will of the patient. I think that with some normal persons, under peculiarly favourable conditions, such as the public stage and a group of other subjects already hypnotised, and a fear in the subject that he cannot resist and is going to be made a fool of against his will—I believe that under such conditions success may sometimes be obtained. But I have never made the attempt.

This natural resentment of the normal man towards any attempt to overwhelm him against his desire and will, sufficiently accounts for the lack of susceptibility of normal persons towards those hypnotists who use the domineering method. It also accounts for the loss of susceptibility of patients when they have been cured of their neuroses. The patient, broken down in health, perhaps after long suffering from a mysterious and obstinate and distressing disorder, is apt to welcome any procedure that promises relief, and to yield himself passively to his physician, as he would yield his body to the surgeon if he suffered from some acute surgical disorder. But, when he has recovered his health, his self-confidence, and his self-respect, he will no longer consent to yield himself up in this passive fashion; just as he would not consent to be laid on the operating-table. He now resents the hypnotic procedure, and asserts himself successfully against every attempt to repeat it.

On the other hand, the method that invites the intelligent co-operation of the subject, whether for therapeutic or for purely experimental purposes, runs much less risk of inducing any such resentment. A further ground of the discrepancy between Janet's view and the more widely accepted one is that Janet and those who think with him refuse to recognise as hypnosis the lighter stages, and deny the name to every stage short of a deep hypnosis with post-hypnotic amnesia. This refusal is entirely without justification.[2]

The usual procedure, which may vary much in detail, is to ask the patient, B,[3] to recline in an armchair or couch, to make himself as comfortable as possible, and to relax all his muscles. He is told that he will feel restful and sleepy, perhaps pass into sleep, and that he should think of some distant pleasant scene. For a short time, not exceeding one or two minutes at most, he is asked to gaze steadily at some small object held about a foot from his forehead, a little above the level of the normal line of vision. This fixation serves to induce fatigue in the muscles about the eyes. We have seen reason to believe that fatigue-sensations from these muscles are normal stimuli of the impulse to sleep. B is told that his muscles are relaxing more completely, that his limbs feel heavy, that his eyes are growing tired. Presently he is told that his eyes are now closing; and, as by this time he is glad to be relieved of the slightly fatiguing strain, his eyes usually close. The operator continues to talk to him, quietly but firmly suggesting complete rest and relaxation, sense of weight in limbs and eyelids, an increasing numbness, a warm glow, and whatever of the usual experiences that attend the process of falling asleep he may like to mention. At the same time it is well to stroke the patient's limbs lightly from time to time, handle them gently to display and encourage complete relaxation, and to stroke lightly the face, either with or without contact. These contacts and these strokings, the so-called "passes," were formerly supposed to be the essential process of imparting the physician's "animal magnetism" to the patient. There are at the present day a few serious believers in this theory, and it is perhaps impossible to rule out some such influence with complete confidence, in the light of the work of Prof. S. Alrutz. But we realise now that the principal function of the "passes," as of the operator's flow of words, is twofold: first, to supply a monotonous flow of rhythmic sensory stimulations; secondly, to keep the patient in touch with the operator, to keep him aware of the presence of the operator, and thus to contribute to the establishment of *rapport*. In the absence of such reminders, a susceptible subject may quickly pass into sleep, but a sleep without *rapport*; he is then no more responsive to the operator than the normal sleeper, and, in fact, is in normal sleep.

The first definite sign of hypnosis, beyond the successful relaxation of all muscles, is a disinclination to move. This quickly passes into an incapacity to move any part of which the operator suggests that it is now too heavy, too sleepy, to be moved. In this early stage many patients feel and assert (truly enough) that they could move the part if they really wished to, that is to say, if they had a sufficiently strong motive for so doing; but they do not wish to move—to do so would require an effort which they are not disposed to make. This is the critical point of the procedure. If the operator now challenges the patient to make a certain movement, insinuating or boldly asserting (according to his taste and judgment) that the movement is impossible, and if then the patient tries and fails to achieve the movement, the success of this suggestion strongly disposes the patient to the acceptance of further and more difficult suggestions. In many cases the patient is surprised to find that he cannot make the movement, or, if he succeeds, that it required much more effort than he had anticipated. But challenges to movement in this early stage are doubtful policy. If the suggestion fails, the failure is prejudicial, though not necessarily fatal, to the success of further suggestions. For this reason it is, in many cases, good policy to leave the degree of suggestibility undetermined by such challenges until other signs of the hypnotic condition appear. But if a suggestion of incapacity to make a movement succeeds, it may with advantage be followed up with similar suggestions, proceeding from the easier to the more difficult. The easier are suggestions of incapacity to open the eyes, to raise the hand as it lies on the palm of the operator, or to relax and separate the clasped hands. The success of any such suggestions may be accepted as evidence that the hypnotic state has set in. But here we cannot be dogmatic; for it is often possible to succeed with such suggestions to a person who seems to be in a fully waking state. We can only assert that such success shows the patient to be suggestible to the operator, and indicates the probability of successful induction of a distinctly hypnotic condition. In some subjects with whom simple suggestions of incapacity to move succeed, no deeper state can be induced; and it may be a fair question whether they can then be said to have been hypnotised. There is no sharp line between hypnosis and the waking state, or between hypnosis and normal sleep.

Most of the subjects with whom these first suggestions succeed will soon pass, either spontaneously or with the aid of further suggestions, into a more marked stage of hypnosis. In this slightly more marked stage, contracture of muscles may be induced; e.g. the extended arm may be rendered rigid by verbal suggestion aided by a few passes. And now the patient will fail to achieve a forbidden movement, not merely because he cannot or will not, or has not sufficient motive to, make the necessary effort; but because, when he tries to make the movement and succeeds in innervating the proper muscles, the antagonistic muscles come into play and prevent the movement. At this stage, then, there is manifested a certain splitting of the personality, a conflict of one part against another: the muscles of one set obey the one part, the conscious willing subject; the antagonistic muscles obey some other part of the personality, which understands and is subservient to the commands and suggestions of the operator.

This simple experimental evidence of division of the personality is of the first importance; for just such division is the very essence of many functional disorders. All such evidence deserves our closest attention; hypnotic experiment furnishes it in abundance.

WAXY PLASTICITY

A rather more advanced stage which may come on with or without suggestion of it (as I have carefully ascertained in many cases) is a plastic condition of the limbs. This occurs more readily with the arms than with the lower limbs. It is the symptom characteristic of catalepsy. When this condition, generally called "waxy rigidity," has set in, the arm and hand and fingers may be placed by the operator in any position, no matter how grotesque, and the position is maintained without the slightest indication of inclination to change it. A complacent subject who has not reached this stage may retain such positions, but only in an imperfect manner. And there is no better indication of a true and fairly deep hypnosis than a genuine waxy plasticity. When the condition is fully attained, the limb resembles a piece of soft lead piping; it may be bent and twisted into any anatomical position and displays as complete inertia as the leaden pipe similarly bent. And an arm may be maintained in such a position, requiring considerable muscular work for its maintenance, for an indefinite period. I have often observed its maintenance for as many as thirty minutes, but have not cared to push the experiment farther. If the maintenance of the position is due merely to the complacence of the conscious subject, the phenomenon is imperfect in various subtle ways; the limb is less perfectly plastic, and it soon reveals, by tremors and a tendency to drop, that the patient is feeling fatigue. The truly plastic limb, on the other hand, reveals no sign of preference for one position rather than another; *e.g.*, if an arm that has been extended in air for five minutes be given a downward push, in the truly plastic subject it moves exactly as far as it is pushed and no farther (like a leaden pipe); but, in the merely complacent subject, the downward movement is prolonged, and generally is continued until the arm reaches a position of rest.

Sometimes, but not always, the onset of plasticity of a limb is accompanied by complete anæsthesia of it; or the anæsthesia sets in later and gradually becomes complete, with or without the aid of suggestion. The subject may report (either at the time or post-hypnotically) that the limb becomes more and more numb, until he loses all sense of it; he is no longer directly aware of it or of its position; it seems to have passed completely out of his field of consciousness, to have been subtracted from his total consciousness of his bodily self.

Deeper Stages of Hypnosis

Plasticity does not of itself indicate the attainment of a very deep hypnosis. B may continue to be aware of his surroundings and to be able to give post-hypnotically a fairly complete account of his experience at this time. The deeper stages are followed by post-hypnotic amnesia. Whether this is in part due to the suggestion of sleep and the knowledge that normal sleep is followed by amnesia, is not clear. But it seems to result spontaneously in susceptible subjects; and it may be induced in others by suggestion. The deeper stages are revealed also by a more complete subjection to the operator's suggestions than obtains in the lighter stages. For this reason the deeper stages are, on the whole, more favourable to the success of therapeutic suggestion. But many physicians are content to aim at only the lighter stages, finding them sufficient for most therapeutic purposes.

In the deeper stages the motor and sensory functions are completely controlled by the suggestions of the operator. He can at once induce or remove any form of paralysis or contracture and complete anæsthesia of any part or organ. The sceptical observer sometimes is inclined to doubt the genuineness of the anæsthesia, even if the patient shows no flinching when pricked or pinched. I am therefore accustomed to make the following demonstration to my students. Even an educated layman, still more a labouring man, is commonly quite ignorant of the relations between the fields of the two eyes, does not know that in the normal binocular field only the central part is binocular, and that the share of the right eye in it is bounded on the left side by the outline of his nose. I therefore suggest to the subject complete blindness of the left eye, and proceed to demonstrate its blindness as follows: I show the subject, B, a small piece of white paper, and, as he sits with both eyes open, I stand behind him and instruct him to say "now" directly he catches sight of this bit of paper. Holding the paper between finger and thumb, I bring it forward from behind B and on his right side, gently waving it to attract his attention the more readily. As soon as it enters the field of vision of B's right eye, *i.e.*, as soon as it comes beyond the coronal plane on his right side, he answers "now." I then repeat the procedure on the left side. If the suggestion of anæsthesia of the left eye has been successful, B ignores the advancing bit of paper, until the moment at which it crosses the boundary of the field of vision of the right eye (formed by the profile of the nose) when he cries "now." This reaction could be shammed only by a person well acquainted with the functional relations of the two eyes; and, since it succeeds with any good subject, it demonstrates a real anæsthesia, or blindness of some kind, of the left eye.

These motor and sensory phenomena imply clearly some functional dissociation in the nervous system, some rupture of functional continuity within the nervous system. For example, when the left arm is completely anæsthetic, and completely beyond the voluntary control of the patient, whether in a flaccid paralysis or a state of contracture or plasticity, we are justified, as it seems to me, in inferring that the neurones, both sensory and motor, directly connected with the limb and serving to connect it with the brain and the rest of the personality, are somehow shut off or isolated; that their functional continuity with other neurone systems is interrupted. Where, at what level, this rupture of continuity occurs is a difficult question. We may, I think, feel sure that the rupture occurs at synaptic junctions; but whether at those of the spinal, the subcortical, or the cortical level, it is difficult to say. Perhaps it is sometimes at one level, sometimes at another. But there are facts indicating that in some cases the dissociating rupture occurs in the cerebrum and involves a considerable system of neurones. These are the facts of negative hallucinations presently to be discussed.

In the deeper stages of hypnosis not only are B's motor and perceptual powers completely controllable by suggestion; but also he can be made to entertain various delusions and hallucinations. He can be made to see and hear things that are not there, and to believe, or to act as though he believed, all sorts of absurdities. If told that he is Julius Cæsar, he will play the part, and in general will play it far better than he would or could in the waking state. These are the phenomena of which the stage-hypnotist makes use in order to amuse his audience. And these also have been made the centre of a prolonged controversy as to the degree to which hypnotic influence can be used to induce improper or criminal acts.

HYPNOTISM AND CRIME

Since it is possible to put a paper dagger in the hand of a hypnotic subject and induce him to strike it vigorously against the bosom of a bystander, or to induce him to put what is alleged to be poison into his neighbour's cup, it was natural that the question should arise—Can a man be induced by hypnotic suggestion to commit a crime? Some distinguished authorities, notably Delbœuf and Liégeois, were inclined to support a general affirmative answer. But it has been made clear that, though it is not possible to assert that hypnotism may not be used to bring a criminally disposed person to the point of action, it is not possible to induce criminal actions on the part of a normal person by simple direct suggestion. Prof. Janet illustrates the point with an amusing story. A great authority had demonstrated to a group of professors and students how easily he could induce his patient, a respectable young woman, to commit enormities with paper daggers and harmless poisons. Then the professors left the patient to the tender mercies of the students, who suggested to her that she strip off all her clothes. At once the young woman came out of her hypnosis and went home in a state of moral indignation. The story represents the truth; namely, that the patient cannot easily be induced to perform any action to which his moral character is decidedly opposed.

Again we have evidence, in these phenomena, of a temporary disintegration or splitting of the personality. While one part accepts absurd suggestions and acts them out in systematic fashion, another part silently watches, aware that the whole thing is as it were a game; and, if the game threatens to go too far, to overstep the limits prescribed by the moral nature of the subject, this part becomes active, steps in, and puts an end to the game by terminating the hypnosis and effecting the reintegration of personality; that is to say, a sufficiently strong motive succeeds in effecting reintegration.

NEGATIVE HALLUCINATIONS

"Negative hallucinations" provide interesting evidence of the splitting of the personality. The phenomenon may be illustrated in the following way.

B is told that one of the persons present is no longer present. He then be-haves as though A were imperceptible by him. If told to go over and sit on the chair occupied by A, B will go and sit down on A's lap, and then perhaps appear puzzled by the strangeness of the chair. If asked whether he can see or hear or touch A, he stoutly denies that he can perceive him. But if you watch B carefully, it is obvious that in some sense he does perceive A; for in going about the room he avoids him, and he also avoids looking directly at A.

A more elaborate demonstration is the following, which I once made with a Hindu subject. I place five new postage stamps upon a white card and ask B to count them, which he does correctly, pointing his finger to each in turn. I then point to two of the stamps and tell him they will be no longer there when he again looks at the card. I then ask him to count the stamps again, and he points to and counts the three stamps and denies that the others are there. I then shuffle the stamps, while hidden from his vision, and ask him to count again. In spite of the changes of position of the stamps, B still neglects and denies the two tabooed stamps. This illustrates two points: first, that the two stamps are really in some sense perceived; secondly, that they are perceived and finely discriminated from the other three; for, if they were not thus perceived and discriminated, they could not be singled out for neglect. But, nevertheless, the two stamps are in some sense really in-visible to the subject. For, after rousing him from his hypnosis, and when he is apparently fully awake and normal, I again ask him to count the stamps, and again he neglects and stoutly denies the forbidden two. I then assure him that five stamps are there, and I point to each in turn; but still he denies the visibility of the two and asserts he sees only three stamps. I then take B's finger, and while he intently looks at the card, I approach his finger to the edge of one of the forbidden stamps. At the moment his finger touches the edge of the stamp, he reports that it becomes visible, at first dimly, then in full colour and form. The same procedure restores the second stamp to visibility.

The paradox that the stamps are seen and yet not seen by the patient can only be resolved by the hypothesis that he at the time is a divided person-ality, one part of which sees the two stamps and prevents the other part from seeing them. In order to describe the facts intelligibly, we must speak no longer of B, the integrated personality, but rather of B1 and B2, B's two separately functioning parts.

The reader must not suppose that the discrimination of the stamps in the foregoing experiment implies some extraordinarily increased perceptual acu-ity; for any normal person can, by close inspection, discriminate and recog-nise one or two postage-stamps among others. The books contain many statements about marvellously increased powers of perception on the part of subjects in hypnosis. To the best of my belief these are in the main errors, founded largely on the reporters' ignorance of the fineness of our discrimination. The limits of such powers seem to be set by such unchangeable anatomical conditions as the size and pattern of the rods and cones of the retina; and most normal men can and do achieve perceptions approaching these natural limitations. The work of the Cambridge Expedition to Torres Straits, in which I took part at the end of last century, showed that even the much-vaunted perceptual acuity of savage men in the main exceeds our own only in respect of those things in which they are particularly interested and practised, and that primitive men's perceptions have the same anatomical limits as our own. Where they excel us, it is due to a mental fineness of discrimination rather than to any considerable superiority of sense-organs. I have, therefore, always been sceptical of the tall stories of hypnotic perceptions, or hyperæsthesia, and I have never found evidence of any considerable extension of power along this line.[4]

The same may be said of the memory functions. It is true that in hypnosis, especially in its deeper stages, the power of recall of seemingly forgotten incidents, especially those of early childhood, is greatly increased; and this is one of the chief uses to which hypnosis may be put in therapeutic work. The increased power of recall renders hypnotism most valuable as a method of mental exploration. But, in the few experiments I have made along this line, I have failed to find evidence of increased retentiveness.

POST-HYPNOTIC PHENOMENA

We may now consider some very interesting post-hypnotic phenomena, which reveal even more unmistakably the fact of dissociation resulting in division of the conscious personality.

If, during deep hypnosis, a subject be told that at a given signal after wakening he will perform some simple action, the action is usually performed in a natural manner. For example, I tell B, during hypnosis, that when I put my hand in my pocket he will open the window. After he has been wakened and has opened the window, I ask him why he did so. If B is not amnesic for the hypnotic period, he will probably say: "Because you told me to do so." But if he is amnesic he will give some plausible reason, *e.g.*, although the air may be cool and fresh, he may say that the room seemed to him stuffy and hot. That is to say, he rationalises; he does not know the motive of his action, and so he discovers a plausible reason for it. Such instances are of immense importance for the theory of motivation, and reveal most clearly the difference between "motives" and "reasons."

In many such cases, if one allows the post-hypnotic action to pass without remark, and a little later inquires about it, B will deny all memory of the action; a fact which shows that the action was performed in an automatic or quasi-automatic fashion. Now suppose we complicate the suggestion and tell B that he will open the window when I put my hand in my pocket for the ninth time. I waken B and engage him in conversation, putting my hand in and out of my pocket occasionally, and he carries out the suggestion. If B is closely observed, it may be noticed that he seems to keep a furtive watch on my hands. Yet if, either before or after carrying out the suggestion, I ask him whether he is aware of any suggestion I have given for post-hypnotic action, he will stoutly deny all knowledge of the instruction. Yet he cannot properly be accused of lying. The part of him, B1, that answers my question speaks the truth in saying that he knows nothing of the instruction. The signals have been observed and counted, and the action carried out by a different part of him, B2.

The same fact, the division of the personality, is revealed also in the following simple experiments. B's hands are clasped together during hypnosis, and he is told that he cannot unclasp and separate them until I blow my nose. He is then wakened. He looks at his hands in astonishment and finds he cannot relax his fingers. He is then challenged to do his best, and putting forth a great effort, he pulls and tugs at his hands. In some cases he succeeds in freeing his hands; in others he gives up in despair. In the latter case, I ask him what signal is to free his hands, and he asserts he has no idea of it. I make various signals; I clap my hands and stamp on the floor. At each signal B makes a hopeful effort, but in vain. Then I take out my handkerchief and blow my nose; and at once he separates his hands with an air of relief. But still, in many cases, B, or rather B1, remains ignorant of the releasing signal, and may even deny that I have blown my nose. The suggestion has been received, remembered, and acted upon by B2.

In another case (I am describing actual experiments) B, a psychologist who is interested in hypnotic theory, is told that at a given signal he will rise from his chair and sit down in another. On being wakened he denies all knowledge of the instruction; and at the signal he sits tight; but he looks at the other chair and shows a certain uneasiness. Presently B says: "I guess you told me that I must go and sit in that chair, but I'm not going to do it." He continues to sit, but he grows more and more uneasy; and presently begins to assert his determination to remain where he is. In the end he says, "Oh, dash it! I suppose I had better do it!" and forthwith gets up and takes the other chair.

In another case B is instructed to perform some absurd action, such as standing on his head, or putting a chair on the table. When the signal is given it becomes obvious that he is the seat of a conflict. His behaviour and his subsequent statements alike show that he wants to perform the action; that he feels an impulse to perform it, but restrains himself because of the absurd nature of the act. In some such instances B succeeds in suppressing the impulse and goes away in triumph. But I have known him to come back after an hour or so and say: "I suppose you told me to put a chair on the table. I shan't be easy till I've done it, so here goes." And he puts the chair on the table and goes off with an easy mind, a "good conscience."[5]

In another case B is told that, when the evening's work is over, he will not go out of the room before the other two persons present. When the time comes to go, B makes no move. Presently we open the door and invite him, as a visitor, to go first. He politely refuses; we argue; he resists. We take him by the shoulders and push him; he struggles against us with all his strength. We give in and let him have his way, and he is satisfied. Being an old subject he suspects it is all due to suggestion, but that does not remove his aversion from going out of the room before us.

In all such instances we have to do with a divided personality; not merely a division of a stream of sensations or atoms of consciousness, but a division involving the conative functions, each of the conflicting conative functions being intelligently directed by memory and sense-perception. They are but accentuated illustrations of a principle which is constantly at work in normal life, a principle defined and insisted upon in Part I [*An Outline of Abnormal Psychology*] as "the subconscious persistence of conation."

How long such suggestions might continue to work effectively I do not know. Presumably they would gradually lose their potency with the lapse of time. But it is obvious that the therapeutic efficiency of direct suggestion depends upon the persistence of such effects; and such efficiency, though often disappointing, is sometimes surprisingly great.[6] There is, however, no room for doubt that the effect may persist over days and weeks.[7] It is sometimes justifiable to make such experiments by way of demonstrating to the patient one's power over him, thus increasing that power. For example, in a very severe case of drug-habit, such means seemed justifiable. In this case B was a soldier in hospital. I tell him in hypnosis that at noon two days hence he will come into my office. As the clock strikes twelve on the appointed day, I see him through the ground-glass door, hesitating outside. He has no business to be there or to come to my office without orders. He paces up and down uneasily for a time; then opens the door and comes in apologetically, explaining that he just wants to see me, he doesn't know why.

POST-HYPNOTIC APPRECIATION OF TIME

Several trustworthy observers, notably Edmund Gurney, Delbœuf, Milne Branwell, and Dr. T. W. Mitchell, have conducted many successful experiments of the following nature. B is told in hypnosis that, after a specified number of minutes, he will write down his name and the time of day on a piece of paper and send it to his physician. The number of minutes mentioned has ranged up to many thousands. Yet, in a large proportion of such experiments with several subjects, the instruction has been carried out, generally with very slight error, the error amounting to less than a minute in some cases, and to a few minutes only in many others. Yet in each case the experienced observer was satisfied that B spoke the truth in asserting that in the waking state he did not know (could not recollect) the instruction given him, was not aware of making any calculation, of counting the passage of hours, minutes, or days, and did not anticipate consciously the moment at which the act fell due until he felt an impulse to execute it.[8]

There is evidence that various methods of calculation, and of counting the lapse of time, were adopted by the several subjects. What I wish to insist on here is the fact that in all cases, whatever the method of calculation or counting or recording, the intellectual operation was carried on subconsciously so far as these experienced and cautious experimenters could ascertain. And in the light of a great mass of other evidence, of which the production of automatic writing is only one, though perhaps the most striking kind, there is no justification for doubting that in these cases the complicated mental process of determining the designated moment was actually performed subconsciously.

Dr. T. W. Mitchell, a most careful and critical worker, has given a report of his own experiments in this line, and a critical survey of those of other workers.[9] He writes: "I have repeated Gurney's experiments on several somnambules, and I find that there is considerable variation in the methods used by them for insuring the fulfilment of the act on the proper day. The method used by any particular subject seems to depend on various circumstances. In the first place it will depend on his standard of education. If, in the waking state, he is not good at mental arithmetic, or if mental arithmetic is distasteful to him, he will probably use the most elementary method of arriving at the correct day, namely, simply counting the days as they pass. But if he can do sums mentally without difficulty, he will generally make some calculation, either in hypnosis or subconsciously in post-hypnosis, so as to arrive at the terminal day, and then fix it in his mind." This passage refers to experiments in which a given day only was designated. But similar varieties were found in dealing with time-intervals specified in minutes; in these cases calculation, rather than mere counting, was the rule. Some of the subjects performed the operations subconsciously more accurately and more rapidly than they could achieve similar operations by conscious waking calculations.

As regards the subconscious calculations, Dr. Mitchell finds the following interested facts well substantiated: some subjects will reveal in hypnosis, intervening between the giving of the suggestion and the designated moment, memory of the suggestion and of the time the act will fall due, although in the waking state they cannot command this knowledge; yet others, even in hypnosis, may have no recollection of making the calculation; in which cases such recollection may sometimes be obtained by plunging the subject into a deeper stage of hypnosis. "If the calculations are made during hypnosis there is, as a rule, no difficulty in remembering in subsequent hypnosis the various steps by which the answer is arrived at." But, if the calculation is made subconsciously in the waking state, then "only under exceptional circumstances and by inducing a very deep stage of hypnosis have I succeeded in reviving in the mind of the subject the slightest recollection of the various stages of the mental process employed in the solution of the problems."

This observation is only one among many evidences that in hypnosis we do not always or necessarily bring to light all that goes on, or has gone on, subconsciously; that the subconscious activities may be of various degrees of remoteness from waking consciousness or, as it is generally said, that there are, in some subjects at least, many strata of submerged or subconscious mental life. These evidences show the inadequacy of that too simplified and schematic interpretation of the subconscious activities which consists in regarding every personality as two-fold, as comprising a conscious and a subconscious personality, or a conscious and an unconscious mind. In other words, though in many cases the phenomena of hypnosis may be intelligibly described by postulating the disintegration of the personality into two parts, B1 and B2; yet in other cases it is necessary to recognise that the disintegration goes farther and results in the independent operation of an undefined number of partial personalities, B1, B2, B3, . . . Bn.

Among all the many instructive post-hypnotic facts perhaps the most deserving of attention (beyond those pointing to the dissociation, splitting, or division of the personality into independently operating parts) are those revealed by the introspective statements of the subject. Upon the arrival of the moment or the signal prescribed for the execution of some post-hypnotic action, the subject commonly becomes aware of an impulse to act. Sometimes this awareness is nothing more than an obscure uneasiness, a sense that something is to be done (comparable to the similar uneasiness which we sometimes feel when we have forgotten some task or errand which we have resolved to execute at some moment in the future) ; sometimes it is experienced as an impulse vaguely directed towards some goal not fully defined; sometimes it is an impulse towards a goal clearly defined in consciousness. Such an impulse is most vividly experienced when the subject for any reason resists its execution and, perhaps, strives consciously, and with varying success, to resist and suppress it.

ORGANIC EFFECTS OF HYPNOTIC SUGGESTION

The therapeutic value of direct suggestion in hypnosis (and however uncertain these effects, they are sometimes striking) depends largely on the fact that by hypnotic suggestion we can sometimes produce upon the organic processes (processes of metabolism, circulation, and other processes which normally go on independently of our conscious control) effects far exceeding any that can be produced by the direct volition of the subject.

These organic processes are normally regulated, in a manner and degree of which we have but little understanding, by the so-called autonomic or sympathetic nervous system. This system is not separate from or independent of the rest of the nervous system; it has, however, a relative independence and is little subject to voluntary control. The degree of such control varies from subject to subject. In rare cases a subject can by direct volition modify the rate of the heart-beat; and others seem to be able to affect directly the circulation of the blood in various parts of the body. For example, I have carefully observed a man who could at will throw himself into a trance-like state, in which his left arm became relatively bloodless, so that no bleeding occurred when a coarse needle was thrust through a fold of the skin.

In all of us these organic, and especially the visceral, functions are modified through nervous action during emotional excitements; and some of us can obtain some indirect control of them, both in the way of inhibition and of increase of function, by provoking in ourselves emotional excitements, a task we can accomplish with various degrees of success by voluntarily thinking of suitable objects and situations. Of the functions of such viscera as the bladder, the bowel, the sex-organs, and the salivary glands, we normally enjoy a partial voluntary control. It is these partial and imperfect routes of control which seem to be more efficiently brought into play by hypnotic suggestion than by any direct effort of the waking personality. The nature and limits of such control are undefined and very little understood at present. But the experimental study of them in hypnosis is of some little interest, if only because in the neuroses similar modifications of organic and visceral functions often constitute a prominent and sometimes a distressing feature of the condition.

I will merely indicate some of the best-established instances of such control by hypnotic suggestion. In many subjects the bowels and bladder may be regulated or disturbed by suggestion. In others the flow of blood to a limb or other part may be increased or diminished; a result which is revealed not only to the eye but also by applying a surface thermometer to the part. In this way I have observed in several subjects changes of surface temperature of 10° Fahrenheit or more, produced after a few minutes of repeated suggestion of heat or coldness in the part.

More difficult to produce, and probably only to be obtained in rare subjects, are blisters, or extravasations of blood and lymph in areas on the skin. I have observed these in one case; and Dr. J. A. Hadfield, at my instigation, has succeeded in obtaining the formation of blisters on one exceptionally good subject. Others have reported similar results. More interesting, perhaps, are the careful observations of the late Prof. Delbœuf, who made the converse experiment of attempting to promote healing by direct suggestion. In two subjects he produced burns on the skin of both forearms, taking care to make them symmetrical and equally severe on both limbs. Taking all due precautions, he found that, when the lesion on one arm was left to nature and that on the other arm was treated by suggestion (suggestion directed against pain and inflammation, and in favor of rapid healing), the latter developed distinctly less inflammation and healed much more rapidly.

We have no positive knowledge of the extent of such mental influences upon bodily processes; but that mental conditions can affect favourably or unfavourably the healing of wounds and the lesions of tuberculosis has long been recognised, even in orthodox medical circles. And the successes of those forms of therapy which invoke the aid of strong religious sentiments (as among Christian Scientists and at such centres of great popular repute as Lourdes) should render us open-minded in this obscure and controversial region.

NOTES

[1] The history is briefly sketched in my article, "Hypnotism," in the Encyclopædia Britannica.

[2] It must at the same time be recognized that some physicians regard as evidence of hypnosis the slighter degrees of influence by suggestion. In popular speech and writing the confusion between waking suggestion and hypnotism is carried farther.

[3] It will be convenient to refer to the hypnotic subject as B.

[4] One of my pupils, Dr. Paul Young, has made a systematic inquiry into this question and reached the same conclusion.

[5] Such experiments should be made with great caution and only on sound subjects. I make it a rule not to leave the subject with any unfulfilled suggestion of this kind. For to do so leaves him with a conflict, which, though a mild one, is uncomfortable and may be harmful.

[6] *E.g.*, I have relieved entirely in a few sittings a neuralgic pain so severe and so obstinate that the patient was on the point of being subjected to the very severe operation of removal of the Gasserian ganglion.

[7] Post-hypnotic suggestions have been carried out after an interval of a year.

[8] Success in such experiments seems to imply a higher degree of that power of waking at any desired time which many persons seem to have.

[9] "Medical Psychology and Psychical Research," 1923.

4.   Suggestion*

By the older British writers on psychology the words "suggest" and "suggestion" were used in senses very close to those which they have in common speech; one idea was said to suggest another when it recalled that other to mind or (in the modern phrase) reproduced it. Modern studies in mental pathology and hypnotism (*q.v.*) have led to the use of these words by psychologists in a special and technical sense. The hypnotists of the Nancy school rediscovered and gave general currency to the doctrine that the most essential feature of the hypnotic state is the unquestioning obedience and docility with which the hypnotized subject accepts, believes, and acts in accordance with every command or proposition of the hypnotizer. Commands or propositions made to the subject (they may be merely implied by a gesture, a glance, or a chance remark to a third person) and accepted with this peculiarly uncritical and intense belief were called "suggestions"; and the subject that accepted them in this fashion was said to be "suggestible." It has also been made abundantly clear, chiefly by the labours of French physicians, that a high degree of "suggestibility" is a leading feature of hysteria, and that this fact is the key to the understanding of very many of its protean manifestations.

It is also becoming widely recognized that the suggestibility of hypnosis and of hysteria is conditioned by a peculiar state of the brain, namely a cerebral or mental dissociation, which in hypnosis is temporarily induced by the operations of the hypnotist, and in hysteria arises from some deficiency

* Article written for the *Encyclopædia Britannica*, 11th ed. (1911), Vol. 26, pp. 48-50.

of energy in the whole psycho-physical system. In respect to these points there is now a wide consensus of opinion among the leading authorities; but as to the range and scope of suggestion in our mental life great differences of opinion still obtain. We may distinguish three principal views. Firstly, it is maintained by a number of physicians (notably by Professor Pierre Janet, whose profound studies of hysterical patients are justly celebrated) that all hypnotizable persons are hysterical and that suggestibility is a condition peculiar to hysterical subjects. In view of the assertions in recent years of several physicians of high repute to the effect that they find more than 90% of all subjects hypnotizable, it would seem that this view cannot be maintained, and that this restriction of suggestion to hysterical subjects only, and the stigmatization of suggestibility as in every case a morbid symptom, are errors arising from too exclusive occupation with its manifestations in this field. A second group consists of writers who admit that suggestion may operate in normal minds, but who, while recognizing that it is not an essentially pathological process, maintain that it is a process of very peculiar and exceptional nature that has little or no affinity with normal mental operations. They hold that suggestion, whether it occurs in morbid or in healthy subjects, always implies the coming into operation of some obscurely conceived faculty or region of the mind which is present in all men, but which usually lies hidden or submerged beneath the flow of our more commonplace mental activities. This submerged faculty or system of faculties, which is held by these authors to be operative in all processses of suggestion, is variously designated by them the secondary or submerged stratum of consciousness, the subconscious or subliminal self (see SUBLIMINAL SELF). The writers of this group insist upon the more startling of the effects producible by suggestion, the more profound changes of bodily and mental processes, such as paralysis, contracture, hyperaesthesia, increased power of recollection, hallucinations (*q.v.*), &c.; and they regard dissociation as the process by which the submerged and supernormal faculty (or faculties) that they postulate is liberated from the dominance of the normal waking self.

A third view has been rapidly gaining ground and is now predominant. It connects itself with, and bases itself upon, the view of Professor Bernheim and his colleagues of the Nancy school of hypnotism. According to this view all men are normally suggestible under favourable conditions, and the hypnotic subject and the hysteric patient differ from the normal human being chiefly in that their normal suggestibility is more or less (sometimes very greatly) increased, owing to the prevalence of the state of cerebral dissociation.

According to this third view, suggestion may be defined as the communication of any proposition from one person (or persons) to another in such a way as to secure its acceptance with conviction, in the absence of adequate logical grounds for its acceptance. The idea or belief so introduced to the mind of the recipient is held to operate powerfully upon his bodily and mental processes in proportion to the degree of its dominance over all other ideas or mental processes; and the extraordinary character of the effects, both bodily and mental, of suggestion in hypnotic and hysterical subjects is held to be due to the fact that, in these conditions of mental dissociation, the dominance of the suggested idea is complete and absolute; whereas in the absence of such dissociation the operation of the suggested idea is always subject to some weakening or inhibition through the influence of many opposed or incompatible tendencies and ideas, even if these do not rise into explicit consciousness.

This third view seems justified by the facts that no sharp line can be drawn between the suggestibility of normal men and that of hypnotized or hysterical subjects, and that under favourable conditions many of the most striking results of suggestion (*e.g.* hallucinations, contractures, inability to move, insensibility of various sense-organs, and so forth) may be produced in subjects who present at the time no other symptom of the hypnotic or hysterical condition.

If, then, we recognize, as we must, that the alogical production of conviction is the essence of suggestion, and that this frequently occurs in normal minds as well as in those suffering from various degrees of dissociation, it becomes necessary to define the conditions that favour the operation of suggestion in normal minds.

These conditions are resident, on the one hand, in the recipient of the suggestion, and, on the other hand, in the source from which the suggestion comes. Of the conditions of the former class three seem to be of principal importance.

(*a*) Defect of knowledge: the defect may be quantitative or qualitative, *i.e.* it may consist in the lack of knowledge or of firmly established beliefs about the subject of the proposition, or it may consist in the lack of systematic organization of such knowledge as the mind possesses. The well-trained mind is relatively insuggestible, firstly because it possesses large stores of knowledge and belief; secondly, because this mass of knowledge and belief is systematically organized in such a way that all its parts hang together and mutually support one another. On the other hand, the young child, the uncultured adult, and especially the savage, are apt to be suggestible in regard to very many topics, first, because they have relatively little knowledge; secondly, because what little they have is of a low degree of organization; *i.e.* it does not form a logically coherent system whose parts reciprocally support one another. Suggestion in such cases may be said to be conditioned by primitive credulity or the suggestibility of ignorance. (*b*) But the same person will not be found to be equally suggestible at all times under similar external conditions. There are changes of mental state which, without overstepping the limits of the normal, condition varying degrees of increased suggestibility. A man is least suggestible when his mind works most efficiently, when he is most vigorous and most wide awake; every departure from this state, due to fatigue, bodily ill-health, emotional perturbation, drugs or any other cause, favours suggestibility. (*c*) Persons of equal degrees of knowledge or ignorance will be found, even at their times of greatest mental efficiency, to be unequally suggestible owing to differences of native disposition; one person is by nature more open than another to personal influence, more easily swayed by others, more ready to accept their dicta and adopt their opinions for his own. Differences of this kind are probably the expression of differences in the native strength of one of the fundamental instinctive dispositions of the human mind, an instinct which is called into play by the presence of persons of superior powers and the excitement of which throws the subject into an attitude of submission or subjection towards the impressive personality.

Considered from the side of the agent, suggestion is favoured by whatever tends to render him impressive to the subject or patient—great bodily strength or stature, fine clothes, a confident manner, superior abilities of any kind, age and experience, any reputation for special capacities, high social position or the occupation of any position of acknowledged authority; in short, all that is summed up by the term "personality," all that contributes to make a personality "magnetic" or to give it prestige renders it capable of evoking on the part of others the submissive suggestible attitude. A group of persons in agreement is capable of evoking the suggestible attitude far more effectively than any single member of the group, and the larger the group the more strongly does it exert this influence. Hence the suggestive force of the popularly accepted maxims and well-established social conventions; such propositions are collective suggestions which carry with them all the immense collective prestige of organized society, both of the present and the past; they embody the wisdom of the ages. It is in the main through the suggestive power of moral maxims, endowed with all the prestige of great moral teachers and of the collective voice of society, that the child is led to accept with but little questioning the code of morals of his age and country; and the propagation of all religious and other dogma rests on the same basis. The normal suggestibility of the child is thus a principal condition of its docility, and it is in the main by the operation of normal suggestion that society moulds the characters, sentiments, and beliefs of its members, and renders the mass of its elements harmonious and homogeneous to the degree that is a necessary condition of its collective mental life. Normal suggestion produces its most striking effects in the form of mass-suggestion, *i.e.* when it operates in large assemblies or crowds, especially if the members have but little positive knowledge and culture. For, when a belief is propagated by collective suggestion through the large mass of men, each falls under the suggestive sway of the whole mass; and under these conditions the operation of suggestion is further aided by the universal tendency of mankind to imitation and sympathy, the tendency to imitate the actions of, and to experience the emotions expressed by, those about one.

Conditions very favourable to mass-suggestion prevailed during the middle ages of European history; for these "dark ages" were characterized by the existence of dense populations, among whom there was free intercourse but very little positive knowledge of nature, and who were dominated by a church wielding immense prestige. Hence the frequent and powerful operations of suggestion on a large scale. From time to time fantastic beliefs, giving rise to most extravagant behaviour, swept over large areas of Europe like virulent epidemics—epidemics of dancing, of flagellation, of hallucination, of belief in the miraculous powers of relics or of individuals, and so forth. In these epidemics all the conditions favourable to normal suggestion were generally present in the highest degree, with the result that in great numbers of persons there were produced the more extreme effects of suggestion, such as are usually associated with the hysterical or hypnotic state. At the present time similar manifestations occur in a modified form, as *e.g.* the popular pilgrimages to Lourdes, Holywell and other places that from time to time acquire reputations for miraculous curative powers.

Auto-suggestion. Although auto-suggestion does not strictly fall under the definition of suggestion given above, its usage to denote a mental process which produces effects very similar to those producible by suggestion is now so well established that it must be accepted. In auto-suggestion a proposition is formulated in the mind of the subject rather than communicated from another mind, and is accepted with conviction in the absence of adequate logical grounds. Generally the belief is initiated by some external event or some bodily change, or through some interpretation of the behaviour of other persons; *e.g.* a man falls on the road and a wagon very nearly passes over his legs, perhaps grazing them merely; when he is picked up, his legs are found to be paralysed. The event has induced the conviction that his legs are seriously injured, and this conviction operates so effectively as to realize itself. Or a savage, suffering some slight indisposition, interprets the behaviour of some person in a way which leads him to the conviction that this person is compassing his death by means of magical practices; accordingly he lies down in deep despondency and, in the course of some days or weeks, dies, unless his friends succeed in buying off, or in some way counteracting, the malign influence. Or, as a more familiar and trivial instance of auto-suggestion, we may cite the case of a man who, having taken a bread pill in the belief that it contains a strong purgative or emetic, realizes the results that he expects.

LITERATURE.—H. Bernheim, *De la Suggestion, et de ses applications à la thérapeutique* (2nd ed., Paris, 1887) ; Pierre Janet, *The Major Symptoms of Hysteria* (London, 1907) ; Otto Stoll, *Suggestion und Hypnotismus in der Völkerpsychologie* (2nd ed., Leipzig, 1904) ; Boris Sidis, *The Psychology of Suggestion* (New York, 1898) ; W. M. Keatinge, *Suggestion in Education* (London, 1907) ; F. W. H. Myers, *Human Personality and its Survival of Bodily Death* (London, 1903; 2nd ed., abridged, 1907) ; A. Binet, *La Suggestibilité* (Paris, 1900). See also literature under HYPNOTISM.

5.   The State of the Brain During* Hypnosis

~~~~~~

The attempt to formulate a theory of the hypnotic state has been approached by two very different roads. On the one hand there is the road along which the late F. W. H. Myers so brilliantly led the attack. Those who follow this road fix their attention on the most strange and perplexing of the phenomena of hypnotism; they seek to exhibit the gulf between the normal and the hypnotic states as very wide; they incline to regard the hypnotic condition as essentially one of extended faculty and increased mental power; and they value hypnotic experiment as one way of approaching the study of alleged supernormal and marvellous phenomena, belief in which orthodox science regards as a delusion bred by erroneous observation and engendered by an incorrigible yearning after empirical evidence of a realm of purely psychical existence.

The other more sober way in which the task of explaining hypnotic phenomena may be approached is to concentrate attention upon the simplest and least astonishing of them, to seek out and establish the affinities of hypnosis with better-known mental states, and to try to find some hypothesis that will account for these simpler facts and will bring our knowledge of hypnosis into line with the facts of our normal mental life and with theories that have proved their value in other departments of research; for, if any such working hypothesis can be formulated, it may be hoped that its field of application may be gradually enlarged and that the more perplexing phenomena may be brought within its range as our knowledge of them increases.

Though I would not disparage or undervalue speculations of the former

* Originally published in *Brain*, Vol. 31 (1908), pp. 242-258. [To avoid lengthy duplication we have reprinted here only the first third of this article, the remainder of which appears intact in the following selection, "Theory of Hypnosis and Suggestion." *Ed.*]

kind, I believe that the second way of approach is more consistent with scientific principles, and the following pages present the results of my own gropings along this road.

The aim of this paper is to render a little clearer and more definite in detail a hypothesis which has been gradually taking shape during recent years under the hands of a number of writers, and which goes by the name of the *theory of cerebral dissociation;* for certain unorthodox views as to the nature of cerebral processes set out by me in former numbers of this Journal [6], and elsewhere seem to lend themselves very well to this purpose.

The current loose usage of the phrase "theory of dissociation" tends to the confusion of several different hypotheses which have little in common with one another, and some of which are held by authors who follow the former of the two roads distinguished above. There is the doctrine (or group of allied doctrines) which teaches that each normal personality comprises two selves, two personalities or strata of personality, which normally are in some sense fused together—the waking and the subwaking selves of Boris Sidis [8], the *Doppel-Ich* of Max Dessoir [2], the waking consciousness and the dream-consciousness, the primary and secondary personalities, of other authors[1]; and that mental dissociation somehow consists in the freeing of the lower, or normally submerged and hidden, stratum from the dominance and control of the upper stratum. I do not think that at the present time we are compelled to make, or are justified in making, the assumption that the normal human mind comprises any such submerged and coherent system of faculties as is implied by each and all of these allied doctrines.

More nearly allied to the form of the theory of dissociation that I am concerned to support is Pierre Janet's doctrine of mental disaggregation [4]. Janet speculates only in terms of psychical material, and refuses to attempt a corresponding neurological hypothesis; but I am very decidedly of the opinion that here, if anywhere, attempts at purely psychological explanation are out of place. I believe that any explanation or theory of the hypnotic state and phenomena must be psycho-physiological; for it seems clear that, during hypnosis, the brain is in some abnormal condition and functions in some manner different from that of the normal waking state, and that therefore we cannot claim to understand hypnosis until we learn the nature of this abnormal brain state; that, in short, a description of the abnormal state of the brain must be an essential, if not the essential, feature of any explanation of the facts.

Th. Lipps [5], of Munich, also has proposed an explanation which, although he states it in terms of psychical dispositions only, and so limits its usefulness, seems to me very helpful; and it can easily be translated into terms of psycho-physical dispositions and developed on those lines.

Lastly, I would mention the speculations of Oscar Vogt [10] (accepted and endorsed by Forel [3]) as those with which my own views, although independently reached, have the closest affinity.

It is held by many authors, notably by Bernheim—rightly, I think—that hypnosis is a state closely allied in many respects to normal sleep, although it presents important differences. The onset of the two states is very similar in many (if not all) cases, and it is favoured in both cases by the same influences and conditions, namely, by the withdrawal of all strong sense-stimuli, by restful position, by monotonous gentle stimulation of one or more of the senses, by expectation and habit, and by the banishment of exciting thoughts and the concentration of attention on some unexciting object or sense-impression.

Another point of similarity of the onset of the two states is the heaviness of the eyelids, which is generally the first symptom of both sleep and hypnosis, and which, in both cases, is generally accompanied by a general drowsiness and disinclination to make any effort or movement.[2]

In both states the subject lies inert and passive; his mind is less responsive than during the waking state to most of the sense-impressions from the outer world; and, although it is not completely shut off from their influence, it is apt to interpret them falsely. In both states the subject may entertain the most fantastic ideas, ideas absolutely incompatible with his actual situation or his best-established convictions, without recognizing their absurdity; and such ideas are apt to undergo some fantastic elaboration in keeping with any prevalent emotion; in both cases these ideational processes are characterized by a lack of the voluntary and critical control which is habitual and normal in the waking state. In both cases the subject not infrequently desires to move his limbs, but finds himself incapable of doing so. In both cases, again, the subject is very apt to have, when awakened, no spontaneous recollection of the ideas of the period (of sleep or hypnosis), though recollection can generally be evoked by appropriate questioning. Some subjects may be induced to display an abnormal suggestibility during normal sleep, and in some the cataleptic plasticity of the limbs, which is a so frequent symptom of hypnosis, may be induced during normal sleep.

Lastly, if the subject in hypnosis is left to himself, he is apt to pass spontaneously into normal sleep, the transition from the one state to the other being perfectly gradual, so that no line can be drawn between them; and, conversely, the state of normal sleep may be converted into hypnosis.

The resemblance between hypnosis and sleep is, in some respects, still closer in the case of ordinary sleep-walking or somnambulism, which may perhaps be regarded as a state intermediate in character to these two.

On the other hand, hypnosis differs from normal sleep in that it has certain positive characteristics that are not found in the latter. A large proportion of these may be summed up by saying that the subject remains peculiarly sensitive to the hypnotizer, and that ideas introduced to his mind by the hypnotizer operate with unusual energy and effectiveness, or, as we say, the subject in hypnosis is very suggestible towards the operator, or readily takes suggestions from him.

The obvious line of approach is, then, to find a good working hypothesis as to the state of the brain in normal sleep; and, having formulated this, to try to understand what further peculiarities of the state of the brain are connected with the positive features in which hypnosis differs from sleep.

Unfortunately we have as yet no generally accepted theory of sleep. We have a number of partial theories or views—the view that sleep is due to the action of waste products of metabolism on the nervous tissue; the view that it is due to cerebral anæmia; the view that it is due to auto-suggestion; the recent view of Claparède [1] that the onset of sleep is an instinctive process.

There is probably some truth in all of these views, as well as in others; but neither individually nor collectively do they give an answer to the essential question: How does the state of the nervous tissue of the brain during sleep differ from its state during waking life?

It seems clear that during sleep the nervous substance of the cerebral hemispheres is either less excitable than during waking life or transmits any excitement less readily from part to part; and in all probability both these statements are true. A high degree of excitability and great freedom of transmission of excitement between all parts—these seem to be the essential positive characters of the waking brain that are lacking to the sleeping brain. Our definition of the state of the brain during sleep must, then, be a negative definition; it must consist in denying it the condition which underlies this proneness to activity characteristic of the waking state.

What, then, is this peculiarity of the waking state? The clue to the answer to this question is given, I think, by those rare cases of very widespread anæsthesia, of which the most striking and most frequently cited example is the case described by Strumpell [9]. The patient was a boy completely anæsthetic as regards all his sense-organs and sensory surfaces, with the exception of one eye and one ear. Whenever the sound eye was closed and the sound ear stopped, this patient fell almost immediately into deep sleep, and could then only be wakened by flashing a light into the sound eye or shouting into the sound ear, or otherwise stimulating violently one or both of these organs. That is to say, in this case the waking state was maintained only by the constant incidence of impressions on these sense-organs.

Now, it seems in the highest degree probable that the constant rain of stimuli upon our sense-organs plays a similar part in maintaining the waking state of the normal man; but the fact is obscured in two ways: firstly, by the great variety and sensitivity of the sense-organs of the normal man and the impossibility of shielding all of them from stimulation; secondly, by what may be called the capacity of the human psycho-physical organism for maintaining an endogenous excitation. We must briefly consider these in turn.

Even if one lies still on a soft bed in a quiet dark place, the nervous system is yet liable to receive many stimuli, especially through the sense-organs of the kinæsthetic and visceral systems. Under these conditions we often become aware of these impressions, and often they excite some sense of discomfort, some need of movement or change, so that one may be kept turning restlessly without sleep. The most striking example of the power of these vague sense-impressions arising within the body to prevent sleep is afforded by those which excite the sensation of hunger.

Nevertheless, save in conditions of great fatigue, the withdrawal of stimuli from the principal sense-organs is a favourable and, for most of us, an essential condition of the onset of sleep. When sleep comes, its continuance depends upon the absence of strong sense-impressions; it may normally be terminated at any time by a sufficiently strong sensory stimulus, or by the summation of effects of a series of sensory stimuli, each of which is too weak to produce any marked change of state;[3] and even after sleep is thus banished we do not usually feel ourselves to be fully awake and alert until a further stream of stimuli has impinged upon our sense-organs.

NOTES

[1] Possibly the doctrine of the Sublimal Self, elaborated by the late F. W. H. Myers, belongs to this group of theories, but I do not feel myself competent to class it.

[2] I am, of course, aware that some subjects exhibit while in hypnosis a degree of liveliness and excitability apparently greater than the normal, and that some of their faculties may seem even more alert and active than during their normal waking life. But these are distinctly exceptional cases, and usually, I think, this lively state is only arrived at after some training. We have to concentrate our attention on the more usual type of hypnosis; for the symptoms of the state are so bewilderingly diverse and numerous that, if we attempt to form a theory which shall account at once equally well for all of them, it is obvious we shall fail. Very much depends upon the handling of each case by the operator. In my own experience I have generally aimed at inducing a sleep-like condition, and have always obtained this result, except where I have failed to induce any degree of hypnosis.

[3] I have described and discussed this process in some detail in the pages of *Mind* [7].

REFERENCES

1. CLAPAREDE, E. "Théorie du sommeil," *Arch. de Psych.*, 1906.
2. DESSOIR, MAX. "Das Doppell-Ich," Leipzig, 1896.
3. FOREL, A. "Der Hypnotismus," Stuttgart, 1902, S. 118.

4. JANET, P. "L'automatisme psychologique," Paris, 1903.
5. LIPPS, TH. "Zur Psychologie der Suggestion," Leipzig, 1895, a reprint from *Zeitsch. f. Hypnotismus.*
6. MCDOUGALL, W. "On the Seat of the Psycho-physical Processes," *Brain,* vol. xxiv.; and "The Nature of Inhibitory Processes within the Nervous System," *Brain,* vol. xxvi.
7. *Ibid.* "Physiological Factors of the Attention-Process," *Mind,* N.S. No. 47.
8. SIDIS, BORIS. "Psychology of Suggestion," New York, 1898.
9. STRUMPELL. *Deut. Archiv. f. klin. Med.,* Bd. xxii.
10. VOGT, O. "Zur Kenntniss des Wesens und der psychologischen Bedeutung des Hypnotismus," *Zeitsch. f. Hypnotismus,* 1895-6.

6. Theory of Hypnosis and Suggestion*

We are now in a position to attempt a theory of the hypnotic state and its peculiar phenomena. Any such theory must consist of two parts. First, it must describe the peculiar condition of the brain which obtains during hypnosis. Secondly, it must give some account of the *rapport*, the peculiar relation between the hypnotiser and his subject.

In discussing sleep and in pointing out that hypnosis is closely allied to sleep, I have already suggested the former part of the theory. At the risk of repetition, I cite here part of an article published in *Brain*,[1] entitled "The State of the Brain during Hypnosis," in which the analogy between sleep and hypnosis was developed at some length. After pointing to the resemblance between sleep and hypnosis and the fact that both are favoured by the absence of strong sensory stimulations, I went on as follows:

"Unfortunately, our knowledge of the immediate effect of stimulation of a sensory nerve is still very imperfect; but there is much to be said for the view that the immediate and essential effect is a katabolic process which liberates chemically stored energy in the substance of the neurone, and that the spread of excitation consists in the discharge of this freed nervous energy from neurone to neurone across the synapses or places of junction of the neurones. This distinction between chemically stored or potential nervous energy and the liberated active nervous energy is, I feel sure, one of the first importance for neurological speculation, although but little attention is commonly paid to it. Oscar Vogt has recognised its importance and has proposed to mark it by calling the freed nervous energy 'neurokyme.' Some

---

* Originally published as Chap. V in William McDougall's *An Outline of Abnormal Psychology*. London: Methuen & Co., Ltd., 1926.

years ago I, in ignorance of Vogt's work, proposed to call it 'neurin.' What name we use does not much matter, so long as we hold fast to this distinction and to this conception of liberated active nervous energy; but for this purpose some name is essential; since Vogt's proposal was prior to my own, and since my proposed name is so similar to neurine, the name of one of the chemical compounds found by the chemists in nervous tissue, I adopt Vogt's term 'neurokyme' in place of 'neurin.'

"During waking life, then, stimuli rain unceasingly on all the sense-organs and liberate in all the sensory nerves streams of neurokyme, which ascend by the sensory tracts of the cord and lower brain to the cerebellum and cerebrum. The brain is thus fed and its activity is sustained by these streams of energy, which keep it charged with neurokyme at a varying tension or potential; and this charge of free energy is constantly being worked off by thought or mental activity of any kind; for all mental activity involves the discharge of neurokyme from the sensory to the motor side of the brain, in accordance with James's law of forward conduction.

"Now consider a second condition that obscures the importance of sense-stimuli for the maintenance of the waking state—what was called above the capacity for endogenous or automatic maintenance of the state of excitation.

"The organism comprises certain hereditary psychophysical dispositions, which, in the evolutionary sense, are essentially continuous with, or to be identified with, the instincts of the animals. In what each such disposition exactly consists we do not yet know, though no doubt an essential feature of it is a complex system of sensori-motor arcs. In the present connection the important fact is that each such disposition is a great spring of nervous energy; when any one of them is excited in any way, it liberates a great quantity of neurokyme that raises the activity of the brain to a higher level, a fact which manifests itself in symptoms of general excitement, in very energetic thought and action and, subjectively, in the form of impulse, desire, and emotion.

"These dispositions can be excited by way of sense-presentation; hence sense-impressions contribute to the maintenance of the state of general excitation of the brain, not only in proportion to the intensity of the stimuli and the extent of sensory surface affected, but also in proportion as they lead to the excitement of any of these special springs of energy. In most of the animals these dispositions can be excited only by sense-impressions, but in the human being they can be excited also by way of representative or ideational processes. Hence the human mind and brain do not necessarily come to rest as soon as all sensory stimuli are withdrawn; the activity of an excitable brain may continue to be sustained by this process of endogenous liberation of energy, by the power of the impulses awakened through ideas and recollections. When this is the case, sleep can only be secured by the avoidance of emotionally exciting ideas, *i.e.*, by turning the attention to indifferent things—to sheep jumping through a gap in a hedge, to counting, or to some faint bodily impression.

"The presence in the brain-neurones of a store of free energy or neurokyme derived from these two sources is, then, a prime condition of the waking state; but there is a second important condition, dependent in large measure upon this one, which underlies the freedom of transmission of excitation from point to point of the brain, the free interplay of all parts of the brain, that is characteristic of the waking state; this is the state of the synapses.

"We can confidently infer that the neurones that make up the nervous tissue of the cerebrum are connected together to form functional groups, the members of each group being so intimately connected that excitement of any one member of the group tends to spread at once throughout the group to every member of it.

"Such a group of neurones is a functional unit, and we may call it a psychophysical disposition; of such groups the hereditary dispositions mentioned above constitute a very important and peculiar class. We may infer also that these dispositions are connected with one another with various degrees of intimacy to form systems; these, again, with less degrees of intimacy to form larger systems; and these yet again with still less intimacy to form still larger systems; and so on, until we reach the most comprehensive system, which is the whole of the central nervous system.

"Each disposition is an intricately woven chain of neurones making up a complex sensori-motor arc or system of arcs. All thought, all perceptual or ideational mental process, involves the perpetual shifting of the main nervous current from one disposition to another; at any one moment some one disposition being the main path of discharge of neurokyme from the sensory side of the brain, where it is constantly accumulating, to the motor side; and, while any one disposition thus predominantly active is the principal focus of excitation, those most intimately connected with it are in a state of subexcitement. When any one disposition thus becomes the main path of discharge, it is because, owing to a favourable conjunction of circumstances, it has become for the moment the path of least resistance from sensory to motor side of the brain. The discharge through any one disposition is the neural concomitant of the rise to consciousness of a corresponding presentation or idea; and the shifting of the main stream from one disposition to another is the neural concomitant of the play of ideas, of the succession of presentations at the focus of consciousness, which continues so long as we are awake.

"An essential feature of the view I am expounding is that the various degrees of intimacy of connection between neurones and between groups and systems of neurones are held to be functions of the synapses or junctions of neurones. If excitement spreads readily from one group to another, it is because the synapses on the path connecting those two groups present at that moment a low degree of resistance; if it spreads less readily to another group, it is because the synapses on this connecting path present a greater resistance. Now there are many good reasons for believing that the resistance presented by any synapse is not a fixed quantity, and that it is not only permanently diminished in some degree by repeated transmission of the excitation process, but that it is a quantity which varies from moment to moment under a number of influences, of which the most important are fatigue of its own substance, chemical influences from the blood, and the charge or potential of charge of neurokyme in the neurones between which the synapse forms a junction. That is to say, it is maintained that each synapse (in the resting condition of the part) presents a certain normal degree of resistance which varies from synapse to synapse, and is in each case a fixed quantity (or one only slightly or slowly changeable) determined by heredity and the course of individual experience; but that this normal degree, to which the resistance of each synapse returns when the brain is at rest, is constantly liable to be modified by the influences named above, being raised by fatigue and anæsthetic drugs such as alcohol and chloroform, diminished by strychnine and tetanus-toxin and by the excitement of the neurones between which the synapse lies.

"This last condition is the most important one in view of the problem in hand. I assume, and the assumption is not without positive evidence in its favour, that the resistance of the synapse falls as the potential of charge of neurokyme rises in both, or in either one, of the neurones between which it lies, and that it rises as this potential falls.

"In the waking state, then, the hemispheres being constantly supplied with large quantities of neurokyme from the two sources indicated above, the main mass of cortical neurones is kept moderately charged with this free energy, the result of which is that all synapses, and therefore all connecting paths, are kept in a state of partially lowered resistance; and there is, therefore, a constant free interplay between all parts of the brain, the main current of energy shifting freely from one disposition to another and from one system to another, each disposition tending to draw to itself a maximal stream of energy, each competing with all the rest for the fullest share of energy according to the principle of drainage.

"Now, when we lie down to sleep in a quiet dark place, we shut off as nearly as possible all stimuli from the sense-organs, and we divert our thoughts from all emotionally exciting topics. The supply of neurokyme to the brain is thus diminished, the charge present in, or banked up in, the neurones of the afferent side of the brain falls to a lower potential, and, consequently, the resistance of the synapses in general rises. When sleep ensues from great general fatigue, another factor probably plays the principal part —namely, the waste products of metabolism, which, accumulated in the blood and lymph that bathe the synapses, act upon them, like chloroform or alcohol, as poisons which diminish their metabolism and so raise their resistance. Also, in the production of the sleep that ensues from deficient energy of the heart's action or from diminished circulation of blood in the brain, however produced, this second factor probably plays a large part, the waste products being allowed to accumulate locally. In normal falling asleep these two conditions—the general accumulation of waste products in the blood and the general slowing of the circulation—co-operate with the diminution of supply of neurokyme to raise the resistances of the synapses of all parts of the brain.

"This general raising of the synaptic resistances throws the whole brain into a condition of *relative dissociation* or functional dissociation; that is to say, the dispositions and systems of dispositions, as well as the neurones comprised within any one disposition, become in some degree functionally isolated or separated from one another. And this functional discontinuity will be most complete in the case of the least intimately connected systems, less complete between the more intimately connected dispositions of any one system, and least between the neurones that are united in one disposition; for the resistance of each synapse will be reduced to, or near to, its normal resting-degree.

"Normal sleep implies, then, a state of relative dissociation of the brain, and the many points of similarity noted above between sleep and hypnosis indicate that hypnosis also involves relative dissociation of the brain; on the other hand, some of the phenomena of hypnosis, to be noticed below, afford positive evidence that such dissociation obtains, and so confirm the indications afforded by the foregoing consideration of the general physiology of the brain and of sleep.

"We have to inquire: How does the state of the brain during hypnosis differ from this state of general relative dissociation of normal sleep? The answer to this question suggests itself when we consider the way in which hypnosis is commonly induced. The onset of hypnosis is favoured by the influences which favour sleep (with the exception, possibly, of fatigue), namely rest and quiet (*i.e.*, the withdrawal of sensory stimuli), the slowing of the circulation, the banishment of emotionally exciting thoughts, and by the expectation of sleep. How expectation operates remains a very obscure problem, but it is clear, I think, that in neither case is it an essential factor.

The important influences brought to bear in the induction of hypnosis, in addition to those which normally produce sleep, are: (1) monotonous stimulation of sense-organs, either continued (as by visual fixation of a bright point) or intermittent (as by passes); such monotonous stimulation is favourable also to the onset of normal sleep; (2) the personal contact of the hypnotiser, who, by speech, by verbal suggestions, and by manipulations, keeps the subject constantly aware of his presence.

"The monotonous stimulation seems to aid in bringing the whole brain to a quiescent condition, by facilitating the continued direction of attention to an object or impression of an unexciting uninteresting character, and thereby preventing the free play of ideas which otherwise may maintain itself for a considerable period in the way noted above. In terms of neural process we may say that the monotonous stimulation tends to keep some one minor disposition or small system of dispositions in dominant activity, keeps open this one path of discharge, so that this one channel, constantly draining off from the sensory side of the brain the supply of neurokyme, depresses, or tends to prevent, the activity of all others.[2]

"The personal contact of the operator contributes to produce the same result. His passes, his manipulations, his verbal suggestions, all serve to keep the idea of the operator present to the mind of the subject, to keep the subject's attention (no doubt an attention of low grade or potential) directed to the operator, *i.e.*, in terms of neural process, they serve to keep in a state of excitation one system of psychophysical dispositions, the system whose activity underlies the presence to consciousness of all thought of the operator; or, again, they tend to keep the main current of nervous energy shifting from one disposition to another within this one system. In this way, while all the rest of the brain is allowed to sink into a state of quiescence and of relative dissociation similar to that which obtains in normal sleep, this one system is kept active and waking, so to speak. It thus serves as an open channel through which ideas can be introduced to, or evoked in, the mind of the subject; as a single focus of nervous activity in a quiescent brain, from which focus other parts of the brain may be brought into play. Any proposition made by the operator to the subject is then accepted uncritically and acted upon because accepted with belief—that is the essence of suggestion— whereas the subject is blind and deaf to impressions from all other persons and objects, except in so far as they are connected in his mind with the operator, *i.e.*, except in so far as they belong to the same system of ideas.

"Now a leading feature of hypnosis is that ideas or propositions suggested by the hypnotiser not only are accepted, but, being accepted, operate with a quite unusual force or effectiveness in the mind and on the body of the subject. The state of the brain described above, the state of relative dissociation of all systems except the one, enables us to suggest an explanation of this feature also. In the normal waking state any proposition about any topic or object is received more or less critically, and is only accepted with conviction if it is not incompatible with the organised body of knowledge or belief about that topic or kind of object already established in the mind. Every idea, we may say, has to withstand or overcome the inhibiting tendencies of these other ideas connected with the same topic, before it is fully accepted, before it can prevail stably and determine action in the way characteristic of belief. But in the state of relative dissociation, any idea introduced to the mind by the operator prevails stably and determines action—is, in fact, accepted with belief—just because the ideas which could check or weaken its operation are not aroused, are not brought to bear upon it in criticism, owing to the state of relative dissociation which renders all interplay of ideas more difficult, more sluggish, than in the waking state. Further, in the waking state, not only contradictory ideas, but all ideas whatsoever that have any tendency to rise to consciousness at the moment, play a similar part, weakening to some extent the force with which the dominant idea at the focus of consciousness operates in the mind and on the body.[3] The refined experimental researches of G. E. Müller upon reproduction and association seem to have established this fact.

"We may try to express these relations in physiological terms. We must remember that in the waking state of the brain all dispositions and systems of dispositions are in relation of reciprocal inhibition with one another, such that the activity of any one tends to inhibit the activity of every other; and we may fairly suppose that between dispositions whose activities underlie incompatible or contradictory ideas about any object, this relation of reciprocal inhibition is peculiarly intimate and direct.[4] All dispositions, then, compete with another, except those that form a harmonious system and tend to express themselves in some particular mode of co-ordinated bodily activity. In the waking state, then, the energy with which any idea tends to express itself, or realise itself through bodily action, is thus diminished by the competition of all other ideas that have any tendency to rise to consciousness; or, in neural terms, the energy with which any disposition functions is normally to some extent depressed by the competition of all other dispositions that are in any state of subexcitation, and especially of those of contradictory ideas. In hypnosis, on the other hand, this depressing, weakening influence, this partial inhibition, is abolished or diminished in virtue of, and in proportion to the degree of, relative dissociation or functional isolation of dispositions from one another. Hence, any idea suggested by the hypnotiser is not only accepted uncritically, but operates with greater force than any idea accepted with conviction in the waking state.

"The absence or diminution of all such inhibitory weakening and restraint, and the correlative concentration of all available neurokyme along the channels of one disposition, seem to be the principal factors to be taken into account when we seek to explain all the commonest and most easily produced results of hypnotic suggestion, namely, the illusions, positive hallucinations, delusions, the control of the voluntary muscles and (to some extent) of the involuntary muscles and of the visceral processes, secretion, nutrition, and so forth; while, as Pierre Janet has suggested, cataleptic plasticity of the limbs may be equally well regarded as due to the functional isolation of the cerebral tracts by which the afferent impulses ascending from the organs of the 'muscular sense' return to those motor elements of the cortex from which the same movements and positions of the same parts are voluntarily effected (in accordance with the principle of the upper motor circuits). The weakening or abolition of reflexes, which, I believe, occurs only in very deep stages of hypnosis, may be regarded as due to the dissociation having attained so great a degree as to affect the functional continuity of the neurones composing the lower reflex arcs.

"To negative hallucinations, and to the execution of post-hypnotic suggestions by a subject who remains unaware of the nature of the suggestions given, these principles of explanation are not so easily applicable; that is to say, while cerebral dissociation is implied by them, the principle is not in itself adequate to shadow forth an explanation of them; some further principle is implied. But these processes are especially interesting from the present point of view; because they prove, more clearly than any other of the phenomena, that some functional dissociation of the brain is really present. In both cases we have unmistakable evidence that some process goes on in the brain independently of, and without affecting or being involved in, the main stream of psychophysical process. Such, for example, is the deliberate ignoring by the subject of an object of which he has been told that it is no longer present; for, although he certainly does not perceive the object in normal fashion, and is apparently not conscious of it, his neglect and active avoidance of it show that the object is in some sense recognised; and when a post-hypnotic suggestion is executed after a given number of repetitions of some signal, the signals clearly have been in some sense counted; and yet the subject remains unconscious of them. It is the facts of this order that have led so many authors to postulate a co-consciousness, a secondary stream of consciousness split off from the primary consciousness and flowing independently of it; for the processes involved seem to be distinctly mental processes, such as normally involve consciousness. There is much to be said for that view, and also there are difficulties in the way of its acceptance. But, though we may leave the reality of such co-consciousness an open question, we are compelled by the facts of this order to believe that a complex and orderly sequence of nervous processes, dissociated from the main stream of brain activity, is involved in the execution of such tasks; the dissociation seems to circumscribe the independently operating systems.

"Anæsthesia also affords good evidence of dissociation; the sensory areas concerned with the reception of afferent impulses from the anæsthetic part seem to be profoundly dissociated from the rest of the brain; though whether this neural dissociation suffices in itself to account for the anæsthesia, and whether we are justified in assuming, as Janet does, that the sensations of the anæsthetic limb exist, or occur, as isolated sensations or sensations of a slender stream of secondary consciousness—these are very obscure questions which also we may leave open, while we accept the anæsthesia as positive evidence that at some point in the sensory path from the anæsthetic organ, probably a point within the cortex of the brain, resistance is abnormally increased in the way which constitutes dissociation.

"The discontinuity between the memory-trains of the hypnotic and those of the waking state, which so commonly obtains, is another piece of direct evidence of the reality of dissociation; although here, as in the preceding cases, it remains a very obscure problem: How can verbal suggestion determine the position of the line of cleavage or dissociation that separates the two systems?

"A few words may be ventured as to the bearing of the views set forth above on the therapeutic applications of hypnotic suggestion. If these views represent an approximation towards the truth, it follows that the therapeutic value of hypnotic suggestion consists principally in the fact that it is a means of concentrating powerful currents of nervous energy in any required direction and of withdrawing them from other parts. By thus withdrawing the nervous currents from an overworked or unduly irritable nervous centre or bodily organ, and by isolating it through induction of a relative dissociation of the centre, rest may be secured and a bad habit of over-action may be suspended, as *e.g.*, in neuralgia; while, by repeatedly directing a powerful stream of innervation through some other channel, a too sluggish organ (*e.g.*, the bowel) may be brought back to a more active and healthy functioning, a habit that has become disordered or unduly weakened may be restored, or a new habit may be set up to supplant, counteract, or suppress some undesirable habit. Under these two heads, the increase or the diminution of the metabolism and functioning of organs, most of the therapeutic effects of hypnotic suggestion may, I think, be classified.

"There are a number of phenomena that remain very obscure, and it is not claimed that the theory of cerebral dissociation as here presented provides a complete explanation of any of the facts. But that cerebral dissociation of some degree is at least one of the essential features of the hypnotic state can, I think, hardly be doubted; and though it may be questioned by some whether even a complete account of the cerebral changes would afford anything like a complete explanation of the facts, it can hardly be disputed that any complete theory of hypnosis must take the cerebral changes into account. I venture to think that the foregoing hypothetical description of the state of the brain during hypnosis may render the conceptions of cerebral dissociation, of the peculiarity of the hypnotic dissociation, and of the process of its induction, a little clearer and more definite than they have hitherto been. It is but just to point out that the hypothesis of cerebral dissociation which I have endeavoured to develop seems to have been first suggested by Hughes Bennett, and that therefore, if it should ever attain to the rank of a generally accepted theory, the credit of having first enunciated it must be assigned to him." [5]

At the time of writing the article from which the foregoing passage is here cited, I was aware that it dealt only with one of the two great problems of hypnosis. I had not developed a theory of suggestion and of the *rapport* which is so striking a feature of the hypnotic state. The solution of this second problem was indicated in my "Social Psychology" at the same date.

THEORY OF SUGGESTION

We have had many theories of suggestion ranging from the commonplace to the mystical. The intellectualist psychologists have struggled in vain with the problem. They tell us that suggestion is the implantation of an idea. And if, like Janet, they seek to explain why "an idea" implanted during hypnosis seems to have a potency quite foreign to ideas imparted or implanted during waking life, they can only say that during waking life an imparted "idea" has to work against the criticism and control of other "ideas"; whereas in hypnosis the general sluggishness of the mental stream, or the state of relative dissociation, permits any one "idea" impressed upon the subject to work with full force, without the inhibition of rival and perhaps contrary ideas. This is as far as any intellectualist or "idea" psychology can go. There is a certain truth in it as regards hypnotic suggestion. But it does not cover the ground; it is hopelessly inadequate. In the first place, it makes the erroneous assumption of the ideo-motor theory, the assumption that "ideas" are forces which in some sense tend to realise themselves. I have sufficiently combatted this error in Part I [*An Outline of Abnormal Psychology*]. Secondly, it leaves suggestion in the waking state entirely unexplained. Yet any theory of suggestion must take into account waking suggestion equally with hypnotic suggestion; there is no line to be drawn between them. Thirdly, it leaves the facts of *rapport* entirely unexplained; yet *rapport* is of the essence of suggestion in hypnosis.

Similar objections lie against the more mystical view of F. W. H. Myers, that "suggestion is a successful appeal to the Subliminal Self"; or of W. J. Hudson and of Sidis, that suggestion is the appeal to "the subconscious self." We are given no light on the essential problem, namely: Why does one appeal to "the subliminal self" succeed and so constitute suggestion, while other appeals, the appeals of other persons, fail? For that is the essential problem of suggestion and of *rapport*.

It is the great merit of Prof. Freud's teaching, here as elsewhere, that he has realised fully the inadequacy of the intellectualist views; and that he seeks the explanation of the potency of suggestion where alone it can be found, namely, among the instinctive bases of the mind, the conative tendencies that sustain and energise all our strivings and operations, no matter how purely intellectual they may appear to be. But here as elsewhere he makes the error (as I see the matter) of representing the one form of instinctive energy, the sexual, as responsible for much that springs from other roots. I shall return to consider the Freudian sexual theory of suggestion after stating my own theory, as developed in my "Social Psychology" and later writings.[6]

I have concisely restated my theory in a recent article[7] as follows:

"My theory sets out from the fact of observation that among animals of gregarious species we commonly find relations of dominance and submission; we see some members of a herd or flock submitting tamely and quietly to the dominance, the leadership, the self-assertion of other members. This submission does not always or commonly seem to imply fear. Yet it is unquestionably instinctive. I have argued, therefore, that such behaviour is the expression of a distinct and specific instinct of submission: an instinct which is apt to be evoked by the aggressive or self-assertive behaviour of other, especially larger and older, members of the group, and whose goal or function it is to secure harmony within the group by prompting the junior and weaker members of it to submit to the leadership of others, to follow them, to 'knuckle under to them' without protest, to accept their slightest word as law, to feel humble or lowly in their presence, and to adopt lowly or 'crestfallen' attitudes before them. My theory maintains that the human species also is endowed with this instinct of submission; and that, with the development of language and intellect, verbal indications of the attitudes of the strong become very important means of evoking and directing this submissive impulse; that the impulse, the emotional conative tendency of this instinct, is the main conative factor at work in all instances of true suggestion, whether waking or hypnotic. Further, that, in human societies, reputation for power of any sort becomes a very important factor in evoking this impulse, supplementing and, in fact, largely supplanting the bodily evidences of superior powers which, on the animal plane, are the principal excitants of this impulse; such reputation constitutes the essence of all that we call prestige, the power of using suggestion, of compelling bodily and mental obedience or docility, without evoking fear. The theory maintains that, if the human species were not gregarious, and if its native constitution did not comprise also this special submissive instinct, human beings would not be suggestible; and, therefore, the social life of man would be profoundly other than it is." [8]

In another place I have defined suggestion as the imparting of a proposition in such a manner that it is accepted with conviction, independently of any logical grounds for such conviction. And in Part I [*An Outline of Abnormal Psychology*] I have pointed out that we do not arrive at conviction or belief without the operation of some conative energy. The theory proposed is, then, that, in the case of belief established by suggestion, the conative energy at work is that of the submissive instinct; and it is evoked by the person (or persons) from whom the suggestion comes in virtue of some quality, or supposed quality, that renders him imposing to the person whom he influences, gives him prestige, authority, or power to throw the other into the submissive attitude, power to evoke in him obedience, respect, admiration, gratitude, in all of which affective attitudes the submissive impulse is an essential factor.

This view meets adequately all the facts of suggestion during the waking state, whether the suggestion comes from an individual, or from a mass, a crowd, a community.

THEORY OF "RAPPORT"

It remains to explain the *rapport* of hypnosis, the essence of which is that this power of suggestion, of inducing submission and complete docility, is much exaggerated as between the operator and the subject, while in respect of other persons it seems to be diminished to the point of extinction. Let us look a little more closely at the facts of *rapport*. In the majority of cases the hypnotised subject displays extreme sensitiveness to every suggestion of the hypnotiser, obeying every indication, however slight, of his will; while, at the same time, the suggestions of other persons seem to leave him unaffected. Commonly, he seems absolutely indifferent or impervious to the suggestions of others. It is easy to make the error of assuming that he does not hear or understand their verbal suggestions; but commonly he does hear and understand, as may be ascertained by questioning him. Consider the following simple experiment.

I tell B to clasp his hands, and that they are now inseparably locked; and I challenge him to do his best to separate them. B tries and struggles in vain to separate his hands; the antagonistic muscles continue to contract so strongly that he cannot free them. A bystander, C, then intervenes and assures B that he can separate his hands, that he can do it quite easily, etc., etc., and urges him to try again. B tries again, but in vain. And no matter how often, how firmly, how loudly the third person repeats his suggestions, the result is the same; and the same also if a whole roomful of people join in implanting this "idea" in B's mind with the utmost energy. The *rapport* seems to be exclusive and complete. Now I tell B that C has just as much control over his muscles as I have. C then intervenes again, and at his suggestion B's hands at once relax and are separated without difficulty. In this way, by a few words, the *rapport* between A and B can be extended by A to C, so that B becomes suggestible to C. It is probable that C cannot immediately be given the influence wielded by A in its full extent; but he can be endowed by A with sufficient prestige for B to enable him to control B's movements effectively. This phenomenon of "the transference of *rapport*," as it has been called, seems to dispose of any such view as that the *rapport* between A and B is due to any "magnetic" influence in a physical sense exerted by A on B; and to me it seems to refute equally completely the Freudian theory, namely, that A's influence on B is due to the fact that B is in love with A, or that, as Ferenczi puts it, B is submissive to A because he intensely desires to be loved by A.

It is not true that *rapport* is absolutely exclusive; that the hypnotic subject is capable of being influenced only by A, the hypnotiser. This fact was illustrated by the following instructive experiment, made by one of my colleagues and myself. The patient, a regular soldier of excellent type, had been cured by my colleague with the aid of hypnosis, and remained highly suggestible to my colleague, A. A induced hypnosis and, placing a cigarette on the table before B, told him that he could not take it from the table, and challenged him to try. B advanced towards the table, and, though he seemed to make an effort, found himself unable to reach the cigarette. I, playing the part of C, then intervened. I had not hypnotised B on any occasion, and the *rapport* was not extended to me by A. But I had the advantage that, while B was a regular soldier of long service, I was a senior officer of rank superior to A's. I told B that he could now reach and take the cigarette without difficulty, and instructed him to do so. Still he remained suspended; but it was obvious that he understood my words, and that they were influencing him, but that A's influence was still the stronger. I renewed my suggestions, and presently B made a new effort, and slowly, seemingly with great difficulty, accomplished the act forbidden by A.

This experiment illustrates the fact that the *rapport* between A and B is not absolutely exclusive, does not preclude all possibility of suggestion from other sources, but merely consists in greater susceptibility to suggestion from A than to suggestions from other sources. Just as the suggestions of A may fail, if they conflict with B's moral nature, or with other strong conative tendencies (I shall later illustrate such failure of suggestion when opposed to the conative forces that maintain a repression) so they may be overcome by suggestion from another source, under conditions exceptionally favourable to that other source. It is a question of the relative strengths of the conative tendencies brought into action. There is no warrant for assuming that the old soldier was in love either with A or with C. He merely knew me by sight as a senior officer, and a lifetime of obedience and respect towards such officers had rendered him peculiarly docile to suggestions from such a quarter. I think it is safe to assume that, if C had been of the same or of lower rank than A, C's suggestions would have failed to make any appreciable effect upon B.

Rapport, then, is not an utterly mysterious phenomenon inexplicable by psychological principles. It is utterly inexplicable by mechanical, sensationist, and intellectualist psychologies, by any psychology that ignores the conative nature of man and the instinctive bases of all our mental life. But in that respect it is in line with all other manifestations of our purposive, our conative, nature. The *rapport* between the operator and the hypnotic subject is essentially the relation of prestige and submission which renders possible all waking suggestion; but for the hypnotic subject the prestige of the operator is indefinitely increased by the success of the latter's suggestions, and the docility of the former is correspondingly augmented.

It remains to consider briefly why the suggestions of A work upon B with so great power. The *rapport* established between A and B, when A has hypnotised B, the moral relation of ascendancy, of prestige, does not cease when B is restored to the waking condition. It grows stronger with every repetition of the hypnosis, so long as A uses his ascendancy tactfully; so that by a mere word or a mere snap of the fingers, A can plunge B into profound hypnosis. There is, then, something in the hypnotic condition very favourable to the working of A's suggestions over and above the *rapport* between A and B.

The great influence of A's suggestions upon B while in hypnosis may, I think, be sufficiently explained by two considerations. First, the state of relative dissociation obtaining during hypnosis hampers or clogs or depresses all the intellectual operations by means of which the suggestions received might be criticised, and tendencies other than the submissive tendency brought into play.

Secondly, A, keeping in mental touch with B as B sinks into hypnosis, increases his prestige with every successful suggestion; that is to say, A is all the time playing upon and keeping in action the submissive instinct; whereas all the other conative tendencies of B are allowed to sink into quiescence, as when he falls into normal sleep. There is thus formed in B, with various degrees of success, according to the depth of the hypnosis, a secondary split-off personality on the very restricted conative basis, consisting of the one instinctive tendency to submission; and the impulse of this instinct is wholly directed to A. The tendency works, therefore, in a free field, without rivalry or modification or restraint from other conative tendencies. It is perhaps true to say that during hypnosis the whole of the vital or hormic energy of B's organism is concentrated along this one of the great conative channels; hence it is capable of producing exceptionally great effects. This system, with its single conative root, forms the split-off personality B1; while the rest of the normal personality remains relatively latent, quiescent, unless roused into activity by some challenge to its fixed and strong moral sentiments. When post-hypnotic suggestions are carried out subconsciously or automatically, it is this split-off secondary personality, B1, which executes the task, or enters into conflict with the waking personality. And in those cases in which the waking personality becomes aware of an impulse to perform the prescribed action, it is the subconsciously operating personality B1 which communicates or imparts or forces this impulse upon the conscious personality. We shall find in later chapters abundant evidence that, in pathological splitting of the personality, the splitting is determined by conflict between the conative tendencies and involves a division of them between the partial personalities; and, further, we shall see that the subordinate, hidden, or subconscious personality manifests in many cases power to communicate an impulse to action to the conscious personality, and thus to force the latter to involuntary or automatic action, just such power as we see exercised in the post-hypnotic state by the secondary personality B1.

We have now a fairly complete theory of the phenomena of hypnosis. It must, however, be admitted that some facts remain obscure. It is possible to understand in general terms, in the light of the theory sketched above, how simple dissociations, both motor and sensory, may be brought about; how, for example, all the motor and sensory functions of one limb may be dissociated from the main personality and left under the control and in the exclusive service of the secondary personality, B1. But, when we have to do with elaborately systematised anæsthesia, there remains much that is obscure. For example, B may receive the suggestion that he cannot see any word containing the letter T. When such a suggestion succeeds, as it does with some subjects, its success involves an elaborated interplay of give and take between the two personalities which beggars description. Nevertheless, I venture to think that, even in face of such most complicated and baffling hypnotic phenomena, explanation may be looked for along the lines of our theory.

According to the view expounded in the foregoing sections, suggestion is essentially a process of communication from one personality, A, to another, B; A exerting upon B a moral influence that inclines B to accept with conviction whatever proposition comes from A.

It is customary to recognise "autosuggestion" as a process by means of which the individual (or some individuals) can induce in themselves effects similar to those producible by suggestion. Some authors, notably Dr. S. Ferenczi, rightly recognising that the essential energy which works to produce the effects of suggestion comes from within the subject, and is not in any way imparted to him by the operator, but rather only released and set in action by him, propose to regard all suggestion as essentially autosuggestion. This is a quite unwarranted deduction from the facts, as may be illustrated by the analogous case of fear. If I meet an angry bear in the woods and take to my heels in fear, it would be true to say that the energy which sustains my efforts comes from within my organism, and is not in any sense supplied by the bear; the bear merely releases this energy within me. But it would not be true or useful to say that my fear was self-inspired and that the bear had nothing to do with the case, or played but a secondary rôle in the drama.

M. Coué has recently carried this view to its logical extreme in his popular campaign of instruction in "autosuggestion." He asserts that all he does is to instruct his patients in the art of "autosuggestion." His famous phrase, "Every day in every way I am better and better," is supposed to work miracles of healing by way of pure autosuggestion. And M. Coué may, no doubt, truthfully claim to have aided, and perhaps to have cured, a number of his patients. Coué is no theorist, and is content to practise his methods with simple and infectious faith in their efficacy. M. Badouin has made himself the exponent of the theories underlying Coué's practice. But I fail to discover in his expositions any intelligible theory of the alleged process of autosuggestion. Without taking up an attitude of dogmatic negation, I am strongly inclined to invert the formula of this school and to assert that all so-called autosuggestion is, in reality, heterosuggestion; and for the following reasons. In the first place, the term "suggestion" essentially implies the influence of one person upon another; and it is a misuse of the term to apply it to any process in which no such influence is exercised. Secondly, it is clear, from the published accounts of Coué's procedure, that he begins by exercising suggestion; by means of such demonstrations before a group of patients he increases his prestige, already great by reason of his fame. It is probable that he even induces a light stage of hypnosis in many of them. Further, according to his own account, he instructs his patient to think of him (Coué) when he repeats, night and morning, the prescribed formulæ. This is a method that I have myself used with success, more especially in cases of insomnia. But it seems obvious that in such cases the so-called autosuggestion is, in reality, suggestion from the operator, renewed in his absence by the repetition of his words accompanied by the imagination of his personality.

It is, I think, probable that, apart from all suggestion, some individuals may secure beneficial results by repeating suitable verbal formulæ during moments of relaxation of mind and body. But, if so, the process would seem to be more properly regarded as a subtle form of volition rather than of suggestion. There remains, however, the possibility of a purely endogenous process which might perhaps be validly called autosuggestion. Namely, where division of the personality obtains, it would seem that one of two partial personalities may exercise suggestion upon the other. We shall see, in a later chapter, that something of this sort seems to have occurred in one at least of Dr. Morton Prince's cases of profound division of the personality, and in other cases of this class. If we adopt provisionally the theory of personality expounded in the final chapters of this volume—the theory, namely, that normal personality is a synthesis, an integration, of minor selves in a hierarchy ruled by a dominant member—it may perhaps be held that processes analogous to suggestion, and therefore properly to be called autosuggestive, may go on in the normal personality.

SUGGESTIBILITY

A few words may be added on the meaning of the words "suggestible" and "suggestibility." We are apt to assume that individuals may be ranged in a serial order of degrees of suggestibility or proneness to the influence of suggestion. But this assumption is ill-founded. The suggestibility of any subject is a function of several factors, and varies with these factors; some of these are resident in the subject; others lie in the environment. Of the non-resident factors the chief is the prestige of the source from which suggestion comes. This prestige may attach to an individual or a group of individuals by reason of reputation for power or knowledge or achievement. It may be due to an outward aspect of power or dignity, to that subtle combination of physical and mental qualities that we call "personal magnetism"; or to the external trappings of dignity and power—wealth, titles, fine clothes, robes of office, crowns and sceptres.

Of the resident factors of suggestibility three are of chief importance. First, ignorance of the topic concerning which suggestions are made. This is of the first importance in all medical suggestion. The profound ignorance of the layman concerning his bodily constitution and functions renders him suggestible in all that concerns health and disease, not only towards members of the medical profession, but also towards the advertiser of remedies and the exponent of esoteric systems of treatment. The suggestibility of children, savages, and the uneducated in general is largely due to this factor; they lack any body of established knowledge or belief that may conflict with and counteract suggestions concerning a vast range of topics.

The second and third great resident factors of suggestibility are constitutional. One is the native strength in the individual of the submissive tendency. Those in whom it is strong are apt to remain suggestible even in respect of those topics about which they are well informed. Those in whom it is weak, and especially if they possess a strong self-assertive tendency, are apt to remain self-confident and unsuggestible even though ignorant.

The third factor is susceptibility to dissociation. This undoubtedly is a constitutional peculiarity; the extrovert being more liable than the introvert to dissociation, and therefore more susceptible to hypnosis.[9] When medical authors write of degrees of suggestibility, they commonly have in view degrees of susceptibility to hypnosis. But this is a misleading usage; we have seen that the suggestibility of the hypnotic subject is not altogether a function of the degree of dissociation attained, but is rather chiefly a function of the *rapport* between him and the hypnotiser; and we have seen that the subject in hypnosis is commonly suggestible only towards the hypnotiser and any other person to whom the *rapport* may be extended by his suggestion; and that in some cases he remains unsuggestible towards the hypnotiser also.

Nevertheless, in the main, suggestibility increases with increasing general dissociation; hence all things that conduce to dissociation, such influences as fatigue, drowsiness, and alcohol, enhance the suggestibility of the subject.

Lastly, it may be noted that emotional excitement conduces to suggestibility, not because, as Janet would have it, emotion depletes the energies of the subject, but because every state of emotional excitement involves a tendency, or tendencies, towards accepting whatever propositions are congruous with that tendency or tendencies.

NOTES

[1] Vol. XXXI, 1908.

[2] That inhibition within the nervous system is always and at all levels a process of drainage of energy from one path or system to another in virtue of the lower resistance presented by the inhibiting path is a view that, as I have tried to show in a previous paper (*Brain*, vol. XXVI), is compatible with all the facts and seems to be the only tenable working hypothesis.

[3] I am, of course, using the word "idea" to denote the whole psychophysical system of activity which reveals itself in consciousness as a presentation.

[4] The hypothesis of inhibition by drainage seems to lend itself well to the explanation of this kind of inhibition, although, of course, it is not possible to apply it in detailed fashion. We may liken the relation between the disposition of contradictory ideas to the relation (so brilliantly studied by Sherrington—see "Integrative Action of the Nervous System") obtaining between the reflex arcs innervating antagonistic muscle groups; and this case is not only truly analogous, but is probably more than analogous; it is probably the simplest example of the same type of functional relation. Contradictory ideas about an object tend to issue in opposed systems of muscular activity.

[5] I am indebted to Dr. Milne Bramwell for having drawn my attention to this fact on the occasion when the substance of this paper was read to the Medical Society for the Study of Suggestive Therapeutics over which he presided. It would seem that the theory was first implied by Bennett in a lecture entitled "The Mesmeric Mania of 1851," delivered and published at Edinburgh in the year 1851. I have not been able to refer to a copy of this lecture.

[6] Especially, "A Note on Suggestion," *Journal of Neurology and Psychopathology*, vol. I.

[7] "Freud's Group Psychology and His Theory of Suggestion," in *Studies of Personality*. In this article a fuller exposition of Freud's theory may be found.

[8] I say that this instinct of submission is evidenced by the animals of many gregarious species. But I maintain that it is distinct from the gregarious instinct itself; that there are species of animals which have the gregarious instinct, but lack the submissive instinct; just as there are men who are strongly gregarious, but in whom the submissive instinct operates very little, if at all; that is to say, I maintain that the gregarious and the submissive tendencies are independent variables and, therefore, cannot be properly ascribed to the same instinct. In this I dissent strongly from the teaching of Mr. Wilfred Trotter, who, throughout his famous little book on "Instincts of the Herd in Peace and War," assumes without question that all the phenomena commonly classed under the head of suggestion are sufficiently explained by invoking the "herd instinct."

[9] Cf. Chapter XXVIII [*An Outline of Abnormal Psychology*].

PART IV

Conclusion: Animism*

In this final chapter [*Body and Mind*] it remains to draw together the threads of the long discussion and to state succinctly what conclusions seem to be justified by the evidences and reasonings we have reviewed.

We have seen how the great successes of the mechanical principles of explanation in the physical sciences, and their more limited success in the biological sciences, have led the greater part of the modern world of science confidently to assume that these principles are adequate for the explanation of all biological phenomena, and to reject as unnecessary the hypothesis of the co-operation of some teleological principle in their determination. We have seen how this opinion has seemed to find support in the law of the conservation of energy, in the Darwinian principles, and in the modern developments of cerebral anatomy and physiology. We have seen that the belief thus engendered in the adequacy and the exclusive sway of mechanical principles in both the inorganic and organic realms has been and remains the principal ground of the rejection of Animism by the modern world. We saw also that the more enlightened of the opponents of Animism, recognizing the uncertain nature of this ground, have rested their case mainly upon certain metaphysical arguments that make against the acceptance of the notion of psycho-physical interaction. We then examined the chief types of the current monistic formulations of the relation of mind to body; and we found that each of them encounters great difficulties peculiar to itself, as well as others common to all of them. After ascertaining that there is no escape from the dilemma, Animism or Parallelism, we proceeded to the defense of

---

* Originally published as Chap. XXVI in William McDougall's *Body and Mind*. London: Methuen & Co., Ltd., 1923.

Animism; and first, we found that none of the arguments, neither those of a metaphysical or epistemological nature, nor those drawn from the natural sciences, render impossible or untenable the notion of psycho-physical inter-action. We then surveyed a mass of evidence which shows that the mechanical principles are not adequate to the explanation of biological phenomena, nei-ther the phenomena of racial evolution nor those of the development of indi-vidual organisms, nor the behaviour of men and animals. In the psycho-logical chapters evidence was adduced which conclusively proves that a strict parallelism between our psychical processes and the physical processes of our brains does not as a matter of empirical fact obtain; and it was shown that facts of our conscious life, especially the fact of psychical indi-viduality, the fact of the unity of the consciousness correlated with the phys-ical manifold of brain-processes, cannot be rendered intelligible (as admitted by leading Parallelists)[1] without the postulation of some ground of unity other than the brain or material organism.

The empirical evidence, then, seems to weigh very strongly against Par-allelism and in favour of Animism. And we saw that, though the acceptance of either horn of the dilemma involves the acceptance of a number of strange consequences and leaves on our hands a number of questions to which we can return no answer, Animism has this great advantage over its rival, namely, that it remains on the plane of empirical science, and, while leaving the metaphysical questions open for independent treatment, can look forward to obtaining further light on its problems through further scientific research. It is thus a doctrine that stimulates our curiosity and stirs us to further efforts; whereas Parallelism necessarily involves the acceptance of metaphys-ical doctrines which claim to embody ultimate truth and which set rigid limits to the possibilities of further insight into the nature of the world, and it finds itself forced to regard certain of its problems as ultimately inex-plicable.

Finally, we have seen that Parallelism rules out all religious conceptions and hopes and aspirations, save those (if there be any) which are com-patible with a strictly mechanistic Pantheism, a Pantheism which differs from rigid Materialism not at all in respect to practical consequences for the life of mankind; whereas Animism in this sphere also leaves open the whole field for further speculation and inquiry, and permits us to hope and even to believe that the world is better than it seems; that the bitter injustices men suffer are not utterly irreparable; that their moral efforts are not wholly futile; that the life of the human race may have a wider significance than we can demonstrate; and that the advent of a "kindly comet," or the getting out of hand of some unusually virulent tribe of microbes, would not neces-sarily mean the final nullity of human endeavour.

These seem to me overwhelmingly strong reasons for accepting, as the best working hypothesis of the psycho-physical relation, the animistic horn of the dilemma. I shall now very briefly consider the principal varieties of the animistic conception, and attempt to estimate the relative strengths of their claims on our acceptance.

We may consider first a peculiar view, which might be called Animism of the lowest or most meagre degree. It is not perhaps new in the history of speculation, though it was not, I think, clearly formulated until recent years.[2]

It is allied to the view of Ostwald, Bechterew, and others,[3] which regards consciousness as a form of energy that undergoes transformations to other forms and is generated by transformations of the other forms of energy. It may perhaps be most easily described by saying that, like *Epiphenomenalism*, it regards consciousness as generated by the physical processes of the brain, but (unlike Huxley's doctrine) conceives the elements of consciousness as forces that influence one another and, in turn, react upon the brain-processes. It might also be described as the combination of the notion of the "Actuelle Seele"[4] with the belief in psycho-physical interaction. It sacrifices the advantages of Parallelism, namely, those which follow from the acceptance of a clean-cut mechanistic scheme of things, and involves many of the difficulties of Animism without bringing its important advantages. Its chief merit, and its only superiority to Epiphenomenalism, is that it finds a place, a function, and a *raison d'être* for consciousness as a factor in biological evolution, and avoids the absurdity of postulating effects which have no causes.

A second type of animistic theory is that advocated by William James[5] and Prof. Bergson. It was called by James "the transmission theory" of the function of the brain in relation to consciousness. It holds that consciousness is a stuff which is capable of being divided and compounded like putty or any plastic matter, its parts enduring or retaining their identity in the various aggregations into which they enter. It is conceived as existing independently of material organisms, either "(*a*) in disseminated particles; and then our brains are organs of concentration, organs for combining and massing these into resultant minds of personal form. Or it may exist (*b*) in vaster unities (absolute 'world-soul,' or something less); and then our brains are organs for separating it into parts and giving them finite form."[6]

According to this view, then, the brain is the ground of our psychical individuality. Matter is regarded as "a mere surface-veil of phenomena, hiding and keeping back the world of genuine realities,"[7] and our brains are regarded as translucent spots or systems of pores in this veil, whereby beams of consciousness "pierce through into this sublunary world." And all the beams thus transmitted by one brain are regarded as normally cohering to form a stream of personal consciousness, which swells and grows rich, or contracts and grows thin and poor, according to the functional condition of the brain.

This theory seems to me very unsatisfactory for the following reasons:[8] (1) It is open to all the objections that are made against psycho-physical interaction, since it implies such interaction and the rejection of the mechanistic dogma. (2) It is open also to all the objections to the notion of the compounding of consciousness, the notion that a number of elements or fragments of consciousness can cohere together to form a logical thought, or that a thought may be formed by the chipping off of a fragment of a larger whole of consciousness, and the notion also that each fragment of consciousness functions simultaneously as an element of larger and smaller aggregates.[9] (3) Like Parallelism, it leaves the fundamental fact of psychical individuality completely obscure and unintelligible; for we can see no reason in the nature of things, or of the hypothesis, why the several beams or elements of consciousness transmitted through any one brain should normally cohere to form the thoughts of one personality, while those transmitted through separate brains should remain separate. (4) In identifying mind with consciousness (i.e. making consciousness coextensive with mind or soul and its operations) it holds out no prospect of aiding in the solution of the physiological problems that remain refractory to mechanical principles, and it would seem to necessitate the assumption of the operation in organisms of a second teleological factor other than consciousness. (5) It seems incapable of giving any intelligible account of the facts of memory.[10]

It seems, then, worth while to inquire why James, one of the most prominent exponents of this form of Animism, preferred it to what he called the soul-theory. The history of James' thought on this question, as revealed in his published works, is interesting and relevant to our discussion. James approached the study of the mind, in which he attained so pre-eminent a mastery, from the side of physiology, and, in accordance with the dominant physiological teaching of that time, he identified thought and feeling and will with sensation; and throughout his first great book[11] he endeavoured to build up a consistent account of our mental life on a sensationalistic basis. At the same time he rejected the mechanistic dogma and affirmed the reality of psycho-physical interaction; he gave a brilliant and convincing refutation of the notion of the compounding of consciousness, and frankly recognized that the soul-theory seemed to him the necessary alternative to that doctrine. He affirmed the logical respectability of the soul-theory, gave a sympathetic statement of it, and confessed "that to posit a soul influenced in some mysterious way by the brain-states and responding to them by conscious affections of its own, seems to me the line of least logical resistance, so far as we yet have attained."[12] Nevertheless, he did not accept the soul-theory, though he gave no reasons for his hesitation, unless his characterization of it as the doctrine of Scholasticism and of common sense can be regarded as such. In his later works he showed himself more decidedly opposed to the soul-theory. In the Ingersoll Lecture of 1898 he hardly mentioned it, but advocated the "transmission theory." And, in his Oxford lectures of 1908,[13] he definitely rejected it in favour of the conception of a hierarchy of consciousness such as Fechner had dreamt of, the members of each level being conceived as formed by the compounding of lesser streams of consciousness of a lower level. In doing so, he recognized that he was repudiating his own demonstration of the illegitimacy of the notion of the compounding of consciousness, and explained that, after a long struggle with the problem, the magic of Prof. Bergson's attack upon the human intellect had given him courage to throw logic to the winds and to accept the notion of the compounding of consciousnesses in spite of its logical absurdity. He struggled in vain to reconcile with logical principles the notion that a consciousness can be at the same time both itself and an element or part of a different and more inclusive consciousness. "How can many consciousnesses be at the same time one consciousness? How can one and the same identical fact experience itself so diversely? The struggle was vain; I found myself in an *impasse.* I saw that I must either forswear that 'psychology without a soul' to which my whole psychological and Kantian education had committed me—I must, in short, bring back distinct spiritual agents to know the mental states, now singly and now in combination, in a word, bring back Scholasticism and common sense—or else I must squarely confess the solution of the problem impossible, and then, either give up my intellectualistic logic, the logic of identity, and adopt some higher (or lower) form of rationality, or, finally, face the fact that life is logically irrational. Sincerely, this is the actual trilemma that confronts every one of us."[14] And James chose to give up logic and the soul, and to accept the Fechnerian conception.

There can be no doubt that James, in making choice of this alternative, was greatly influenced, on the one hand, by the modern studies in psychopathology, which seemed to him to have shown that the normal stream of personal consciousness may be split into two or more coexistent streams, and, on the other, by his studies of those experiences of mystics in which they seem to themselves to transcend the normal limits of individuality and to become one with some larger whole of consciousness.[15] But he did not claim that these considerations compel us to this renunciation of our most fundamental logical principles. Rather he seemed driven to this renunciation by his strong objection to the soul-theory, which, as he so clearly showed, is the only alternative to it. What, then, are the grounds of this objection put forward by James? They are stated in less than two pages of large print; and for the purpose of our inquiry it is so important to have these grounds fully before us that I quote the entire passage. "It is not for idle or fantastical reasons that the notion of the substantial soul, so freely used by common men and the more popular philosophies, has fallen upon such evil days, and has no prestige in the eyes of critical thinkers. It only shares the fate of other unrepresentable substances and principles. They are, without exception all so barren that to sincere inquirers they appear as little more than names masquerading—*Wo die Begriffe fehlen da stellt ein Wort zur rechten Zeit sich ein.** You see no deeper into the fact that a hundred sensations get compounded or known together by thinking that a 'soul' does the compounding than you see into a man's living eighty years by thinking of him as an octogenarian, or into our having five fingers by calling us pentadactyls. Souls have worn out both themselves and their welcome, that is the plain truth. Philosophy ought to get the manifolds of experience unified on principles less empty. Like the word 'cause,' the word 'soul' is but a theoretic stop-gap—it marks a place and claims it for a future explanation to occupy.

"This being our post-humian and post-kantian state of mind, I will ask your permission to leave the soul wholly out of the present discussion and to consider only the residual dilemma. Some day, indeed, souls may get their innings again in philosophy—I am quite ready to admit that possibility —they form a category of thought too natural to the human mind to expire without prolonged resistance. But if the belief in the soul ever does come to life after the many funeral-discourses which humian and kantian criticism have preached over it, I am sure it will be only when some one has found in the term a pragmatic significance that has hitherto eluded observation."[16]

In spite of my profound admiration for William James, I am driven to exclaim—Could anything be more perverse! On one page he tells us that the only alternatives to the acceptance of the soul-theory are either to give up our belief in logic, or to declare that life is logically irrational.[17] On the next page he tells us that the conception of the soul is otiose, that it explains nothing, that it has no pragmatic significance and does not help us to any understanding. But surely, if any hypothesis is so logically necessary that its rejection must involve the rejection of our belief in the most fundamental logical principles, it is, *ipso facto*, justified, and bears the highest possible credentials. Has any scientific hypothesis any better justification, or can any better one be conceived? Why do we believe that the earth is round? Surely only because to deny it would involve the mistrust of logical reason! No one has directly perceived the earth as a round object. Why do we be-

* ["Where concepts are lacking, a word appears just at the right time." *Ed.*]

lieve that the earth was at one time a fiery mass; that it is not now a hollow shell; or that the remote side of the moon, which no man has seen, is approximately spherical and is illuminated by the sun at new moon? Why do we believe in those "unrepresentable principles and substances," the ether, energy, magnetic force, electricity, atoms, electrons? These and many other things we believe in for the same good pragmatic reason, namely, that our intellect finds the conceptions of these things necessary for the building up of the conceptual scheme of things by means of which we seek to render intelligible the facts of immediate experience. If we choose to resign our belief in man's powers of reason, we may believe in the flatness of the earth, in perpetual motion, in the existence of atoms of mind-stuff, in the compounding of consciousnesses, or in any other absurdity. "But I can take no comfort in such devices for making a luxury of intellectual defeat. They are but spiritual chloroform. Better live on the ragged edge, better gnaw the file forever!"[18] Or—as a less desperate alternative—retain a modest confidence in human reason, and accept the hypothesis of the soul!

In the passage quoted above (page 294), James places the notion of the soul on a level, as regards pragmatic significance, with the notion of causation. I am very willing to accept the classification; for no conception has proved of greater pragmatic value than that of cause. Wellnigh the whole of such superiority to savagery as our civilization can boast is due to our successful application of the conception of causation.

If James had belonged to that group of high and dry methodists who frown on all hypotheses, and teach that the function of science and philosophy is not to explain facts or render them intelligible, but merely to describe them with the utmost accuracy, his position would be comprehensible. But he explicitly demands explanation and intelligibility, and, in order to explain certain results of "psychical research," himself propounds the hypothesis of a cosmic reservoir of consciousness, or the existence in the universe of "a lot of diffuse mind-stuff, unable of itself to get into consistent personal form, or to take permanent possession of an organism and yet always craving to do so."[19]

I conclude, therefore, that the transmission theory, implying as it does the overthrow of human reason, encounters immense difficulties and gratuitously raises more problems than it solves, and that James' objections to the soul-theory were of the flimsiest, were in fact little more than the current prejudice in favour of that "psychology without a soul" to which, as he said, his whole psychological and Kantian education had committed him.[20]

Those readers who prefer the soul-theory will perhaps bear with me a little longer, while I inquire how we may best conceive and describe the soul in the light of the empirical evidence now available.

First, let us see what negative assertions can be made with some confidence. We can say that the soul has not the essential attributes of matter, namely, extension (or the attribute of occupying space) and ponderability or mass; for if it had these attributes it would be subject to the laws of mechanism; and it is just because we have found that mental and vital processes cannot be completely described and explained in terms of mechanism that we are compelled to believe in the co-operation of some non-mechanical teleological factor, and to adopt the hypothesis of the soul.

The Scholastics and Cartesians have generally described the soul as an inextended immaterial substance. In doing so they meant not only to deny it the attributes of matter, which they defined as extended substance, but, in applying the term substance, they meant also to imply certain positive attributes, especially the attribute of permanence or indestructibility; and, curiously enough, they seemed to believe that, by applying this word substance in their description of the soul, they guaranteed the immortality of human personality. Now, it is hardly necessary to say that we cannot prove the immortality of the soul by this simple expedient. Nor can we accept the description of it as substance in the old scholastic sense of the word. In that old-fashioned sense of the word, substance denoted a core or substratum underlying and distinct from all the attributes of a thing; which substratum might in principle remain unchanged as the identical substance, though all its attributes were changed or stripped off it; a sort of inert lay figure that might be dressed up in many garments. That is a notion which pretty nearly all moderns are agreed to reject; for a thing can only be known through the effects or activities it exerts, and its capacities for exerting these effects are its attributes, and we can only conceive the thing as the sum of its attributes. But we may conceive the thing as possessing these capacities for action or influence, not only at the moments at which they are exerted, but also during periods in which they remain latent. A material thing or being is then a sum, not only, as J. S. Mill said, of "permanent possibilities of sensation," but also of enduring possibilities or capacities of definite kinds of action and reaction upon other material things.

In a similar way we may describe a soul as a sum of enduring capacities for thoughts, feelings, and efforts of determinate kinds. Since the word substance retains the flavour of so many controversial doctrines, we shall do well to avoid it as the name for any such sum of enduring capacities, and to use instead the word thing or being. We may then describe a soul as a being that possesses, or is, the sum of definite capacities for psychical activity and psycho-physical interaction, of which the most fundamental are (1) the capacity of producing, in response to certain physical stimuli (the sensory processes of the brain), the whole range of sensation qualities in their whole range of intensities; (2) the capacity of responding to certain sensation-complexes with the production of meanings, as, for example, spatial meanings; (3) the capacity of responding to these sensations and these meanings with feeling and conation or effort, under the spur of which further meanings may be brought to consciousness in accordance with the laws of reproduction of similars and of reasoning; (4) the capacity of reacting upon the brain-processes to modify their course in a way which we cannot clearly define, but which we may provisionally conceive as a process of guidance by which streams of nervous energy may be concentrated in a way that antagonizes the tendency of all physical energy to dissipation and degradation.

These are the fundamental capacities of conscious activity that we may assign to the soul, and we may say that in the laws or uniformities that we can discover in these processes we may discern the laws or the nature of the soul; and the view that the soul is this sum of psychical capacities we may express by saying that the soul is a psychic being.

The Cartesians described the soul as a thinking being, using thinking (cogitatio) as the most inclusive term for what in modern terminology we call being conscious. But we cannot accept this description without reservation. Our evidence at present allows us to say only that the soul thinks or is conscious (realizes its capacities or potentialities) when interacting with some bodily organism; psycho-physical interaction may be, for all we know, a necessary condition of all consciousness. For all the thinking or consciousness of which we have positive knowledge is of embodied minds or souls; and a great mass of evidence goes to show that whatever prevents the body from playing its part in this process of psycho-physical interaction arrests the flow of consciousness, i.e. brings the soul's activities also to rest, at least so far as they are conscious activities. Rather than say that the soul is a thinking being, we must then say that it is a being capable of being stimulated to conscious activities through the agency of the body or brain with which it stands in relations of reciprocal influence.

Further, we must maintain that the soul is in some sense a unitary being or entity distinct from all others; for we found that prominent among the facts which compel us to accept the animistic hypothesis are the facts of psychical individuality, the fact that consciousness, as known to us, occurs only as individual coherent streams of personal consciousness, and all the facts summed up in the phrase "the unity of consciousness." We found that these facts remain absolutely unintelligible, unless we postulate some ground of this unity and coherence and separateness of individual streams of consciousness, some ground other than the bodily organisation.

This conclusion seems to rule out the notion that the soul of man or of any complex organism may be compounded of the souls of lesser organisms, or of the cells of which the body is made up. But it does not rule out the possibility that more than one psychic being may be associated with one bodily organism. It may be that the soul that thinks in each of us is but the chief of a hierarchy of similar beings,[21] and that this one alone, owing to the favourable position it occupies (I do not mean spatial position), is able to actualize in any full measure its capacities for conscious activity; and it may be that, if the subordinated beings exercise in any degree their psychic capacities, the chief soul is able, by a direct or telepathic action, to utilize and in some measure control their activities. We may see in this possibility the explanation of those strange and bizarre phenomena which have been so zealously studied in recent years under the head of secondary or dual personality, and which constitute evidence that has seemed to many to justify the notion of a division or splitting of the mind of a human being into two minds.[22] The animistic hypothesis may seek to explain also in this way the fact that the bodily organism of certain animals may be divided into two or more parts, each of which continues to lead indefinitely an independent existence and develops all the parts and functions of the complete organism. For we may hold that, as Lotze wrote, "Section would have cleft in two, not the soul of the polyp, but the corporeal bond that held together a number of souls, so as to hinder the individual development of each."[23]

The unity of the soul does not necessarily imply that all impressions made upon it and all its activities must be combined in the stream of personal consciousness. It remains open to us to suppose that, as Prof. Pierre Janet maintains, the bringing together or synthesizing of many impressions in the unitary field of attentive self-consciousness is only effected by the expenditure of psychical energy, the available quantity of which varies from time to time, and that the quantity of this energy is deficient in those states of "psychical poverty" (la misère psychologique)[24] characterized by sub-conscious mental activities of an abnormal kind.[25]

We may, then, suppose that abnormal conditions of two distinct types are commonly confused together under the head of co-consciousness or subconscious activity. In the one type (of which Sally Beauchamp remains the best example) the co-conscious activities become so highly developed and organized that we cannot refuse to recognize them as the activities of an independent synthetic centre, a numerically distinct psychic being, which, owing to insufficient energy of control of the normally dominant centre, escapes from its position of subordination and repression, and, not without a prolonged struggle,[26] actualizes and develops in an abnormal degree its latent capacities. In the other type we have to do with a mere insufficiency of synthetic energy of the one centre, from which results a temporary narrowing of the field of attentive consciousness, and the automatic or semi-mechanical functioning of parts of the psycho-physical organization. Into this class would fall all or most of the cases of functional anæsthesia and most of the instances of post-hypnotic obedience to suggestion in spite of lack of all conscious memory of the nature of the suggestion given.

The capacities and functions enumerated above seem to me the minimum that can be attributed to the soul. If we assign it these, while denying it any share in memory (regarding all mental retention as conditioned by the nervous system), we have a peculiar view of the soul, which might be concisely expressed by saying that the soul conditions the forms of mental activity, while the bodily processes (through the senses and the mechanically associated memory-trances of the brain) supply the content of consciousness. According to this view [27] the soul is to be regarded as undergoing no development in the course of the individual's life. Rather, the soul is a system of capacities which are fully present as latent potentialities from the beginning of the individual's life; and these potentialities are realized or brought into play only in proportion as the brain-mechanisms became developed and specialized. The mental differences exhibited by any person at different stages of his life would thus be wholly due to the developmental and degenerative changes of his brain-structure. And it would follow also that the mental differences between one person and another may be, and presumably are, wholly conditioned by differences of brain-structure. It would follow also that just as we should have to conceive the soul of any human being as an unchanging system of potentialities at all stages of the individual life, mental development being purely development of the bodily mechanisms by which the psychical potentialities are brought more fully into play, so we might conceive the mental differences between man and animals of all levels as wholly due to differences of kind and degree of bodily organization; the souls of all animals, from the lowliest upward to man, would have the same potentialities, and these potentialities would be actualized in proportion to the degree of evolution of the bodily organization. Mental evolution would thus be regarded as consisting wholly in progressive evolution of bodily organization; a view which is implied also in the "transmission theory" of James and Bergson. [28]

This view of the soul would satisfy all the empirical evidence, except that which points to "memory" as being, in part at least, immaterially conditioned. But, though this view is compatible with the belief that the soul survives the death of the body, and even with a belief in its immortality, it signally fails to satisfy those demands of our moral and æsthetic nature which have in all ages inclined the mass of men to believe in the life-after-death. In accordance with these demands the popular view has always held that all "memory," all mental retention and reproduction, all mental and moral growth, is rooted in the soul, that, in short, the soul is the bearer of all that is essential to the developed personality of each man. For the demand for a future life has two principal sources (beyond the promptings of personal affection and the mere personal dislike of the prospect of extinction), namely, the desire that the injustices of this life may be in some way made good, and the hope that those highest products of evolution, the personalities built up by long sustained moral and intellectual effort, shall not wholly pass away at the death of the body. And the survival of a soul which bears nothing of that which distinguishes one personality from another, one which bears no marks of the experiences it has undergone in its embodied life, and enjoys no continuity of personal memory, would satisfy neither this desire nor this hope. But the popular view, though it has been maintained in modern times by Lotze, a philosopher of the first rank, cannot be reconciled with the fact that the make-up of human personality includes many habits that are unquestionably rooted in the structure of the nervous system. It conflicts also with all the large mass of evidence which indicates the dependence of all the sensory content of consciousness, all sensation and all imagery on the integrity of the brain.

If we accept the hypothesis of the dual conditions of memory set forth and defended in Chapter XXIV [*Body and Mind*], we are led by it to a conception of the soul intermediate between these two extreme views, that [view] on the one hand which denies to the soul all development and therefore all that constitutes personality, and on the other hand that popular view which ascribes all development of mental power and character to the persistence of psychical modifications. For though, according to that hypothesis, all habits belong to the body, the soul does undergo a real development, an enrichment of its capacities; and, though it is not possible to say just how much of what we call personality is rooted in bodily habit and how much in psychical dispositions,[29] yet it is open to us to believe that the soul, if it survives the dissolution of the body, carries with it some large part of that which has been gained by intellectual and moral effort; and through the acceptance of the view we have suggested as to the essential part played by the body in conditioning the sensory content of consciousness, would make it impossible to suppose that the surviving soul could enjoy the exercise of thought of the kind with which alone we are familiar, yet it is not inconceivable that it might find conditions that would stimulate it to imageless thought (possibly conditions of direct or telepathic communication with other minds) or might find under other conditions (possibly in association with some other bodily organism) a sphere for the application and actualization of the capacities developed in it during its life in the body.[30]

Before bringing this long inquiry to an end, it is necessary to touch on the very obscure and difficult problem of the part played by the soul in the development of the body and the control of the organic functions. We have seen that many of the thinkers of earlier ages regarded chiefly these bio-logical functions in considering the nature and activities of the soul; and we have seen that there has appeared and on the whole has increasingly predominated a tendency to separate these from the distinctively mental func-tions, and to ascribe the vital and the mental functions to distinct principles, to the soul and to the spirit respectively, or to the vital force and to the soul or mind. Among those modern writers who have continued to accept the notion of the soul, this tendency has culminated in the view, first definitely propounded by Descartes and in more recent times best represented by Lotze, which regards all bodily processes, except those of the central nervous sys-tem, as wholly withdrawn from direct psychical influences, and as governed by purely mechanical principles.

But we cannot accept this position, for we have found reason to believe (*Body and Mind*, Chapter XVI) that the bodily processes, especially those of growth and repair, are not susceptible of purely mechanical explanation. If, then, we deny to the soul or thinking principle all part in these bodily proc-esses, we shall have to postulate some second and distinct teleological factor operative in organisms. The principle of economy of hypothesis, therefore, directs us to attempt to conceive that the soul may be operative in the guid-ance of bodily growth, either directly or by means of a general control exercised by it over some system of subordinate psychic agents.

Lotze rejected the view we are considering for two reasons: first, because in the adult human being all the direct interactions of soul and body seem to be confined to certain parts of the brain; secondly, because we are not normally conscious of exercising any control over the body, otherwise than in the production of voluntary movements through the contractions of the skeletal muscles. These objections may be partially answered or diminished by the following considerations. The lowliest animal organisms exhibit no specialization of organs and tissues; and whatever psychic powers they enjoy must be exercised equally in or through and upon all parts of the body; and it is not until in ascending the evolutionary scale we come upon animals of very considerable complexity, that we find a centralized nervous system which we must suppose to be the organ specially concerned in psycho-physical interactions. And even in the vertebrate phylum we find good reason for believing that in the lower members the psychical functions are distributed throughout all parts of the central nervous system, at least, and that only gradually, with the increasing specialization of the brain, do they become more and more restricted to its higher levels.

It is, then, reasonable to believe that in this respect, as in so many others, the human and higher animal organisms recapitulate in their individual development the history of the evolution of the race. If we take this view, we may believe that in the early stages of bodily development, during which the main lines of the bodily structure are laid down, the direct influence of the soul makes itself felt throughout all parts of the body as a controlling power, and that only gradually, as the specialization of the tissues progresses, it becomes circumscribed and confined to higher levels of the central nervous system. These psychic operations of embryonic life may well be in some sense conscious; but we can hardly expect to have any power of recollecting them, seeing that we consciously remember little or nothing of the experiences of early childhood, although in those early years we make a greater volume of acquisitions than in any later period. And we must not forget that, even when the early years are past, and all the bodily organs have been developed to their full size, our mental life still exercises a very considerable influence upon the bodily form, moulding our features and, to a less extent, our general structure and bearing to the more adequate expression of our characters.

It is in harmony with this view that the lower vertebrates, when deprived of the brain, exhibit more spontaneity and adaptability of movement than the higher members of the group; that the lower animals exhibit a much greater power of repair and regeneration after injury or ablation of parts of their bodies, a power which is reduced to its minimum in man; and that in every species this power of repair and of rectification of disturbances of the normal growth of the body seems to be greater, the earlier the stage of development at which such disturbances are inflicted.

To the other objection to the notion of control of growth by psychical influences, namely, that we are not conscious of exerting any such control, no great importance can be attached in view of the modern demonstrations of the large range and scope of subconscious processes, processes which imply intelligence and yet find no expression in consciousness that can be introspectively seized. Lotze himself recognized in several connexions the necessity of postulating psychical activities that remain unconscious or subconscious, though forming essential links in the chain of psychical process. And, since he wrote, evidence of the great extent of such processes has accumulated rapidly. The clearest of such evidence is perhaps that afforded by automatic speech and writing; but every successful experiment in post-hypnotic suggestion affords similar evidence. Successful therapeutic suggestions and others that effect definite tissue changes are especially significant in the present connexion; for in all such cases we have definite evidence of control of bodily processes which, though unconsciously effected, must be regarded as psychical. Of the limits of this power of mental control over the organic processes of the body we are altogether ignorant, and new evidence, much of it ill-reported and therefore valueless, but much of it above suspicion, repeatedly warns us against setting up any arbitrary limit to what may be effected in this way.

The view that the soul, even in the human adult, may exercise extensive vegetative functions finds some support in the following considerations. All routine bodily functions may be regarded as habits or as closely allied in nature to habits. And, if there is any truth in what was said above as to the psychical control of the growth of the embryo, we may regard each routine function of the body as originally acquired and fixed, like the motor habit of the skeletal system, under conscious psychical guidance. Now, though our motor habits or secondarily automatic movements undoubtedly imply the existence of well-organized systems of neurones, there is some ground for saying that they never become purely mechanical processes, but that rather they always retain something of the character of psycho-physical processes. For, first, they are initiated, controlled, and sustained by volition; even so thoroughly ingrained a habit as the movements of the legs in walking continues (as was pointed out in Chapter XXIII [of *Body and Mind*]) not merely as the repetition of a self-sustaining mechanical sequence, but in virtue of the intention or volition to walk, which continues to be effective, even when the attention is wholly withdrawn from the process. Secondly, the least disturbance or obstruction of a habitual movement causes the process to spring back into full consciousness, thereby showing that the soul has, as it were, its hand upon the process, ready at any moment to intervene and consciously effect the adjustment of the process required by the unusual situation; at the least we feel, however obscurely, an impulse, an unrest, until the obstruction is overcome or the adjustment achieved.

The same is obviously true of those old racial habits by which our organic life is so largely regulated, e.g. our respiratory movements. Of these movements, so long as they go on gently and smoothly, we remain unconscious; they seem to be purely mechanical. But let there arise any obstruction or mal-adjustment of the processes, and we become acutely aware of them; they become conscious and distinctly volitional processes; and if the obstruction is serious, as in an attack of asthma, our whole psychical activity becomes concentrated in the effort to maintain and reinforce the process, to the almost complete exclusion from consciousness of all other things. In this respect, then, these processes closely resemble our secondarily automatic movements; and there is nothing fanciful or improbable in the view that, like these, they are habits which have been built up under psychical guidance, but at an early period of life of which no recollection is possible. These organic hereditary habits form, then, a link which connects the habits, of whose formation under psychical guidance we retain a distinct memory, with other routine processes of the body, the acquirement of which we cannot recollect; and analogy justifies us in maintaining the possibility that these also have not been established without psychical control.[31] Biologically regarded, the function of mind is the effecting of new adjustments of the bodily processes; consciousness plays its part only in the process of adjustment, and the more completely the adjustment is effected, the more completely is the process withdrawn from consciousness; hence the routine processes of our bodies normally find but very obscure expression in consciousness, contributing only to that vague background which is usually called the *coenæsthesia.*

An alternative to this view would consist in adopting the conception that each complex organism comprises (or consists of) a system of psychic beings of like nature with the soul, but subordinated to it; it might then be held that each such being is a centre of a partially independent psychical control of some part of the organic processes.

Lastly, I would maintain that if the soul is to be taken seriously as a scientific hypothesis, we shall have to face the question of its part in heredity and of its place in the scheme of organic evolution. I do not propose to attempt any speculation on these extremely difficult and obscure problems, but merely to point to them as rising above the scientific horizon. We have found reason to believe that the germ-cell, by the growth and repeated division of which the body of each organism is generated, cannot contain material dispositions that shall suffice to determine in purely mechanical fashion the course of the development of the complex organism with all its myriad specific characters and its personal and family peculiarities. How is the teleological immaterial factor, which we are driven to conceive as controlling the development, related to the parent forms, each of which contributes its share to the determination of the nature of the new organism? In face of this tremendous problem, I will only say that to me it seems easier to believe that two souls may somehow co-operate in giving origin to a new one, than that two machines of incredible complexity and delicacy of constitution should combine (in the fusion of male and female germ-plasms) to form a new one, in which half the parts of the one parent machine become intricately combined by a purely mechanical process with half the parts of the other in a structure which minutely reproduces the essential features common to both, as well as many of the individual peculiarities of either one.

As regards the evolutionary problem, I would say that, if heredity is conditioned, not mechanically by the mere structure of the germ-plasm, but by the teleological principle, it follows that the factors which have produced the evolution of species must have operated on and through this principle.

Is it possible that the phrase "the soul of a race" is something more than a metaphor? That all that wonderful stability in complexity combined with gradual change through the ages, which Weismann attributes to the hypothetical germ-plasm, is in reality the attribute of an enduring psychic existent of which the lives of individual organisms are but successive manifestations? [32] However the continuity of psychical constitution of succeeding generations of a species, a stock, or a family is maintained, it seems not improbable that the experience of each generation modifies in some degree the psychic constitution of its successors. The Neo-Darwinians have denied that any such modification takes place, chiefly because it seems impossible that such experiences should impress themselves upon the structure of the germplasm. But if the structure of the germ-plasm is not the only link between the generations, this positive objection to the Lamarckian principle disappears; and we are free to accept the mass of evidence which points to some partial transmission of the effects of experience. Such modification of the hereditary basis would be least in respect of those characters which have long been established in the race and are least susceptible to modification in the individual by psycho-physical activities; among these would be all the specific bodily characters and all the fundamental forms of psychical activity. It would be greatest in respect to those more recently acquired mental characters which are the peculiar property of man; and it is just these characters, such as mathematical, musical, and other artistic talents, and the capacity for sustained intellectual and moral effort, that seem to exhibit the clearest indications of the effects of experience and of psychical effort, cumulative from generation to generation.

I will illustrate the conception of the evolutionary process that I have in mind by reference to a single psychical capacity, namely, our capacity of spatial apprehension. Whether or no space and spatial relations be objectively real, it seems to me quite indisputable that Kant and Lotze (among many others) were in the right in regarding the capacity of spatial apprehension as an innate power of the mind, which awaits only the touch of experience to bring it into operation. Space in the terminology used in these pages, is a meaning rooted in an enduring psychical disposition, [33] a disposition which, like others that we are constantly building up and extending as experience enriches the meanings that we have made our own, has been elaborated and fixed by the experience of countless generations, but which nevertheless may be capable of still further development.

According to this view then, not only conscious thinking, but also morphogenesis, heredity, and evolution, are psycho-physical processes. All alike are conditioned and governed by psychical dispositions that have been built up in the course of the experience of the race. So long as the psycho-physical processes in which they play their part proceed smoothly in the routine fashion proper to the species, they go on unconsciously or subconsciously. But whenever the circumstances of the organism demand new and more specialized adjustment of response, their smooth automatic working is disturbed, the corresponding meanings are brought to consciousness and by conscious perception and thinking and striving the required adjustment is effected.

NOTES

[1] I remind the reader of Paulsen's dictum, "Die Seele ist eine auf nicht weiter sagbarer Weise zusammen gebundene Vielheit innerer Erlebnisse." ["The soul is, in a manner not further susceptible of expression, a bound-together plurality of inner experiences." *Ed.*]

[2] It was advocated in my first publication touching on the psycho-physical question ("Mind," N.S., vol. vii., 1898), and has more recently been urged by several writers, especially by Dr. Archdall Reid ("Laws of Heredity," London, 1910) and by Mr. E. B. M'Gilvary (*Journ. of Phil., Psychology and Sci. Method*, 1910).

[3] See p. 130 [*Body and Mind*].

[4] Wundt's notion of the "Actuelle-Seele" (as consisting in the stream of consciousness composed of elements that causally interact with one another and synthesize themselves undergoing transformations in the process) differs from this view chiefly in that it denies any causal relation between the elements of the stream of consciousness and the brain-processes of which they are the invariable temporal concomitants.

[5] "Human Immortality," Ingersoll Lecture, 1898. The Animism of Bergson as expounded in his "Evolution Créatrice" is in many essential respects similar to James' view. But though Bergson has more fully elaborated this doctrine, I have chosen to present it in the form given it by James. Their formulations agree in the following essential points: both reject the claims of mechanism to rule in the organic world; both regard all psychical existence as of the form of consciousness only; both assume that consciousness exists independently of the physical world in some vast ocean or oceans of consciousness; both maintain that the consciousness or psychical life of each organism is a ray from this source; that the bodily organisation of each creature is that which determines individuality; that the brain is a mechanism which lets through, or brings into operation in the physical world, a stream of consciousness which is copious in proportion to the complexity of organisation of the brain.

[6] James, *op. cit.*, note 3. James distinguished these two views as alternatives in his Ingersoll Lecture, but later ("Pluralistic Universe") he seems to have realized that they imply one another; that if consciousness can be split off from larger wholes, its fragments must also be capable of being compounded. Elsewhere he speaks of a cosmic sea or reservoir of consciousness in impersonal forms. James, in fact, recognized that the transmission theory implies the doctrine of mind-stuff, the metaphysical notion that consciousness as we know it consists of compounded or aggregated atoms of mind-stuff.

[7] James, *op. cit.*, p. 33.

[8] My very condensed statement of it inevitably fails to do justice to it, and the reader should consult the original sources. Mr. Schiller's very readable "Riddles of the Sphinx" presents a psycho-physical hypothesis which in some respects is allied to the "transmission theory."

[9] See p. 169 [*Body and Mind*].

[10] I cannot discover that Prof. Bergson has brought the theory of memory of the "Matière et Mémoire" into intelligible relation with the psycho-physical doctrine of the "Évolution Créatrice."

[11] "The Principles of Psychology."
[12] "Principles," p. 181.
[13] "A Pluralistic Universe."
[14] "A Pluralistic Universe," p. 207.
[15] "Varieties of Religious Experience," 1902.
[16] "A Pluralistic Universe," p. 209.
[17] Surely these are but two ways of stating one alternative, the radical mistrust of the intellectual powers of the human race.
[18] James, "Principles," vol. i. p. 179.
[19] Article on "Psychical Research," in the "American Magazine" for 1909, p. 588.
[20] It seems necessary to insist in this connexion that agreement with conclusions of "common sense" or even of scholastic philosophy does not in itself suffice to render an hypothesis absurd or untenable.
[21] I remind the reader of the metaphysical doctrine (of Leibnitz, Lotze, and others) that the body is in its real nature an organized system of beings of like nature with the soul.
[22] The cases of alternating personality are not in question here, but only the rarer cases of seemingly concurrent dual personality or co-consciousness. Almost all those who have treated of these cases have started out from the assumption that, if the two streams of consciousness and mental activity coexist, they must be regarded as formed by the splitting of the normal stream of consciousness; the uncritical acceptance of this assumption renders these writers incapable of impartially weighing the evidence. Now, if we examine the very full and careful description of one of the most striking of these cases, that of Sally Beauchamp ("The Dissociation of a Personality," by Dr. Morton Prince, London, 1906), we find that there were two or more alternating personalities, both of which were continuous with the original normal personality, and by the synthesis or combination of the memories of which the normal personality was restored. These alternating personalities may, therefore, properly be regarded as formed, not by the splitting of the normal stream of consciousness, but by the alternation of two phases of the empirical self, or of the organic basis of personal consciousness, each of which brings back to consciousness only memories of experiences enjoyed during former periods of its dominance.

But the most striking feature of the case was the existence of a personality (Sally by name) which dominated and controlled the whole organism at times, and claimed to be conscious, though incapable of expressing herself (save in a fragmentary manner) in bodily movement, during the periods of dominance of the other personalities. This claim was supported (1) by the fact that Sally seemed to have knowledge of all or most of the experiences, even the dreams, reflections, and emotions of the other personalities; claiming to become aware of them in some immediate fashion, though regarding them always as not her own experiences, but as those of the other personalities; (2) by the fact that during the dominance of these others, involuntary, forced, or automatic movements, sometimes speech or writing, expressing the personality of Sally, were sometimes made by the bodily organs; which movements Sally claimed to have willed, when afterwards she came into full control; (3) by the fact that the other personalities were liable to unaccountable inhibitions of the will, which also Sally claimed to have effected in some direct fashion.

Now the point I wish to insist upon is this: there is in the whole very full account no evidence to support the view that Sally, the seemingly co-conscious personality, resulted from the division of the normal personality. Rather there is positive evidence that she was not so formed; she claimed to have existed before the time of the emotional shock which led to the alternation of phases of the original personality, and (what is more important), when the normal personality was restored, this was effected by the recombination of the alternating phases, and there was no indication that Sally was in any sense synthesized within this normal and complete personality; rather she gave indications from time to time of her continuance in a repressed and relatively inactive condition.

I would put alongside this fact the following remarks of Prof. Pierre Janet, who has had a very large experience of cases of this type, and to whose statements great weight must be assigned. After expressing the opinion ("L'Automatisme psychologique," p. 343) that, if in such cases of co-consciousness as he describes a complete cure were effected, the normal personality would regain the memories of the co-conscious secondary personality, he adds, "I ought to say that I have never observed this return of the memory, and that this opinion is founded upon the examination of my schematic diagram and upon reasoning rather than upon experience. . . . *I have never seen these hysterical persons recover after their apparent cure the memory of their second existences.*" And he adds that he supposes, therefore, that, though they seemed cured to his experienced eye, they were nevertheless not completely cured.

I submit, therefore, that we have no sufficient ground for the assumption that the co-conscious personality is formed by splitting off from the normal personality, that rather the facts justify the view that they are radically distinct. The facts may, therefore, be reconciled with the Animistic hypothesis by assuming that a normally subordinate psychic being obtains through the weakening of the control of the normally dominant soul an opportunity for exercising and developing its potentialities in an unusual degree.

[23] "Microcosmus" (Eng. trans.), vol. i. p. 154.

[24] *Op. cit.*, p. 444.

[25] "Comme le disaient les anciens philosophes, être c'est agir et créer, et la conscience, qui est au suprême degré une réalité, est par là même une activité agissante. Cette activité, si nous cherchons à nous représenter sa nature, est avant tout une activité de synthèse qui réunit des phénomènes donnés plus ou moins nombreux en un phénomène nouveau différent des éléments. C'est là une veritable création, car, à quelque point de vue que l'on se place, la multiplicité ne contient pas la raison de l'unité, et l'acte par lequel des éléments hétérogènes sont réunis dans une forme nouvelle n'est pas donné dans les éléments. . . . La conscience est donc bien par elle-même, dès ses débuts, une activité de synthèse" (*op. cit.*, p. 484).

[26] The feature of the Beauchamp case which most strongly supports this view is, perhaps, the occurrence of sustained and seemingly very real conflicts of will between Sally and the alternating phases of Miss B.'s personality; these, if we accept the description given (and it is perhaps permissible to say here that the good faith and scientific competence of the reporter of the case are indisputable), were no mere conflicts of opposed impulses, such as anyone of us may experience, but conflicts of the volitions of two organized and very different personalities. Another fact brought out clearly in the description of this case, one very difficult to reconcile with the view that Sally was merely a fragment of the normal personality, is that Sally's memory was more comprehensive than that of the normal personality, since it included all or most of the latter's experiences as well as her own. Now, in what manner or under what form Sally became aware of the thoughts and emotions of Miss B. remains one of the obscurest and most interesting of the problems presented by this and similar cases. For Sally seemed to become directly aware of these thoughts and emotions and yet to know them as Miss B.'s, and to regard them in a very objective manner. I may say that, thanks to the kindness of Dr. Morton Prince, I have had the opportunity of closely questioning upon this point a secondary personality very similar to Sally, and though she seemed highly intelligent and willing to reply to the best of her ability, it was impossible to obtain any light on this problem. I have discussed the case of Sally at more length in the Proc. S.P.R., vol. xix.

[27] This is the view sympathetically presented, if not actually accepted, in James' "Principles of Psychology" and defended by myself in my "Primer of Physiological Psychology." James, after expounding the laws of association and reproduction, wrote, "The schematism we have used is, moreover, taken immediately from the analysis of objects with their elementary parts, and only extended by analogy to the brain. And yet it is only as incorporated in the brain that such a schematism can represent anything *causal*. This is, to my mind, the conclusive reason for saying that the order of *presentation of the mind's materials* is due to cerebral physiology alone. . . . The *effects of interested attention and volition* remain. These activities seem to hold fast to certain elements, and by emphasizing them

and dwelling on them, to make their associates the only ones which are evolved. *This* is the point at which an anti-mechanical psychology must, if anywhere, make its stand in dealing with association. Everything else is pretty certainly due to cerebral laws" ("Principles," i. p. 594).

And again he wrote: "The soul *presents* nothing herself; *creates* nothing; is at the mercy of the material forces for all *possibilities;* but amongst these possibilities she selects, and by reinforcing one and checking others, she figures not as an 'epiphenomenon,' but as something from which the play gets moral support" (*op. cit.,* ii. p. 584). That this view is not consistent with James's transmission theory and later utterances seems to me clear.

[28] Lotze expressed himself as follows on this view of the essential similarity of all souls: "What causes determine the various levels of development reached by the various races of animated beings? Now here it was a possible opinion that all souls are homogeneous in nature, and that the combined influence of all external conditions, as well those whose seat is the organization of the body as those which supply the seat and issues of life, is the cause of the definite psychical development of each species, in one case of the inferiority of the animal kingdom, in the other of the superiority of human civilization. We did not feel ourselves justified in decidedly rejecting this opinion; on the contrary, one cannot help following its attempts at explanation with interest, for undoubtedly they are to a great extent justified" ("Microcosmus," Eng. trans., i. p. 643).

[29] It must be admitted that the distinction appears especially difficult on the side of the volitional and emotional developments of personality.

[30] I venture to throw out to those who are interested in the problems of "psychical research" the suggestion that in this line of thought may be found the explanation of the fragmentariness, the seeming triviality, and the inconsistencies of so many of those "automatic movements" which claim to be expressions of surviving personalities, defects which are generally felt to be a serious difficulty in the way of accepting these expressions as what they claim to be.

[31] It should be remembered also in this connexion that in many of the lower animals instinctive behaviour is so intimately interwoven with processes of structural development and modification, that it is impossible to draw any sharp line between them. As a single illustration of the facts I have in mind, I remind the reader of the process of "autotomy" observed among various species of arthropods; this consists in shedding a limb or appendage by means of violent muscular action.

[32] Its recognition of the continuity of all life is the great merit of Prof. Bergson's theory of creative evolution; its failure to give any intelligible account of individuality is its greatest defect. I venture to think that the most urgent problem confronting the philosophic biologist is the construction of a theory of life which will harmonise the facts of individuality with the appearance of the continuity of all life, with the theory of progressive evolution, and with the facts of heredity and bi-parental reproduction. By conceiving the animating principle of each organism as but relatively individual, as a bud from the tree of life, all of whose parts draw their energies from a common stem and root, it seems possible dimly to foreshadow a synthesis of the Animism of James and Bergson with the hypothesis discussed in these concluding paragraphs. To any reader familiar with the works of Samuel Butler it will be apparent that the conception which I am attempting vaguely to foreshadow is allied to the biological doctrines of his earlier works, but not to the Hylozoism to which he inclined in his later years.

[33] It has been argued in Chapter XXI that no system of neural elements, however complex, can be the sufficient ground of the capacity of spatial conception. But, even if we put aside those objections and adopted Herbert Spencer's view of the conditions of spatial conception as some immensely complex inherited system of associated nerve-cells, the impossibility of this view would force itself upon us again when we sought to conceive how this enormously complex system could be hereditarily transmitted by means of the structure of the germ-plasm.

Epilogue

In a letter to the Hon. Secretary of the S.P.R., written a few weeks before his death, Professor McDougall concluded with a valedictory message which the Council decided should be communicated to the Society. It was published in the Journal *of the S.P.R., Vol. 30 (1938), p. 294. Professor McDougall wrote as follows:*

I take this opportunity to say goodbye to all my friends on the Council of the Society and to express my great regret that I have not been able to do more to promote the work both in America and Great Britain. The small bulk and value of my contributions by no means represent fairly the importance which seems to me properly to attach to all good work in this field. Whatever the ultimate outcome is to be, it has been a privilege to be associated, continuously and through so many years, with a group of persons who have shown themselves so well able to sustain the high standard of critical judgment combined with openness to all new possibilities which was the absolutely indispensable condition of all useful work in psychical research. And if I may feel that I have contributed something, however small, toward the maintenance of that so rare combination, I shall be well satisfied.

Index

abreaction, 125
absolution, 91
"Actuelle Seele," 291, 306 n.
Adams, D. K., 32
Alrutz, S., 243
American Society for Psychical Research, 42, 44, 49, 50, 90, 180, 187
animal magnetism, 223 ff., 239 ff.
animism, 17, 19, 64, 96 ff., 289 ff.
apparitions, 137 ff., 143
Atlantic Monthly, 185
atomic theory of chemistry, 7
automatic writing, 94, 113, 114, 116, 122, 146, 150, 151, 216, 234, 235, 302
automatisms, 119 ff., 174 ff.
automaton theory, 96 (*see* parallelism)
autosuggestion, 283 ff.

Balfour, Lord, 39
Barrett, Sir William, 49
Beauchamp, Sally, 56, 152 ff., 298, 307 n., 308 n.
behaviorism, 5, 14, 15, 27, 126 n.

Bennett, Hughes, 277, 286 n.
Bergson, Henri, 39, 88, 173, 291, 293, 299, 306 n., 309 n.
Bernheim, H., 226, 239, 257, 261 n., 264
Bertrand, Alexandre, 224, 239
Binet, Alfred, 131, 261 n.
Bird, J. M., 198
Bird, Malcolm, 184, 192
Boston Society for Psychical Research, 31, 84
Boyle, Robert, 223
Braid, James, 225, 239
brainwaves theory, 18, 64 ff.
Bramwell, Milne, 68 n., 69 n., 236, 251, 286 n.
Brown, William, 241
Browning, Robert, 12
Burt, Sir Cyril, 3, 20, 22 ff., 30
Butler, Samuel, 309 n.

Cambridge Anthropological Expedition to the Torres Straits (1899), 27, 249
Cambridge University, 9, 10

313